Graham Lord is the author of seven novels, including *A Party to Die For*; an acclaimed autobiographical travelogue, *Ghosts of King Solomon's Mines*; and a bestselling biography of James Herriot. He is a former Literary Editor of the *Sunday Express*. He lives in the South of France.

D1637838

Also by Graham Lord

NOVELS
Marshmallow Pie
A Roof Under Your Feet
The Spider and the Fly
God and All His Angels
The Nostradamus Horoscope
Time Out of Mind
A Party to Die For

AUTOBIOGRAPHY
Ghosts of King Solomon's Mines

BIOGRAPHY
James Herriot: The Life of a Country Vet*

*Available from Headline

Just the One

The Wives and Times
of Jeffrey Bernard 1932–1997

Graham Lord

HEADLINE

For Keith Waterhouse,
*who let the genie
out of the bottle*

Copyright © 1992, 1997 Graham Lord

The right of Graham Lord to be identified as the Author of
the Work has been asserted by him in accordance with the
Copyright, Designs and Patents Act 1988.

First published in 1992
by Sinclair-Stevenson

First published in paperback in 1993
by HEADLINE BOOK PUBLISHING

This revised edition published in 1997
by HEADLINE BOOK PUBLISHING

10 9 8 7 6 5 4 3 2 1

All rights reserved. No part of this publication may be
reproduced, stored in a retrieval system, or transmitted,
in any form or by any means without the prior written
permission of the publisher, nor be otherwise circulated
in any form of binding or cover other than that in which
it is published and without a similar condition being
imposed on the subsequent purchaser.

ISBN 0 7472 6004 4

Printed in England by
Clays Ltd, St Ives plc

HEADLINE BOOK PUBLISHING
A division of Hodder Headline PLC
338 Euston Road
London NW1 3BH

Contents

Acknowledgements

I must of course first thank Jeff Bernard himself, who gave me hours of remarkably open interviews and who answered the most offensive and impertinent questions with startling honesty, even though he knew that I would publish everything I learned about him, no matter how reprehensible it might seem. Such honesty is rare and deserves to be saluted.

His three living ex-wives, too, could not have been more helpful: Jackie Heard, Jill Wilsworth and Sue Gluck. And some of his five hundred lovers were also generous with their memories: Marsh Dunbar, Fenella Fielding, Debbie Geller, Finola Morgan, Jill Neville, Deirdre Redgrave, Wendy Richard, Jan Rowell, Juliet Simpkins.

Most of Bernard's relatives, friends, enemies and acquaintances were equally co-operative, and I am grateful to dozens of them for talking to me about him, sometimes in long, revealing interviews and sometimes by lending me unpublished diaries, letters and typescripts. The list reads like a roll-call of the Boozy, Bohemian or Chattering Classes of the late 20th century: Tom Baker, Norman Balon, Carol Bennett, Gaston Berlemont, Bruce Bernard, Isabel Bernard, Oliver Bernard, 'Sally Bernard', Ian Board, Hilary Bonner, Sally Bonney, Deborah Bosley, Derek Brook, Craig Brown, Michael Bywater, Carmen Callil, Fergus Cashin, Alexander Chancellor, Victor Chandler, Carolyn Cluskey, Clare Colvin, Peter Cook, Adrienne Corri, Simon Courtauld, Julian Critchley, Beverley Cross, Hunter Davies, Dan Farson, Christopher Fernau, Nick Garland, Martyn Goff, Giles Gordon, Bill Haddow, Bill Hagerty, Joe Haines, Allan Hall, Susan Hampshire, Anna Haycraft, Colin Haycraft,

Tim Heald, Michael Heath, Susan Hill, Dr Harry Hoffman, Anthony Howard, Barry Humphries, Bobby Hunt, John Hurt, Richard Ingrams, Derek Jameson, Dr Anthony Kurtz, Irma Kurtz, Fran Landesman, Jay Landesman, Julian Lewis, Jean Leyland, Eddie Linden, Magnus Linklater, Neil Mackwood, Frank Mahon, Patrick Marnham, Bunny May, Jonathan Meades, Bill Mitchell, Mike Molloy, Bel Mooney, John Moynihan, Jenny Naipaul, Conan Nicholas, Miriam Nicholas, Jimmy Nicholson, Geraldine Norman, John Osborne, Anthony Powell, Jonathan Powell, Dominic Prince, Peter Rankin, Ned Sherrin, Gordon Smith, Lionel Stephens, Dudley Sutton, Taki Theodoracopulos, Leslie Thomas, Mick Tobin, Martin Tomkinson, Sally Vincent, Peter and 'Bonk' Walwyn, Keith Waterhouse, Auberon Waugh, John Wells, Richard West, Geoffrey Wheatcroft, Bill Whelan, Owen ('Oska') Wood, Noel Woodin. Thanks to all.

For help with major items of research I am very grateful to Keith Beard, Sonia Lambert, Juliet Lewis and Charles Seaton. For individual items of research I am grateful to Keith Beaston of the Coal Board, Isabel Brotherton-Ratcliffe, John Coldstream, Martin Coveney, Stephen Fothergill, Michael Gallemore, Jenie Glover, Jane Holbrey, Philip Howard, Robert Parfitt, Penny Perrick, Joanna Prior, Tony Rushton, Michael Williams, *The Times* archive library and the Ministry of Defence Record Officer, A. Churchill.

I have also quoted from the following books and plays and am grateful for permission to do so:

Jeffrey Bernard, *Low Life* (Duckworth, 1986)
Jeffrey Bernard: unscreened Play For Today, *Starting Tomorrow It's All Going To Be The Same* (1975)
Jeffrey Bernard: *Talking Horses* (Fourth Estate Ltd, 1987)
Oliver P. Bernard: *Cock Sparrow* (Jonathan Cape, 1936)
Oliver Bernard: *Getting Over It* (Peter Owen, 1992)
Tom Cross: *Artists and Bohemians* (Quiller Press, 1992)
Jane Ellison: *Another Little Drink*

Daniel Farson: *Soho In The Fifties* (Michael Joseph, 1987)

Patrick Marnham: *The Private Eye Story* (Andre Deutsch, 1982)

John Moynihan: *Not All A Ball* (MacGibbon & Kee, 1970)

Frank Norman: *A Kayf Up West* (1964 play script, Geraldine Norman)

Frank Norman: *Why Fings Went West* (Lemon Tree Press, 1975)

Frank Norman and Jeffrey Bernard: *Soho Night And Day* (Secker & Warburg, 1966)

Anthony Powell: *Infants of the Spring* (Heinemann, 1976)

Ken Russell: *A British Picture* (William Heinemann Ltd, 1989)

Ned Sherrin: *Theatrical Anecdotes* (Virgin Publishing Ltd, 1991)

Frances Spalding: *Dance Till The Stars Come Down* (Hodder & Stoughton, 1991)

L. C. Stephens: *Pangbourne College* (Pangbourne College, 1991)

Rosemary Sullivan: *By Heart* (Lime Tree and Penguin Books Canada Ltd, 1991)

Keith Waterhouse: *Jeffrey Bernard Is Unwell* (Keith Waterhouse Ltd, 1989)

I have also quoted from the following publications, with thanks: Country Life, Daily Express, Daily Mail, Daily Mirror (and Mirror Magazine), Daily Telegraph, Evening Standard, Mail on Sunday, Harpers & Queen, Men Only, Midweek, New Statesman, Private Eye, Queen, She, Spectator, The Sporting Life, Sunday Mirror, Sunday Telegraph, Sunday Times, Telegraph Magazine, Time Out, Town, You.

Finally I must thank Eve Pollard, the Editor of the Sunday Express, for her understanding in helping me to meet the deadline for this book, and Michael Corkrey and Guy Hart for permission to use Corkrey's brilliant portrait on the jacket.

Foreplay

On the evening of 26 September 1989 I shepherded the fifty-seven-year-old alcoholic journalist Jeffrey Bernard to the world premiere in Brighton of *Jeffrey Bernard is Unwell*, the Keith Waterhouse play that starred Peter O'Toole and was to become a major West End hit and make Bernard internationally famous.

It was an amazing accolade for any journalist to have a play named after him, let alone a journalist who boozed himself to oblivion every day in the Coach and Horses pub in Soho and whose reputation was based on writing about little more than his incredibly heavy drinking, smoking, womanising and gambling. He was the most unlikely cult figure, yet what other living writer had ever been portrayed like this on stage in what was virtually a one-man monologue? Even so, Bernard (the stress was on the second syllable so that his name rhymed with hard) was very subdued at first that evening. He had with him no party of friends and admirers to support him, as you might expect, so he met me alone for a drink at our hotel before we went on to the Theatre Royal to see the play. He was noticeably nervous, perhaps because he had managed miraculously to keep off the booze all afternoon. By that time of the evening he would normally have been comatose with alcohol.

As he tottered into the theatre foyer – his leg muscles had long been wasted by his drinking and smoking – we were approached by the wonderfully wacky, sexy, glinty-eyed actress Fenella Fielding.

'Who the hell is that old cow?' enquired the short-sighted

Bernard too loudly, peering at her. 'It looks as though she knows me.'

'Fenella Fielding,' I said.

'Christ, is it? I once lived with her for a year.'

He staggered towards her. It was difficult to imagine that they had once been lovers.

'What are you doing here?' he demanded.

She gave him the full benefit of her seductive, throaty voice: 'I couldn't wait for the opening night in the West End, *daaah*ling.'

Bernard tottered on towards the bar for 'just the one' before curtain-up.

In his column in the *Sunday Mirror* the following week Bernard wrote of Fenella Fielding's reaction to him that night: 'I suspect that the sight of O'Toole playing me drunk and lurching all over the stage may have reminded her of the time she had the good sense to give me the elbow twenty-five years ago.'

In fact they had lived together for only a few weeks. Seeing Jeffrey she had been tremendously saddened by the wasted sight of her old lover that night. He was only fifty-seven but he looked at least seventy-five. 'I saw this old man coming towards me,' she told me later, 'and he said in courtly fashion, "Oh darling, how nice to see you", but I didn't know who he was! I hadn't recognised him. I was appalled. As a young man he was gorgeous.'

He was certainly no longer gorgeous, but he was by now widely recognised as the finest journalistic diarist of his generation, the Pepys of the 1980s. Each week he described his bohemian existence in his 'Low Life' column in the upmarket weekly journal the *Spectator*. It was a woebegone but exhilarating diary of life at the blunt end among boozers, lay-abouts and tramps of both sexes that had been described by Jonathan Meades in *Tatler* as 'a suicide note in weekly instal-ments'. And Bernard wrote his column with such verve and cool intelligence that his fans and friends included Graham

Greene, John Osborne, Francis Bacon and John Hurt. Even before the play became such a hit strangers would loiter in the Coach and Horses hoping for a glimpse of Bernard's lurching, wasted figure and would ask for the honour of buying him yet another large vodka. He would always accept, and then quite often would tell them to sod off. By some strange alchemy this seemed to turn the honour golden for them: he had lived down to his boozy reputation as a curmudgeonly old bastard; he had treated them just as he treated his friends. He drank in those days a bottle of vodka a day, which was unwise for an alcoholic who was also a diabetic, and sometimes he failed to write his column, when there would appear instead in the *Spectator* the wry line *Jeffrey Bernard is Unwell*, which had given his old friend Keith Waterhouse his title for the play.

Some who did not understand the appeal of Bernard's writing were baffled that a mere drunk should have such a devoted following, but they made the mistake of overlooking the fact that not only did he write with astonishing clarity, fluency and raw honesty but that he had also had a vividly colourful life. He had been married four times and divorced thrice – it would have been four divorces but his first wife committed suicide. He had scrounged 'freebie' Press trips all over the world. He could tell stories about scores of famous friends, household names, yet he had also been a gigolo, labourer, miner, fairground boxer, stagehand, actor, racing tipster, *Private Eye* gossip. And perhaps his greatest appeal as a writer was that he saw the world, himself and all of us as monstrously absurd but entertaining black jokes and wrote about it all with irresistible self-deprecating charm and melancholy common sense.

It was his uniqueness which the play celebrated. It was based on his witty *Spectator* articles and depicted the immensely drunken but also extremely funny Bernard reminiscing about his extraordinary life, just before dawn, after being locked by mistake overnight in his favourite pub, the Coach and Horses in London's Soho. Even the brilliantly clever, uneven set by John Gunter appeared to be drunk. The play began in darkness with a verse that Bernard's dead poet friend Elizabeth Smart had written seven years previously for his fiftieth birthday, extolling his virtues. It started: 'My dear Jeff,/I can't say enough/how much I admire/the way you have/conducted your entire/life, and the way you have/used your marvellous Muse.' At the end of this eulogy the darkness was disturbed by the sound of O'Toole – playing the drunken Bernard – groaning on stage, stirring from the floor and hitting his head against a piece of furniture. 'Shit!' he muttered. He reached for some matches in the darkness and spilled them. 'Fuck,' he said, and the play was up and away, two shocked laughs already with just two words, and plenty more to come. The play was essentially a two-and-a-half-hour monologue by O'Toole but he was interrupted constantly by one-liners from a small cast of four actors who played Bernard's: barracking ex-wives, mistresses, editors, writers, actors, publicans, policemen, waiters, jockeys, trainers, doctors, nurses, drunks and tarts. They also portrayed real friends of Bernard's: the painter Francis Bacon, the jockey Lester Piggott, the Fleet Street editor Mike Molloy, the actor John le Mesurier, the Soho lady No Knickers Joyce and even Keith Waterhouse himself, who had been a boozy acquaintance of Bernard's in Soho and Fleet Street ever since the early Sixties.

From the moment that the lights went up on a wonderfully boozy but witty O'Toole the audience was with him. He looked uncannily like Bernard as he staggered about the stage chain-smoking, chain-drinking and trembling and few of us in that audience can ever have laughed so much in two hours. For here was the best of Jeffrey Bernard, the best jokes from his columns, the best anecdotes, the best of his bizarre view of the world from the other side of that bottle of vodka a day – and the best of a brilliant O'Toole. But here also was the best of Keith Waterhouse. After the play became a hit Bernard liked to claim that almost all the words in the play were his alone and that Waterhouse had merely assembled them like jigsaw pieces. This was quite untrue.

Waterhouse's work was a triumph. He had indeed skimmed the cream from Bernard's *Spectator* columns, but he had also whipped into it his own wit and style to fashion something quite independent, a confection that was also a work of art and the funniest play in years. And Peter O'Toole gave the part a magic, zest, dignity and unexpected poignancy that was to make the real Bernard such a media star that before long even American and Japanese tourists were gathering in the Coach and Horses to gape at him as he slid each morning into yet another bottle of vodka as soon after breakfast as possible. This was a drunk with a difference, a piss-artist who was by some amazing chance also extremely funny, perceptive and well read and who could also when he chose be utterly engaging, charming men as well as women. There was, for instance, in the play the line from the jockey and racehorse trainer Fred Winter when Bernard observed that his horses looked remarkably healthy: 'That's because they don't sit up all night playing cards and drinking vodka.'

There was the line that appeared in the *Spectator* in 1987: 'Jeffrey Bernard's column does not appear this week, as it is remarkably similar to that which he wrote last week.'

And there was the hysterical egg trick, where so many things could go wrong, and an avalanche of hilarious set-piece anecdotes. The one about the gambling fanatic who was made so restless by the lack of horseracing one frozen winter that he staged races between cats galloping along the corridor of his flat in Battersea towards a whiff of salmon. The one about the anonymous racehorse trainer (in fact Richard Hannon) who played Find The Lady with his gambling chums one boozy night by shuffling his infant triplets – only one of whom was female – on the sofa. The one about Bernard waking up drunk and baffled in the bottom drawer of an Edwardian wardrobe and desperate for a pee: 'Imagine trying to open a drawer from the inside . . .' The one about the day that he woke up drunk in the restaurant of the Groucho Club in Soho thinking he had gone blind: 'I was scared shitless. It turned out I'd been resting my head on a grilled turbot and I had tartare sauce all over my reading glasses . . .'

Despite such hilarity the play's ending was surprisingly touching. The ageing Bernard/O'Toole has run through his review of his life, the oceans of booze, the aeons of forgotten time, the four ex-wives, the countless mistresses and illnesses and hospital visits, the gusts of laughter, the fat catalogue of unforgivable drunken misbehaviour. He is homeless yet again and still locked in the pub but the dawn is coming up at last. It has been a wasted life, perhaps, and yet this stage Bernard goes out at the end with an indomitable dignity that leaves the audience wondering whether it has in fact been wasted after all. The landlord of the Coach and Horses, Norman Balon, has finally arrived to release Bernard from the pub and as Balon's key scrapes in the lock Bernard/O'Toole lifts his suitcase and tatty carrier bags and braces himself to face whatever bleak future he might have left. 'Life does go on,' he says, 'whatever proof there may be to the contrary. Last week . . . Last week I had an erection. I was so amazed I took its photograph. Life after death! What more do you want? Come on, Norman!' And the curtain falls.

Long before then it was obvious that O'Toole, Waterhouse and the director Ned Sherrin had a hit on their hands and I said so the following weekend in my column in the *Sunday Express*. Jeffrey too knew immediately that his life was about to be transformed. He was about to become a star. He was about to be recognised wherever he went, recognised almost as much as O'Toole himself, asked for his autograph, interviewed and photographed (as he would have put it himself in his column) from Marble Arch to Christmas. It was uncanny to see the frail, white-haired Jeffrey in the box and just yards away on-stage another frail, white-haired 'Bernard' as depicted by Peter O'Toole. 'We broke the champagne sales record on the first night at Brighton,' the producer, Ned Sherrin, told me afterwards, 'and the old barmaid nearly resigned because Jeff was so rude and said she was too slow with his vodkas.'

He needed the vodka badly for he was dazed by the play's

immediate success; the flashbulbs, the autographs. Within a few months the name Jeffrey Bernard was known to almost everyone in the British Isles.

I had known him well since meeting him in 1978 when we both moved out to live near the racing village of Lambourn on the beautiful Berkshire Downs, he with his new, fourth wife Sue and I with my then wife Jane. We had journalism in common and a liking for pubs and nobody had ever made me laugh as much as Jeff did. I was also astonished to see how he seemed to be able to get away with the most disgraceful behaviour, rudeness and drunkenness, and like so many other middle-aged married men with children, mortgages, insurance policies and pensions I envied the ease with which he simply ignored the problems and pressures of everyday living and just determined to enjoy himself. His life was astonishingly selfish and yet that was oddly part of his charm. He didn't seem to give a damn for anybody else or any thing. He was completely self-centred. He was free. And always he was funny.

For years I tried to persuade him to write his autobiography but he was always too lazy (and often too 'unwell') to do more than doodle a few notes. This did not of course prevent him from accepting several large advances from naively optimistic publishers for this non-existent autobiography – provisionally entitled *A Downhill Struggle* or *Reach For The Ground*. He once even went as far as to begin some serious research for the said work by writing a letter to the *New Statesman* asking: 'Can anyone tell me what I was doing between 1960 and 1974?'

'Yes,' replied the editor of the *Daily Mirror*, Mike Molloy. 'On a certain evening in September 1969 you rang my mother to inform her that you were going to murder her only son.'

The problem is of course that as a writer Bernard is a 750-word sprint man, not a 100,000-word long-distance runner, and he is also strangely superstitious. To write his own life-story would have seemed to him like writing his own obituary and tempting fate. So when I told him in August 1991 that I wanted to write his biography he was not only flattered but also relieved: now there really was no need for him to do the job himself. I warned him that he might not like the finished article and that I was determined to publish everything I discovered about him, however reprehensible or embarrassing. It was a measure of his amazing honesty (or masochism) that not only did he agree that I was right to do so but he also gave me numerous interviews, answered every question I put to him with startling frankness, and wrote in his Low Life column in *The Spectator* that he expected everyone I interviewed to tell me the whole truth. He has had no control whatever over the contents of the book. I suspect he regretted that when he finally read the typescript, for this is indeed a warts-and-all biography and parts of it must have upset him deeply. But as he himself wrote in that *Spectator*: 'I see no point whatsoever in an autobiography, or a biography for that matter, that isn't one-hundred-per-cent honest and reveals the sordid nitty-gritty of the years since 1948 when I left school.' That seemed to be a licence to try to tell the whole truth, however unpleasant it might be.

Some suggested when I began my research that this book would be superfluous since Bernard had written his own life story in his column. They were wrong. His columns were not always completely accurate or consistent and although he had always exposed himself in his writings to an extent unmatched by any other modern writer there were numerous secret corners of his life that he had kept hidden or been less than candid about. He had never, for instance, written much about his older brothers Oliver and Bruce. 'It would embarrass me to say what I really thought of them,' he told me. Slowly the secrets started emerging. That his childhood had shimmered with lust for his mother. That his 'mad' sister Sally had been certified and committed to an asylum in 1953 but was still living in South London in 1992. That many of his friends are convinced that he went through a homosexual phase in his late teens and early twenties. That his first wife Anna's real name wasn't Anna at all, a revelation that astonished Bernard when I told him. That she was forced to give up her illegitimate daughter Alfreda for adoption and regretted it ever after. That her mysterious – perhaps sinister – suicide happened neither when nor how he had thought it had. That Alfreda herself later changed her name to Sally Bernard and claimed to be the mother of Jeffrey's grandchildren. That Bernard too made several suicide attempts. That his third wife's daughter, Isabel, was not his child and that Isabel, now twenty-two, had known this for five years but had kept it from him to protect his feelings. That he had in fact been sterile from puberty. That his marriages had been disturbingly violent.

I was astounded by the number of secrets I stumbled across. These were not things that Bernard himself had ever written about. For a man as public as Jeff Bernard, for one who exposed himself so brutally each week that he was almost an exhibitionist, so pitilessly that he seemed almost masochistic, he was in fact turning out to be very private indeed. Even his old friend of forty years, Gaston Berlemont, who was for decades the landlord of the York Minster pub in Dean Street ('the French Pub'), told me: 'Strangely enough, although I have known Jeffrey and his brothers and sister for more years than I care to think about, there is little I can tell you about his personal life.' As I proceeded with my interviews and research it seemed increasingly astonishing how *little* we all really knew about Bernard. By pretending to tell the truth, the whole truth and nothing but the truth, he had brilliantly deflected attention from those aspects of his life that he preferred to forget, those very aspects that explained precisely why he had become the man he was. He had covered his tracks as adroitly as the most skilful desert tribesman will disguise his passing by leaving behind him the hoofprints of a very different animal.

I warned him in the Coach and Horses that I was discovering more than he can have expected or wished. 'I don't care what you write so long as it's true,' he told me. 'I'm a witness to that,' said his friend Bunny May. I knew then that Jeffrey and I would fall out over the book just as he had eventually fallen out with almost every friend he had ever had. In fact at one stage, after about six months of research, I had discovered so much to suggest that on the far side of this twinkling star there was a deep dead darkness so desperate that I began to dislike more than I liked. But three months later the dislike had matured into an understanding of and sympathy for a painfully complex man and a finer, more balanced admiration for his work and courage. One of the joys of writing the book was the chance to reread every one of Bernard's Low Life columns. I had almost forgotten how very funny he had been. Not many journalists can make you laugh aloud again and again. At his peak, in the 1970s and 1980s, he was quite superb. That alone is sufficient justification for this book.

There were, of course, special problems attached to writing a biography of Jeff Bernard.

Bernard seemed to have no diaries (though he had kept them intermittently many years before) and he appeared to have kept no cuttings of all the millions of words he had written for dozens of publications. I suspected too that he was still trying to hide some things from me. He lent me a brown John Menzies exercise book in which many years ago he had scribbled notes for his autobiography, but five of its pages had been torn out. What was he trying to hide? And then when I asked him to list his enemies – telling him that we are all best defined not by our friends but by the calibre of our enemies – he pretended that he had no enemies at all. He was wrong.

Some potential interviewees were less helpful than I had hoped they would be. Some old friends of Bernard's could not be bothered even to write the word 'no' on the stamped addressed return envelopes I sent them along with my polite request for interviews. Germaine Greer replied loftily that she knew almost nothing of Bernard despite the fact that I had been told by several people that she had met him many times. Bernard himself told me that he and Dr Greer once went to the Festival Hall together to hear Pollini play Mozart and that although they had never been lovers they had discussed the possibility. Indeed, at one *Private Eye* lunch at the Coach and Horses they sat opposite each other and enjoyed a long discussion about oral sex, much to the bewilderment of Derek Jameson, who was sitting beside Bernard. Richard Ingrams also told me that he had heard Dr Greer telling Bernard in her inimitable Australian accent after a *Private Eye* lunch: 'Jeffrey, you've just talked yourself out of a fuck.' I was sorry she was unwilling to discuss such touching moments.

I was also baffled by Peter O'Toole's response to my request for a brief interview. 'Mr O'Toole thanks you very much for the kind invitation to participate in your book,' his assistant Sue Burchett wrote. 'Unfortunately, Mr O'Toole is currently engaged in his own writings and is therefore unable to contribute to your book due to his copyright contract.' I wrote back, suggesting diffidently that as his memoirs would be published before this book and would obviously sell many more copies, my book would not be able in any way to anticipate or detract from his. Ms Burchett's reply was baffling: 'Mr O'Toole has asked me to convey to you his general rule of thumb which is not to comment about his friends whether they be dead or alive.' Really? What about the memoirs, then? Will they refer only to his enemies?

Oddly enough, Bernard's own long-term memory seemed surprisingly good though he often had trouble remembering what happened the previous night. Even Richard Ingrams, who hadn't touched a drop for many years, was quite wrong about the date that he started writing for the *Spectator* and confessed that he could not remember much about the 1970s. He could not remember how he had hired Bernard to write the Colonel Mad column in *Private Eye* and he could not remember how he had fired him in 1980. You would have thought that some of these witnesses had been talking about the Middle Ages. Most of Bernard's friends kept warning me against his other friends. 'Don't believe *him*,' they would say, 'he's a notorious liar.' Some were terribly unreliable and kept promising to send me information, cuttings or photographs and then failing to do so. Nor did it help that Bernard kept asking me who I was seeing next. I suspect he would then ring them up and be nice to them so that they would be nice about him to me.

Perhaps the most engaging witness of all was Norman Balon, the legendary landlord of the Coach and Horses, who gave me an endearingly furtive interview in his pub, muttering out of the corner of his mouth, while Bernard drank a few yards away and pretended not to notice us. Norman first made me sign an undertaking that I would not quote him in the book but swiftly changed his mind the following day when he discovered that everyone else was prepared to be quoted and that he would be appearing in the index forlornly as A Certain Publican if he insisted on remaining off the record.

Three final memories remain. I will not soon forget Bernard's expression of irritation when I told him that it was Keith Waterhouse who had made him famous but I who would make him immortal. Nor the way that he wept on the afternoon that his first wife Anna's long-lost forty-two-year-old illegitimate daughter Alfreda turned up with a rare photograph of Anna: he had not seen her face for nearly forty years. And finally there was the exhausting, heavy-drinking day that I spent interviewing Bernard's boozing friends in the Coach and Horses and the Groucho Club after which I woke the next morning to find that I had lost my spectacles. I rang everyone who might have found them: the pub, the club, Bernard himself; to no avail. And then eventually my consort discovered them nestling among her knickers. It was a truly Bernardine moment of truth. When I told Jeffrey where the glasses had turned up there was a stunned silence, then he said: 'I think this book is beginning to get to you, Graham.'

I felt at last that I was properly qualified to write it.

1

Bunny and Fedora

His name was not even Jeffrey, for a start. He was born Jerry Joseph Bernard, and Jerry he stayed until he was eight and begged his mother to let him change it to something else – *anything* else – because they were teasing him at school.

He was born in North London at his parents' home at 11 Hampstead Square, Hampstead, on 27 May 1932, the son of Oliver Percy Bernard, a successful architect, and Edith Dora Bernard (*née* Hodges), a snobbish working-class opera singer who preferred to be known by her stage name Fedora Roselli. He was born appropriately under the sign of Gemini, the split-personality sign of the twins. In later life he liked to joke that because he was born under the sign of Gemini he should have become a barrister, con-man or actor. Some would say that he was a con-man and an actor all his life.

He was born into a family where there were already an eight-year-old sister, Sally, and two older brothers, six-year-old Oliver and four-year-old Bruce. After Bruce there had been another sister, Susannah, but she had died of lead poisoning when she was eighteen months old after sucking a door handle.

Jeff Bernard always liked to fantasise about his ancestry and pretended that he had aristocratic origins and was descended from Richard Neville, Warwick the Kingmaker. He would claim that his great-uncle had been a Cornwallis-West and had been related to Winston Churchill's mother's second husband, George, and had changed his name to Bernard because of the scandal when George Cornwallis-West left Churchill's mother to marry Mrs Patrick Campbell.

Bernard even tried to persuade me once that his great-uncle had actually *been* Jenny Churchill's husband and he wrote once of 'my stupid ancestor, Lord Cornwallis, who surrendered to the Americans at Yorktown'. It was all nonsense. The family name was changed from West to Bernard – by Jeffrey's grandfather, Charles, who had a French aunt called Bernard – long before Captain George Cornwallis-West even met Jenny Churchill, let alone left her for Mrs Campbell in 1913. George West did not die until 1951, which would have allowed ample time for any of the modern Bernards to confirm the legend, which was spread by Jeffrey's snobbish mother.

Jeffrey Bernard's true ancestry was on his father's side theatrical and on his mother's side very working class. His paternal grandfather, Charles West, was an actor-manager impresario who also wrote music-hall songs, among them *Think Yes But Say No*. His paternal grandmother was an actress. His maternal grandfather was an itinerant horse-and-cart pork butcher, Joseph Hodges, who retired to live in poverty at Norman's Bay, near Pevensey. His wife, Jeffrey's grandmother, is believed in the family to have been a gipsy. In those genes – the theatrical, the working-class, the gipsy – lay much of the explanation for the man that Jeffrey Bernard was to become, and since both his parents were in the theatre it would not have been at all surprising if he had become an actor.

His mother, Dora, who was born in 1896, was the youngest of six children, the only girl. She was pretty and talented, with a good voice and a comic touch, and she was sent to a small music/drama school where she was soon noticed sufficiently for her to start to get work when she was very young. She became an opera singer under the exotic stage name Fedora Roselli, which she used increasingly in private, too, rather than the dreaded Dora Hodges. Typically, when Dora married in 1924 she wrote on the marriage certificate (under Rank or Profession of Father) the shameful word

'Butcher' and then added defiantly '(Master)'. 'She was phoney, pretentious, certainly a snob,' her eldest son Oliver told me. 'She did a certain amount of talking about my father's parents and grandparents and ancestry but none about her own. She didn't realise that her father was one of the sweetest persons, and her mother was absolutely charming, and very funny and loving. The first night that we arrived to stay with her mother in Norman's Bay during the holidays she said, "You'll find it all quite strange, we have oil lamps, paraffin, and the toilet is outside but you'll find *this* useful" and she held a chamberpot up, and we giggled, and she put it on her head and she danced. She was about sixty, *wonderful*.'

In later life Jeffrey too would sneer at his mother's snobbery even though he was to become a notorious snob himself. He inherited more from his mother than her theatricality, her talent for comedy and her gipsy blood. You had only to look at his entry in *Who's Who* where he listed his mother as Fedora Roselli.

Apart from a couple of idealised stage shots that have survived, Dora looked in most photographs like a tough, dumpy peasant. Obviously they did not do her justice, for she was certainly interesting enough for Epstein to sculpt her head in bronze and good-looking enough to attract the roving eye of Augustus John – and, when she was twenty-eight, of the resident scenic designer at the Royal Opera House in Covent Garden, Oliver Bernard, a divorced man of forty-three who liked to be known by his nickname, Bunny, and who was a friend of Caruso. Bunny was also an architect who was to design the revolutionary Art Deco interiors of Lyons Corner House restaurants in the 1930s and the facade of the entrance to the Strand Palace hotel, which is preserved in the basement of the Victoria and Albert Museum in London. When he was looking for a godfather for the boy Jerry he chose a man who was to become the Queen's furrier and an expert on Venice, J. G. Links, for whom Bunny had designed his first showroom.

In many ways Bunny Bernard seems to have been a blueprint

for Jerry, a dry run, for the boy was to inherit an impressive array of his father's talents and weaknesses, from his pugnacity and compulsive womanising to his dapper style, absurdly expensive tastes and constant flirtation with bankruptcy. 'My mother said I was exactly like him,' Jeffrey told me. 'I look like him. I think it's in the genes, though he wasn't a pisspot like I am.'

'I would think that Jeffrey *was* quite like him in some ways,' his brother Oliver agreed. 'They were both *fucking* irritable and aggressive, and they were never at any pains to smooth anybody down at all. Also of course, like Jeffrey, my father was *very* sweet at times. He'd sit us all round him and make us read *The Merchant of Venice* when we were boys.'

Jeffrey certainly hero worshipped his father. 'He was a remarkable man,' he told me. 'Unlike his sons, he pulled himself up by his fucking bootstraps and from that to an office in Park Lane and a house in Cheyne Walk is not bad going. He was a tough nut. He was only about 5ft 5ins but could knock shit out of anyone. He was a bit of a womaniser. He used to go to lunch at the Ritz every day, or the Dorchester, where he helped to design the interior, when he had his office in Park Lane, and he wore Savile Row suits. He was very small, an extravagant, flash little bastard. When he worked for a short time as a bookmaker's clerk there was one incident that sums him up. A bloke disputed a bet with him, so my father whacked him and knocked him flat on his back. Someone said, "Do you know who you've just hit?" and he said no. He had just floored a gypsy called Pedlar Palmer who was the bantamweight champion of the world! There's also a 1920s Chelsea Arts Club complaints book in which someone had written this complaint about him and Augustus John: "I would appreciate it if members would not have fights after the bar closes at 11 p.m." '

Even though Bunny Bernard (who had been born Oliver Percival Bernard) was to die when little Jerry was seven he obviously had a large impact on his son. His own parents

had let him 'go to the devil', he wrote in his autobiography
Cock Sparrow (Cape, 1936). His mother, Annie, Jeffrey's
grandmother, had been 'a belle of Glasgow' who had not
been impressed by the duties of motherhood. When Baby
Bunny was first shown to her she said 'very nice but please
take it away'. She 'cared less about sons than many of
her pampered sex do for pet poodles' he wrote. 'Could
anything be so contrary to nature as a heartless, beautiful
woman?'

His father, Charles, the theatrical manager, toured England with his own company, had founded the Queen's Royal
Minstrels and had owned several theatres. He had also sung
for the Prince of Wales at the Savage Club.

Bunny's father had also been handy with his fists and
had 'thrashed' his own brothers as well as one of his touring
managers 'for ill-treating the children who formed the entire
cast of a novel production of *Les Cloches de Corneville*.'

'This was a father,' reported Bunny, 'who had helped to
keep the ring for Tom Sayers when he fought Heenan into
blindness in pouring rain; who upheld Quaker descent only
to the extent of never going to law; who boasted he could make
anybody like him. Queen Victoria regarded him as a favourite
minstrel at Balmoral, and even John Brown approved . . . His
own father carried him as an infant prodigy into country inns
and stood him on taproom tables, to work out mathematical
propositions for the best wits of the west countryside.'

Bunny's parents died within six months of each other,
leaving him to be raised in Manchester by relatives – 'a half-
educated, penniless orphan' of thirteen – just as Jeffrey was to
be left a penniless orphan of eighteen in 1950. Like his son,
Bunny had a nice cynical line in pawky black humour and
irony: writing of teachers, he observed that 'those which are
supposed to instruct often destroy; those which are intended
to destroy are always instructive – especially the gallows,
guillotine, and electric chair.'

In Manchester he previewed Jeffrey's own theatrical career
by becoming a stagehand errand-boy. Like Jeffrey later

Bunny became a useful amateur boxer and he even suffered the 'indecent advances' of 'the travelling manager of a well-known troupe of dancers': unlike his son, who was to make the most of besotted old queers, Bunny punched his own 'perverted guardian' senseless.

Like Jeffrey too he had to suffer some dreadful jobs as a young man. At a fearfully early age Bunny became a cabin boy on the transatlantic run from Manchester to Montreal, working seventeen hours a day – like his son later, he wanted to be an officer in the Merchant Navy – and he then worked before the mast as a twenty-year-old deck boy on a Norwegian barque for £1 a month, sailing in a windjammer from Liverpool to Finland through the Gulf of Bothnia, climbing high in the rigging and once spending fourteen hours clinging to the wheel in winter snow and ice well into the night, 'forgotten all day except by cook, who sent Bert aft with foul coffee and stale rye bread'.

So portentous and prophetic is the story of Bunny Bernard's early life that it comes as a shock to discover that he sneered at people amongst whom his son was to spend most of his life, 'people whose adventure happens in public-houses, on golf courses, or within some kind of mental slum'. He wrote of 'those derelicts who owe their downfall to three busy B's – bookmakers, billiards, and booze'. And although he seems to have enjoyed going racing almost as much as his son was to do, he said that people 'who matched their wits against the combined forces of horse racing, bookmakers, tipsters, jockeys, horses, trainers and owners, were adjectived fools'. Yet when he died in 1939 his obituary in *The Times* remarked in an eerie premonition of Jeffrey's future career: 'He saw the low life of billiard halls and race-courses.'

In 1905, at the age of twenty-four, the adventurous Bunny Bernard crossed the Atlantic again to work in the theatre as a scenic artist on Broadway and later in Boston, Philadelphia and Chicago. He was for a while a resident technician at the Boston Opera House. He stayed in America for eight years until he received a letter from a dancer he had known in Manchester who offered to marry him. In a surge of romantic emotion he returned to England in 1913 to work at Covent Garden, where he met the great operatic tenor Enrico Caruso, only to discover that he didn't love his dancer after all. An Italian prima donna promised to marry him – they even fixed the date – but jilted him when her Italian lover threatened to kill her if she did so. Many opera singers were 'beasts and bitches', Bunny moaned: 'the exaggerated accomplishments and tiresome peculiarities of artists too frequently cover up complete lack of principle'. This opinion did not bode well for his second marriage, to Jeffrey's mother, an opera singer. Bunny's love life was beginning to become as fraught as Jeffrey's was to be. When a friend remarked cheerfully that 'there's always something around the corner', Bunny replied, 'Yes, it's either death or a woman, and who's to say which is best?'

Like Jeffrey, Bunny was obsessed by class and wrote of 'his unhappiness, his contempt for the snobbery of England' and explained: 'Americans hate discipline any way; English officers practise a different sort of swank, in their clubs, on their parents' money, in other people's houses, hunting and shooting boxes; country squires, feudal fiddlesticks, the back streets of Manchester would teach them something about King and Country.' If Jeff had a chip on his shoulder his father was humping a whole bag of them – with salt, to rub in to the wound.

After just a year in Britain Bunny was back in the United States in November 1914 and working as a stage designer and illustrator just as the First World War was starting. He hankered to do his duty and join the army and returned in May 1915 on the *Lusitania* – his twelfth trip across the Atlantic. It was in fact twelfth time lucky, because the ship was torpedoed by a German submarine and sank off Ireland; 1198 passengers died, but Bunny was one of the 761 survivors even though (like Jeffrey) he never learned to swim.

In 1915 Bunny married for the first time, to a Muriel

Theresa Lightfoot, who was perhaps an actress and maybe the daughter of an Essex colonel, but his references to his marriage in the book are so fleeting that it is impossible to tell precisely who was doing what to whom when. He does mention that his mother-in-law was the Commandant of the Red Cross Hospital in Burnham-on-Crouch – an excellent title for a mother-in-law, *Commandant* – and he refers in passing to his unhappiness and 'matrimonial turmoil' and 'the bitterness of matrimonial error'. Luckily Bunny and his first wife had no children and he escaped as soon as possible, in January 1916, to face the lesser miseries of the trenches in France, where he began his service as a subaltern in the Royal Engineers, a Camouflage Officer whose job included disguising snipers' posts and planting hideout spy-trees made of steel. His experiences on the Western Front made him suspicious of authority and he sneered at 'the medieval qualities which percolate so persistently through social sieves into the highest posts of military authority throughout the armies of Europe.' Decades later his son Jeffrey, too, was to exhibit nothing but contempt for authority.

On 4 August 1916 Bunny was wounded just below the kneecap by a machine-gun bullet that passed through the bone. 'He was in great agony,' Jeffrey recalled, 'and staggered in to a field station and the nurse in charge slapped him across the face assuming that he was pissed because he couldn't stand up properly!' The wound sent him back to Blighty and won him the Military Cross.

After recuperation he returned to France in 1917, was made up to Captain, sent to Italy, became a Major, and eventually in 1919 received his MC and an OBE at Buckingham Palace from George V, with his hoarse voice and 'a kindly weatherbeaten smile and the tiredest eyes he had ever looked into'.

Bunny and Dora met in the early twenties, perhaps at the Palace Theatre, where she was singing in *Chu Chin Chow* and he was the designer. Their son Oliver believed that they were forced into a shotgun wedding because he thought that their first child, Sonia, was born very soon after their wedding in June. But in fact Bunny and Dora were married on 17 April 1924, at Chelsea Register Office, and although it is possible that Dora was already pregnant – Sonia was born nearly eight months later, on 29 November – Dora would have been no more than six weeks pregnant when the wedding took place and could hardly yet have been absolutely certain that a child was on the way. If Bunny were being forced into marriage he would surely have waited a little longer to be in no doubt that it was absolutely necessary. Certainly the arrival of Sonia interrupted Dora's career at a crucial stage – she was singing in *The Beggar's Opera* during her pregnancy – and she may well have felt bitter towards the child for blighting her future. Things might have been happier if Sonia had been a boy because Dora much preferred her sons, but as it was she was to be dreadfully cruel to her daughter. The tragedy of Sonia, who was known throughout her childhood as Sally and who was later to be committed to an asylum, had started its long unhappy journey.

Oliver and Bruce always blamed their parents' subsequent unhappiness on the fact that they had been forced to marry – Bruce even thought that the gap between wedding and birth had been just three months – and that Dora blamed Sonia for destroying her career. 'My father was not untypical in a person of his class in refusing to let her work and earn money,' said Oliver. 'She could earn lots of money at the time she was married. She was doing really well on the stage and she was both an actress and a singer in musicals and musical plays.' But an equally important cause of their parents' marital misery might have been the gap in their ages. Bunny was fifteen years older than Dora: when they married he was forty-three and she was twenty-eight. Not only was he probably set in his ways by then but he may well have had a natural disposition towards unhappiness, just as Jeffrey was to have. Perhaps Bunny Bernard was simply no

more cut out for marriage than any of his own children were
to be: one of them never married and the other three ran up
a total of eight spouses between them. And unhappiness can
surely also be hereditary. Bunny's own parents had been so
unhappy together that his mother did not even go to his
father's funeral.

Whatever the reason, it was to be a bitter marriage.
Bunny seems to have stayed away from home as often
as possible but Bruce remembered: 'My father and mother
had terrible rows, really dreadful. It made for an anxious
home because we were all very keen on them both. They
were both very interesting and they both had very strong,
attractive personalities, so one's loyalties were very divided
when there was tension between them.' He also remembered
his father throwing things at his mother but did not think he
ever beat her up.

Oliver, perhaps because he was a little older, could remember violence. 'They used to have *terrible* rows,' he told me,
'and I can still see him with his hands round her throat.'
Bunny had been trying to strangle his wife on that occasion
because they could not agree as to which cinema they should
try. 'They obviously *really* got on each other's tits in a very
serious way.' Nor could Bunny's behaviour, like Jeffrey's so
often later, be explained by drink. 'At that time he didn't
drink at all,' said Oliver, 'but he was an irritable man.'

The obvious unhappiness of the parents severely infected the
children, all four of whom grew up lonely to the bone. 'By
the time I was eight or nine I used to loathe going anywhere
with the family or having anything much to do with them,'
said Oliver. 'I disliked my family from quite an early age. I
used to wish I was an orphan and that everybody would die.
It was a *bloody* unhappy family.'

– 2 –

Had little Jerry's parents been happier together he should
have had an idyllic English middle-class childhood. They
moved house often – from Hampstead, where Jerry was born,
to Oxshott in Surrey, then to two flats in Great Portland
Street (one for Bunny and Dora and one for the children)
and then to Upper Cheyne Row in Chelsea, and the same
house in Oxshott again and then for a year to a house on the
towpath near Richmond Bridge, in Cholmondeley Walk, and
finally to Dilke Street in Chelsea. Dora may not have been
able to stand her husband but at least her gipsy blood must
have been singing, and the snob in her must have relished it
when occasionally Sir Thomas Beecham would come to stay
for the weekend. Although Bunny always rented their homes
– for some romantic reason he was determined never to own
one – he was increasingly successful and wealthy enough to
have an office in Park Lane and to lunch regularly with his
mistresses at the Dorchester and the Ritz. His children had
a series of nannies – their favourite was Nanny Boys – and
he was sending them to expensive private schools. When
Jerry was born in 1932 and raised in leafy, genteel Southern
suburbs, much of Britain was gripped by Depression and the
desperate unemployed were tramping across the country on
the Jarrow hunger marches. Boys of his generation were being
born to exhausted mothers in the cramped attics of grimy
cobbled back streets of industrial towns where the only light
at the end of the tunnel seemed to be the welcome glow of
the furnace in the crematorium. Privileged little Jerry was
luckier than he was ever prepared to admit. Apparently he
was very pretty and a jolly baby who laughed a lot. He had
a lot in those days to be jolly about.

He would have known nothing of the family crisis, when
he was two, when his sister Sally fell desperately ill and her
mother, who was a Christian Scientist, refused to call a doctor. A woman friend insisted on doing so instead and Sally's
life was saved by a Chelsea doctor, R. C. Jewesbury.

Jerry's first memory, appropriately, was of his first sip of alcohol, in 1937, when he was five. Bunny took the boy to his office in Park Lane to watch George VI's coronation procession and he was given a glass of champagne or possibly cider. 'I've often wondered if that was when the rot set in,' he wrote forty years later.

At that time they were living in Oxshott, at Pachesham Lodge, where they stayed for two years. They had a tennis court, servants, nannies, temperamental cooks – even alcoholic gardeners – and in the large garden were several ponds, into one of which weedy little Jerry was pushed by Bruce, which no doubt explained why he never learned to swim and was always in later life to exhibit the deepest distrust of water unless it came in a glass disguised as ice cubes.

The Bernards' family background was so comfortably bourgeois – Bruce even played the violin – that in later life Jeffrey Bernard could surely have qualified as a recipient of a handout from the Distressed Gentlefolk's Association.

It was certainly a typically privileged 1930s childhood. Jerry was sent at six for a few weeks to a school in Oxshott run by a Mrs Haines, who was instrumental in initiating him into the second great passion of his life: he spent a great deal of time trying to look up her skirt. He was very pleased with himself when he was seven and the little girl who lived next door asked him to pop in one night and see her in her bath at bedtime.

Sadly he had few memories of his father, who was to die the following year, although he remembered that Bunny would take him into the garden every morning, before he went to Park Lane, to cut himself a rose for his buttonhole and that they once went together to the Oval to see Surrey play Nottinghamshire at cricket. 'Jeffrey was terribly in awe of him,' Bruce recalled. 'We all were. He was a very small man but very dynamic, quite frightening but also very engaging and one wanted him to like one. I remember Jeff's absolute mortification one Christmas when he went

up to my father with a balloon and my father just popped
it with his cigarette. Jeff regarded it as a terrible putdown
but of course my father meant it as a joke. Jeff was a very
sensitive child indeed and he wet his bed a lot. It must have
been some nervous problem.'

It was a problem that was to be exacerbated when Jerry
was sent off to join his brothers at a boarding school called
Belmont at the age of six and became desperately miserable
and homesick. He simply could not understand why his
mother wanted to get rid of him and claimed later that for
the next ten years, until he was sixteen, he was never happy
again unless he was playing cricket, boxing or fencing.

In 1939, when Sally was away at a Swiss finishing school
in Gstaad, the family returned to live in London at 11 Dilke
Street, a weird modern house on the Chelsea Embankment
which had been decorated most depressingly. The bathroom
walls and ceiling were both painted the deepest black and it
had a turquoise bath and lavatory. Oliver's bedroom had
black walls and a blood red carpet.

In April 1939 Bunny fell suddenly ill with a 'perforated
ulcer' and was rushed to St Thomas's Home in Lambeth.
His children were never to see him again. Callously Dora
sent them to stay separately with strangers on the South
Downs. He died of peritonitis on 15th April, aged only
fifty-eight. None of the children was allowed to attend his
funeral.

'That was really *bloody* odd,' Oliver told me. 'My father
was taken ill with an ulcer one afternoon. A week later we
were told that he was dead. Then she took us all off to the
South of France! Very strange.'

'I've always missed not having a father,' Jeffrey told me fifty
years later, when he was himself fifty-eight. Jeffrey was always
to claim that *his* sadness was quite different from depression
and that it was a chronic, lifelong, incurable illness contracted
at about the age of seven, the time Bunny died. His father's

death must surely have left him bereft and devastated, like so many other children who were to lose their fathers in the world war that was about to begin.

But dreadful though the effect was to be on all Bunny's sons, the impact of Bunny's death was worst of all for Sally, whom he had described as the apple of his eye. His death was literally to drive her mad.

2

An Engaging Little Ruffian

Bunny Bernard died leaving his widow £2,000, no property and huge debts. Dora immediately decided to splash out on a holiday she could not afford. In July 1939, three months after Bunny's death, as Europe trembled on the brink of another world war, she took the three boys on holiday to Roquebrune in the South of France. Typically, fourteen-year-old Sally was not included in this holiday but was packed off back to her finishing school in Switzerland. Dora's anti-Sally campaign had begun. There was also one very odd episode during this holiday that still disturbed Oliver's memory fifty years later: he was now thirteen but during a bus ride from Menton to Roquebrune his mother told him to sit on the lap of a man who then fondled him quite blatantly. It was later a weird sexual quirk of Dora's that she never minded her sons' homosexual friends – indeed, she encouraged them – but she resented their girlfriends. Because they were potential sexual rivals? It was something that could perhaps explain her jealousy of Sally.

The family returned to England in August just two weeks before war was declared on 3 September. They went to live in a Victorian house in Holland Park, at 19 Lansdowne Walk, and Dora told Oliver that he was now the Man of the House. The house, which had three floors, a basement and a garden with a summer house, was in fact for sale at £600 but Dora could not afford that much and had to rent it.

Young Jerry was very conscious of ghosts in Holland Park, where he felt aware of the shades of a gamekeeper and a Regency buck: 'Every time I went down to the basement I got as cold as ice at the top of the stairs,' he said fifty years later. 'I felt someone was there.' The landlady's small son also told him that he had seen more than once the figure of a man with a tall black hat and a buckle on it. Death certainly seemed to be close about them. Jerry's first pet died too, a white mouse called Wolfgang Amadeus Mozart, which he gave a full ceremonial funeral in a flower bed.

Bunny had died without leaving a will and Letters of Administration of his estate were granted to Dora and his old friend Sir Evan Owen Williams, a Mayfair engineer who was Oliver's godfather and had designed the black glass *Daily Express* building in Fleet Street. Bunny's estate was valued at £2,950 1s. 1d., a poignantly precise amount that was worth in modern terms about £120,000. But he also left huge debts. Oliver kept Bunny's diaries for 1939 and they revealed how close he was to bankruptcy. Bunny Bernard had enjoyed a few too many mistresses and lunches at the Ritz and his widow and children ended up paying the bill. Bruce believed that when his father died he was earning well over £5,000 a year [£200,000 today] and perhaps as much as £8,000, but he never insured his life and his family was left with little. His financial profligacy and his refusal to insure himself or think about tomorrow were two more traits that he shared with his youngest son.

Sir Evan Owen Williams may have helped Dora financially and the family of course was still far better off than the majority of Britons during the war, but their sudden comparative poverty was to leave a deep bitterness in Jeffrey, who developed in later life such a chip on his shoulder about money and his lack of it that you would have thought that he had been cheated out of a fortune. He was never to lose the childish feeling that he had been done down and that the world now owed him a living.

Despite the hardships she faced, Dora was determined that her sons would grow up as proper gentlemen and she vowed to keep them at their boarding schools for as long as possible even though she had to swallow her middle-class pride and rely on charities to pay the school fees, beginning with the Architects' Benevolent Fund. 'She was very good at persuading people like that to help her and us,' Bruce remembered. Perhaps it was her genteel scrounging that was to teach Jeffrey how to borrow and scrounge himself in later years. Dora needed to get a job, of course, but she had long wanted to return to the stage and Bunny's death had removed his disapproval and released her to do as she wished at last. It is revealing that on Bunny's death certificate she signed herself 'E. D. Bernard' but by the time she was granted Letters of Administration she was calling herself Fedora Bernard. Until now she had been Edith Bernard officially and Fedora Roselli in the theatre. To merge the two names and call herself Fedora Bernard suggests a deliberate blurring of her roles as widow, mother and singer. As soon as possible after setting up the family in their new home in Lansdowne Walk she joined ENSA, the Entertainments National Services Association, which sent performers out to entertain the troops. It was during her six years with ENSA that she met Joyce Grenfell, a fellow Christian Scientist who was to become a great friend and to pay Jeffrey's school fees for a year after the war.

Now that Dora was back in showbiz, Oliver remembered that she tended to adopt an irritatingly theatrical manner and 'alternated between intense affection and a kind of fury'. She certainly exhibited a strikingly dramatic personality. She once had to appear in court for failing to keep up with hire-purchase payments on some furniture and when she was haranguing the prosecuting counsel she was told by the magistrate that if she continued to speak like that he would have to commit her to prison for contempt of court. She fixed him with a haughty look and remarked: 'Make that *utter* contempt.' The magistrate was so astonished that he merely ordered her to pay off a small amount of the debt each month. On one occasion, when she was in a lift with a woman who bent to smack her child, Dora smacked the woman as well and declared: 'Don't you *dare* hit a child.'

Even the terrifying crashing of Hitler's bombs all over London did not seem to bother her at all.

Oliver may have been now The Man of the House but he came close to hating his mother, though he admitted that she had been 'a heroine' in managing to keep the whole family going 'in the most amazing way'. His considered verdict on her fifty years later – in his autobiography *Getting Over It* (Peter Owen, 1992) – was devastating. 'I admired my mother,' he wrote, 'but didn't trust her.'

'Bruce was my mother's favourite, without any doubt,' he told me. 'I was the person who should have been coping with everything and taking the place of my father but instead I was miserable and cried a lot and was always gloomy and I wouldn't brighten up when I was told to brighten up.' Dora considered him to be the scholar of the family and he was now at Westminster School, where a friend of Bunny's helped her to pay the fees and where one of Oliver's contemporaries, a year older than himself, was the future politician Tony Benn, then still Anthony Wedgwood-Benn. But Bunny's death had hit Oliver hard. He had always been very withdrawn and tearful and he too, like Jeffrey later, wet the bed even as a teenager, which was surely a sign of domestic tension and distress. But in 1940 he had become a sulky, morose fifteen-year-old and seemed to be in serious danger of going to the bad: he stole a cigarette case from a woman who seduced him, a ten-shilling note at school, and for five or six weeks he earned a bit on the side by becoming a male prostitute in the West End, a rent boy. He even took one of his customers back home to his bedroom at 19 Lansdowne Walk. Perhaps Dora would only have minded had he had a girl with him.

Oliver was particularly upset by the way Dora treated Sally, who had been Bunny's favourite child. She was devastated by his death yet Dora seemed not to care how much she hurt her, sending her back immediately to her Swiss finishing school and treating her as a third-class citizen at home. Until the death of her father Sally was a perfectly normal teenage girl who enjoyed her friends and the usual teenage interests:

make-up, fashion, acting. Slowly, over the next twelve years, Dora drove her daughter mad. Oliver remembered 'squabbles at mealtimes, my mother's overriding voice, my sister's wail: "It's always the boys! The boys this, the boys that!" ' Later Jeffrey said that the slamming of a door still filled him with gloom, 'evoking as it does memories of childhood scenes'.

As the baby of the family, Jerry was becoming a deeply unhappy, lonely child shunned by his brothers because he was so much younger than they, and he was even less happy when Dora sent him to join Bruce at a boarding prep school called Belmont, which had just been evacuated because of the Blitz, from London to Cockermouth in Cumberland, more than two hundred miles away. He hated every minute there. 'I didn't understand that my mother had to work to make money,' Jeffrey told Rosanna Greenstreet of the *Telegraph Magazine* in 1991, 'and that kids are a bloody nuisance anyway.' To me he said: 'I was a weak, frail, miserable, unhappy little bedwetter with skin trouble and hayfever.' Bruce's memory of him at this time, however, was much less pathetic: 'I thought he was an engaging little ruffian. He was pretty anarchic and pretty untidy, a little rebel, very stroppy. He had his legendary charm very early on.' It is difficult not to feel in all of Jeffrey's horror stories about his childhood and schooldays that perhaps he was exaggerating and playing the young soldier, though Bruce agreed that all the boys had been lonely and had had few friends because they had moved houses and schools so often that they never had any roots anywhere.

Dora must have realised that the boys were too far away up in Cumberland, especially in wartime, and she sent them instead to a Christian Science prep school much closer to home, to Fan Court in Surrey. Little Jerry did not appear to be much happier here and it was now that he was teased about his name so much at school that he persuaded his mother to let him change it. 'I got teased a lot at school in the war,' he explained, 'because Jerries were Germans – and chamberpots were jerries. I came home crying one

day because of it and my mother said, "Well, we'll call you
something else beginning with J", and she chose Jeffrey.' In
later years he was not particularly taken by Jeffrey, either,
when he came to realise that it was a name 'frequently given
to moronic but decent cow hands in Hollywood Westerns'.

For all his later claims that he was a snivelling little
erk in the early Forties he was also remarkably lively,
mischievous and adventurous. He was certainly not one
for sitting at home in a corner weeping. The incendiary
excitements of the war, with bombs and buildings crashing
all over London, had fired his imagination and he would
sit on the roof at Lansdowne Walk and bomb passers-by
with milk bottles. He threw stones through people's windows and popped thunderflashes through their letter boxes.
On a grander scale he also succeeded in burning down the
summer-house and Dora's favourite lilac tree. When he was
a little older he used to buy sulphur from a local chemist to
make gunpowder: 'The noise of the air raids deceived my
mother into thinking that I was in my room gently reading
Treasure Island.' He would compress the gunpowder into tins to
make bombs, and at school he designed a torpedo with which
to sink other boys' boats as they sailed them on public ponds:
a 12-bore cartridge with the shot removed and powered by
sodium. His most explosive triumph came on the night of
5th November 1944, when he was twelve. He climbed onto
the roof of a neighbouring house – where there was a Guy
Fawkes party and dance in the drawing-room, which was
being warmed nicely by a blazing fire – and fired a rocket
down the chimney. When the firework hit the grate beneath,
hot coal shot across the room and the waltz suddenly became
a lively polka.

'I thought the war was a hell of an adventure,' he was
to say. 'I used to watch dogfights in the sky, and in the
mornings after air raids I used to walk round these streets
collecting shrapnel. I found an incendiary bomb once. I don't
know why it didn't kill me. I just picked it up. I must have
been crazy.'

Dora was by now a merry widow and attracting admirers, 'but not impressive ones,' according to Bruce. 'I can remember a very nice American officer who obviously loved her,' he said, 'but I think she resisted respectable interest. I don't think she wanted to know again, actually.' Bruce had in fact by now become her closest confidant, even though he was only thirteen and was about to go to school at Bedales, which she had chosen for him because he was the 'artistic' one of the family: 'My mother would talk to me about things that she wouldn't talk about to the others.' In 1992 he still found the memory of that closeness and responsibility 'burdensome'. Jeffrey thought that his mother did have other lovers after his father died: 'I know she did. She wasn't a very promiscuous woman but she was obviously a highly sexed woman, no doubt about that. She was a middle-class, beautiful bum.'

By now Sally had decided that she wanted to be an actress and had won a place at the Royal Academy of Dramatic Art, but she soon had to leave. There was simply not enough money. 'She had a lot of wit as well as beauty and she'd have been a bloody good actress,' said Oliver, 'but my mother *had* to cut down on these enormous fees that she was paying for everyone to be at school. She had me at Westminster, Bruce at Bedales and Sally at RADA.' Oliver himself had to leave Westminster after he had been there only a year and a term, and was then sent to a tutor for six months. Dora must have been desperate for money in those days and she borrowed a great deal from Bunny's friends. 'I think she tapped a few of them once too often,' said Oliver, 'but when Sally and I were off her hands it was perhaps easier to keep Bruce and Jeffrey going.'

Even though she had to curtail her children's education Dora still managed to keep up a stylish front. 'My mother had impeccable taste in furniture, considering how broke we were,' Jeffrey claimed. Her drawing room 'was full of Dresden and there was a beautiful grand piano . . . We had a lot of parties – theatrical people, showbiz people. I suppose she was what you might call middle-class bohemian . . .' One can imagine the nine-year-old Jeffrey observing the noisy antics of this thespian Holland Park salon from the kitchen where his mother forced him to remain. Jeffrey made the most of the situation by blackmailing his mother: he threatened her by saying that if she did not give him money he would tell her posh friends that her father had been a butcher. She paid up.

Jeffrey was in fact by now becoming decidedly precocious. In 1941, when he was nine, he had already started smoking and he was sent for two years to another prep school in Herefordshire, Doone House at Peterchurch, which boasted a ghost, a homosexual geography master and the delectable Miss Browne, who taught history and English. One day Jeffrey, who was becoming increasingly interested in the curious appendage that he had discovered between his legs, suddenly lunged for Miss Browne's thighs, perhaps to discover whether she had one too. She slapped his face. He crept away to tremble and smoke Black Cat cigarettes behind the gardener's shed.

There were two other major excitements in 1942. There was the November night that Jeffrey and the rest of his dormitory were awakened by an excited master who switched on the light and announced: 'Monty's got Rommel on the run.' Then Oliver, who was now sixteen, finally ran away from home after Dora had slapped him during a row about his staying out later than ten o'clock at night. His mother was not to see him or hear from him for three years.

The effect of Oliver's sudden disappearance must have been electrifying for Bruce and Jeffrey but Dora appears to have taken it quite calmly. 'She only liked me and Jeff,' said Bruce, 'she didn't like Sonia and Oliver. I don't know why, it's irrational. It's funny for a mother not to like her oldest son. She thought I was an artistic type and I'd be a musician and she liked the idea of that. She was very fond of Jeff and thought he might do great things. She didn't think my sister was anything much. She was dismissive and patronising and my sister didn't have the sympathy that she needed, which is partly why she's a mental invalid now.' He was sure that his mother's antagonism towards Sally had nothing to do with jealousy even though Dora had by now lost all chance of becoming the star that he felt she could have been. 'She had no reason to resent Sally because Sally wasn't rival material whatever,' he said. 'She was quite pretty but she wasn't going to be an actress.'

Oliver disagreed: 'I *know* she disliked my sister and felt jealous of her: later on my sister became very pretty and very witty and very funny. She was *extremely* good-looking. People who remember her as a child or a young woman say she was *absolutely* beautiful. What happened was that my mother loved to surround herself with her *boys*. We were pretty well let know that we were loved and that my sister wasn't. She knew this and I think that's what made her mad. I really *do* think so.'

It also seems that there was a strong sexual undercurrent in Dora's relationship with her sons. 'I felt a little bit sort of *chased* by my mother as if she was sort of *after* me, sexually,' said Oliver. 'I couldn't bear it. I just hated the idea.'

— 2 —

In 1943 Doone House was closed when the headmaster died and Jeffrey was sent to yet another prep school, this time in Kent, the New Beacon in Sevenoaks, which he described later as 'a ghastly school' of 'bullies and self-abusers presided over by a mad ex-Major'- who had by chance the same name as the Cockney playwright who was later to become Bernard's best friend in the 1960s, Frank Norman. The novelist Anthony Powell had been a pupil there twenty-five years earlier, from 1916 to 1919, when most of the boys were the sons of army officers. The school 'would rank high in any competition for dearth of cultural enlightenment,' he wrote in his memoirs *To Keep The Ball Rolling* (Penguin, 1983). 'Nothing picturesquely horrible ever happened to me there, though I should be unwilling to live five minutes of it again.' While Powell was there (along with Henry Yorke, who wrote under the name Henry Green) a boy who had been accused of dishonesty was publicly given thirty-two strokes of the birch so viciously that he urinated on the floor of the classroom. The thrashing was administered by the headmaster, who then forbade the other boys to speak to the victim. A few weeks later the boy was found to be totally innocent.

'I think it was probably much the same as any other prep school at that period,' Powell told me in 1991. 'I was heartily glad to leave, but my chief objection, looking back, was that the teaching was bad. It was during the first war, and teachers were hard to come by, but I think some schools managed better.'

The place did not seem to have improved much in a quarter of a century, though Jeffrey did admit later that the school had two good points. One was a beautiful botany mistress, Miss Burt, up whose skirt Jeffrey would peer as often as possible by dropping a pencil as she passed his desk. The other was a music mistress who played the piano with her legs so wide apart that the boy suddenly developed an avid interest in Bach and would sit on the floor in front of her piano with an eager expression. Jeffrey had now also discovered masturbation, thanks partly to the proximity of the music and botany mistresses but mainly to the advice of his friend, Watson, who told him that he had discovered something called masturbation during the hols and it was really 'rather extraordinary'. Curious about this, Jeffrey researched the matter and delightedly agreed. He now made every effort to sit at the back of the class to play with himself during lessons. He seems also to have corrupted some of the other boys because in 1944 he was suddenly expelled. His mother came down to Sevenoaks from London one day to take him home, gave him tea at the Royal Hotel and announced that he had been kicked out for persistent bedwetting and 'for being a bad influence', which usually in the prep school code of those days meant sexual misbehaviour. Major Frank Norman did however see him off with a reference admitting that he had the makings of a 'fine seam bowler'.

Back in London for the holidays Dora seems to have been living quite a normal middle-class life in Lansdowne Walk despite some of Jeffrey's later stories about her. To boost her finances she was now taking in occasional lodgers, usually American officers, and although she was perhaps a little grand and tended to consider herself superior to more people than was perhaps justified, she also had theatrical friends and fellow singers in for noisy sherry parties when they gathered around the piano and laughed and drank and smoked a lot, both men and women. In fact she sounds just the sort of woman of whom the adult Jeffrey would have approved, especially when she left the house one day in April with their ration books to buy food and returned instead with a candlestick. 'My mother was always terrible with money,' he said. 'There wasn't any food in the house at all, not even a loaf of bread, and she went out to Notting Hill Gate to get the weekend shopping. When she came back she didn't even have a loaf of bread for us: she brought back a Dresden candlestick which she said she couldn't resist. I loved her for that. I thought that was style. Fuck the bread!' True, she embarrassed him when she sang Mahler at the piano beside the candlestick, and her friends made him blush when they insisted that he should sing *O For the Wings of a Dove* but they did give him half-crowns with which he bought Dinky Toys.

He seems to have had few friends. Sally tended to stay in her room and Bruce was out of the house a lot with his chums; he was planning to leave home and often did not return until late at night. But a lonely childhood does not always mean an unhappy one. It did, however, mean that Jeffrey was in danger of falling in with the wrong sort of company, like the fireman who lived nearby and played the harpsichord and took him home to show him pictures of naked women. Jeffrey was also quite capable of amusing himself. He had now graduated to smoking Park Drive cigarettes and in May set the dry grass of Lansdowne Gardens alight with such success that the firemen had to rush to the scene. His incendiary talent was to last him all his life.

By the end of the month Dora had found yet another prep school that was brave enough to take him, this time in Sussex, and he went off to Fonthill School, East Grinstead, which was presumably sufficiently far from Sevenoaks for any rumours of his behaviour to have failed to reach them. He was put into Form IIIB, enjoyed the admiration of a homosexual Latin master, and discovered only too soon to his horror that the headmaster, the Reverend Walpole E. Sealy, liked when caning boys to clear his study of all furniture but for the chair over which they had to bend. It gave him more room for his swing, he explained. The Rev. Sealy came up with an even more exquisite torture for young Bernard when he learned that the boy was still wetting his bed at the age of twelve: he made him carry his wet sheets every morning through Assembly to the jeers of the other boys. Whenever he wet the bed the matron, Mrs Spencer-Payne, would slap his face.

Eventually Dora became so desperate to cure Jeffrey's bedwetting that she arranged for a genito-urinary surgeon to operate twice on his urethra. 'He put rods of steel up my cock to try to widen the urethra to make it easier to pee in the daytime so that I wouldn't pee at night,' Jeffrey told me. 'It was very frightening. I had to have a general anaesthetic and I woke up in great agony and saw that my cock was covered in blood-soaked bandages, which was traumatic for a boy of twelve. You can't *punish* children for wetting the bed, and that operation was a punishment of a sort. And I had two of them – I went back about six months later! It put me off my mother for a bit, I can tell you.' The two operations may have caused untold psychological damage, but failed to cure his bedwetting. They also damaged his reproductive capacity and left him sterile for the rest of his life.

It was at Fonthill that he thought it was time that he tried to kiss his first girl rather than merely lunging at her thighs. The school was so short of money that the Rev. Walpole E. Sealy had taken in a few day girls, one of whom was a diplomat's daughter, Norma King. Jeffrey was by now in the responsible position of being either the 'ace right-winger' or the goalkeeper in the school's 2nd XI football team and one day when Norma was hanging about behind the goal it seems that he happened to have a bottle of cherry brandy that he was swigging whenever the play was up at the other end of the field. It is possible that this was when he had his first proper alcoholic drink, since the sip of cider or champagne that his father had given him in his Park Lane office when he was four hardly counted. There is unfortunately some doubt about this momentous occasion of the First Drink. Jeffrey himself retailed several versions in later life. In one he claimed that his mother gave him a glass of sherry when he was ten and he was so revolted by it that he told her: 'I shan't drink when I grow up. It tastes awful.' But twice he reported that it was when he was the goalkeeper in the school's 2nd XI football team. What makes the 2nd XI claim particularly momentous, however, is that it combines Jeff Bernard's First Drink with his First Kiss and so manages to combine the genesis of his two lifelong obsessions. As he told it, just one swig fired him with that miraculous Dutch courage for the first time in his life and he suddenly grabbed Norma King behind the goalmouth and kissed her. She tasted of Dolly Mixture, he reported later. 'You dirty little guttersnipe,' she said. At Christmas the prelude to Jeffrey's sex education proper was almost complete: he went shopping at Harrods and Santa groped him in the grotto.

There were more inaccuracies to come in his later memories of taking his first drink. In one article in the *Spectator* he claimed that he had swigged the bottle of brandy while playing cricket and fielding at deep long leg that summer. In the *New Statesman* he claimed that his first drink had been a glass of Algerian wine that his mother gave him on VJ-Day on 15th August 1945. Two years later, in the *Daily Mirror*, he said that this had been on Christmas Day that year. By 1985 he was reporting in the *Spectator* that after the glass of North African plonk he had not only promised his mother that he would never touch another drop but had actually been physically sick. By 1991 he was telling the *Telegraph Magazine* that he had had his first proper drink in a pub round the corner from his home at Lansdowne Walk when he was fourteen: 'The Castle was the first pub I ever went into. I went with some friends of my mother's and they slipped me a couple of ciders.' Although the differences between the various versions are unimportant in themselves they do show that some of Bernard's anecdotes were polished so vigorously and so often over the years that eventually the shine came off them and left them tarnished. The precise date of his first swallow will remain for ever a mystery and of course – as he might have observed himself – one swallow doesn't make a summer. But it seems reasonable to assume that he had tasted the forbidden nectar well before he was fifteen.

– 3 –

In later years Jeffrey would paint a pathetic picture of his two years at Fonthill, claiming that he was thrashed constantly by the Rev. Walpole E. Sealy – he always managed to misspell Sealy's name – and that he was bullied by two boys called Stainthorpe and Leckie and spent much of his time in terror. An article he wrote for *Town* magazine in 1967 was enough to bring tears to the eyes: 'Dear God, please God, don't let me wet the bed tonight, but if you do, make sure that it's dry by the time matron sees it in the morning . . . Make me good for just one day so that they can see that I am good. Make Mummy send me some sweets and a postal order for 2s 6d and make the Germans bomb the headmaster's study tonight, but let us win the war.'

That summer of 1945 should have been perfect for young
Jeffrey. The war had just ended, he was now one of the
oldest boys in the school and in the cricket First XI. The Rev.
Walpole E. Sealy had even made him a prefect. Many years
later Jeffrey even admitted that he had been an extremely
unpopular prefect: 'I was very strict and discovered a nasty
puritan streak within me,' he wrote in the *Spectator*, which simply does not square with his usual whimpering self-portrait.
Once again he seems to have been exaggerating his misery.
He was to continue to do so.

   He had, for instance, by now decided that he wanted
to be a marine engineer. He found steam engines exciting
and was to build a railway around the garden for a working
model of the Royal Scot that he got from a boy at school who
swapped it for a rare triangular Victorian Cape of Good Hope
stamp that Jeffrey had stolen. He was especially fascinated
by ships' engines and very much wanted to go to the Naval
College at Pangbourne to allow him to join the merchant
navy. He admired naval uniform and dreamed of dressing in
braid. Yet when Dora managed valiantly to raise the money
to send him there he was utterly ungrateful. In 1989 he told
Martyn Harris of the *Sunday Telegraph*: 'What I'd really like
to have been is a solicitor with a house in Haslemere. A
wife, a boy and a girl, a Ford Escort and a Flymo, with
a pint of bitter on Sunday lunchtime. But my mother sent
me to Pangbourne naval college and that messed me up.
She wanted me to be an officer and a gentleman.' In print
and in private he blamed her bitterly for the rest of his life
for sending him to Pangbourne, but he himself had chosen
it.

   Jeffrey's sneering at his mother in later life was grossly
unfair, especially as he knew precisely how hard she had
had to struggle to pay for his education. Fifteen years later
he was to tell his second wife, Jacki, that Dora had even had
to do occasional cleaning work as a char to help pay the bills.
'She was doing whatever sort of job she could do to keep him
there,' said Jacki, 'and maybe the guilt was too much for him.

On the surface it was a middle-class upbringing but it wasn't really at all because she was driven to desperate straits to try and keep it so. It gave him a huge burden of guilt.'

He was also rather too young when his mother foolishly allowed him to feast his greedy little masturbator's eyes on the succulent flesh of all the pretty young chorus girls who appeared with her on stage in *The Lisbon Story*. Now that the war was over there was no more work for her in ENSA and she had to take what she could get in the theatre, even to the extent of demeaning herself by appearing in the chorus. Thirteen-year-old Jeffrey was allowed to sit in her dressing room and watch the girls undress. This was not a good idea. He became fixated on stockings, suspender belts, high heels, and his mother's salmon-pink underwear. Eventually they were to become sexual obsessions and they fuelled his furious interest in masturbation, a cause that he adopted with all the fervour of a missionary, persuading so many other boys of its pleasures that in his last term at Fonthill the habit spread so far and wide that it attained the status of a new Craze. When the Rev. Walpole E. Sealy discovered that his entire establishment had suddenly been gripped by the vitals the boys were questioned and Bernard was fingered as the culprit after Mrs Spencer-Payne had discovered that he was regularly 'playing with himself'. This led to a three-week enquiry into masturbation by the Rev. Walpole E. Sealy, who discovered in addition that young Bernard and his disreputable friend Thorley had also begun seriously to smoke themselves to death. Sealy gave Bernard nine of the best with the cane, doubtless clearing his study of furniture to allow for the swing. The headmaster also wrote to Dora to complain of her son's corrupting influence. She in turn sent the blushing Jeffrey to an Austrian psychiatrist in Wimpole Street, who enquired: 'Tell me, do you ever play wizz your leetle man?'

'Do you mean masturbate?' asked Jeffrey.

The shrink burst out laughing and explained: 'I'm amused by your insistence on using its *legal* term.'

It was an ignominious end to the prefect's career at

Fonthill and in the circumstances he was handsomely treated by the Rev. Walpole E. Sealy, who wrote a glowing letter of recommendation to the Pangbourne College secretary on 12 February 1946, though this may of course have been inspired by an urgent desire to be rid of the troublesome little chain-smoker as soon as possible. It was a letter worthy of H. F. Ellis's immortal fictional prep school master A. J. Wentworth (B.A.) or of Captain Grimes in Evelyn Waugh's *Decline and Fall* and was written in eloquently tiny, crabbed handwriting. The Rev. Walpole E. Sealy obviously did not clear the furniture when he sat down to write:

> This boy has only been in my school since May, 1944. When he first came, we did not find him a very satisfactory boy, as he apparently had the wrong attitude towards authority; and being a strong personality, he was beginning to influence other boys in this direction; but as soon as we realised this, we took a very firm line with him, in consequence of which his attitude has undergone a marked change; so much so, that we have felt justified in giving him posts of responsibility in the school, which he has fulfilled satisfactorily. He is a very promising cricketer, his bowling being exceptionally good; he is in the school soccer team. He is quite a capable boy, but he didn't start working really hard until this last year, so that the standard of his work is not yet as high as it should be in a boy of his ability. He is a boy with a considerable amount of charm and a good sense of humour; he gets on well with the other boys. He is very musical and has a lovely voice.

There is also a delightful letter in the Pangbourne College files, dated 15 February 1946, from a Captain G. A. Kitchin, who lived just around the corner from Dora at 32 Ladbroke Grove, commending young Jeffrey: 'He is, in my opinion, a most suitable candidate for the College, a quiet and serious boy with good manners and a wise head on his young shoulders.' The following day the Reverend Reginald

Churchill, CBE, RN, wrote from the naval air station at
Worthy Down, near Winchester, that he was very pleased
to be able to recommend Mrs Bernard's son: 'He is very
bright.' He added somewhat optimistically that he was sure
that the boy would be 'a very great credit to the school'.

He was wrong.

3

Idle and Untrustworthy

He arrived at the Nautical College, Pangbourne, on the River Thames near Reading in Berkshire, on 25 April 1946, a month before his fourteenth birthday, thanks to the first of several charity handouts that were to keep him there for two years, a £50 grant from the Royal Asylum Assistance Society. The school's official history, *Pangbourne College*, published in 1991, reports that 'the object of education at Pangbourne was to send cadets to sea, particularly to the Merchant Navy'.

The book mentioned Bernard briefly, with sadness rather than anger: 'All schools have their misfits – Pangbourne perhaps more than most because of its rigorous discipline. The majority disappear into obscurity, but two such products of Pangbourne have achieved fame and rarely miss an opportunity of hurling abuse on "this disgusting naval academy". The first is Ken Russell (1940–1943), the *enfant terrible* of British films; the second is Jeffrey Bernard (1946–1948) who was totally unsuited to any orthodox boarding school.'

Jeffrey hated the place for ever after with a loathing that was to embitter even his old age. Not only was the headmaster known as the Captain Superintendent, the teachers were also dressed as naval officers, the boys ('cadets') wore white peaked caps and rows of brass buttons and stood at attention. For a teenager with Bernard's lackadaisical, fatherless, bohemian background such discipline was beyond endurance. In rejecting it, as he did, he was charting the course of his entire undisciplined life to come. Never again would he be able to live by any rules other than those of his own making, and his rejection then at Pangbourne of any form of discipline was to make him in later life virtually unemployable and unmarriageable. At Pangbourne he chose to go against the grain. He refused, for the first but not the last time in his life, to change and settle down.

Arriving at Pangbourne in the same term as Bernard was young Johnny Webster, later Admiral Sir John Webster, who was at the college from 1946 to 1950. Another contemporary who went on to become an admiral was John Barker (1944–1948), as was Rear Admiral Sir Paul Greening, KCVO, who was to become Master of the Queen's Household in 1986. It is sobering to realise that of all the boys who were at Pangbourne when he was there it was only the wretched Bernard who was to become famous even though five of them went on to become admirals. In 1990, while theatre-goers were guffawing night after night at the Apollo Theatre in Shaftesbury Avenue at the seriously unnautical antics of the unwell Jeffrey Bernard, the fortunes of the Royal Navy were still held in the firm, dependable grip of one Old Pangbournian Vice-Admiral, three Old Pangbournian Rear-Admirals, twenty-one O.P. Captains and more than fifty Commanders and Lieutenant-Commanders. As Bernard admitted himself, the nation is fortunate that one of those nuclear admirals was not himself.

The film director Ken Russell gave a graphic portrait of the college in his autobiography *A British Picture* (Heinemann, 1989) and claimed that all he ever learned there 'was how to speak proper and the rudiments of direction and choreography' when he was involved in theatrical productions. Otherwise: 'Every night row upon row of metal bunks rattled to the rhythm of mass masturbation. I suppose it was because we missed our mums . . . At thirteen and a half I found life could be hell. Everything about me was wrong, from my accent to my uniform. Suddenly I discovered I wasn't talking proper. I didn't talk posh. I said Mum instead of Mater. One of my chief tormenters was Cadet Leader Forbes-Marlborough, who told me, "I say, Russell, you sound like a common dockland matey." ' Russell was bullied for months by Forbes-Marlborough, who encouraged his cronies to throw Russell 'fully clothed into a stinking bog' while chanting:

Our Ken's a dirty nipper,
He stinks just like a kipper.
Let's fill his ass
With broken glass
And circumcise the skipper.

Russell was also beaten: for being suspected of stealing a five-pound note; for breaking bounds; for reading *Picturegoer* in the chapel; for talking after lights-out. 'Soon, I thought, they'd be able to play noughts and crosses on my ass,' he wrote in his book, which seemed to bear out Bernard's complaint that he was thrashed constantly. But three or four beatings in three or four years hardly seems excessive for a boarding school of that era, especially when you consider that Russell and Bernard must have been quite impossible as teenagers.

It is not however difficult to sympathise when reading Ken Russell's description of a day in the life of Pangbourne: 'Reveille sounds. We tumble out of bed, put on our plimsolls, pull up shorts and stumble out of the dormitory and down the stairs. Six-forty-five on the parade ground. There's a cold wind blowing as we shiver in untidy ranks waiting for directions from the Cadet Captain.

' "Around the piggeries, through Seniors' Wood, across Big Side and up Bartholomew's Bottom . . . Go!" The Cadet Captain yawns and returns to his bunk, leaving the rest of us to trot off on the first cross-country run of the day.

'Twenty minutes later we take a cold shower, dress and march to breakfast.' Later 'the Chief Cadet Captain barks, "Cadets 'shun, right tun, quick harch." Under the arch, clatter, clatter . . . Biscuit farts again, march to lunch, march to afternoon studies, march back, recreation – sawing logs – march to supper, march to evening studies, march to ablutions. Stand by your bunks, one bell, kneel and pray. Silence,

Biscuit farts, stifled laughter. Two bells, turn in, lights out, toss off.'

It is not surprising that as soon as he arrived at Pangbourne Jeffrey Bernard felt decidedly unwell.

When he arrived there on 25th April he was put into the junior house, Port Jackson, and placed in Form IIIB with twenty-four other boys. He had a bewildering first term, coming bottom of the class, surprisingly, in English, and very low in History, Mathematics, Seamanship and Signals. 'He seems to be rather at sea at the moment, and does not appear to have really settled down,' the Director of Studies, Frank Woodall, wrote on his end-of-term report, without apparently realising that being at sea was precisely where a naval cadet ought to be. 'His preparation is very poorly done – he seems not to be able to concentrate.' Woodall also observed that Bernard had a poor memory and was not a very hard worker. His Divisional Tutor, Ernest Beet, wrote that Bernard was 'a rather highly-strung boy who found College life difficult in some ways'. On the credit side he had joined the Choral Society and was keen on cricket.

At the start of the new term, in September 1946, the Professional Classes Aid Council awarded Dora £75 towards Jeffrey's school fees for the coming year, a gesture of rescue that they were to repeat in June the following year. But it was not enough to save her from losing her home. To pay for Jeffrey's education she had to move in 1946 for the first time since Bunny's death seven years previously. She left 19 Lansdowne Walk to live at 161 Maida Vale, W9 and later she had to move again to 15 Leinster Gardens, W2. Each time she was moving downmarket to pay for her youngest son's education. Whatever mistakes she may have made she was a dogged fighter, had obviously tried very hard to give him a decent start in life and was to be given no thanks for it. He seemed to make even less effort in his second term than he had in his first. He was promoted to Form IIIA where he was one of only eleven boys but managed to come bottom in

Mathematics and Seamanship, tenth in Physics ('Very poor work') and ninth in English ('Poor. Must make more effort'). On the credit side he had become a keen boxer and the Captain Superintendent (in effect the Headmaster), Commander Hugh Skinner, wrote on his report: 'I was impressed with his showing in the boxing ring where he showed a good spirit', though he added: 'At his age he should no longer be quite such a scrubby little boy.'

Beverley Cross, whose plays have included *Boeing-Boeing* and *Half a Sixpence*, was a little younger than Ken Russell ('I remember him doing his impersonation of Carmen Miranda') but a year older than Bernard. He remembered Bernard as being 'very amusing and academically quite bright'. Cross denies that the bullying at Pangbourne was any worse than anywhere else at that time: 'There may be some exaggeration on Jeffrey's part. I never knew of much bullying, and in fact he was always very good at answering back. He did have a very ready wit. And he could box: everyone did boxing there.'

Much of the problem was of Jeffrey's own making. 'I spent all my schooldays sitting in the back row of the classroom fantasising about either fucking Ava Gardner or opening the batting for England at Lords against Australia,' he told me, 'so not a lot of work got done. There were two subjects that I enjoyed: History and English, but I couldn't add 2 and 2 until I started backing horses and it was only through racing that I got to be quite good at mental arithmetic.'

Nor did it help that he had discovered during the summer holidays the liberal joys of Soho thanks to Oliver and Bruce, who had joined the Young Communist League and was at St Martin's School of Art in the Charing Cross Road. Bruce introduced Jeffrey to friends of his who seemed incredibly glamorous to the little naval cadet. 'Bruce said come and have a cup of coffee in this marvellous place, and that was it,' Jeffrey told Dan Farson in 1989. 'He messed up my life completely. I was fourteen. Soho was a liberation after the horror of English public schools with their cry of "Don't!" and the discipline of Pangbourne where the masters thrashed me.

Suddenly I was surrounded by pretty girls, booze, nutcases, painters and writers. It was magic, like walking out of Belsen into Disneyland and I've been drunk ever since.'

Bruce remembered that Jeffrey took to hanging around the café they used regularly in Manette Street, the Swiss Café, near Foyles bookshop, 'and everybody thought he was amazing, everybody liked him, his precocity. He was thoroughly engaging to most people and he embarrassed me by actually standing outside the Pillars of Hercules. I could get into pubs and *he* wanted to get into pubs too, but there was no *question* of the landlord serving him because he was quite small and looked so young. For him Soho was total liberty, and I suppose friends at last – he *was* friendless – and I had tons of friends all doing rather dodgy, forbidden things.'

And then Oliver took Bruce and Jeffrey to eat at Bianchi's restaurant in Frith Street on 3rd August and the boy fell in love immediately with the whole bohemian atmosphere. He was already marked out for life. It was the start of Jeffrey's long love affair with Soho.

– 2 –

1947 was to be a crucial year for Bernard in what he later referred to as his lifelong 'downhill struggle'. At last he stopped wetting his bed. In July he lost his virginity. And in September he was to have his first bet on a racehorse, Black Tarquin in the St Leger. The year did not however start well.

For all his apparent timidity he was already bold enough to be smoking illicit cigarettes behind the boathouse and organising masturbation races. He was caned once for reading a Somerset Maugham novel during prep and he was given three 'cuts' by the Master at Arms for having a photograph of Ava Gardner pinned beneath the lid of his desk. He had a friend, Grove, with whom he would hide in a hut in the woods at weekends, smoking and making toast. Bernard even managed to persuade an eccentric maths master, a

Mr Dixon, to take him and Grove to a tea shop in Goring
and let them smoke. This earned Dixon the sack. And he
became insufferably cocky, writing fan letters to the actress
Veronica Lake. 'At Pangbourne I suddenly discovered I was
able to hold my own in a boxing ring and overnight I became
a little tearaway,' he told me. 'Boxing in a funny sort of way
saved me a bit from being petrified. It made me not scared
of life. All you need to face life is to have a fiver for yourself,
and a fuck, and the world is your oyster.'

The boy was obviously heading for trouble and he ran right
into it. One day one of the Cadet Leaders pushed in front of
him in the tuckshop queue and Bernard remarked 'fuck these
CLs'. It earned him his one brutal beating at Pangbourne, ten
strokes that made his buttocks bleed. The Captain Superintendent told him, 'There's a tradition in the Royal Navy,
Bernard, that we do not swear' and he was thrashed by the
Master at Arms. 'I nearly fainted,' he said. 'It was literally
like Nelson's day, and the Chief Cadet Captain had to count
each stroke. He'd say "ONE" – *whisht* – "TWO" – *whisht* –
and at the end of it: "Ten strokes delivered, sah." It was like
being flogged round the fucking fleet. There was a boy with
a hard arse, Vickers-Armstrong, there was something wrong
with him, with his nervous system I think, he had an arse
made of leather, he went to the Master at Arms after six
that were really nasty and said in an oily voice, "Thank you
very much, sah." They were fucking choked. They'd made no
impression on him.'

His report at the end of that term was disastrous. His
teachers commended his singing and boxing but had serious
doubts about his work: 'Still finds it difficult to concentrate,'
said one. 'Spends too much time drawing ships instead of
learning about them,' said another. As for his future, 'It is
abundantly clear that he is making very little progress. He
will have to improve or he will find himself leaving with only
a 3rd Class Certificate.' And ominously: 'I am beginning to
feel that he is not wholly suited to the exacting demands of
a Service career.'

In fact he did seem to try harder during that summer term of 1947 and startled everyone by suddenly coming equal first in English even though there were now twenty-two boys in Form IIIA. He was still bottom in Seamanship ('Very disappointing') but otherwise his teachers were delighted: 'A welcome improvement'; 'He has made distinct progress'; 'I congratulate him on an all round improvement in effort and attitude.' Bernard was now in a senior house, Harbinger, and seemed to be settling down better and playing good cricket for the house team and school's junior XI.

Perhaps the improvement had something to do with the fact that he had at last stopped his bedwetting. He was nearly fifteen and it must have been a huge relief to him. Dora had sent him in despair to a psychoanalyst. 'I only saw him once,' said Bernard, 'and he actually cured me by just talking for half an hour. He was terribly nice about it. He was the first person who never fucking berated me for wetting the bed. He just said "don't worry about it, it's all right", and it was.'

The cure may also of course have been connected with his burgeoning sexuality. He always dreaded the arrival of his mother at Pangbourne at half-terms because she made him squirm, he once wrote in the *Spectator*. 'Her arrivals were like the entry of the Queen of Sheba. All the other boys knew that she was on the stage – tantamount to being a tart during the war years' and the days out always ended with 'a ghastly tea in a Pangbourne tea shop'. But he could just as well have been embarrassed by her presence because he very much wanted to ravish her. He was consumed by fantasies of incest. 'I didn't like her very much,' he told me. 'She was a bit austere and she frightened me. She would be nice grudgingly and she was a terrible snob. But for thirty years I've felt guilty for fancying her, the old Oedipus Complex. I realised when I was fourteen or fifteen that I fancied my mother very very much indeed and I was consumed with guilt about it. She was a very glamorous, beautiful woman.'

Jeffrey found instead another object for his urgent teenage

lust, Anna Grice, a promiscuous eighteen-year-old girl, 'part of the Soho crowd', who was at last, to his huge relief, to Make Him A Man. During the summer holidays he started going to Soho every day to see Bruce and his friends, telling his mother that he was going to the Science Museum. He met Anna, the daughter of Edward Grice, an *Evening Standard* journalist, in a Soho café. 'She was one of the brightest girls I've ever met,' Bernard told me. 'I was fifteen and with my Pangbourne cadet's uniform I used to be able to pretend I was eighteen, which is what she was.' His pretence was so successful that on the night of 2 July 1947 she took him out onto the open spaces of Hampstead Heath and at 10.45 p.m. relieved him of his virginity. 'Just to make sure I'd lost it,' he reported thirty years later in the *Daily Express*, 'I lost it again the following evening.'

Another young Soho girl at that time was Yvonne Marsh, who preferred to be known by her surname and was later to become Marsh Dunbar and to have an affair with Bernard in 1959. 'I knew Anna,' she told me. 'She was extremely bright but she was not only older than Jeffrey but also much more mature. She was a bit intimidating because she was a very tough talker. I think she probably frightened him. She was very handsome, not pretty – beautiful.'

She was also frighteningly volatile and unstable. Bernard did not see her again until 1951. In the autumn of that year, 1947, Oliver and Bruce went off to live and work in Paris for a while and Anna joined them there for two weeks and became Oliver's lover as well. When Jeffrey did bump into her again in Soho four years later she was very quickly to become his first wife. Their story was to end in tragedy.

– 3 –

When Jeffrey went back to Pangbourne in September 1947 his performance of the previous term had so impressed the

Union Castle Line steamship company, which ran the distinctive cream-and-lilac Royal Mail liners between Southampton and South Africa, that he returned with an £80-a-year Union Castle Line cadetship. This could eventually have led him into an engineering job servicing Union Castle liners anywhere from Southampton to Port Said, Suez, Dar-es-Salaam, Zanzibar or Lourenço Marques, Mozambique. Perhaps the prospect appalled him but in any case he never really took the chance. During that term he improved his piano playing so that he began to play quite well in a simple way but that was about all.

But he had also discovered horseracing. It was to become one of the loves of his life. A boy called Tosh was caught gambling on racehorses and was given twelve strokes of the cane. Bernard reasoned that if you could get twelve of the best for gambling it *had* to be immensely exciting. He claimed later that he put a 2/6d bet on Black Tarquin to win the St Leger in 1948 and won £10. Many years later he cursed himself for winning on his first bet because it gave him the ridiculous idea that he could win every time. He was to gamble on horses, dogs, cricket, football and almost everything else that moved, including women, for the rest of his days. He later claimed in the *Sporting Life* that it was also now that he started his career as an illegal bookmaker: he and another boy took bets for the Stewards' Cup on a horse called Dramatic and apparently lost 237 weeks' pocket money 'and if you've never tried welshing on 150 boys at a boarding school miles from anywhere – then don't'. If this story is true it is further evidence that he cannot have been as miserable and ostracised at Pangbourne as he claimed. An unpopular boy would never be able to strike such bets with 150 of his fellows: they would have had nothing to do with him.

His initiations into the joys of Soho, drinking, fornication, horse-racing and gambling, at this early age of fifteen, finally wrecked his naval career at Pangbourne. He could no longer be bothered to go through the motions of pretending that he wanted to be an officer with the Union Castle Line on the Cape Town run. Except for his parade work and rifle shooting his record in the last term of 1947 was disastrous. He was now in Form IVA, with twenty-three others, but despite being older than most of them he was suddenly twenty-third in English, bottom in Mathematics and down among the last three in French, Physics and Navigation. The new Director of Studies, Kenneth Topliss, was brusque. 'There are few redeeming features in this report,' he wrote with a touch of menace. 'He is above the average age of his form and I do not believe that he is below the average in ability. All he has to do is work. I expect him to do so.' Robinson, his Divisional Tutor, called the boy in for a frank talk and told him he was not happy about him but was not among those teachers who were convinced that he was simply not making an effort. 'He worries if things are wrong,' said Robinson, 'and this does not help. A friend to confide in would help.' The Executive Officer, Commander Ronnie Hoyle, agreed: 'He must realise that authority is not against him but would willingly help if more co-operation came from him', a remark with which Commander Skinner agreed entirely. 'He should not get depressed if things do not always go right for him,' wrote Skinner. 'He knows the standard of conduct expected here and there is no reason why he should not do well.'

Telling Bernard not to be depressed was as futile as suggesting that he should pull himself together or pointing out that you only get out of life what you put into it. He simply gave up. After Christmas he returned to Pangbourne for the worst term of his school career and seemed to make no effort at all. Robinson called him in early in the term and warned him that he could no longer make excuses for him and that he had to make a real effort. The charity that was helping his mother with the fees was being sent regular reports and must have been beginning to wonder if the feckless young Bernard was after all a worthy case to support. But the pep talk had no effect whatever. Just two terms after being top of the class in English and astonishing everyone with his sudden improvement in almost everything, Bernard crashed to the bottom of the class in almost every subject. Out of twenty-five boys, almost all of them younger than himself, he came last in Physics and Chemistry, second last in French, Mathematics and Navigation and very low in Geography and Signals. Even in English he was only thirteenth.

He did win the Junior Reading Prize, but even then he managed to incense his teachers. His prize was to be a book. You were supposed to ask for something like *Nelson And His Captains*, but Jeffrey chose quite blithely *Sons and Lovers* and wondered why it caused a fuss. Commander Skinner was already beginning to suspect that Bernard was a bad influence on some of the other boys – even though he seemed to have no real friends except for a boy called Yeoman – and after his excursion with Anna on Hampstead Heath Bernard had certainly developed an even keener interest in smoking and masturbation, though not necessarily at the same time. For the first time there was a real chance that he might be expelled. 'If he wishes to remain here,' Skinner warned, 'he must show much more desire to work. He is idle at present and cannot afford to be.'

Dora must have been at her wits' end by now. Already she was relying on Joyce Grenfell to pay Jeffrey's fees, and for what? And what would become of him if he failed the School Certificate examination in December? He must have returned from 15 Leinster Gardens to Pangbourne for the summer term of 1948, for what was to turn out to be his last term at school, with threats and warnings ringing in his ears.

In that final term he was among the bottom four (out of twenty-five boys) in six out of ten subjects. Even in English he was only eighth. In the overall class results only one boy was worse than he. There was no point in anyone pretending any more. This boy was never going to make an officer. Indeed, there were serious doubts that he would ever become a gentleman, either. Robinson was by now thoroughly fed up, especially since the boy had now developed a 'supercilious outlook' that hardly seemed justified considering his poor performance. 'His idea that people are against him is really fantastic,' said Robinson, 'but one loses patience when the response is practically negligible.'

Commander Skinner had also had enough. He had always had a reputation for being good at dealing with difficult boys but this particular one, he told Dora, was so 'idle and untrustworthy' and 'not justifying his retention here or the financial help given him' that he would be expelled at the end of the following term if he did not make a dramatic improvement.

Bernard beat Skinner to the draw – just. During the summer holidays he persuaded Dora tearfully that he was miserable at Pangbourne and begged to be allowed to leave. She agreed. Had he stayed any longer he would have been kicked out anyway. In later life he always denied that he was expelled from Pangbourne but it was a damned close run thing and in 1992 there was still in the College files a letter that Commander Skinner wrote six years later, in 1954, to a London probation officer after Bernard had been arrested and charged with stealing a book. 'He was removed by his mother at my request,' wrote Skinner.

Bernard never returned to Pangbourne. Dora simply telephoned Skinner to say that he would not be back. There must have been some raucous carousing in the masters' common room when the news came through. One can imagine the entire Pangbourne staff dancing the Hornpipe with relief. In November Dora asked Commander Skinner for some sort of reference for Jeffrey, presumably to help him to get a job. Skinner's reply was brusque. 'To Whom It May Concern,' he wrote. 'This is to certify that Jeffrey Joseph Bernard was a cadet R.N.R. at this College from 25th April 1946 to 27th July 1948. Whilst here his conduct generally was good, but psychologically I do not consider that he is suitable for boarding school life.'

He was not in fact psychologically suitable for anything, but that was another matter.

4

The Sport of Queens

Dora was baffled. What was she to do with this impossible youngest son? He had become at sixteen quite as difficult as any of her other boys. Jeffrey had been expelled even from the South Kensington troop of the Boy Scouts after only six months, for smoking, and now he was shaving and had suddenly disappeared to Jersey after hearing that he could earn the huge sum of £20 a week picking tomatoes. He ended up broke and sleeping on the beach and was arrested for vagrancy. He was put into a detention centre but escaped and went to a pub where he charmed a rich homosexual who spent a week trying to get him drunk so that he could have his way with him. Eventually the old queen bought the boy an air ticket back to London, where his furious mother insisted that it was time he went to the Labour Exchange.

That autumn he worked briefly in Holland Park as a temporary gardener, burning leaves. Dora was still as determined to get him into the Navy as any eighteenth century press gang might have been. In November she sent him off to Aberdovey on the Welsh coast to join a three-month Outward Bound course where the boys were woken at five-thirty, sent for a two-mile run, forced to have breathtakingly icy showers on their return and then sent out onto Cardigan Bay to sail in the cold November breeze. No wonder he kept so remarkably fit in later life and staved off death despite his suicidal lifestyle. He claimed later that his fellow Outward Bounders were working class idiots and that he was the only one who knew anything about navigation, which would have interested Commander Skinner. He failed the course because of his smoking.

Back in London he was mesmerised by Soho. Every night as he went to bed his mother said firmly 'Labour Exchange for you in the morning' and every morning he went to Soho instead. He took the tube from Holland Park to Tottenham Court Road to work for Victor Sasse in the Budapest restaurant in Dean St, a forerunner of Sasse's famous Greek Street restaurant the Gay Hussar, which was to open in 1953. He worked there as a part-time dish-washer in return for 'a cup of tea, a bun and a ten-bob note'.

Soho simply delighted him. The poet Elizabeth Smart discovered its joys at about the same time and its appeal is described well by her biographer Rosemary Sullivan in her book *By Heart* (Lime Tree, 1991): 'For those who went there in the late forties, Soho was a refuge against the grey uniformity of London. It was a place where the rules didn't apply . . . Soho still had the integrity of a village. It was a pleasant backwater, a place where there were numerous pubs within walking distance of each other, and drinking clubs that were entitled to open in the afternoon, with a backdrop of delicatessens, off-licences, small shops, and restaurants.'

He was particularly taken by the York Minster, which was also known as the French Pub after the war because of its popularity with General de Gaulle and his Free French exiles. He gawped at the French prostitutes who seemed irresistibly elegant as they sipped their Ricard and gave the place a whiff of Parisian café society. In the restaurant upstairs there was an eccentric waiter who fancied himself as a spoof player (the pub game in which you guess how many objects are being held in the hands of all the players) and who would spoof for the bill with the diners, double or quits. For the misfit from Pangbourne this was heaven.

He also arrived just as the legendary lesbian Muriel Belcher was opening her outrageously camp and bitchy Colony Room Club in Dean Street and was about to bribe

the homosexual painter Francis Bacon £10 a week to bring
in his friends to drink there. Muriel called Bacon 'daughter'
(he called her 'ma'am') and although the Colony was no more
than a first-floor one-room bar it was the sort of club where
anything went, though Brendan Behan and Dylan Thomas
did manage to go too far even for Muriel when they tried
to vomit on the carpet and were barred. Bernard was to
come to love the Colony. For him it was to epitomise
everything that he adored about Soho. When Elizabeth
Smart came to write Muriel Belcher's obituary many years
later she catalogued the Colony's thousands of members thus:
'painters, writers, tinkers, tailors, sailors, editors, art editors, cartoonists, singers, African chiefs, burglars, strippers,
composers, dress-designers, lords, landowners, barrow-boys,
advertising people, and unclassifiable people.' It was raw and
raunchy and raffish. Muriel perched on a stool at the bar and
welcomed members as they arrived with the greeting 'Hello,
cunty'. When Bernard discovered Muriel's he felt that he had
come home. He had also of course discovered his own doom.
But how could he resist it? He did go once to the Islington
Labour Exchange, which sent him to work in a factory near
King's Cross, which claimed to make hot-water bottles. It
did indeed, but its main product was condoms. Bernard
declined the job. Eventually he couldn't stand his mother's
nagging any more and simply left home – by taxi, of course
– abandoning what he called 'her Dresden-littered drawing
room' to rent a £3-a-week bedsitter off a Mrs Shillibeer at
54 Queens Gate in South Kensington even though he had
no money. He tried at first to pay the rent by 'borrowing'
2s 6d from twenty-four people in Soho every Friday night in
the hope that they were drunk enough to have forgotten the
'loan' by the next Friday. He also humped planks in a timber
yard off Greek Street for £2 15s a week and started drinking
halves of bitter in the Pillars of Hercules next door.

Mrs Shillibeer was 'a completely barmy Polish woman,'
Bernard once said. 'At first we got on like eggs and bacon.
I used to visit her in her flat in the basement and she

played Chopin on a clapped out piano and fed me glasses
of Slivovitz and cream cakes. But came the inevitable day
when I was unemployed and utterly skint and I hadn't got
the rent. When I crept out of the house the following morning – silently, I thought, and unseen – she aimed a chamber
pot at me. The pot missed me by inches and shattered on
the pavement with such an explosion I resolved to go to the
Employment Exchange immediately.

'Eventually, I paid the back rent, thanks to some ghastly
night work in a bakery, and moved on. As luck, or bad luck,
would have it, my next landlord was also a Pole.'

He moved to a room in Little Venice where he said that
the frogs jumped out of the canal and hopped up the stairs.
Later he earned 4s 6d an hour as a labourer, navvying on
London building sites and moving on to a new one almost
every week. Occasionally he would take on brief dishwashing
jobs. Whenever he could not pay the rent he would do a
Moonlight Flit, travelling light with just a carrier bag full
of shirts, a saucepan, a frying pan and a gramophone.

'It's quite frightening not being equipped to do anything,'
he later told *Midweek*. 'I could still tell you the date of the
Battle of Bosworth, or The Great Reform Bill, but it doesn't
equip me to earn a living, does it?' At times he was so down-
and-out that he kept moving from one bedsitter to another
and spent several nights (about twenty in all) in a Camden
Town dosshouse, Rowton House. He was even reduced to
sucking up to the rich homosexuals who hung around Soho
looking for pretty boys like him and managed to survive for
years by accepting money from old queens: bumming, you
could call it, though he always denied that he was ever a
rent boy or actually pleasured them physically. 'I treated
several old poufs quite badly,' he told the homosexual writer
Dan Farson for an article in *Harpers & Queen*, 'but I had to
grasp on to anything I could. I became a sort of heterosexual
tart. In those days poufs only liked heterosexual men and
having just left a naval college may have appealed to them.'
Francis Bacon, another homosexual who became very fond of

Bernard, used to call him 'an honorary pouf' and Bernard admitted to me: 'I suppose I *was* a sort of cockteaser when I was young because I was pretty. It was embarrassing and I hated it, but the poufs bought me drinks and meals.'

One of them, John Minton, the thirty-one-year-old Professor of Painting at the Royal College of Art, did a great deal more than that. He became Bernard's protector, sugar daddy and would-be seducer and took him on holidays to France and Spain. They met almost as soon as Bernard arrived in Soho, in the Black Horse, when he was sixteen, and Minton was soon putting him up for the night. It was Minton, he told Dan Farson, who got him 'out of an awful rut' by introducing him to witty people and making him realise that his mother was 'a middle-class fool. It was a new world: I got pissed with Augustus John in the Caves de France.' Minton would take him and several other young friends – Bobby Hunt, Peter Dunbar – out for meals or the cinema and buy them drinks. 'Poufs in those days seemed to get as much pleasure out of this as a young boy being treated and spoilt,' said Bernard. 'It was through Johnny Minton that I got to know the sort of Names, the people with talent, the writers, painters and poets, people that made life more interesting, like Louis Macneice and Dylan Thomas and Francis Bacon and composers like Malcolm Arnold. I suddenly wasn't with *bums* any more.'

All three Bernard boys became part of Minton's Soho 'Circus' of boozy young hangers-on and spongers who infested Soho and Minton's home in St John's Wood at 37 Hamilton Terrace. The Bernards 'were at this time a little like characters out of a Chekhov play, searching and bewildered,' wrote Frances Spalding in her biography of Minton, *Dance till the Stars Come Down* (Hodder & Stoughton, 1991). 'Minton was fond of all three, but it was the seventeen-year-old Jeffrey, thin, nervous, articulate and funny, who caught his fancy.'

Minton paid him an allowance of ten shillings a week, and they went together to the cinema, restaurants, pubs like the Black Horse and the French, drinking dens like the Colony Room Club and the newly opened Caves de France, and clubs like the Gargoyle and the Mandrake – for all of which, of course, Minton paid. The generous Minton would also suddenly give him £10, the equivalent of a month's wages. Being picked up by Minton, Jeff said, made him feel as though he resembled Long John Silver's parrot (who's a pretty boy?).

'Minton was not a sodomite,' Bobby Hunt remembered. 'Buggery was the one thing he hated. He liked fellatio, sucking boys off. Francis Bacon would say to him in his high-pitched voice: "Why don't you do it properly and get up the arse, where you can really enjoy yourself?" We used to hear these silly conversations going on in the pub.'

Bernard always denied that he had had any homosexual involvement with Minton. 'I *stayed* with him, for about three months, I didn't *sleep* with him,' he told me. 'I was always staying with him, even at the end of his life, at Apollo Place.' Even so, Martyn Goff, the writer and bookseller who was later to run the Booker Prize, remembered that Minton and Bernard were living together as 'an item'. Bernard was 'beautiful', said Goff, himself a homosexual, and he invited the couple down to his cottage at Dallington in Sussex for the weekend. 'I was aware that Jeffrey was not gay or only fractionally gay but that wasn't unusual for Minton who tended to fall for people who were not gay. After they'd gone on the Monday my dark blue blazer had also gone. I asked Minton about it and he said, "oh, Jeff just borrowed it because he was cold" but I never saw it again. Jeffrey was quite engaging but certainly on the make in those days.' Forty years later, when Bernard was basking in the success of *Jeffrey Bernard is Unwell*, Goff approached him in the Groucho Club in Soho and asked him teasingly if he might now return the stolen blazer. Bernard was not amused.

Many of Bernard's friends believed that he never told the truth about his relationship with Minton or, indeed, with some of the other Soho queens who pursued him in his youth and throughout the 1950s. One old homosexual who was in Soho in those years claimed that Bernard turned queer tricks for money, even that he 'used to cane old queers for money'. 'He's a closet queen, I reckon,' said another old friend, Jay Landesman. 'In those early days he might have been a little in the meat market.' His wife Fran protested at this but remembered: 'In the Colony Muriel used to refer to him as one of her beautiful hostesses.' Irma Kurtz, the magazine agony aunt, did not meet Bernard until the Sixties but remembered noticing 'the very *butchness* of him. He was a right little rooster. The way he walked, the way he moved, worries me now. I know that there are a lot of men who dislike him intensely and I feel that there's a sexual element in that.' Another old girlfriend, Sally Vincent, was blunt: 'I don't think he was averse to selling his arse a bit,' she said. He was, after all, notorious for hating authority and for embracing anything exciting and illegal, and homosexuality was illegal in 1949 and could result in a prison sentence. How could he have resisted it?

Even a decade later, when the author and literary agent Giles Gordon met Bernard in 1963, he had 'a menacing air of homosexuality,' said Gordon. 'He wore black and was very sinister and threatening, with slicked-back hair. He was like a B-movie character.' Gordon claimed that Frank Norman's homosexual publisher, David Farrer, was convinced that Bernard was Norman's boyfriend.

Several surviving photographs of Bernard in his younger days make him look decidedly homosexual, especially one taken in a country garden and showing him naked to the waist. Another old friend, Allan Hall, was convinced that Bernard had 'no homosexual leanings whatsoever' but told how Jeffrey had once been invited to Paris in the early Sixties by an older man, 'a peculiar man, very camp and very amusing', to stay at his apartment for £200. Hall remarked that this was an expensive way of acquiring £200 and realised that the man was after Bernard's body, but Bernard went to

Paris just the same to collect the loot. 'Jeffrey showed no particularly strong sense of morality in any direction whatsoever,' said Hall. 'I thought perhaps there'd be some sort of . . . accommodation . . . I suppose it's just like a guardsman who does his best for a client in Hyde Park in order to take his girlfriend out.'

Bernard's fourth wife, Sue, never suspected him of being at all homosexual but considered that 'he might have done it for a drink. He was always trying to get money for a drink.'

Many other friends, however, were convinced that Bernard had never had even the mildest homosexual relationship. 'I don't think he's homosexual because if he was he would have written about it,' said his old friend and journalist colleague Richard West. 'He's too bloody honest and outspoken.' Even his friendship with Minton 'was simply opportunist,' said Oliver Bernard, 'perhaps a bit predatory but in fact they did like each other. Jeffrey was quite amusing company and Minton was a very nice man, very happy and generous'. Oliver said that he himself had actually slept in the same bed as Minton 'and he'd put his arm round my shoulder and say goodnight' but that would be all. 'He wasn't an aggressive homo at all.' Minton's young painter assistant Bobby Hunt also slept with Minton in the same bed 'but we never had sex', he told Farson. This so frustrated Minton that he gnawed his fingers with such ferocity that the sheets were blood-stained. Frances Spalding certainly believed that Bernard was no more than a 'prick teaser', and pointed out in her biography of Minton that Minton preferred to associate with heterosexual men and boys, perhaps because they offered more of a sexual challenge.

Bernard never lost his habit of fleecing homosexuals. As late as the Seventies Francis Bacon was still slipping him the odd £50 note, though Bacon did once enquire in his high, piercing voice: 'What are you going to do now, Jeffrey, now that your looks have gone?' Bernard denied that Bacon had ever tried to seduce him: 'Good God, no. He preferred rough trade or very smart businessmen.' In fact Bacon preferred such rough trade that one of Bernard's favourite stories in later years related to Bacon's £1,500 Cartier watch and the sailor whom he picked up one evening and inveigled home for a night of joy. Bacon despatched the sailor, 'a rough person', to the bathroom to wash, and as he reclined in bed awaiting his return was suddenly convinced that the matelot would mug him and steal the expensive watch, so he hid the watch under the carpet and lay back in bed to await his love. On returning from his ablutions the sailor, whose huge feet were just right for the roll of the ocean swell, trod on the watch and smashed it.

But the most convincing witness of all was the openly homosexual Ian Board, who was Muriel Belcher's barperson at the Colony Room Club and succeeded her when she died. If anyone would have known about Bernard's possible homosexuality it would have been Board but he told me: 'He didn't come across for any of them.'

It is worth remembering, as Bernard's fourth wife Sue pointed out, that in his earliest days in Soho Bernard bummed off *everybody* without necessarily sleeping with them. He was very good with rich older women as well as homosexuals, and one fur-coated, elderly aristocratic lady who met him in the French Pub bought him numerous drinks and trinkets. He appealed to both sexes and claimed that an older woman once paid him £20 to service her. 'He was a *toyboy* in those days, you see,' said Sue, 'before a toyboy was invented.'

Other friends of both sexes would look after him and give him treats without expecting any sexual favours. He always dreamed, for instance, of being taken to Wheelers fish restaurant in Old Compton Street and finally managed to persuade an old prep school contemporary to take him there, Tony Hubbard, a Woolworth heir. Later Bernard often persuaded richer friends to take him to Wheelers: Alan and Isabel Rawsthorne, Frank Norman, Francis Bacon. He never paid himself. One Wheelers visit with Bacon many years later was to pass into Soho legend.

'Who would you most like to fuck in the entire world?' enquired Bacon in his loud, high-pitched voice.

Christ, thought Bernard, I don't know. Cyd Charisse? Sophia Loren? Monica Vitti?

'Out of everybody in the world,' Bacon shrilled, 'I'd like to fuck Colonel Gadaffi.'

Four American tourists at the next table rose and left the restaurant.

– 2 –

In April 1949 Bernard met young Yvonne Marsh from Beckenham, 'Marsh', later Marsh Dunbar, who was to become his lover ten years later and a lifelong friend. Marsh was eighteen and living with Minton's twenty-year-old assistant and boozing friend Bobby Hunt in Hampstead where Oliver Bernard was their lodger and was earning a sort of living as a road labourer at Chalk Farm. Jeffrey was not quite seventeen but already irresistibly attractive. Marsh met him with Minton and Hunt in the Black Boy in Rathbone Street one Saturday evening. 'I must say I did fancy him even then,' she admitted. 'He was stunning, and *surly*. I suppose he was the James Dean type, sulky, and I think he was really like that. He was James Dean *before* James Dean, Jeffrey was the *first* James Dean.'

He scraped a living in the next two years doing almost anything that came his way. He sat as a model for ten shillings an hour for Minton privately and for Minton's students at the Royal College of Art. Minton gave him a couple of drawings he had done of him, one of which Bernard was mortified to discover years later was hanging on Sir John Waller's lavatory wall. He modelled with a naked girl for a work by a German sculptor entitled *The Lovers*, which allowed him to seduce the girl. He worked as a navvy. Later in the year he and a young Soho friend, Pete Arthy, worked in a travelling fairground run by gypsies. They had been hitchhiking through Kent, doing odd jobs, picking apples, working on fruit farms, a few days here and there, when they reached the village of Mereworth and asked the fairground boss for a job. He hired them to assemble, manage and dismantle the roundabouts and dodgem car tracks at each stop. 'I enjoyed that,' said Bernard. 'It was quite fun.'

Most extraordinary of all, he became a professional, licensed, featherweight boxer, a dainty 5ft 7ins and weighing in at 8st 10lbs. 'I was obsessed with boxing,' he told me. He started in a boxing booth at Tottenham, where for three weeks he took on all comers of the right weight for ten shillings a bout. 'It seemed quite a lot,' he said. 'I never got a whacking because all the opponents were tearaway kids who wanted to show off in front of their girlfriends. If you could box a bit you could stay out of trouble, the left jab, give them a bloody nose. I stopped some painful punches but I never got floored or knocked out. That's one of the few virtues I've ever prided myself on throughout this ghastly life. I've always been quite brave although I say it myself, in every way. I don't frighten easy.'

He claimed that he won six straight fights but Bobby Hunt, who saw him box and said that Minton bought him his boots and boxing gear, had less rosy memories of Bernard's career in the ring. 'I saw Jeff being knocked out three times in the first round,' he said. 'I couldn't understand why I was invited!'

Bernard went on to spar with the real pros at Jack Solomons' gym in Windmill Street. 'It was an amazing building,' he recalled, 'with a snooker hall on the first floor, full of layabouts and gangsters, and his gym was on the floor above it and all the champions from everywhere, even America, trained there. I used to spar with the European and Empire featherweight champion, Al Phillips, who was known as the Aldgate Tiger, and he knocked *shit* out of me one morning, then took me downstairs to the billiard hall, where there was a coffee bar. He bought me a cup of tea, a cheese roll and five Woodbines. I was still swaying. He patted me on the head and said, "Thanks, Jeff. Remember, try not to step out of your class." I felt really humiliated at that.' Bernard was so desperate for money that he even sparred for a couple of rounds and £8 with Sandy Saddler, the featherweight champion of the world, and was soundly thrashed.

His last fight was at Slough Town Hall, four three-minute rounds against a boxer called Jeff Holdsworth, for which he earned £5, a good beating, and had to give his manager and second ten shillings each and to pay his train fare to Slough and back so that he was left, for all his pain, with £3 15s. He remembered that awful night vividly. 'From the moment the bell went I was fucked because at that second as I came out of my corner I noticed a fantastic looking bird sitting in a ringside seat. I looked at her for a split-second too long and got a tremendous right cross to my jaw. I hung on for as long as I could but he was quite a hard nut and just before the end of the first round the referee stepped in and stopped the fight. I foolishly didn't go down and take a rest and clear the head.

'In the end, I gave up because I wasn't good enough. Now I think boxing's pretty disgusting.'

His life was by no means all work and no play. He had started drinking regularly, halves of bitter beer, because he had no friends of his own age and he wanted desperately to look grown-up and drinking seemed to be glamorous. It was a way of meeting people and picking up girls and was successful enough for him and a friend to take two girls on holiday in a rented caravan in Newhaven but Bernard's girl went off him after they went to Brighton and he was hit on the head with a billiard cue – and then the caravan's calor gas stove blew up. He made his first trip to a racecourse, Alexandra Park, and was immediately hooked for life. 'I was suddenly overcome by a flow of adrenalin,' he recalled years later in the *Sunday Times*. 'I don't know of anywhere else other than a racecourse bar where you could meet and drink with a Cabinet Minister, navvy, alcoholic, industrialist, con-man, dwarf, duchess and waitress.' Inspired by Minton, he even painted his only still life canvas, *Orange on a Formica Kitchen Table*, otherwise known as *Notting Hill Gate at Dawn*. Bernard wisely decided not to pursue this new interest.

– 3 –

In the summer of 1949 Minton, racked by lust, decided on a final extravagant assault on his pretty little seventeen-year-old toyboy's virtue. He took him on holiday to Spain with the full agreement of Bernard's mother, who seems to have been strangely naive considering she was in the theatre. 'She thought he was after my mind and not my beautiful body!' said Bernard. Minton took him to Granada, Barcelona, Alicante, Majorca and Ibiza. He took him to several bull-fights. It was all apparently in vain. Bernard reported later that 'there was a tremendous amount of sulking' by Minton because he would not have sex with him but Minton had obviously by now accepted the inevitable because when they stopped off in Paris on the way home he was even generous enough to pay for Bernard to enjoy regularly the services of Mimi, a Montparnasse prostitute who charged 500 francs a time. Mimi worked with a clutch of other whores – among them Fifi and Tiger – who hung out in the Hotel Select and at the Café Ambiance. 'I was very randy in those days,' said Bernard. 'I couldn't leave her alone. I was up and down stairs all day long.' He seems to have felt no guilt in sponging so shamelessly off the glum, unrequited Minton, whose long, sad face reminded Bernard of a tragic clown.

Minton finally gave up his pursuit of Bernard and at the end of the year met Ricky Stride, an ex-sailor and club doorman who soon moved in with him. The end of the affair did nothing to whittle away the chip of resentment on Bernard's shoulder, which was destined to become larger as the years passed. Suddenly he found himself on the breadline

again, and he was to remain there for nearly ten years. There
is no doubt that he was indeed often extremely poor but some
of his stories of the poverty of those days are too incredible to
be taken seriously. In 1969, for instance, he was to write in the
Mirror Magazine a tearjerking description of that Christmas
of 1949, just after Minton had dumped him, that made him
sound like a Dickensian waif and that simply defied belief. It
was called *Christmas Eve in the Doss-House* ... and described
his dreadful Christmas 'in cubicle No. 1064':

> It was Christmas Eve and I was living in a Camden
> Town doss-house, hiding from a clutch of bailiffs, a
> bookmaker, a girl friend and my mother. My mother
> simply wanted me to go to the Labour Exchange and the
> others just wanted money. It was a desperate situation
> and life was hard for a dropout ... Somewhere in the
> doss-house there hung one piece of berryless holly. In
> the middle of the room was one piece of leafless mistletoe
> and under that sat the most unkissable bunch of people
> you've ever seen.
>
> It really was awful. This was the place where God
> would have put the tube had he wanted to give the
> universe an enema.

And so it went on and on. None of the article rings at all
true: it was obviously sheer fantasy. It is perhaps relevant
that just before Minton and Bernard split up, Jeffrey took his
protector to have lunch one Sunday with Dora at her new flat
in Earl's Court, where she had moved now that all the family
had left home. Minton was mesmerised by the entire family.
They had all been to expensive schools but there was Oliver
digging roads. Bruce was so inarticulate that he could hardly
speak and had been working in a butcher's shop before going
off to Cornwall to paint and to scratch a meagre living doing
odd jobs. Sally was about to see her first psychiatrist. Jeffrey
he knew quite enough about already, thank you very much.
And now here was the mother, who kept saying to him 'But
I can't understand why you're so nice to Jeff, *why* are you

being so nice to Jeff?' Minton told Bobby Hunt that the Bernards were the most bizarre family he'd ever known. The mother, he said, was undoubtedly insane: 'they're all living in a fantasy world'.

Minton did leave a prophetic epitaph to their 'affair' as he set a new course with Ricky Stride towards increasingly desperate drunkenness, despair and suicide. 'Jeffrey has got enormous talent,' he told Bobby Hunt. 'He's going to be a very good writer. But he's bloody lazy.' When Bernard announced that he wanted to be a writer, Minton bought him an Olivetti typewriter. The ungrateful boy sold it a week later. 'I've destroyed you, haven't I?' Minton once asked Jeffrey as he watched him swigging his free drinks. He had certainly tried.

5

Anna and the King's Hussars

Dora died on 21 July 1950, of cancer of the cervix, at St Mary Abbots Hospital in London. She was only fifty-two. The death was registered by Bruce, her favourite son, who claimed on the death certificate that he was still living at her address, 18 Nevern Mansions, Warwick Road, in Kensington. She had been rushed to hospital in February with an 'internal haemorrhage' and Oliver, who had been working again in France, had returned hurriedly to London. But she had had a remission that had allowed her to return home for four months and in May she had given Jeffrey £3 as his eighteenth birthday present. He had spent some of it buying his first legal drinks in a pub, at the Swan in Notting Hill Gate, where he had already been drinking underage and illegally for two years with the poet George Barker. He celebrated by having a fight in the pub with the Right-wing South African poet Roy Campbell, who had fought with Franco's fascist army during the Spanish Civil War. It was not perhaps the fairest fight. Bernard had been a professional boxer and Campbell was forty-nine.

At the end of June Dora had been taken back to hospital where she died three weeks later. She was cremated at Golders Green crematorium, as her husband had been, and her ashes were scattered.

Jeffrey seemed at first to take her death badly. 'At the hospital I actually had a five-minute fight with him,' said Oliver. 'We'd all been there on and off for five days and nights, not sleeping, and there was some confusion about what my mother's will might entail or whether we were going to allow the hospital to muck about with her in terms of cancer research. Jeffrey was showing a lot of emotion and

I couldn't bear him showing it and I told him to shut up or grow up. But that didn't last more than an hour or two. It was genuine emotion. He was distraught, but like all of us, a bit relieved that it was all over. We were all feeling a mixture of guilt and relief.'

'It was the first time I saw a corpse,' Jeffrey said on the television programme *The Obituary Show* in April 1992. 'It didn't look anything like being asleep and I found it rather frightening that the body had been vacated – an empty house.' Bobby Hunt remembered that Jeffrey was so shocked by Dora's death that he went bald: 'He got alopecia sebora, which means your hair drops out from shock. He had to wear a hat. And he got absolutely smashed.' Jeffrey's own story was that he had only a small bald spot 'the size of a half-crown'.

The death of any man's mother is profoundly significant in his life, especially at such a young age. Jeffrey was only eighteen, still technically a minor, an orphan. But in later years he was to make the most dreadful remarks about Dora and her impact on his life. He told one magazine writer, Graham Hassell, in 1989, that he had only ever been happy three times: 'getting out of school, getting out of national service, and my mother dying, which was another escape from authority'. He told Dan Farson that when his mother died he 'felt slightly delighted – a *terrible* thing to say – but I felt free, no longer someone to answer to.' When I mentioned in 1991 that some animals eat their young Bernard responded swiftly: 'Yes, that's what my mother did.' And he once told his journalist friend Mike Molloy that Dora had tried to have him aborted before he was born because she didn't want him.

The most perceptive appraisal of Jeffrey's final attitude towards his mother came from Dan Farson. 'Perhaps he has never forgiven himself for not having loved her more,' he said.

One effect of Dora's death was that Sally, who was now calling herself by her real name, Sonia, started to crack and succumb to her mental weakness. Perhaps she too blamed herself for her mother's death, and the guilt cannot have been helped much when she and her husband moved into Dora's flat in Earl's Court. Marsh Dunbar remembered that until then Sally had been quite bright: 'She was incredibly made up, beautifully done, and she worked for Helena Rubinstein as a young girl, she was properly trained.' Bobby Hunt agreed. Sally was very pretty, he said. Within three years she was to be certified insane and committed to an asylum.

Dora had of course left no money to her children and they all continued to struggle to make ends meet with a variety of dead-end jobs. Jeffrey went back to navvying on a derelict bomb site in Dean Street right opposite the French Pub, where a church had been flattened by a flying bomb in 1944, and helped to clear the rubble and dig there the foundations of a new building, a block of flats, Kemble House. Customers in the French would sometimes pass him a glass of his new favourite drink, Pernod, over the wall, which enraged the foreman. He started drinking every morning with Dylan Thomas, who was usually wearing a hangover – 'nice man sober, impossible drunk,' said Bernard – and began to meet more of Soho's artists and bohemians: Louis MacNeice, Robert Colquhoun, Robert McBryde, Lucian Freud, Cyril Connolly, as well as such denizens of the area as Ironfoot Jack, Handbag Johnny, Sid the Swimmer and the Fox. In the camp Colony Room Club he met and drank with homosexuals like Noel Coward, E. M. Forster and Tom Driberg. 'He mixed with the Bohemian set without actually being one,' the land-lord of the York Minster, Gaston Berlemont, remembered in 1992. 'He bore a kind of mystic aura, an aura of being impor-tant which of course he was not.' Berlemont first met Bernard on a sweltering summer day when Bernard was stripped to the waist 'looking like boiled lobster' as he worked on the Kemble House site. They shared an interest in racehorses, gambling and cooking and became friends, though Berlemont remembered that after a few drinks Bernard would even then become sarcastic and abrasive.

Despite his poverty and the menial nature of his job

he must have had style even then because even the smart
Gargoyle Club used to allow him to go in there in the afternoons straight from the building site 'wearing gumboots with
cement on them' to drink with the actor Robert Newton. And
in the Colony one afternoon he was picked up by the wife of a
very famous Labour MP and taken back to her house for an
afternoon of sex. 'She gave me £20 afterwards,' he said, 'so I
jacked in my labouring job for a couple of weeks.' He would
take any job in those days. In a pub he was once approached
by a solicitor and asked if he would like to earn an easy £10.
What a silly question. Bernard was sent that evening to an
hotel off the Bayswater Road where he had to be 'caught'
in bed with a sad young woman who wanted a divorce. A
private detective witnessed the charade.

He must have been particularly sore when Minton took
Ricky Stride off on holiday to Jamaica in September, but
he was soon to have something much more unpleasant to
think about. He was called up by the army to serve two
compulsory years as a conscript.

On 2 November 1950, the day that George Bernard Shaw
died, he enlisted as a National Service cavalryman in the
Royal Armoured Corps as 22425776 Trooper Jerry Bernard
and was posted to the 14/20th King's Hussars at Catterick
in Yorkshire to become a tank driver earning twenty-five
shillings a week. 'People with high IQs were made tank
drivers,' he boasted years later. 'The working class boys were
made gunners or wireless operators.' His senior officer was a
Colonel Scar, who wore a black eye-patch, but Bernard was
not impressed by his spotty fellow conscripts, who seemed
incapable of talking about anything but cars and football
and were to bore him witless.

John Moynihan, who was sent to Aldershot, did not envy
him his posting to Catterick, which Moynihan described as
'that awful place up north where the winds blew across the
parade ground'. But it was not so much the cold that
depressed Bernard that freezing winter, or shaving in icy
water, or eating lukewarm fried eggs for breakfast, or the

marching, or even the fact that the Second Lieutenant
Stainthorpe at Catterick was the very Stainthorpe who had
bullied him at prep school. What finally got him down was
the relentless boredom. In desperation he volunteered to go
to fight in the Far East with the 8th Hussars in the Korean
War. Colonel Scar would have none of it. 'The trouble with
you is you're bolshie,' he told Bernard.

On 5 February 1951, though, he was posted to the 65th
Tank Regiment and given a weekend's forty-eight-hour leave
in London, his first leave. Afterwards, he simply failed to
return to Catterick. He just went missing: Absent Without
Leave; AWOL. He went to ground in London for four months
while the Military Police looked for him.

He could not stay at his mother's old flat in Earl's Court
because that was the obvious place for them to find him.
Oliver was living there briefly with Sally/Sonia and her
husband and on 7 February the police arrived at the flat,
looking for Jeffrey. He was not there but in Soho, drunk.
Oliver disapproved of Jeffrey going on the run but retained
sufficient brotherly love to send a telegram to Catterick
claiming that Jeffrey Bernard was unwell. Unlike numerous
similar claims years later, this one was accompanied by the
rash promise of a doctor's certificate if necessary. Meanwhile
Jeffrey himself, skulking about Soho, considered doing a bunk
to Cornwall. It was typical of him that he simply refused to
face up to the fact that the army would eventually catch up
with him sooner or later.

During those four months in hiding he stayed all over
London, begging a bed off friends for the occasional night,
sitting slumped and hopeless in deserted, echoing Lyons Corner Houses until dawn, lurking in Muriel's Colony Room and
the Gargoyle Club. Occasionally Oliver would take the risk
of putting him up and Oliver and Bruce would meet Jeffrey
in Soho for a drink and urge him to give himself up and get
it over with. 'I thought he should straighten himself out with
the army and not be furtively sliding around London in fear
of the police,' said Oliver. It was one of the few occasions in

Jeffrey's life that Oliver was really worried about his youngest brother.

Eventually he was persuaded that he could not avoid reality for ever and would have to give himself up. He did so one night in June, telephoning the police from the Gargoyle Club at 2 a.m. and waiting for them to come and fetch him.

It was typically swashbuckling that he should have chosen David Tennant's fashionable Gargoyle nightclub, high in a building in Dean Street, as the place to give himself up to the army, a gesture that would doubtless have incensed every sergeant at Catterick when he returned. It was in the Gargoyle that the Russian spy Donald Maclean was regularly involved in drunken brawls and Robert Newton once stripped naked in public.

It is not difficult to imagine the expressions of the Military Police when they arrived in such a place to arrest the deserter Bernard. The appearance of the police would not even have interrupted the syncopation of the band. When Donald Maclean fled to Russia just a month earlier the management of the Gargoyle simply wrote on his membership card, 'Gone to Moscow'.

The police took Bernard to a military detention centre near Scotland Yard to await an escort back to Catterick. He was there for two days and two nights and claimed that a Scots Guards sergeant kicked him every three hours to make him wake and scrub his wooden plank bed, and he would then have to wait for two hours while it dried before he tried to sleep again and was kicked once more. This treatment seems to have simply made Bernard even more determined to buck the system and never again be told by anyone what to do. The general public, however, was much more sympathetic to conscript deserters and when he was being hauled across the concourse at King's Cross to return to Catterick, handcuffed to a Military Policeman, he said that strangers came up and gave him cigarettes, money, sandwiches and a magazine and shouted 'good luck, mate' and 'don't let the bastards get you down'.

Back at Catterick he was put in a cell, where he claimed that he was inspected by the Duke of Gloucester, who peered at him through the bars of his door. 'Only in England,' Bernard wrote later, 'could you be up to here in it and get a visit from the King's brother.' It is possible, however, that he was confusing his royalties, because in 1991 he wrote in the *Spectator* that the Duke of Gloucester ('a right old pisspot') inspected the Catterick conscripts one day and had the soldier standing next to Bernard put on a charge for not polishing the *back* of his cap badge. There is no mention that this took place in any prison cell and it is unlikely that the Duke visited Catterick twice in the ten months that Bernard was there.

One of his punishments while awaiting judgment was to undertake the endless task of replacing the dirty snow on the parade ground with clean snow, but not all was misery. Oliver and Bruce had both written to Colonel Scar to say that Jeffrey was still distraught after the death of his mother and the authorities accepted their pleas and decided to treat him leniently. Even when he was in confinement the Provost Sergeant let him out of his cell to make a book on the next day's horse races, and there was a friendly NCO who nicknamed him 'Scruffy' and always seemed to have a fat bundle of banknotes which he would wave at Bernard, shouting 'Horses, horses. It's the only way. You'll never get rich by soldiering.' When it finally came to a sentence for what was generously described as 'overstaying his leave' he was given just one week in the guardhouse. Normally a four-month absence would have earned him six months in prison but the letters from Oliver and Bruce had rescued him.

Far from being particularly grateful, Bernard now determined to get himself out of the army altogether by pretending to commit suicide. 'I took a lot of sleeping pills and drank some revolting stuff called maraschino, which is made of

cherries,' he told me. 'I was very glad that I didn't succeed.
I woke up in a military hospital in Woolwich and a wonderful
doctor, a lieutenant, a sadistic bastard, shook me and said,
"You should have jumped out of a fucking window instead of
messing about with pills: that would've worked." ' Eventually
he was taken to see an army psychiatrist who was alarmed
when Bernard yelled at him 'I can't stand it' and who sent
him to a military mental hospital near Southampton, Netley,
where he joined a ward of soldiers shell-shocked from the war
in Korea. Psychiatrists came to eye him every day and after
a month he was called before a medical board where he was
asked what he wanted to do if he were discharged from the
army. He said that he thought he would like to be a writer.
'It was the first time I'd ever *said* that,' he remembered, 'and
they immediately stamped my paybook with a rubber stamp
Mental Stability NIL and let me go.'

He left on demobilisation leave in August 1951 – he
was not to be formally discharged from the army until
24 September – and even forty years later the Ministry of
Defence replied to several requests for information about his
brief military career: 'you are advised that the military service
records we hold are not open to public scrutiny' though it did
confirm his dates of service and Cause of Discharge, 'Ceasing
to fulfil Army Medical requirements', i.e. presumably 'Mental
Stability NIL.' The last line of the Ministry of Defence letter
was particularly engaging. It read: 'Medals issued: None
Recorded.'

It was one more victory for Bernard over authority, compulsion, normality. Dora, the Rev. Walpole E. Sealy, Pangbourne and now the army had all failed to tame him: what
hope was there going to be in the future for mere bosses,
girlfriends and wives?

– 2 –

He was to marry his first wife just six weeks later even

though he had emerged from the army to face a bleak future. He was nineteen and had no money, no qualifications, no obvious skills or particular talents. While boys of his age were going off to university he was spending his first week of freedom dossing down at the Camden Town Rowton House for down-and-outs and working on a building site. His dream of becoming a writer was probably not even a serious ambition. Bruce for one had never heard him even suggest it before and except for one term his English reports at Pangbourne had been dreadful. Within a couple of weeks he had nowhere to live and was too proud to ask the sister he so disliked for a bed at Dora's old Earl's Court flat, so he was trying to sleep during the day in friends' beds while they were out and again spending many nights sitting in the very Lyons Corner Houses that his father had designed.

He decided to go to the National Assistance Board labour exchange in Knightsbridge to look for a job and ask for a social security handout to allow him to pay rent. While there he bumped into Anna Grice, who had so generously relieved him of his virginity on Hampstead Heath four years previously. It was the first time he had seen her since that summer of 1947 and she was applying for National Assistance as well, despite being obviously intelligent and working occasionally in advertising. She was now twenty-two and very pretty and the young couple were gripped by a sudden youthful madness. He moved in with Anna at her room in north London, at 23 Alwyne Road, Islington, and they were married within a couple of weeks.

'I married her for all the wrong reasons,' he admitted forty years later. 'It was very difficult for a young bloke to get a girl to bed in those days but I suppose I married her so that I could get regular sex. They're frightened of Aids now, in those days they were frightened of getting pregnant.'

This was perhaps particularly so in Anna's case and with good reason. Since he had last seen her she had become a wild, promiscuous girl who was so easy to get to bed that at one time two years previously she had been having affairs with five men simultaneously. She became pregnant, had no idea who the father was, gave birth in London in 1949 to an illegitimate daughter, Alfreda, and gave the child away for adoption, which she was later to regret bitterly.

'I liked Anna,' said his brother Oliver, who had had a brief affair with her in Paris in 1947 after she had seduced Jeffrey. 'She was silly and romantic and she'd been messed about very badly by some older bloke, seduced or abused by her teacher or something. She was very good natured and nice but unstable. She'd get very drunk – young women don't usually get as drunk as that – and she'd be infantile and get like a dependent child when she was pissed.'

In fact one of her many lovers of those years, Christopher Fernau, told me in 1992 that Anna had been expelled from school 'when she was 16 or 17 for having an affair with the headmaster. It was at the instigation of the headmaster's wife who discovered it.' Fernau added: 'I daresay that Anna was the prime mover in it.'

Jeffrey believed that the father of Anna's child was an older man who was still living in Canada in 1992: 'He conned her. She was in love with him and he said to her "I'll live with you if you get rid of the daughter", so she had it adopted and then he left her. She was fucked up all her life.'

There was one further complication about Anna that explained her neuroticism and instability. She told Bernard that as a child she had returned home from school one day to find that both her parents had hanged themselves in the same room. The truth is that her mother, Sarah Grice, had died of asphyxia due to carbon monoxide coal-gas poisoning in the family home at 22 Collinswood Drive, Hastings, on 6 November 1938. She was only thirty-three. At the inquest two days later the coroner found that there was insufficient evidence to show whether the death had been 'accidental or otherwise'. The next day, on 9 November, three days after his wife's death, Anna's distraught (or guilty) father, Edward Grice, who was forty-two, committed suicide by throwing himself from a top-floor window at 1 Wellington Square, Hastings. He landed on his head.

It is hardly surprising that Anna was unstable after such a tragic childhood or that Bernard's first marriage was doomed from the start. He did not even know until I told him in 1992 that his first wife's name had not been Anna at all but Mary Patricia.

They were married on 18 September 1951 at Islington Registry Office, he in his birth certificate name of Jerry, she as Mary Patricia. He gave his 'rank or profession' as 'Pugilist' even though he hadn't punched a glove for more than a year. She had no job and left the space blank. The witnesses were Jeffrey's brother Bruce and Anna's sister. Perhaps he had been inspired in his lunacy by the fact that Oliver had just married *his* first wife Wendy three months earlier: perhaps Jeffrey thought that it would be quite a grown-up thing to do to get married as well. Oliver was appalled. 'I didn't approve when Jeff married Anna,' he said. 'I thought they were both unstable and they wouldn't help each other very much.'

Bobby Hunt remembered the wedding. 'One story I heard was that as soon as they came from the Register Office he went off to play snooker with some friends. He was drinking like mad even then.' They went to North Wales to a friend's cottage for a short honeymoon 'but we rowed all the time,' said Bernard, 'and came back to London' and moved into a bedsitter in Notting Hill. The marriage was almost over already. After one fight she stabbed him in the arm with a kitchen knife, when she was drunk, and within two weeks of the wedding she tried to commit suicide again, on 3 October.

That night, after taking pills and Pernod, she wrote what appeared to be a suicide note to Christopher Fernau in which she said that committing suicide gave her 'the same sort of surprise I feel when I see the name bernard [*sic*] on my identity card, a faint feeling that the sequence of things has become disordered.' She added: 'I feel, in fact, vaguely like dancing, I would like to dance unobserved on a beach in wet sand, how sad that I shall never feel wet sand over my feet and between my toes, and see the imprint of a living foot left by me.' She went on: 'But now there is nothing' despite 'Jeff who I love to look at, and who I thought might pull himself together if he married me so that we could both be happy.' On the second page of her letter she wrote 'please do convince Jeff that the cause of this were lain long before I met, and particularly before I married him' and she concluded on the third page: 'I leave it to you to make J. realise that far from being responsible, he is far too young to have any conception of the causes of any of this.'

'In the very few months we were together,' Bernard explained, 'I daily began to resent having to work really hard on building sites and doing shitty jobs like that, and it must be said that it *was* tough. This was in the days before pre-mixed concrete and diggers, and digging clay for foundations and running concrete in barrows. It was a *killer*. That was for 3/6d an hour and I couldn't take it any more and we had a couple of nasty rows and split up. I resented having to keep her at that sort of work. She used to do bits and pieces for advertising, but not regularly. She was dealt a bad hand, and of course she was dealt a bad hand with me because I never had any money. We lived on the breadline.'

They did spend Christmas with Oliver and his new wife on an old Thames barge at Southwold but a few days later they parted – 'hysterically', according to Bernard – and it was all over after just a few weeks. Chris Fernau knew many of Anna's boyfriends but believed that she was 'more genuinely attached to Jeff than anyone else but she realised that there was no future with him and he wasn't capable of supporting her.'

For the next seven years Anna drifted inevitably towards suicide. She lived in London with Brian Berry for some time and then went to Gloucestershire with a Soho poet, Noel Woodin, and worked on farms as a dairymaid. Bernard once went to stay with her in the country and discovered that she had become 'hefty' from lifting milk churns but that did not stop him sleeping with her again. 'I caught clap from her, which didn't delight me,' he said. 'It must be the last time I saw her. She was putting it about a bit with American airmen based at Cheltenham.' Woodin was living in Wales in 1992 and told me that Anna had been 'very unstable' while she was with him and was put on probation for attempted suicide, which was then a criminal offence. Part of the probation was to work on a farm as a dairymaid at Sudeley Castle, Winchcombe, near Cheltenham. 'We swapped ration books,' said Woodin, 'so for nine months I was Jeffrey Bernard.'

In January 1954 Anna was found guilty at Middlesex Sessions of trying to smuggle £1653-worth of gold and platinum in a pouch strapped to her back after being stopped and searched at London Airport. She had been recruited into crime by Andrew Dirac, who was probably the father of her illegitimate daughter Alfreda. She admitted in court that this had been her third smuggling trip to Paris, for which she was paid £20 each time, and was remanded in custody for a month in Holloway Prison, where she complained in letters to Christopher Fernau that nobody bothered to visit her. Certainly Bernard made no effort at all to comfort her in her unhappiness, even though they were still married. She was already on probation for trying to kill herself and the probation officer's report claimed that Bernard had left her after six weeks of marriage. She pleaded guilty and was given a light sentence – two years probation – and told the *News of the World* that Sunday that Jeffrey was 'a film actor, whom she first met at a party. Hardship followed.'

On 22 February 1959 Anna committed suicide at 'Cedrych', Leas Green, Chislehurst, Kent, the home of Dr Harry Hoffman, the forty-one-year-old local G.P., and his wife Pamela. Anna was twenty-nine. On her death certificate her address was given as 39d, Belsize Avenue, Belsize Park, Hampstead,

NW3 and she was described as a Market Research Interviewer and 'Wife of Geoffrey Bernard, Occupation unknown'. At the inquest four days later, on 26 February, the cause of death was given as barbiturate poisoning and Anna was found to have killed herself 'whilst the balance of her mind was disturbed'.

She died as she had lived, in a mess, a mystery woman. In 1992 there seemed to be no records at all of her end apart from her death certificate, no reports at any of the surviving merged coroners' offices. Nobody who had known her, not even Bernard himself, could provide a photograph of Anna until eventually her daughter Alfreda/Sally produced one a month before this book went to press. Bernard claimed in 1992 that he had not attended the inquest or her funeral or even received her last effects or seen a death certificate. It was almost as though Anna had become a Non-Person.

But then in the very week that this book went to press, in August 1992, I discovered that Dr Hoffman, now seventy-four, was living in a cottage in Wiltshire with his third wife. Anna had indeed left a suicide note, he told me, and she is buried in an unmarked grave in Chislehurst cemetery. He said that Anna (who was then drinking a bottle of whisky a day and was still depressed by the loss of her child) had been living in 1959 with Brian Berry in Belsize Avenue, but had spent that final weekend with the Hoffmans. They had sat up drinking until 4 a.m. on the Sunday and Anna and Pamela Hoffman had had an argument about motherhood. Dr Hoffman told the inquest that his wife had said to Anna: 'You are no good. Why don't you kill yourself? I will turn the gas taps on for you.' The next morning he had taken Anna a cup of tea in bed and had found her dead. Beside the bed was an empty bottle of pills and she had left a note saying how fond of him she was and how much she disliked his wife. She had promised spookily: 'I will meet you at dawn every morning in the garden.' On 27 February, the day after the inquest, every national newspaper carried prominent stories about the case. There were pictures of Anna and the *Daily*

Mail described Bernard (without mentioning his name) as a 'film actor'. It is difficult to see how he could possible have not known of her death immediately. Yet he did not bother to attend her funeral on 9 March, when her sister's husband, John Crowe, somehow managed to have her interred in consecrated ground even though she had committed suicide.

When Bernard compiled his first entry for *Who's Who* in 1989 he left her out altogether and his second wife, Jacki, was listed as his first. Anna might never have existed.

6

Jeff the Ripper

When Bernard's first marriage broke up in January 1952 it was the start of five desperate wilderness years in which he lived on the edge of disaster and never had a proper home or a moment's real security. It was during these terrible lean years of the early 1950s that he really learned how to live on his wits, to scrounge off others, to 'borrow' money and never repay it, to charm the rich and 'sing for his supper', to 'skate on thin ice' as he liked to boast in later years. It was now that he turned the occasional free meal of lobster and champagne at Wheeler's with the likes of Francis Bacon into high art. It was now that he honed his social skills so finely that even when his acquaintances felt that he somehow seemed to have picked their pockets, they did not mind too much because he had done it with such engaging panache. He charmed both men and women. He was not so much Fagin as the Artful Dodger. It was now that people began to feel sorry for him: 'oh, *poor* Jeffrey' was a refrain that could be heard all over London for the next forty years. People started tucking £5, £10 and even £50 notes discreetly into his top pocket, patting it smugly as they did, so that eventually he came to expect it but also to despise and possibly even to hate those who had patronised him by helping him out. He had felt tainted at Pangbourne because his fees had mainly been paid by the do-gooders at whom he was to sneer for the rest of his life. It must have been difficult for a middle-class boy with Bernard's pride to admit to himself that despite the nannies and servants in childhood, the big homes in the country, the rich father with an office in Park Lane, he was himself in his twenties little better than a beggar with a posh voice and a pretty face. His life forever after was to be stained with charity.

'I didn't know what to do,' he told me. 'I wasn't *trained* to do anything. I had vague ideas about wanting to write but I remember thinking that being a copywriter in an ad agency was frightfully flash because you could earn £20 a week – it was a magic figure, £1000 a year. But I didn't know what I wanted to do. I suppose that until I started journalism I was lost. I was a bit like Micawber, waiting for something to turn up.'

He worked again as a dishwasher. Now and then he was a builder's labourer again. For a spell he was a freelance decorator tarting up flats. He wandered the streets with a bucket and chamois leather, offering to wash cars: he was particularly successful among the rich nightingales in Berkeley Square. He also became a barrow-boy, selling books that his friends would otherwise have thrown out from a hired barrow in Earlham Street, off Cambridge Circus, outside the Marquis of Granby pub. 'The bloke with a barrow next to me was a playwright, Bernard Kops, selling junk, antiques,' he told me. 'I'd sell a book, close the barrow down and go into the Marquis of Granby for just the one.'

This did not guarantee him much of a living. Years later he estimated that in the early Fifties he may have moved from one small, grim bedsitter to another as many as a hundred times. 'I was always on the move,' he told me, 'and getting slung out by landladies for taking girls back after 10 p.m. That was very infra dig in those days, taking girls back to your bedsitter. Landladies used to listen to your footsteps going up the stairs at night.' Every now and then he would be reduced once again to spending the night in the Rowton House dosshouse in Camden Town for 2s 4d a night or the Turkish baths in Russell Square, where he could spend the night for ten shillings, though his virtue was endangered by the eager homosexuals.

'Rowton House was very lowering,' he told me. 'They had a thousand beds in cubicles and it was very Orwellian.

To get up in the dark in the freezing winter in a dosshouse and then to have to go to a building site and shovel clay . . . The most rock bottom was one freezing night when I slept with a mate of mine in a bombed house off the Tottenham Court Road that was derelict. We slept on straw.' At this time his older musician friend Edward Williams was remarkably kind and let Bernard use his credit account in a restaurant in Old Compton Street, where he could eat risotto for just three shillings. 'That saved my life,' he told me. 'When I was out of work it wasn't just laziness, I was so *miserable* doing these jobs, it was awful.' He and his friend Terry Jones would survive in Soho on cheap curry and rice and try to make two pints of beer last all night.

There was no one to whom Jeffrey could turn for help. Bruce was navvying as well. Oliver was in the process of becoming a teacher, living in Norfolk for most of the 1950s and teaching in Corsica in 1954 and 1955. And Sally had finally been committed to an asylum.

Not surprisingly Jeffrey began to find himself running up against the police. In 1954 he stole an expensive book, *The History of Byzantine Art*, from a bookshop in Notting Hill Gate and was arrested for shoplifting when he tried to sell it in the Charing Cross Road. On 10 March 1954 the West London Magistrates Court probation officer wrote to Commander Skinner at Pangbourne College to report that the twenty-two-year-old Bernard had been remanded on bail on a charge of stealing a book from the Java Head bookstall and was due to appear again before the magistrates on the 15th. He asked Skinner for his opinion of the boy. Hugh Skinner replied sadly two days later: 'He was unfortunate in his family background – I never knew of a father – and his mother who was a professional singer could not take care of his upbringing and it seemed that he had mixed with some very odd types during his youth . . . Whilst here, his conduct was never entirely satisfactory and he never seemed happy or inclined to settle down. Much of this, I am sure, was due to his home life or lack of it . . . I was always sorry for the boy and felt that with more help at home he might have developed quite well.'

He never seemed inclined to change and *settle down*. It was a phrase that was to haunt Bernard for the rest of his life. Settling down was never to be one of his talents.

Skinner was a magistrate himself, a Justice of the Peace, and concluded his letter: 'I feel that with adequate supervision something might be made of him . . . I think that he is a case that might be dealt with by a good psychologist.'

Thanks to this letter, the probation officer persuaded the magistrates on 15 March to remand Bernard for three more weeks for a full psychological report. Sadly there seems to be no sign of it. It would make intriguing reading. Forty years later Bernard himself had little good to say of his probation officer and claimed that he was a homosexual who had tried to seduce him.

He was given probation for a year – the first of his three criminal convictions. The other two were to come in the 1980s for causing criminal damage to a car and for evading VAT as an illegal bookmaker. Because of his youth he was ordered merely to report once a week to his probation officer. 'I also reported *him* to the police for sexual harassment,' said Bernard. 'He was a pouf. He implied that if I didn't go to bed with him he'd report me for breach of probation. They rapped him across the knuckles, I believe.'

Then the police picked Bernard up one night in the Mandrake Club, took him to West End Central police station, showed him a Colt .45 automatic and accused him of being the owner. 'It took hours and a public-school accent to convince them that I was a harmless layabout,' he said later. On another occasion an acquaintance called David Litvinov was arrested with a stolen car and told the police that he had bought it from Bernard, who was arrested, taken to Scotland Yard and interrogated.

He was in fact close to becoming a petty criminal. Rodrigo Moynihan told his son John that he was sure that Bernard had stolen small items from their Chelsea home at 155 Old

Church Street, where he and his wife Elinor ran an artistic salon near the Chelsea Arts Club for the likes of Francis Bacon and Lucian Freud but also made young Jeffrey welcome.

It was Bacon who passed on to Bernard a philosophy of life that he was to adopt for the rest of his days. 'The only way you can possibly survive is to regard everything as being totally unimportant,' Bacon told him. But Bernard also adopted a motto of his own with which Bacon would have disagreed. 'I realised in those dives in Soho that there is no virtue in work for its own sake,' Bernard wrote later in his anthology *Low Life*. The importance and pleasure of hard creative work was a vital lesson he was never to learn.

By now, despite his poverty, Jeffrey was meeting and regularly drinking with all the most famous 1950s denizens of Soho: Louis MacNeice, Robert Newton, Tambimuttu, the painter Nina Hamnett, the composer Alan Rawsthorne and his wife Isabel Lambert, the deaf poet David Wright, the blind Notting Hill poet John Heath-Stubbs, the poets George Barker and Elizabeth Smart. In the Colony Club one afternoon he so impressed the homosexual novelist E. M. Forster that Forster wrote him several letters. And Bernard was meeting those who were unknown then but were to become famous themselves, one of whom was to make him famous too – Keith Waterhouse. There was also Gavin Lambert, the editor of *The Monthly Film Bulletin*, who was to publish Bernard's first article in the 1950s, a film review, and to pay him ten shillings for it.

Among the new friends he made now in Soho was the future cartoonist Nick Garland, who was then an art student at the Slade. 'Soho then was extremely attractive,' Garland told me, 'and Jeff was a sort of pet, everyone liked him. He was everything you shouldn't be: completely feckless, self-destructive, irresponsible. He was also highly intelligent and witty. There was this strange mixture of someone who ought to be a write-off but was terrifically good company. You wanted to *save* him.

'He was terrifically fond of Frank Norman – the Cockney playwright and ex-convict – and there was an awful scene once in the Mandrake Club when Frank had offended some gangster and there was a fight and Frank was attacked and screaming "Is he tooled up? Is he tooled up? Has he got a knife?" It was absolutely terrifying but Jeff immediately hurled himself into the fight. He got thumped but it was his complete courage that impressed me enormously.'

Dan Farson, who was five years older than Bernard and soon to become a major television personality himself and the star of several interview series and documentaries like *This Week* in the late 1950s, remembered Soho then as being an extraordinarily closely knit community. 'We were almost like a band of brothers,' he told me. 'We were all hustlers in our way. Even people like Bacon were hustling but on a rather grander scale. Money was so different then: it was very much a matter of getting through the day and if someone had a bit of luck there was a camaraderie that made them share it. Because of this closeness we became very fond of each other.'

Every now and then Jeffrey would decide that he was fed up with London and that it was time to see something of England and he would take off into the unknown, working his passage as he did so. He took a job as a labourer on a farm in Suffolk, at Roamwood Green Farm, Debenham. He went to stay with Anna in Gloucestershire, where he toiled briefly at a 'ghastly' job in a paper factory in Winchcombe and spent all day cooking rags in caustic soda in a boiler into which he later had to climb to empty it. The stench was appalling. He would try to wash the smell from his throat by drinking in a pub run by the England cricketer Tom Graveney. And it was then that Anna gave him the pox and he had to attend a VD clinic in Cheltenham. She finally sent him packing when she screamed one day in the kitchen that a bumble bee was inside her jersey and he ran away, slamming the door behind him. He never saw her again.

Perhaps the most unlikely job he ever claimed to have had was as a miner for six months – from November 1952 to May 1953 – at a pit in Staffordshire called Hanley Deep, near Stoke-on-Trent, where he said that he had been a 'ripper', which involved cutting the rock after the other miners had cut the coal.

'I was fascinated to see what it would be like down there,' he told the *Telegraph Magazine* in 1992. 'I think that I had read too much D. H. Lawrence,' and he told me: 'I went first into a training pit for a month, an old pit called Kemble. I lived in a strange hostel mostly inhabited by strange, lovable, drunken Poles, all bonkers' and a 'big black Jamaican called Winston Churchill who beat me up in the lamp shed one day. The miners were some of the nicest people I've ever worked with but the job was very boring and very hot. We were working 3,000ft deep and it was hard work.'

He also claimed that at Hanley Deep he was threatened with a beating when he took his 'snapping' (lunch) down the pit wrapped in a copy of *The Times* and an angry miner accused him of being 'a fookin' Tory'. Apparently it did not help when he replied airily that he only bought *The Times* for the crossword and the cricket.

Bernard claimed once that his old Soho friend Terry Jones, who later worked with him as a stagehand in London, went down the mine with him at Hanley Deep but sadly Jones was dead in 1992 and unfortunately the Coal Board had no record of Bernard's spell as a ripper. 'There's nothing,' said A Spokesman, 'in fact there's no record of such a mine anyway. Perhaps it was a private mine or the colloquial name for a coal mine. That often happened.' A Spokesman offered one glimmer of hope in solving the mystery of Jeff the Ripper. Would Mr Bernard have been a likely contributor to the Miners' Pension Fund, of which they did indeed have records? I had to admit that this seemed unlikely. Bernard was not a man to invest in the future, particularly at the age of twenty. The only Pension Fund to which he ever contributed, even indirectly, even by the time he was sixty, was the Norman Balon Pension Fund, into which Bernard paid every day for fifteen years from 1978 to 1992 in the form of large vodkas with the kindly intention of easing the old age of the legendary landlord of the Coach and Horses.

Another unlikely job he took – for nine months in 1954 – was as a forester in the wilds of North Wales, near Lake Bala in Merionethshire, where he worked in a gang of six for the Forestry Commission, planting and felling trees. 'With axes,' he said later, 'which was the hardest physical work I've ever done. I lived in a two-hundred-years-old stone cottage on my own, where I had to walk across fields to get to the nearest track. There was no electricity or water and even in winter I had to wash in an ice-cold mountain stream outside. I used to like making fires and chopping up wood and I lived off a continual stew, and on Saturdays I'd go into Bala to the pub to drink pints of bitter. It was very dull but I wasn't unhappy.' Dan Farson remembered visiting him there once: 'We reached it by a marvellous little Sherlock Holmes train, it was like the Alps.'

On Bernard's travels around England he went down to Dorset to live for some time in the village of Piddletrenthide, near Dorchester, with the composer Edward Williams and his wife Zoe, one of Augustus John's daughters. Williams had been responsible, along with John Minton, for raising the money to send Bernard to a film school in Paris when he announced that he wanted to become a film editor and director. Bernard had thanked him by attending the school for just two days before deciding that it was all going to be too difficult and returning to England. He now compounded his ingratitude by having an affair with Williams' wife, Zoe, who was thirty-one. 'Now I think it's wicked and evil to do that, to screw friends' wives, because it just makes people unhappy,' Bernard told me in 1992. 'I feel ashamed now about it. I fucked up two marriages when I was young and it's not on. I did it to show off and to say to the world "I'm grown up, too, I can pull women." It was the beginning of the end of the marriage even though he was broad-minded.'

Zoe Williams was just one of a clutch of mistresses during those years. One of the few diaries that Bernard kept into his sixties was a brown John Menzies exercise book in which he listed various lovers, starting with Anna in 1947, and going on to Janet, Francesca, Avril, Scotch Annie, Georgiana, Penelope, Rose, Marsh, Margaret, Sally, Irma, Georgia, Jenny, Mimi, Wendy, Shirley, Alix, Inge, Susannah.

It must have been a relief to escape to St Ives in Cornwall with his friend Pete Arthy to try to get a job on a fishing boat. 'I thought that would be a romantic adventure,' he said, 'but I couldn't get a job and I bummed around for a bit.' He even managed to rent a proper flat, the first he had ever had, and persuaded the unfortunate local tobacconist and grocer to give him credit. After running up some impressive bills in the local shops he simply did a Dawn Flit one morning at six o'clock and hitchhiked back to London. Even in 1992 he showed no remorse about cheating the small local shopkeepers.

Back in London he was going racing increasingly with another new Soho acquaintance, Conan Nicholas, an admirer of the Sherlock Holmes books who had been named after Sir Arthur Conan Doyle and was sixteen years older than Bernard and to become a close friend. Nicholas was then a public relations officer at the Turkish Embassy, which meant that he was 'modestly affluent' and could take long lunches. 'Jeffrey was an engaging chap,' Nicholas told me, 'and we shared an interest in racing, Sherlock Holmes and cricket. We would often have lunch together at the Café Bleu in Old Compton Street.' Nicholas's interest in racing was indeed so strong that it was he who inspired the famous Battersea Cat Race that was to bring the house down night after night in the theatre during the West End run of *Jeffrey Bernard is Unwell* in 1989 and 1990. In 1969 Bernard was to describe him in the *Mirror Magazine* as his 'Most Unforgettable Character' after Nicholas's wife had confronted him as he left the marital home on their daughter's birthday to go to the races yet again to back a horse called Ribot and had asked him which was more important to him, his daughter's birthday or Ribot. 'Frankly,

m'dear, Ribot,' said Nicholas, closing the door. His daughter
Miriam was later at great pains to assure me that when her
father had raced the family cats along the passageway of their
Battersea flat she had not allowed him to treat them cruelly
by handicapping them with weights from the kitchen scales,
as legend had it.

Bernard was already acting as an unofficial bookmaker
and taking bets on horse races, without of course paying
tax, a hobby that was to earn him a criminal conviction
more than thirty years later. 'We used to drink in the
Caves de France,' Conan Nicholas told me, 'and Jeff took a
large amount of money on the favourite in the 1955 Derby,
Daemon, and whispered to a friend "We'll have to leave the
country if Daemon wins." But Phil Drake won. I had money
on it and Jeff hated me for backing a French horse. He felt
it was unpatriotic.

'In those days we used to go to the races at Hurst Park
and Alexandra Park, two courses that no longer exist, and
once we went to a dog track at New Cross, where we were
on the balcony when a man gave Jeff a tip on a particular
dog just before the race started. Jeff had had a few drinks,
pulled out a fiver, stepped down the steps to get the bet on
in a hurry and fell head over heels – but he tumbled and
bounced up again right in front of the bookies, holding the
£5 above his head and right under their noses just in time
for the off.'

But most of those years of the Fifties were spent in and
about the pubs and clubs of Soho, Chelsea and Notting
Hill. However, Bernard did actually get down to writing
another article, this time about his experiences working on
the fairground dodgems in 1949, and Stephen Spender published it in *Encounter*. It was to be the first cuckoo of his real
career. And in the end of course nothing had been wasted,
none of those awful years, not the dreadful jobs, not the
poverty, not the drunkenness, scrounging, hopelessness, nor
the sense of waste and loss, for all of them were to become

a deep inspiration for him when he finally realised that he was indeed a writer, whatever the army medical board had said. He was to recycle those memories over and over again for thirty years and finally make himself famous.

7

Jacki and the Flyman

In 1956 Jeffrey started at last to do a job that interested him. He began to work in the theatre, just as his parents had done, but in a lowlier role, that of stagehand, for £12 a week at the Old Vic. It was his first regular employment and the first that he really enjoyed, even though he did once lower the backdrop of *The Merchant of Venice* into the final act of *Much Ado About Nothing*. He was a dayman, making scenery and props and working regular hours. The leads in the Old Vic company then were Coral Browne, John Neville and Robert Helpmann – and one of the actresses was the twenty-two-year-old Canadian Jacki Ellis, who was to become Bernard's second wife three years later.

Jacki (Jacqueline Sheelagh) had come to Britain from Ottawa and was the daughter of a retired Canadian Director of Naval Intelligence, Captain Martin Ellis. She was an ex-convent girl 5ft 6ins short and stunningly beautiful, with long blonde hair. She had come to London in September 1952 to attend the Central School of Speech and Drama, where a fellow student was Wendy Craig. By the end of 1954 she had an agent, Coral Browne's husband Philip Pearman.

In April 1955, when she was only twenty, she took a gamble by skipping her last term at drama school to appear on the West End stage with Bernard Lee, Diana Churchill and Barry Foster in *The Desperate Hours*, an American thriller by Joseph Hayes, that played for six months at the Hippodrome, where Jeffrey's mother Dora had appeared in the chorus of *The Lisbon Story*. It was a gamble that paid off. She spent six months with the Oxford Repertory Company and appeared at the Oxford Playhouse in Christopher Fry's *A Phoenix Too Frequent*, Terence Rattigan's *The Browning Version* and a modern musical version of *The Comedy of Errors*, in which she was described by Harold Hobson (in the *Sunday Times*) as 'shatteringly attractive'.

By May 1956 she was on a two-year contract with the Old Vic, playing an extra in *King Richard III*, but in June she was suddenly catapulted for two weeks into a leading part – the Queen in *Richard II*, opposite thirty-year-old John Neville – while the regular Queen, Claire Bloom, was away making a film. Jacki was still only twenty-one. 'My ambition is purely and simply to make my living as an actress,' she told a Canadian news agency. 'I wouldn't want to do anything else, ever – so I guess I'll have to make sure I marry an actor.' Instead she was to marry Jeffrey Bernard.

In August she was appearing with Sir Ralph Richardson in *Timon of Athens*, a tiny part of just twelve words, but her sudden success was such that in October *Maclean's Magazine* published a six-page profile of her headlined 'Imagine *me* playing Shakespeare at the Old Vic!' . . . and illustrated with nine pictures of her, including one showing her leaving her small Hampstead flat.

It is easy to imagine the lusty twenty-four-year-old stage-hand Jeffrey Bernard in the wings at the Old Vic watching this luscious young blonde and drooling. They met in the Old Vic canteen and he fell for her immediately. She was not only beautiful, she was also obviously an actress full of promise: in the three years after she had first appeared on the West End stage she had never been out of work and soon she was making television films as well. And then Bernard got his hands on her and, according to some, destroyed her career.

John Moynihan remembered that the courtship was 'rather stormy'. 'I was very fond of Jacki and fancied her like hell,' he said, 'but I thought Jeffrey was a bit shabby to Jacki, and she was too kind to him. I had a friend called Heather Sears who knew her at the same time and who did make it. Heather was in *Room at the Top* and went on and became a star, but Jacki seemed to fade in the most extraordinary way after Jeffrey. She drank a lot and came into Soho a lot.'

By the most extraordinary coincidence Oliver Bernard had already been Jacki's lover before Jeffrey met her, just as he had had an affair with Anna Grice before Jeffrey married her. It seemed that the Bernard brothers had very similar tastes in women.

One witness who was amused by the Jeffrey/Jacki courtship at the Old Vic was Ned Sherrin, who was to direct *Jeffrey Bernard is Unwell* thirty-two years later. He remembered that when Jacki was playing Lady Anne in *Richard III* Jeffrey was ravishing her in the flies right up to the moment that she was due to come on stage and mourn: 'She arrived on-stage late and covered in grease.' The affair caused quite a stir. Actresses simply didn't have affairs with stagehands. 'The company was quite appalled,' said Bernard. 'Nothing like that had ever been *heard* of. In actual fact it wasn't much of an achievement because ninety per cent of the men in that season at the Old Vic were poufs anyway. If I'd run off with the leading man instead of the leading lady they'd have felt jealous! They were such snobs about it. At first they were fascinated by me because we used to share the same canteen under the stage and I remember them all nudging each other one morning because I looked absolutely awful with a hangover and I'd just had a fight with a girlfriend and I was scratched and head thumping and one of them noticed I was reading Turgenev and there was a lot of nudge-nudge, what's a stagehand doing reading Turgenev? That amazed them.'

It was to be a long courtship and it was not until more than a year later that Bernard left the flat he shared with Moynihan to move in with Jacki at her flat in Bywater Street, Chelsea, and later in Hampstead, at 58 Fitzjohns Avenue. He was still married to Anna, and he and Jacki were to live together for another year before Anna committed suicide in 1959 and he was free to marry again. Jacki was eventually to keep him for six years and to pay for almost everything, even though he was three years older than she was. He had already become the eternal toyboy, always expecting to fall on somebody else's feet.

Even at the start of their affair they did not feel that it was necessary to be faithful to each other. At one first-night party at the Old Vic Jacki was flirting so strongly with another man that Bernard went home afterwards to his flat in World's End with Jan Rowell, a mischievous beauty who looked like Juliette Greco or Audrey Hepburn and who had worked at the Old Vic and was now with the Royal Shakespeare Company in Stratford making props and costumes. As she joined Bernard in his narrow single bed he announced that there was 'no need' for them to use any contraception since he had had mumps as a child and was sterile. 'The rest of the night passed delightfully,' she told me, 'and he asked me to stay the next morning, but Jacki was a blonde beauty, very pretty and very nice and I knew she would be back. I went back to Stratford.'

Among Bernard's many rivals for Jacki's favours was Peter O'Toole, who was starring in *The Long and the Short and the Tall* at the New Theatre in St Martin's Lane and who was to immortalise him on the West End stage thirty years later in *Jeffrey Bernard is Unwell*. One night Bernard was sitting in the Salisbury pub in St Martin's Lane, a favourite drinking place for theatricals, 'eking out a half of bitter and feeling particularly dejected', when O'Toole came up to him and gave him a £5 note and told him to have a drink.

The boozing was non-stop. It is astonishing that any of Bernard's circle of friends from the Fifties remembered anything at all about those days. They did not even seem to care much about the occasional tragic casualties of their frenetic way of life, like John Minton, who killed himself with sleeping pills at his home at 9 Apollo Place, near Cheyne Walk, on 20 January 1957, finally driven to suicide by hopeless alcoholism, self-hatred and despair. He had been drinking ferociously for several days. Just before he died –

when Bernard must surely have known that Minton was just about at the end of his tether – the painter who had been so generous to him as a young man asked him to buy for him a skull as a prop for a play with which he was involved and gave him some money to do so. Frances Spalding claims in her biography that Bernard made no effort to find a skull. He spent the money on booze. Perhaps he was bitter that Minton had cut him out of his will and left his house to Henrietta Moraes, the wife of one of his earlier boyfriends, Norman Bowler, and £100 each to his acolytes like Bobby Hunt but excluding Bernard.

In 1957 Bernard shared a basement flat with John Moynihan in Trevor Place, Knightsbridge. Moynihan's girlfriend Rita Wheatley also lived there. Moynihan had to pay all the bills for gas, electricity and the telephone. Bernard pleaded poverty despite the fact that he had now landed a job at the Old Vic and was earning a good wage. 'We put up with it because of his charm,' said Moynihan. 'Life was less obligated to paying your way in those days: you tended to allow people to get away with it if they were old friends; now one thinks "dirty mean swine". My father lent him some money and didn't expect to get it back but then my father had used to borrow money himself. People who had been borrowing money were now growing up, becoming middle-aged, and they remembered the hard times themselves.'

Moynihan had just bought a huge, cumbersome tape recorder which Bernard liked to use to make fantasy recordings pretending that he was the cricket commentator E. W. Swanton. He also enjoyed hiding it under the bed to record the love cries of Jacki or any other woman that he managed to inveigle into the basement. Moynihan and Bernard would also gatecrash the bohemian parties at the Chelsea Arts Club by climbing over the garden wall and once witnessed the club's Chairman being punched so hard that he landed in the pond. 'People seemed to be hitting each other much more in the Fifties,' mused Moynihan. 'Jeffrey used to go looking for it, I think.'

But the endless boozing was already becoming a problem. Early in 1958 the stage carpenter at the Old Vic sacked Bernard for being drunk one night too many. 'Suddenly drinking had ceased to be a leisure-time occupation,' he recalled in the *Daily Mirror* in 1975. 'The fun had gone and it had become a way of life. What had merely been a bad habit had become a compulsion.' He was only twenty-five. He became a freelance flyman, working high above the stage in the flies for twelve shillings a show, taking shows on the road and assuming responsibility for all the scenery equipment that is 'flown' in the theatre – scenery that comes in from the grid, not a standing set.

He quickly found work, in March, when he joined the production of *Expresso Bongo*, in which Paul Scofield, Charles Gray, Hy Hazell and Millicent Martin appeared and the very young Susan Hampshire was a backstage assistant. She was a gofer trying to learn something of the craft although she also had a small part in the nightclub scene playing a débutante, a part she did not find too taxing since she had been one herself. It was said that she was so kind and obliging that when she was off-duty she washed Bernard's socks, but unhappily in 1992 she could not remember this. Bernard, however, remembered her extremely well. 'I once gave Susan Hampshire a bollocking,' he claimed. 'She'd been a deb and was Assistant Stage Manager but I said "those fucking props should have been here half an hour ago." ' He admitted, however, that he was not perfect himself during his theatrical career: 'During rehearsal I once dropped a hammer on stage from the grid, more than 100ft up.' He also greatly impressed the cast by dropping a chandelier onto the head of the unpopular director during a rehearsal at the Oxford Playhouse when the show was on its four-week provincial tour before it opened in London at the Saville Theatre. Paul Scofield was so delighted by the chandelier incident that he took the young flyman out for a drink.

Mick Tobin, a Cockney carpenter who was also working backstage on *Expresso Bongo* and was to become a great friend

of Bernard even though he was ten years older – they were
still drinking together in the Coach and Horses in 1992 –
remembered that 'he was a comical, witty, sharp kid. I
took to him straight away even though he wasn't really
interested in stage work.' They took the show to Newcastle,
Birmingham, Leeds and Oxford. 'It was hard work,' Tobin
remembered. 'On Saturday night you were pulling down,
loading the lorries, travelling all through the night, getting
in Sunday, putting it all up again.'

It was also thirsty work and they drank heavily wherever
they went. Bernard was being very well paid for those days
– £13 a week plus subsistence allowances – and he could at
last afford to drink spirits rather than beer. Tobin introduced
him to whisky, a dangerous development that was to have him
seriously ill in hospital eight years later. In the meantime it
was also to make him very intoxicated. He got so drunk on
the *Expresso Bongo* tour that on the first night in Newcastle
the local stagehands took the cue out of his pocket and left
him to sleep it off. But usually he was still reasonably reliable, said Tobin: 'If I wanted a flyman I'd hire him. On the
next show we had forty-nine flying cues, that's a lot of cues,
actions, movements on cue, so I used to have him, he knew
the cues.'

There was one other job that Bernard always remembered
with affection: the *Folies Bergères* nude show where one of the
perks was to stick stars on the dancers' nipples. There were
thirty girls in the show: 'Jeffrey went half way through the
cast,' Tobin chuckled.

– 2 –

It was during that winter of 1958 that the Great Battersea
Cat Race took place in Conan Nicholas's flat.

'That winter we were living in Prince of Wales Drive
facing Battersea Park,' Nicholas told me, 'and I said to
Jeffrey, "Since there's no racing why don't we go back

and race the cats?" We had two or three cats and a long
L-shaped hall where each part of the L was about 15 yards
long. The winner got a sardine.' Nicholas believed that the
cat racing was his thirteen-year-old daughter Miriam's idea.
Bernard himself confessed to me that both he and Nicholas
had exaggerated the story. 'Well,' said Nicholas, 'I'll tell you
this: Jeff even had a board up in the hall offering odds on
the cats, and a piece of chalk to mark it up, and eventually
we even handicapped the cats by tying small weights around
their middles – 1oz, 2oz and 4oz weights from the kitchen
stove, nothing to hurt them. And we put up strings so that
they had to do hurdles. I suppose we raced those cats three
or four times, for a fortnight, until the cold spell was over.'
Miriam Nicholas agreed that she used to race the cats –
Suki, Selima and Sammy – down the corridor towards the
kitchen at feeding time. 'I put obstacles in the way: a string
across the corridor, a pile of books or cushions, but I think
my father's exaggerating when he says they put weights on
the cats' backs.'

Around this time Jacki was working hard and earning
enough to support them both. She appeared in plays with
Daniel Massey, Robert Beatty, Anna Massey and Beatrice
Lillie, including *The Happiest Millionaire* with Wilfrid Hyde-
White, and made several television films. When she was not
working she would join Bernard in Soho and drink all day
in the French Pub or the Colony. 'He would take bets for
people,' she remembered. 'He was a bookie's runner for some
time and a couple of times he'd think that a particular horse
had no chance and he would keep the money and not put it
on with the bookie. He got into terrible trouble if the horse
won because people would expect to be paid their winnings.'

He also worked part-time in the evenings in an illegal dirty
bookshop in Soho. The job was well paid, £5 for a two-hour
shift, and he was astonished to discover that many of the
customers were famous: among them were several Members
of Parliament and the theatre critic Kenneth Tynan, who
collected books on flagellation. One evening Bernard was

also visited by an armed robber who pointed a Colt .45 automatic at him and raided the till. Bernard was terrified and handed over even the few banknotes he had in his own back pocket.

On 22 February 1959 his long-lost wife Anna committed suicide and Anna's death may in fact have affected Bernard more than he remembered later because a few weeks afterwards he and Jacki separated for five months. The widower went to stay at Pebmarsh with Peter and Marsh Dunbar and promptly seduced Marsh even though Dunbar had done him the honour of asking him to be his baby son Sean's godfather six months previously. At one stage Bernard inveigled Jacki down to Pebmarsh so that he could enjoy both his women at the same time. 'Jacki was very pretty and very funny, a lovely girl,' said Marsh, 'but it was a bit traumatic because they were staying in our little back cottage and not only was their bedroom wall right next to ours, so we could hear everything, but Jeffrey still slipped in to see me while Pete was away. It was all squalid to say the least. Nobody made a scene but it was all pretty uncomfortable.' Jacki told me in 1991 that she had never been unfaithful to Bernard until she realised that he and Marsh were lovers.

Marsh's affair with Bernard lasted just five months but it was so intense that although Marsh had three very small children she left her husband to follow him back to London, taking the children with her. 'I really was insane about Jeffrey,' she said. 'He wasn't particularly funny, he was mostly sullen and miserable. It really was like an illness. It wasn't even that he was a very good lover. I think it was because he was such a shit. He was a sod unless you did exactly what he wanted. We used to have rows about absolutely nothing. I don't know why and it's really awful, but being a shit is irresistible.'

In London Marsh and the children stayed with her husband's parents – 'I must have had a hell of a nerve, they weren't very pleased, I must have gone mad' – only to discover that Bernard had suddenly gone back to Jacki. Marsh realised at last how foolish she had been to run after someone who had never had any intention of accepting any responsibility for anything that he did. She telephoned her husband, who 'kindly' agreed to take her back. 'The next thing I knew Jeffrey and Jacki were getting married. It was like madness.' Peter Dunbar was understandably displeased about the whole business, even though he was himself a notorious womaniser. But Marsh had to admire the way her husband took his revenge on both of them. He promptly had an affair with Jacki and left it to Marsh to tell Bernard. Jacki too was determined to get her own back. 'I think she gave Jeff rather a hard time when they moved to Highgate,' Marsh remembered. 'She went through the card, starting with Peter Dunbar. I thought it was terribly funny at the time.'

– 3 –

Jeffrey married Jacki on the unlucky date of Friday 13 November 1959 at Hampstead Register Office, when he was twenty-seven and she was twenty-five. On the wedding certificate he described his architect father as an 'Artist' and himself as a 'Writer' when in fact he had published only a couple of ten-shilling film reviews in the *Monthly Film Bulletin* and *Sight and Sound*. He was not to become a journalist until five years later. He was no more a Writer when he married Jacki in 1959 than he had been a Pugilist when he had married Anna in 1951.

Jacki was now famous in London and the newspaper photographers were out to record the wedding. She was appearing in the West End with Leo McKern and Nicolette Bernard (no relation) in the French farce *Rollo*, which had opened at the Strand Theatre a fortnight earlier, at the end of October. Because of her West End success the London evening papers, the *Star* and the *Evening Standard*, both carried front-page photographs of the happy couple that afternoon and drew attention to the fact that the bride had defied superstition by marrying on Friday the 13th. 'She chose the date to please her Irish mother, who has always found it her "lucky day",' reported the *Star*, which also described Bernard as 'a writer'. 'Anything with a three in it is usually lucky for me,' Jacki told the paper. The next morning the *Daily Mirror* carried a huge photograph across several columns – on page 13, of course – showing Bernard and his bride smiling beneath a Bus Stop sign. The accompanying story claimed that after their wedding they had taken a bus to a Soho café for a Wedding Breakfast of bacon and eggs.

Typically Bernard had no idea in later years of when he had married Jacki. In *Who's Who* he claimed that it was in 1958 and he told me that he thought it might have been 1957. It is difficult to imagine him remembering wedding anniversaries but he did of course have more of them to remember than most. In 1992 he had no idea as to what Jacki's married surname might be even though he regularly went to see her during the 1980s at the club she ran in Cambridge whenever he became drunk and maudlin after Newmarket races nearby.

It seems that the marriage could have been successful if only Bernard had been less selfish, but he was still too immature even at twenty-seven to realise that it might be rather nice if he considered someone else's feelings as well as his own. 'Jacki was a gentle, attractive woman,' Conan Nicholas remembered, 'and it seemed that Jeffrey was never happier than when he was with her. He was at his best at this time.' Jacki too remembered the good times more than thirty years later: 'He could be very loving and warm and he used to be proud of me if I made people laugh, which was nice. He loved cricket and I watched him play at Battersea Park once, and we went to Lords.'

They kept a cat called Fred Winter and gave riotous parties on Derby day and Grand National day when they moved later to a flat at Hornsey and invited the likes of Frank Norman, Conan Nicholas, Allan Hall, Tony Harris and Sandy Fawkes. 'Jacki seemed a bit detached from Jeffrey in those days,' said Hall, 'probably feeling that while he was into racing and his friends were around him there wasn't really much communication between them.' In Hornsey they also mixed with a disreputable crowd of dirty-book dealers who would come round to the flat to play cards. One night Jeffrey went to bed early and Jacki stayed up late gambling and kept winning, stuffing pound notes into her brassiere. When she got to bed and proudly removed her bra Bernard was littered with fluttering banknotes.'

It was ultimately the suicidal drinking that was to kill the union. Jacki told me that it was a very boozy marriage in which they drank heavily most of the day and were not surprisingly 'pretty much' legless every night. 'Most of our rows were caused by drink,' she said, 'but everyone drank such a lot in those days. Frank Norman used to get absolutely paralytic: I remember beating him over the head with a chair leg to stop him beating up his wife Geraldine. Jeffrey could be very violent. He beat me up and I beat him up. We all used to fight quite a lot. One night Frank Norman got terribly drunk and he felt that we'd all ignored him at a party at Sandy's and he came and smashed his fist through the sitting room window and cut his wrist – blood was everywhere. Sandy said she'd phone for an ambulance, and there I was running down the road trying to catch Frank and bring him back! We both came back covered in blood. Things like that would keep happening. Still, you never got bored.'

By now Bernard was having alcoholic blackouts and he was becoming increasingly aggressive and using Jacki's money to compensate by being grandiosely generous. She ended up paying for everything. 'Jacki was a sweet, innocent actress,' the Colony Club barman Ian Board remembered. 'She was very beautiful and I liked her very much. She'd come here in the afternoon, demure, hardly said a word, didn't drink, in fact she wasn't a boozer, but they got married and it was only a year or so after that she really took to the gin bottle. There was a rapid change in her. She was in *The Reluctant Debutante* with Wilfrid Hyde-White, at the Cambridge Theatre, and he said, "She's a terribly good actress. If she sticks to it she'll go places." I think Jeffrey managed to fuck that up beautifully.' Another friend claimed: 'Jeff destroyed Jacki. She was widely considered to be a most promising young actress but he led her astray. He took her drinking in the pubs and clubs and he would turn up at the theatre roaring drunk.'

Another problem for the marriage was the contrast between Bernard's layabout failure and Jacki's comparative success. Three months after they married *Rollo* was still playing so successfully in the West End that on 1 February it transferred from the Strand to the Duchess Theatre in Catherine Street, the Aldwych. Was Bernard proud of his wife or perhaps beginning to become jealous? Two months later she was appearing at the Pavilion, Bournemouth, with Terry Thomas and Richard Briers in an out-of-town run of another French farce, *It's In The Bag*, which had been adapted by Somerset Maugham's nephew Robin. The play moved on to Edinburgh and Liverpool before opening in London at the Duke of York's Theatre.

Bernard's 'career' was by comparison non-existent. He had decided now that he was going to be a photographer and he and Pete Arthy started to take pictures of well-known people around Soho and photographs of actors and actresses for the actors' magazine *Spotlight*, but it was not until six years later that he finally managed to produce a book of photographs, with text by Frank Norman, called *Soho Night and Day*. He had simply become Jacki's kept boy.

I asked Jacki what had most made Bernard *happy* during their marriage. 'Having a meal off Francis Bacon at Wheelers,' she said. 'Winning on the horses. Being with important people. He's going to deny all this, but he admired money. We had an acquaintance who was a terrific conman, called Charles da Silva, from Goa, and although Jeff knew he would never rise to his heights he used to admire that man. Da Silva sold a "fishing fleet" from Dubai to someone in Norway, he sold "rice fields" in Kuwait ... He was the conman of all time. He used to stick fivers into Jeffrey's breast pocket when he'd done a good con. That was creative conning, that wasn't begging on a doorstep. Do you think Jeffrey's like a lucky mascot for these people? Maybe that's it – he brings them luck. And he used to play on it a bit. First he was the orphan boy finding his way in London, and then he was the down-on-his-luck writer of the Novel of the Century next week, then he became the hack.'

Jacki wondered whether she had molly-coddled him too much when they were married: 'My mother said that Jeffrey would have been a success a lot sooner if I hadn't nursed him so much in his early days. She said I had looked after him too much. But I thought, no – he needed to get as old as he was to be what he was, to write. Her opinion was that I was far too good to him and looked after him far too well. His clothes were a mess and his teeth were all falling out and I sorted him out, sent him to the dentist and paid for it and bought him clothes and now he's quite dapper, and I like to think that some of that was my influence.'

Jacki also used to do what she could for his sister Sally/Sonia, taking her out for the day whenever possible from her mental hospital. Once, when Bruce wanted to have Sally released from a hospital in Tooting Bec, Jacki vouched for her, 'but it was a dreadful mistake and Oliver was furious with us because she really did need more supervision than we could give her. She was totally schizophrenic and she could be perfectly charming and rational and then just go absolutely bonkers. What we hated about Tooting Bec was that they were giving her shock treatment and very strong drugs and you could see all the other ladies sitting around like cabbages and Bruce was frightened that she'd become like that. She looked most like Jeffrey. She must have been very beautiful at one time.'

Yet despite Jacki's kindness and consideration Bernard would often treat her without any consideration at all. Whatever she did to show him her love, he always seemed to be 'dry and bitter', she said.

The marriage was no better in 1961. Even when he went to the Derby at Epsom 'to take some photographs' he claimed later that he had been 'kidnapped by gipsies . . . They bundled me into a beer tent.' Conan Nicholas remembered that between 1961 and 1963 he was freelancing and so able to come and go as he pleased: 'Jeffrey and Frank Norman and I would each always arrive in Old Compton Street in taxis at 11 a.m. – we were known as the Three Musketeers. At this time I was probably closer to him than anyone else. We went racing together – we went with Peter Cook to the 2,000 Guineas – and we used to drink a bottle of scotch a day each in places like the Colony, the French, the Gargoyle and the Rockingham Club, a club in Archer Street that was used by old queers and run by Toby Roe. We did our betting from there – there was a quiet room with phones.'

Frank Norman took Bernard to one very liquid publishing party where Norman Mailer had a fight with Gregory Corso and then invited Bernard back to his suite at the Ritz where they enjoyed 'a very friendly all-night session' drinking together. After drinking all night at Mailer's expense he persuaded him to give him the taxi fare home.

Jacki in the meantime was building a proper career. By now she was well known to television viewers and had appeared in several television plays as well as series like *Danger Man* and *Emergency Ward 10*, and on 22 February 1961 she opened in the female lead – opposite Terence Stamp – at the Wimbledon Theatre in the out-of-town preview of *Why the Chicken* by John McGrath, a play about teenage loneliness in a New Town, with music by Lionel Bart (who also produced and directed) and sets by the acclaimed stage designer Sean Kenny, both of whom had had a previous triumph at the Wimbledon with the smash-hit *Oliver*. The play was not a success but for Jacki to have landed the leading role – and to have been so successful in television – must have made Bernard jealous, and he certainly brooded about her possible promiscuity with her leading man and other actors.

She admitted years later that she had had a lot of

affairs during their marriage ('It was just the way we all were then'). 'After we split up I discovered she'd been to bed with various people I'd put up in our flat out of the kindness of my heart, which upset me a bit, and then she had a big affair with my best friend, Barry Bell, who was an electrician at the Old Vic,' said Jeffrey. 'The final crunch was when she had an affair with an actor who was in *Oh What a Lovely War* called Griffith Davies, who was quite well-heeled and moved in a rather grotty little group with Rita Tushingham. I was jealous about Griffith Davies, and did some damage to Barry Bell. He and Jacki were having a meal in a restaurant and I walked in and he was just putting a fork in his mouth and I walked over and gave his hand a tremendous shove into the roof of his mouth, which made his eyes water.'

Another affair of Jacki's, this time one that Jeffrey knew nothing about, was with Bunny May, an actor/dancer who was later to become a close friend and was still drinking with him in the Coach and Horses in 1992.

Jacki's success cannot have helped the marriage and they drifted apart. The end came in 1962 when he was paid a publisher's advance of £100 for the book *Soho Night and Day*, and lost the lot on ten spins of a roulette wheel in a club one night. Jacki was livid. 'You could hear the slap my lady gave me the length of Greek Street,' he recalled later. Jacki finally threw him out.

Bernard was distraught by the break-up and burning with jealousy. When he was asked whom he was going to cite for adultery in his divorce petition he replied bitterly: '*Spotlight*' [the theatrical casting catalogue]. He was particularly tortured after their separation when Jacki played the female lead in *The Bedsitting Room* at the Comedy Theatre opposite a twenty-nine-year-old Australian comic actor, Barry Humphries, who had been acting in Britain for four years and was later to create that monstrous international Housewife Superstar Dame Edna Everage. 'Jacki and I shared a stage bed and after the performance I'd drive her home to Muswell Hill,' Humphries told me in 1992. 'We had merely a platonic relationship – she was just my actress – and Jeff wasn't living with her any more. But being jealous he'd haunt the stage door when he was drunk.'

The divorce, which went through eventually in 1964 – the *nisi* on 29 July, the absolute on 30 October – was traumatic. It was Jacki who wanted it and as usual, as with everything else during their marriage, she paid for it, though she allowed Bernard to divorce her for adultery. He cited her adultery with Griffith Davies but Jacki had to employ (and pay for) a private eye on his behalf to bear the necessary witness. 'This funny little old man came round to the flat,' said Jacki. 'Griff came to stay the night in our flat and the lawyer told us he had to wear pyjamas – he never wore pyjamas! – because he had to be seen in "night attire"! And so this man duly came and knocked at the door (it was all arranged) and he surveyed this chap in night attire and made a note and went into the sitting room and asked all sorts of questions. It was awful.' In court Bernard's lawyer 'named every person I'd ever met in my life and I was supposed to have slept with them. It was just unbelievable, and in the end I had to pay the most fantastic bill.'

The divorce affected both of them powerfully but in different ways. Just before they separated Jacki had bought him an expensive camera to encourage him to try to make a living on his own as a photographer. In his sober moments, as he flitted homeless and unwanted from one friend's flat to another, he must have wept and hated himself for letting such an affectionate woman go. By now his brother Oliver had a three-year-old son, Joe, and a year-old daughter, Emma, and what did he have himself? A second broken marriage, no home, no job, no prospects. In his misery one night he tried to commit suicide by gassing himself in a flat off Bayswater Road that had been lent to him by Nick Luard. His friend Nick Garland, the cartoonist, was out of London but for some reason telephoned Bernard. 'He came to the phone sounding very strange and sleepy,' said Garland, 'and he told me I had interrupted an attempt to kill himself and that all the gas taps were on. I telephoned the police and then telephoned him again to keep him talking. He told me there was somebody at the door and he was very angry. He said, "That filthy cow has called the police." They took him away. He had left a note for Nick Luard saying "I'm very sorry to do this to you but I'm at the end of my tether." He was serious.'

Jacki married Griff Davies later that year and moved out of London to live in a cottage in the village of Berden, near Bishops Stortford, as she had always wanted. She found that because of her volatile relationship with Bernard she was now constantly trying to rile Davies. 'When I first lived with Griff I used to *instigate* rows,' she said. 'I'd suddenly find myself making him hit me and we talked about it one night and he said this is ridiculous: you're trying to re-enact all the excitement of before and it's not like that now. So we calmed down, but this was still in me, all this violence, and I *missed* it. It was the way of life I was used to. Without it, it seemed, gosh, very dull. I was *enraging* him to the point where we had a terrible fight.' Eventually they too were divorced but in the meantime, mysteriously, her career simply evaporated. She appeared in eighteenth century costume as Berinthia in *The Trip to Scarborough* at the Belgrade Theatre, Coventry and in the Ernest Hecht/Stanley Dubens production *I Want To See Musov*, and in two episodes of *The Ratcatchers* TV series, *Amsterdam Story* and *Dubrovnik Story*, playing Miss Larks, and she looked as gorgeous as ever in all of them. But after that she gave up the theatre to do menial jobs. She worked as a van driver, then in a small electronics factory near Bishops Stortford, then near Saffron Walden in a Dunlop factory making badminton shuttlecocks, then as a barmaid in the Eight Bells pub in Saffron Walden, which she told me in 1992 was much 'like acting'. She married for a third time, Brian Heard, and together in 1980 they took over the running of the County Farmers Club in Cambridge, where they were still working in 1992.

That vital spark of ambition had died within her.

'I'm still fond of Jeffrey and I don't regret having married him,' she told me. 'I think he did change my life quite a lot – for the better, mainly.'

8

A Kayf Up West

Before Jeffrey and Jacki separated he had started to find jobs as a boom-swinger and clapper boy on films for both the cinema and television and over the next three years he worked at Shepperton, MGM and Ealing Studios. Both jobs were possibly the humblest on the filmset floor and involved little work, but he hoped that they would earn him a cinema technician's union ticket and so eventually a job as a cameraman. They could also earn him as much as £35 a week, a very good wage in 1962, and a flattering proximity to the stars. He was a clapper boy on a film called *Zarak Khan*, which featured Victor Mature, Michael Wilding and the stunning Anita Ekberg, for whom he itched in vain, and Bernard himself was so good-looking that when he was working on another film Martita Hunt sat beside him and stroked him and said 'I want to buy you lots of pretty jerseys.' He worked as an assistant editor on *The Guns of Navarone*, with Gregory Peck ('a good man'), David Niven and Anthony Quinn, and as an editor on *Anastasia*, which starred Ingrid Bergman and Yul Brynner. 'Yul Brynner was one of the biggest shits I've ever come across in show business,' Bernard said, 'he was just a pig. But Ingrid Bergman was one of the nicest people you could possibly imagine.' He also worked on *The VIPs* with Elizabeth Taylor and was astonished to look into her violet eyes, a colour that he had never previously encountered on each side of a nose. She was 'a great lady for Bloody Marys', he remembered.

In television he became a BBC trainee in the cutting rooms at Ealing, finally earning his union card, and worked on the first episodes of the television series *Z-Cars* as well as several film obituaries, among them those of the Duke of Windsor and Winston Churchill. Churchill, who was to die in 1965, 'used to come down and see his obituary as often as he could', Bernard remembered. 'He loved it, the vain old bastard! I was editing it, putting it together, putting sound-tracks on, everything.' Another of Bernard's television programmes was *The Death Penalty*, during the filming of which he spent three days in the company of the hangman Albert Pierrepoint, 'a very boring little man, the epitome of everyone's idea of a bank clerk, very insensitive. He had a pub in Yorkshire with notices on the wall bearing stupid legends like NO HANGING ABOUT. I remember one day in the canteen saying "Is it true, Albert, that the prisoner always eats a hearty breakfast?" and he just laughed and said: "I don't know, but I always used to eat a hearty one." The great regret of his life was not being given the job of hanging all the Nazis at Nuremberg.'

After Jacki had thrown Bernard out of her flat in Hornsey he began to live like a gipsy again, camping briefly on and off with any friends who would have him. The comedian Peter Cook took him in for a while at his house in Church Row. 'He was very quiet,' Cook told me. 'I was going through my social worker phase. I must have been mad.' Bernard repaid Cook's kindness by seducing his wife, Wendy. Even worse, he proceeded to rob Wendy Cook. 'She got drunk one night and I tapped her for some money,' he told me, 'so she started to write me out a cheque for £5 and as she wrote the *fi-* of five I got hold of her hand and guided it into another *-fty* so that the cheque was for £50 and I was at the bank the next morning at one minute to ten to cash it. She was pissed but she was loaded. He was very mean, Peter.'

The end of his second marriage marked the beginning of a frenzied period of compulsive one-night-stand promiscuity during which any and every woman he met was a target, no matter to whom she was married. One husband, a friend, came home unexpectedly and found Bernard with his wife on a chaise-longue, stark naked. He later claimed to have destroyed the marriage of one of his oldest friends, Pete Arthy, whose bride-to-be he seduced on the night before the wedding. 'I was ruthless,' Bernard told me, 'besotted with sex. It was all I used to think about. I think maybe I was oversexed. I had had this awful upbringing, being told everything was wicked.' The American writer Irma Kurtz, who met him at about this time and was later to become a close friend and a magazine agony aunt, remembered that one of his seduction ploys was 'to go around saying that he was sterile. God knows how many women went to bed with Jeffrey thinking that he couldn't make babies.' Bernard's women, however, were not all victims. One girl whom he picked up in a club one night was so gorgeous that when he was dressing the next morning – and feeling particularly pleased with himself for managing to seduce her – he told her that he would meet her for lunch. She sat up in bed. 'Listen,' she snapped. 'Today's Tuesday. You were Monday.'

There was also, of course, as a typical Gemini, another side to Bernard. 'He was effervescent,' I was told by the actor John Hurt, who met him in Soho in the early Sixties. 'We were pub friends and occasionally we'd go to a race meeting together. He had – and has – an electricity, presence, and he struggles for honesty. And he was uproariously funny in the old days, when he did cod Shakespeare and would sometimes give a performance which was absolutely hysterical, wonderful. They were roistering days. I don't think that anybody expected to get to thirty.'

Bernard was also starting to live dangerously, to 'skate on thin ice'. One afternoon in the Colony Club he told a fellow drinker at the bar not to be 'such a fucking bore' and discovered later that he had insulted the vicious gangster Ronnie Kray. 'It's a wonder he didn't blow my brains out,' marvelled Bernard. He also bumped into the Richardson gangsters in the Pickwick Club when his journalist friend Fergus Cashin, with whom he was later to share an office at the *Daily Sketch*, made the mistake of informing one of the Richardsons that he was 'an arsehole'. 'I just finished my drink and walked out,' Bernard recalled. 'Cashin said

I'd betrayed him, but I didn't want to get beaten up by the Richardsons.'

And then Bernard's luck seemed to change. He met Tony Hancock one morning in the York Minster – they were introduced by their mutual friend John le Mesurier – and they drank together right through the afternoon. By the early evening Hancock was very drunk, so Bernard hailed a taxi to get him home. Hancock sat on the floor of the taxi and gave Bernard his telephone number. 'Phone me some time if you're ever in trouble,' he said. 'I think you may have a drink problem.' Then the great comic lay back on the floor of the cab and passed out. It seemed to be a happy omen. Soon afterwards Bernard was to be drawn into a chain of circumstances that ended with him appearing on-stage as a comic actor himself, at last.

At the end of 1963 Frank Norman asked Bernard along to the Theatre Royal at Stratford East, in the East End of London, to listen to the first read-through of Norman's new semi-musical play *A Kayf Up West*, based on a real Soho café up West, the Alexandria in Rathbone Place, where Norman and Bernard had met in the 1950s. Norman had become the flavour of the decade after he had been released from prison in April 1957 after serving two years of a three-year sentence (in Wandsworth Prison and at Camp Hill on the Isle of Wight) for bouncing cheques. It was smart to be a dinner-jacketed criminal in the 1960s and Norman had become the darling of fashionable thespian society after writing the 1959 stage smash-hit *Fings Ain't Wot They Used T'Be* (music by Lionel Bart). He was basking by now in the titles of 'the Cockney Brendan Behan' and 'the Cockney Jean Genet'. His new play was to be directed by Joan Littlewood – who had just had a huge success the previous year with *Oh What a Lovely War*.

Bernard sat in the wings but when one actor failed to turn up he was asked by Joan Littlewood to read the part. He was so good at it that when the missing actor had still not arrived by lunchtime Miss Littlewood offered Bernard the part. He was at the time just bumming around Soho pretending to be a photographer, so he jumped at the chance.

By the time of the first night he was in fact playing four parts. 'Just regard it all as messing around on the stage with your mates,' Miss Littlewood told him. 'Pretend you're in a pub telling your friends a joke.' They rehearsed for twelve hours a day and he was paid 'practically nothing', he claimed later – in fact £10 a week – but Joan Littlewood would slip him the odd fiver in the pub afterwards. During one of those rehearsals, on 6 March 1964, the picture that is reproduced in this book was taken, four days before the play opened. It was described on the back of the agency photo as 'a modern Dick Whittington, who finds that the streets of London are not paved with gold. He meets the most diabolical bunch of people one could imagine and falls under their spell.' One of the diabolical bunch of people was Jeffrey Bernard, who seemed to be playing himself.

A Kayf Up West, which starred the young Barry Humphries and Barbara Ferris as well as Bernard, opened at the Theatre Royal, Stratford East, on 10 March 1964, with music by Stanley Myers. It told the story of an innocent young man from the London suburbs, Tommie White, who arrives in Soho and falls in love of course with a golden-hearted whore and is corrupted by the group of drunks, junkies and unemployed layabouts who frequent a seedy café – and by a crook, Bill the Burglar, played by Bernard.

This story of a nice young man going to the bad in Soho and being seduced by tarts and ponces could almost have been the story of Bernard himself. The main character that he played, Bill the Burglar, steals art books, just as Bernard had done. Like Bernard he is also highly knowledgeable about Byron. By Act II Jeffrey was playing a simpering socialite called Gilbert who was shrieking: 'Come along everybody. I want you to have lots and lots of lovely drinks and get terribly drunk and enjoy yourselves.' The stage direction following this remark reads: 'The party trail in behind him, twittering.' For Bernard to play a character keen on getting everyone else drunk was of course excellent casting.

Bernard claimed later that he had played the lead in *A Kayf Up West* but in fact the lead, Tommie, was played by a young actor just out of drama school and taking on his first professional role, Edward Roscoe. Bernard played a Kew Gardener and a prison warder as well as the burglar and the homosexual. He claimed afterwards that he had received the best reviews, much better even than Barry Humphries, and Soho legend has it that he alone was praised by the critics. The truth is less generous. In *The Stage* R. B. Marriott called the play 'a tedious strip of bits and pieces about the sleazy side of Soho in 1949. It is extraordinary how lacking in originality, interest or a personal slant the play is . . . there is a lot of thoroughly bad acting . . . This show is a Littlewood mistake.' Bernard's performance was singled out by two reviewers. 'The only real character among them is the small-time thief, played with brisk belligerence by Jeffrey Bernard,' said the anonymous *Times* reviewer, while Milton Shulman wrote in the *Evening Standard* that 'Howard Goorney, Jeffrey Bernard, Barry Humphries all manage three or four parts extremely well.'

Bernard liked to pretend afterwards that this play had been immensely important in his life, some sort of thespian Everest, but it was obviously a theatrical disaster. Still, it was fun while it lasted and it massaged Bernard's ego wonderfully. 'I didn't know what the fuck I was doing till 1964,' he told me. 'I was just a face in the crowd and didn't like that. I'm ashamed to say I've always *craved* being not just a success but being well known. I didn't like being just a face in a saloon bar. They were dizzy days for me in *A Kayf Up West* because it was my first experience of being able to make 500 people laugh. I loved it.'

It was also fun to work and play with Barry Humphries, and Bernard had by now overcome his jealous suspicion that Humphries might have been Jacki's lover. 'Barry was a practical joker par excellence,' said Bernard. 'One Saturday between the matinée and the evening performance he went out into the street dressed very shabbily, looking a bit like a tramp, and he had some tins of Heinz baby food which he mixed up and poured on the pavement when no one was looking. Then he got down and started eating it with a spoon. People thought he was drinking vomit. After curtain down we used to go to the Pickwick Club in Soho for a few drinks and on the Tube going up Barry would always walk right through the train going from carriage to carriage, which was quite hairy, and in his Australian accent he would ask passengers who were sitting down, nice quiet respectable people going home after a day's work, "Excuse me, can you tell me which end of the train the buffet car is? I'm *desperate* for a drink." '

Barry Humphries told me that Bernard 'was a very good actor indeed. Then, as now, he was an amiable man, though like his friend Frank Norman he could assume a mildly threatening aspect late at night in the Kismet Club. He deeply resented it when I compared his dazzling smile with that of a forgotten cocktail pianist, Russ Conway. Happily, he has outgrown the resemblance. He was very influenced by Frank Norman and modelled his brusqueness and rudeness on him. And he wouldn't thank me for saying it but he *did* look like Russ Conway. He used a Senior Service-type voice and in the Sixties he used to wear blazers, Daks trousers, a cravat. He had a sort of saloon bar raffishness but definitely a military college background was there in wisps.'

Appearing on the professional stage did not seem to interfere with Bernard's drinking at all. He was often tipsy on stage and one afternoon he missed a 2.30 matinée curtain-up because he had drunk too much at lunch, fallen asleep on the Central Line Underground train to Stratford East and had snored all the way to Epping and back. He still drank with gusto until late every night in the Pickwick Club, just off the Charing Cross road, and it was there that he caught the eyes of two actresses, Marlene Dietrich and Jean Marsh.

'Marlene Dietrich came along to see the play one night,'

said Bernard. 'I saw her in the stalls, which unnerved me slightly, and two hours later she came up to me in the Pickwick and said very cornily: "You probably don't know who I am but my name's Marlene Dietrich" and I said "Well of course I bloody know who you are", and she then said "I just came over to tell you that I think you were wonderful." She stayed for half-an-hour drinking with me and an American actor, John Bay, and bought us a couple of drinks, which annoyed the table of people she had left to speak to me, a nonentity.' Even Bernard did not have quite the nerve to try to seduce Dietrich that night but when he returned home he lay awake for hours: 'I just kept staring at the pitch-black ceiling thinking, Marlene Dietrich thinks I'm wonderful.'

He was less reticent with the attractive young woman of twenty-nine whom he noticed staring at him from the other side of the room for several nights running in the Pickwick Club. He was thirty-one, in his prime, and by all accounts devastatingly attractive. Eventually she approached him in the bar. 'I swear this is true,' said Bernard, 'she said, "Hello, I'm Jean Marsh and I must tell you that I'm absolutely besotted with you." She was living with Kenneth Haigh and he was in a play at the Phoenix and used to take her to the Pickwick after his curtain-down. You could have knocked me down with a feather. And what amused me later – it was unpleasant at the time – was that it got up Haigh's nose that he was a star and she'd gone off with a *stagehand*.'

Jean Marsh had already been married to the *Doctor Who* actor Jon Pertwee but divorced four years earlier, in 1960. 'We had an affair,' said Bernard, 'but we didn't live together because I had nowhere to invite her. I was living with Peter and Marsh Dunbar in Canonbury Square and I only had a little room, and Jean Marsh was used to grander things than a bloody bedsitter and I couldn't blame her for that. It went on the whole of the summer. We used to meet at Nick Garland's house. He used to be a very close friend of mine and in those days was stage director at the Establishment Club.'

Bernard's affair with Jean Marsh, who was to become internationally famous in the 1970s playing the housemaid Rose in the TV series *Upstairs, Downstairs* was dramatic, he claimed. 'She and Ken Haigh, who was the first Jimmy Porter, broke up because of me. We had quite a tempestuous little thing. I used to go and see her in her dressing room between the matinée and the evening performance. I'd go to see her anywhere. I remember going down to Brighton to see her in The Cricketers one day. But I never had a penny: that didn't go down well and it never bloody has. Women do mind. You can't buy them a drink, you can't take them out to lunch. Money does help. And I was out of my depth because of not being *posh* enough. Jean was a bit of a snob. She got in a bad state emotionally for a while, she was very upset by the break-up with him, and with me not being able to manage to conduct an affair properly because of a shortage of cash. I was hanging around the Colony and the French pub and getting pissed, which is not really a lady's idea of fun. She was quite cultured, ladylike. She wore remarkably good clothes and had very good taste. She was a bit of a lady – although that mouth of hers always reminded me of *Jaws*. She started avoiding me because she couldn't take the emotional strain of it any more and I think she went back to Ken for a while.'

Opinions were mixed as to whether Bernard ever really could have become a professional actor. Alexander Chancellor, who was to give Bernard his great chance when he asked him to write his Low Life column for the *Spectator* in 1978, spotted even then Bernard's theatricality, his tendency to behave like a luvvie: 'He's like a sort of actor with all his photographs on his walls. He's always had photographs of himself with the famous, like an actor's dressing room.' And Bernard's American writer friend Jay Landesman asserted that 'the acting profession lost a potentially great actor.'

But the professionals were sure he would never have made it. 'He wouldn't have been disciplined enough,' Mick Tobin declared bluntly, and Jacki was equally sceptical: 'He was very good on stage but I think it would have killed him, having to turn up all the time. He was too unreliable. Even as a stagehand he would miss his cues. There's quite a discipline in the theatre: you've got to be there and do it, not just when you feel like it.'

However it might have been, Bernard's life was already changing course in a very different direction. Within a few days of the end of the short run of *A Kayf Up West* he was writing his first regular magazine column. He was to scratch a living from journalism for the rest of his life.

9

Beau Bernard

Early in the Sixties Bernard asked his Fleet Street friend Allan Hall whether it might be worth his trying to be a journalist. 'It's the only thinkable alternative to working,' said Hall. Many years later Bernard complained that Hall had given him tainted advice. 'When you were encouraging me to become a writer,' he said, 'you never told me what fucking hard work it was.'

It was in fact the boozy Soho poet Elizabeth Smart, who was then the Literary Editor of *Queen* magazine, who finally found Bernard his first job in journalism, in 1964. 'We had a few drinks one lunchtime and were a bit tiddly,' he recalled, 'and she took me back to the office and being a bit tiddly she introduced me to Dennis Hackett, who was then the editor. I said to him, "What this magazine needs is a racing column" and to my utter amazement he said, "You're quite right – do it."' Bernard worked as a freelance and was paid only £30 a month but found to his astonishment that here was a job that he actually enjoyed. He was not yet a properly accredited racing correspondent and did not yet have a Press badge, but at last, at thirty-two, he had discovered where he belonged. For many years he had hero-worshipped trainers and jockeys – men like Fred Winter, Terry Biddlecombe, Lester Piggott and Ryan Price. Ever since he had struck his first bet in 1947 he had wanted to get into racing and meet the people who made it. Now he could do it. What was more, he found himself in distinguished company. Other contributors to *Queen* included Quentin Crewe (on restaurants) and the Editor-in-Chief was Jocelyn Stevens.

Marsh Dunbar, who had rented Bernard the top flat in

her house in Canonbury Square, well remembered his first article for *Queen*. 'It took him three weeks to write,' she said. 'He used to sit down making model aeroplanes and wouldn't let the kids touch them. He was supposed to be writing this article but in the end he did it the night before it was due. Pete and I came back very late one night and there was Jeffrey absolutely flat on his back in the kitchen, drunk, and our fourteen-year-old son Robert in his pyjamas had made him a fried egg and kept pulling his head back and pushing this egg down.' It was a warning already, in Bernard's very first journalistic job, of what was to come throughout his writing career. He began to demonstrate, right from the start, the erratic nature that was to infuriate so many editors in later years. Dennis Hackett once asked him to go to Goodwood to write a piece about the racing there but in the bar at Victoria Station Bernard met two friends for 'just the one' and they ended up missing several trains and finally spent the day in a betting shop. On another occasion the production editor of *Queen* was incensed when he was waiting for a last-minute article by Bernard only to receive a telephone call from a girl who trilled: 'I'm ringing for Jeff. He won't be doing the article. He's made another suicide attempt.'

'*Attempt?*' bellowed the production editor. 'Let me speak to the bugger: I'll give him a fucking foolproof method.'

His first column for *Queen*, which was to appear fortnightly, was published on 6 May 1964. It was a collection of racing tips, anecdotes and chit-chat and in his very first sentence Bernard had already found the tone that was to flavour all his future writing. 'The practice of making excuses for beaten horses,' he wrote, 'is not only the punter's greatest expense, but it also allows bookmakers to take off for the Bahamas every winter.' By 17 June he had already discovered the Lambourn jockeys' and stable lads' favourite pub, the Malt Shovel in Upper Lambourn, where he was to spend so many alcoholic evenings in the decades to come and where in 1964 he was talking to jockeys like his lifelong hero Fred Winter, Tom Dearie and Sammy Wragg, who had

won the 1940 Derby. In writing about Royal Ascot that year
Bernard explained straight away the excitement that he was
going to derive from racing and gambling in all the years to
come: 'Apart from the high standard of the racing, the debs,
the hats, the colour and the glamour, there is DANGER.' In
July he was gallivanting at Newmarket with Peter Cook. In
August he was pondering the problem of 'the essential drink'
at the races: 'the next thing you know you've missed them in
the paddock.' In September: 'I made another mistake. I had
a bottle of champagne before setting out for the course.' He
also observed that outside the celebrity tent 'was an actor
celebrated for being the only one who owes me money'. Any
one of those sentences could have appeared in his *Spectator*
column twenty years later.

Even then, so early in his journalistic career, odd things
somehow seemed to *happen* to him. He was always to be the
most unpredictable catalyst. In February 1965 Hackett sent
Bernard to interview the racecourse tipster Prince ('*I gotta
horse!*') Monolulu, the eighty-two year old Abyssinian, who
was himself seriously unwell in the Middlesex Hospital.
Bernard took along a box of Black Magic chocolates and
when Monolulu proved to be too weak to help himself to
one, Bernard pushed a strawberry cream into Monolulu's
feeble mouth. The 'prince' tried to swallow it, coughed, and
started choking. A nurse sent Bernard out of the ward and
drew a screen around the bed but it was too late. Monolulu
had choked to death.

Bernard's articles in *Queen* so impressed Felicity Green of
the *Daily Mirror* that she asked him to write the sort of men's
fashion column that was later to be written by Christopher
Ward and on the *Evening Standard* by Angus McGill. 'I failed
at it,' Bernard admitted, 'because I didn't have any nerve in
those days.' Contemporary photographs do indeed show him
as being noticeably diffident, but that first early foray at the
Mirror did at least bring him the lifelong friendship of Mike
Molloy, the *Daily Mirror*'s Features Art Editor, who was later

to become Editor-in-Chief of the entire *Mirror* Group until he fell foul of Robert Maxwell in the 1980s. 'I was going to lay Jeff's column out,' Molloy told me, 'and we took to each other instantly. I think Felicity was a little glum about this because she thought we'd be a very bad influence on each other, which tended to be the case, of course. Jeffrey's the eternal boy at school that you're not meant to play with or have anything to do with. There's always someone who's the undesirable boy who's always more worldly and knowing than anybody else and you find yourself getting into trouble and you can't help it because he's such wonderful company. So we went off immediately on the batter and played a terrible game of snooker at the Press Club and we've remained friends since that day. The column didn't last for very long, although he did it very well and wrote it beautifully, but Jeffrey's always been somebody that newspapers for some reason found difficult to handle. It wasn't so much that he was so unreliable, it was that he didn't seem capable of knocking off a hack piece. He wasn't malleable: he did one act. He didn't fit into the common newspaper stuff that people wanted in the Sixties and when they asked him to rewrite it he couldn't because he hadn't trained to be flexible. He couldn't fit into someone else's briefing, he had to do his own thing, and he did tend to be drawn off towards Soho.'

Bernard lasted just three weeks in the job but he was soon given a similar job on the *Daily Sketch* by its Editor Colin Valdar. There he shared an office with Fergus Cashin who remembered that Bernard was 'unwell' into his typewriter. He also became a friend of John Taylor, the Editor of *Tailor and Cutter*. He was quite a smart dresser in those days, almost natty, wearing sharp suits all the time, but he did not impress the crime reporter Jimmy Nicholson, who was later to become legendary in Fleet Street for his flamboyance and his nickname The Prince of Darkness. 'Bernard was never one of us,' said Nicholson. 'He was a supercilious smartarse who would walk through the place as though he owned it, very conscious of his good looks and boasting of the birds he was pulling.' That job did not last very long either, but in just one year as a journalist Bernard was already making waves in Fleet Street.

Sally Vincent, also writing for *Queen*, had one disastrous experience with Bernard when they worked together on a double two-day assignment: an interview with Lord Leverhulme followed by another story in Anglesey. Bernard was sent along as her photographer.

'Jeff was looking like Death,' she told me. 'He was wearing a suit for this occasion, a chocolate-brown pin-stripe suit which was covered in fag burns through which you could see his little white leg glinting and he used to chew his fingernails to the bone so you could see little bits of bone glinting through, and he was all bright yellow with nicotine. There was a cock-up at Lord Leverhulme's, it was pouring with rain, we were both drenched to the skin, we'd gone up on the train, and we'd been wrongly briefed. Leverhulme was expecting some people from *Queen* magazine, not these two drenched rats. I thought I was going there to interview him and Leverhulme thought I was going there to admire his house. Jeff went wandering off to look at his horses. I started the interview. Leverhulme went bananas. "How dare you ask me these rude questions?" he fumed. It rained and rained and rained and the Leverhulmes were obviously horrified by us, by the sight of Jeffrey, who said to Leverhulme, "Excuse me but I am an alcoholic, do you have any scotch in the house?" We rang for a taxi but it couldn't come. Lord and Lady Leverhulme were then obliged to ask us to tea. I honestly even then didn't know Jeffrey was middle-class. They had this silver teapot and dainty cucumber sandwiches and I was frozen with horror and Jeff said to Leverhulme, "Christ, we gotta get to Anglesey tonight, I don't suppose you 'appen to know what time the pubs shut in Anglesey, do you?" And every time these dreadful nicotine-laden, bitten fingers reached forward for a cucumber sandwich he would take about six and denude the one underneath so there'd be this cucumber winking horrifyingly at me.'

Bernard was later to claim that Sally Vincent had become one of the great loves of his life but she denied that they had even had a proper affair although she admitted they might have been to bed together a couple of times. 'This "affair" thing is pure fantasy,' she told me. 'I guess he was beautiful but he was not charming. He was *beguiling*, which is very different, and he was dangerous because you never knew when he was going to flip.'

But he was certainly still sufficiently glamorous to appeal to an apparently endless supply of palpitating women and he made the very most of the permissive and promiscuous Swinging Sixties. Sexually, 1965 was 'a vintage year', he wrote later in the *Spectator*. 'Women seemed to be incapable of pronouncing the word "no".' Yet he treated them disgracefully. Molloy remembered bumping into him in the *Daily Mirror* office one morning when Bernard had started working there and finding him boasting that he had seduced one of the beautiful secretaries, 'Mary Smith', the previous night. She had begged him not to tell anyone. Bernard was appalled: 'What a fucking thing to say, "You won't tell anyone, will you?"' and he spent the rest of the day telling everyone about it. 'By the end of the day the entire office knew about it and there was poor Mary Smith typing away, blood-red in the face,' said Molloy. 'He's a rotter, very caddish.'

One woman who could not resist him was the actress Fenella Fielding. Bernard moved on from *Queen* and began to write for *Town* magazine and his first job there was to go and interview the actress late one afternoon. He had had a few drinks first and was so mesmerised by her smouldering sex appeal that he could not concentrate. Halfway through the interview, he claimed later, he put his notebook aside and told her that it was impossible. 'I can't interview you,' he said, emboldened by alcohol. 'All I'm doing is sitting here and thinking how much I'd like to fuck you.'

Miss Fielding was surprised to learn that he had spoken of their affair. 'He gave you my name himself, did he?' she

Bernard's mother,
Dora Hodges,
alias Fedora Roselli

Bernard's father,
Oliver ('Bunny')
Bernard,
at the Boston Opera
House before the
First World War

THE BROTHERS BERNARD
Above: Bruce (left), Jeffrey and Oliver (right) with their mother
in 1939 in the South of France, three months after their father's death
Below: Oliver (left), Jeffrey and Bruce (right) in 1992
in the Coach and Horses pub in Soho [*Times Newspapers*]

Above left: Joyce Grenfell, the actress who helped to pay Bernard's school fees, in *Laughter in Paradise* in 1951

Above right: The young Bernard in Soho in the 1950s

Left: Bernard's mysterious first wife, Anna Grice, who married him in 1951 and committed suicide in 1959 [*Chris Fernau*]

Left: Twenty-seven-year-old Bernard and his second wife, the Old Vic actress Jacki Ellis, after their unlucky Friday 13th wedding in 1959 [*Hulton-Deutsch Collection*]

BERNARD'S ARTIST FRIENDS and benefactors Francis Bacon (left, in 1958, aged fifty) and Lucian Freud (right, in 1954, aged thirty-three) [*Popperfoto*]

Above left: Susan Hampshire, the young Assistant Stage Manager on the 1958 production of *Expresso Bongo:* 'I gave her a bollocking,' said Bernard [*Camera Press*]

Above right: Marlene Dietrich in 1963. A year later she told Bernard how wonderful he was on-stage in *A Kayf Up West* [*Camera Press*]

Below: On the East End stage in *A Kayf Up West* in 1964: Bernard (right) as Bill the Burglar, Barry Humphries (centre) as Gregorious, the Greek café owner, and Howard Goorney (left) as Vivian, the 'resting' homosexual actor [*Barratts*]

Left: Fenella Fielding, the actress, when she met Bernard in 1965 [*Hulton-Deutsch Collection*]

Below left: Jean Marsh, the actress, in 1966, two years after she met Bernard [*Popperfoto*]

Below right: Bernard's third wife, Jill Stanley, when they met in 1966

Bernard and his wife Jill's four-year-old daughter Isabel in 1975

In an English country garden: Bernard in beefcake pose

BERNARD AND HIS HORSERACING HEROES

with Fred Winter (above) and Lester Piggott (below)

said. 'I'm surprised. Over the years in his writings he's always omitted me, I thought deliberately.'

She was enchanted by his version of how their affair began. 'It sounds very funny!' she chuckled. 'I don't remember it at all but I wouldn't put it beyond the realms of possibility.' It was his sense of humour rather than his beauty that first appealed to her: 'I don't care for him too much in his Cosmic Sadness Mode,' she told me, 'but I do like him when he's being terribly funny and he was in those days. He was the most incredible improviser and ad-libber of Shakespearean verse that I've ever come across. He made it up as he went along, perfect iambic pentameters, it was just brilliant. He could do it for hours on end and he incorporated – without stopping – brilliant impersonations of current great classical actors who were totally recognisable. He was *terribly* funny doing that. It was sensational.'

She was less impressed by the chip on his shoulder: 'He used to go on about the fact that he was working class and that I was a sort of duchess, which made life even more difficult for him, but it was all absolute twaddle because he isn't working class and he went to a public school that cost the earth and nor am I a duchess. It was all rubbish. He saw himself as my bit of rough, but it was also all part of his Cosmic Sadness: *I'm only working class, therefore everybody else can tread all over me and I shall never get anywhere.*'

She was also startled when he began to tell everyone that they were engaged: 'It made me feel very claustrophobic. We spent a lot of time in drinking establishments. We'd go from one pub to another and then to a club and to somebody else's place and then it'd be time for the pubs to open again. I didn't do very much drinking myself and if you're not a drinker you find in the end if you're with somebody who *is* a drinker, that there are only about sixty to eighty-five minutes a day when the person concerned is their own glorious self and otherwise they're hungover, drunk, getting maudlin, getting silly, getting aggressive, and it's not that interesting. The fact is that if he hadn't been a great drinker we'd have

gone on much longer: it really is as simple as that. I think
I gave him forty-eight hours' notice: I know that he found
that very striking, to be given notice to quit. He went round
telling everybody!'

Bernard often boasted of the end of their affair to numerous friends, both male and female. 'I stayed with her for
several weeks in her Hyde Park Square flat,' he claimed,
'but eventually she told me to piss off because I drank too
much. I fell asleep once when I was supposed to be screwing
her. That made her angry. She said fuck off so I did. I went
at about five o'clock in the morning. But we've always been
friends ever since. I like Fenella. She doesn't come over to
the public as she is at all. She's a very well read, intelligent
person. She understands English Literature, which is strange
for an actress, and she can write. She's very clever. We had
a fling for about two months.'

Despite all the sudden new journalistic work Bernard was
always broke in these years of the mid-Sixties. He was so
hard-up that he pawned his expensive camera for £10 and
then persuaded Nick Garland to give him the money to get
it out of hock. '£10 was a lot at the time,' Garland told me.
'I was slightly peeved that he wasn't grateful.' One reason
for his poverty was that he was of course drinking more
ferociously than ever. He had started drinking, his brother
Bruce told me, because 'basically he was very frustrated about
what he really wanted to do. By the time he did find out what
he wanted to do he *was* a boozer, and then of course his work
became infinitely bound up with his dissipation. So it was no
good stopping it because he was actually in the end living
off it. I didn't worry about Jeffrey's drinking until he started
to work as a barman at Terry Mottram's Round Table pub
in St Martin's Court in about 1965. Terry encouraged Jeff
to come round at half past nine in the morning and start
drinking scotch, and Jeff would drink scotch all day, and
suddenly he started getting pancreatitis. That phase at the
Round Table was the time that Jeff went over the top with

drink. There was no point trying to warn him. He'd just ignore you. He got made a sort of hero of boozing and dissipation, really. Frank Norman *worshipped* Jeff and took him to Wheeler's almost every day. He worshipped that kind of dissipated streak in Jeff because Jeff pulled off this kind of dissipation in such style, with such panache. He was so funny and his mimicry was as good as Peter Sellers. He's talked to Glaswegians in Glaswegian in a way that he'd be killed for if they found him out. He was amazing.'

Mike Molloy agreed that Bernard was a serious boozer 'but then everyone I knew was a serious boozer: newspapers were full of people who drank a lot. He never seemed to me to be an alcoholic: he seemed to be a heavy drinker. In an odd sort of way I still don't think he's an alcoholic. Jeff always seems to be drinking for the crack, not just having to get a certain amount in him.'

The problem was of course that alcohol simply transformed Bernard from being a shy, morose man into being hilarious company. Allan Hall remembered one notorious race meeting in the Lake District, at Cartmel Races, after which the sponsors, Bass Charrington, refused ever to sponsor a race again because of Bernard's drunken behaviour: 'It was just crazy, the boozing that was going on. He used to get very offensive when he was drunk and his behaviour was deemed so awful that Bass Charrington said that if the PR company couldn't get this kind of thing covered without events of this kind then they'd rather pull out of sponsorship altogether. I think Jeffrey imperilled the whole business of sponsorship since he'd been brought in as a member of the Press. He didn't often rub shoulders with senior figures in the booze trade and he took the opportunity to tell them what he thought about the piss they made. I seem to remember there was one senior director of the brewery who didn't feel he'd paid all this money to take these drunks to Cartmel to be abused.' Bernard admitted that on that first of many freebies he and Hall had done 'strange things with ladies, chasing naked women. They vowed they'd never sponsor a race again.'

Booze could inspire Bernard in those days to the heights
of zany invention. He loved practical jokes. When a friend
once filled his pocket with tartare sauce in the Pickwick Club
he strolled over to a table where the actor Peter Finch was
sitting and asked if Finch would like some sauce. 'Yes,' said
Finch, whereupon Bernard dug into his pocket with a spoon
and slapped a dollop of sauce on Finch's plate. Finch was not
amused.

Another lark was a racing sting that involved defrauding
Tony Harris, a regular French Pub drinker who would
occasionally bet on the evening races with other drinkers.
Bernard's friend Raymond Smith would telephone from a
call box across the road to discover what had just won the
7.30 at Windsor and then signal to Bernard inside the pub
by holding up the same number of fingers as the number of
the winning horse. Because the bottom half of the windows
in the French Pub then was frosted glass but the top half
was clear glass, the seated Tony Harris could not see what
Smith was up to but the standing Bernard could. Bernard
would then bet on the horse that had just won and Harris
would accept the bet because there seemed to be no way in
which Bernard might have known the result already. Bunny
May remembered Bernard and Smith each wagering a fiver
on a horse that had just won at 8–1 and winning £40 each
off Tony Harris, a lot of money in 1965. Harris eventually
took his revenge by accepting bets on how soon Bernard was
likely to kill himself with his drinking.

There were plenty of gamblers in Soho who believed that he
was likely to kill himself very soon indeed. He had now started
drinking early every morning with Allan Hall, who was then
working in Covent Garden on the newly launched broadsheet,
the *Sun*, which was born out of the old *Daily Herald*. Hall wrote
the Henry Fielding diary column, paying Bernard every now
and then 'for information' and printing some of his photographs. He and Bernard would meet for liquid breakfasts in
the Covent Garden pubs that were open from six to nine for
the vegetable market workers, and sometimes they would be

joined by Albert Bright, the dog-racing correspondent of the *Sporting Life* – 'a most amusing character', and as dangerous a drinker as Jeffrey. They had very much in common, they formed a warm bond of morning drinkers in Covent Garden, and this of course was to provide Jeffrey ultimately with the entrée to the *Life* five years later, in 1970.

By now Bernard and Frank Norman had decided to work seriously on their book *Soho Night and Day*, which meant that Norman paid for everything and, according to Bernard, they were 'drunk for a year'. Their alcoholic behaviour was quite shameless. Late one night Frank Norman was sick in the Stork Club over a hostess who screamed with horror.

'What's that?' cried one of the diners.

'That's a lobster thermidor,' said Norman.

Jeffrey's wildness inspired Mike Molloy to see him as a modern reincarnation of a Regency Rake. 'He has always been quite firmly a member of the upper-middle classes,' claimed Molloy a trifle unconvincingly. 'He's a rogue gentleman. He was never a spiv. Very occasionally, under the most unlikely circumstances, suddenly a flash of the gentleman will appear, in the sense of being aloof and educated and rather grand. It's quite interesting when it happens, when it suddenly appears, like the old gunfighter in *Cat Ballou* when Lee Marvin is broken down and then suddenly appears as he was. There's this ghost inside Jeffrey. I've seen him stunningly put people down by suddenly this figure appearing who is rather grand. And he'd have liked to have been an actor and a National Hunt jockey and a painter and all sorts of things. He's a sort of eighteenth century person, really, isn't he? Or early nineteenth. He would have been really happiest as a Regency buck, going racing, bare-knuckle boxing, Squire Bernard, *Beau* Bernard. He'd go to Bath and buy a Damn Fine Pair Of Banana Tongs. I can imagine Jeff as one of those figures cutting a dash, a friend of Byron's, or as a prizefighter who wasted a fortune gambling and ended up putting a bullet through his head in some seedy place, a founder member of the Hellfire Club.'

It is a strikingly perceptive assessment, right down to the inclination to suicide. For all the cosy warmth and camaraderie of drunken pubs and clubs Bernard was lonely after the break-up of his second marriage, and lost, and often close to despair. He attempted suicide several times, though it is difficult to judge whether these were serious attempts or merely unhappy ploys to attract attention and sympathy. 'I used to feel depressed all the time when I was on the whisky,' he told me. 'I was miserable and I never had any money because I never had a decent job. All my friends were in bloody Fleet Street and I wanted a job but didn't know how to go about getting a staff job. I suppose I sat around for years hoping to be offered something. The thing that's upset me most has been women that I've foolishly fallen in love with. I don't know why I took them so seriously, because they're so *silly*. These suicide attempts haven't always been due to women, they've been disintegration because of drinking too much whisky and self-disgust.' 'I've never tried to commit suicide sober: I'd be too frightened, because I don't really want to die.'

Bernard being Bernard, even his suicide attempts were invested with moments of black humour. In May 1966, as he approached his thirty-fourth birthday, he was staying with Allan and Connie Hall in their London flat and became so depressed again that he took an overdose as he lay on the sofa. Connie Hall sent for an ambulance to take him to King Charles Hospital and telephoned Sally Vincent to ask her to come after finding that Bernard had left a suicide note saying 'Dear Connie, I can't bear it, I love you.' 'Connie was panic-stricken,' said Sally Vincent. 'Jeff was a bit comatose like a bad hangover and Connie was weeping and preparing a little note to pin to him, "Darling Jeff, I love you too, please come home quickly" and they wrapped him in the red hospital blanket in that funny little deckchair arrangement that they take you down the steps in and he'd got this billet-doux from Connie Hall pinned to him and I said, "It doesn't do anything for your complexion, that blanket."'

Despite his suicide attempts the booze nearly killed him anyway. In December 1965 he was in Ireland writing an article about racing for *Town* and embarked on a two-week whisky-drinking bout (with his Soho artist friends Robert Colquhoun and Robert McBryde) without eating. When he returned to London he was struck down by an excruciating attack of acute pancreatitis. 'That attack was the initial incident that has completely fucked up my life physically ever since,' he told me. 'Pancreatitis is *so* painful it's just unbelievable.' It was to plague him for more than twenty years, sending him back to hospital in agony seven more times, until his last attack in 1979.

During that first attack in 1965 he was rushed to St Stephen's hospital in the Fulham Road and had to spend Christmas there. Before he came out he was told by the registrar that if he ever had another drink it would kill him, and that he should never sip another coffee or eat another curry because if he did his pancreas would explode. Twenty-six years and gallons of booze, caffeine and curry later, Bernard was still drinking heavily, his pancreas had shrunk to nothing more than a lump of scar tissue, and he was taking great pleasure in speculating as to whether that registrar was still alive.

That crisis in 1965 was the first occasion that Jeffrey Bernard was really unwell. He was to remain unwell for most of the time for the rest of his life and he was to be in and out of hospital constantly, not just for pancreatitis. He would gamble when drunk and sometimes lose a week's earnings in an hour, which would make him feel dreadfully guilty, so he would drink even more to numb the guilt, so fuelling his depression and suicidal tendency. He was of course entirely to blame for his woes, or at least as much to blame as any alcoholic can be. His pain was self-inflicted. But even so it is difficult not to feel at least a glimmer of admiration for the astonishing resilience with which he kept fighting back. Tony Harris may already have made him the 6–4 favourite to be the next in Soho to drop dead but he kept going on and on and on. Ten years later, far from being dead as predicted by everyone who knew him, Bernard was starting to write articles that were to be hailed as the funniest in the land. To achieve that from the depths of his pain and misery in the 1950s and early 1960s at least suggests immense courage.

And yet there was always a ghost fading in and out of the grey, forgotten backdrop of his life: his sister Sally. He might try to forget or ignore her but she was always there to haunt him, like a dark wraith in a Regency romance. In 1992 she was living in a sheltered bedsitter in South London, just eleven stops from Soho on the Northern Line. She turned out to be an obliging, grey-haired widow of sixty-eight. 'It would be nice if my brothers came to see me before I die,' she said.

10

Jill and the Idyll

On 27 May 1966, Bernard's thirty-fourth birthday, a few days after he had tried to commit suicide in their flat, Allan and Connie Hall decided to try to cheer him up by taking him out for dinner. As his blind date, to make up the numbers, they also asked pretty young Jill Stanley, an unmarried twenty-three-year-old seamstress who made clothes for Connie, designed swimming costumes for the swimwear company Slix, and had just left her previous boyfriend, David Wilsworth, after living with him for several months. The Halls could hardly have cheered him up more effectively. Bernard and Jill fell for each other immediately and afterwards he always referred to her as his birthday present. Two weeks later they went to live together in a thatched cottage in Suffolk and two months after that they were married. She was to live with him for six years, longer than any of his other wives.

Jill was the daughter of a policeman, eleven years younger than Bernard but bright and sexy with long blonde hair. One of her jobs was to make costumes for films and soon after they met she took him on location onto the set of *Far From the Madding Crowd* where Peter Finch took one look at him and cried 'oh, my God, take him away. That *profile*, it's better than mine, I can't bear it, take him away!'

The Halls introduced them in a pub in the Portobello Road, the Earl of Lonsdale, and then they went on in a party of six for dinner in Kensington Park Road at the Artiste Assoiffé. Afterwards Connie Hall and the third man decided to call it a night but the other four went off to one of the Mayfair gambling dens, continued to drink in Covent Garden at four in the morning, enjoyed a spot of sexual activity in the car, with Jill and Bernard giggling in the back seat, and ended up in Hyde Park feeding the ducks at six o'clock, by which time Hall found that he was washing his trousers in the Serpentine. 'We were fairly well on by then,' Hall remembered, 'and of course one didn't worry so much about drunken driving in those days.' It would certainly have been difficult for Jill to pretend later that she had not realised that Bernard liked a drink or two. He had made it perfectly obvious that first night.

'I saw this beautiful pair of green eyes staring at me,' Jill told me twenty-six years later. 'It was Jeff. He was *terribly* handsome and he had these huge eyes. I was hooked. In the restaurant he sat next to me and I found my leg being massaged. I was in a bit of a mess and I think now I was rather impressed by this very handsome man who always had a hundred quid in his pocket. I'd never come across anyone like him before. He had an enormous charisma about him.'

Bernard had arranged to go to Essex the next day to spend the weekend with the long-suffering Peter and Marsh Dunbar. He asked Jill to go with him, Marsh put them in a double bed, and from then on they were inseparable. 'It was *months* before Jeffrey and Jill were ever apart,' said Hall. 'That was unusual because normally he got away from his womenfolk fairly quickly to get back to his friends, but Jill was always there. Wherever he was, she went, and that existed for a long time. It was certainly a different kind of life for Jeffrey. She was too intelligent to try to change him but what she did do was recognise that he was exceptionally gifted but not manipulable. I can't remember anybody influencing him.'

Although Jill was impressed that Bernard always seemed to have £100 in his pocket, it was all a show. 'He was permanently broke in those days,' said Allan Hall. The following week Bernard in fact had to borrow £100 to go to the Derby at Epsom and he lost it all in one bet, a sum which in those days was more than a junior Fleet Street reporter earned in a month. 'I'd been convinced for weeks that Charlottown would win the race, as indeed he did,' he wrote in the *Mirror Magazine* six years later, 'but in the paddock, blinded by Bollinger, I'd changed my mind when I'd fallen in love with the looks of Sodium and a gipsy girl who had sold me a sprig of heather for £2 14s 6d.' Sodium came in fourth and he ended his day on the Epsom Downs standing in the rain by a fish-and-chip van eating a bag of chips. 'The most depressing remark I heard at Epsom, after all these years of struggling to pick the winner of the Derby,' he told the *Evening Standard* in 1987, 'was that by my bookmaker Victor Chandler. He greeted me once as I approached him on the rails by turning around and saying to his workmen, the tic-tac man and his clerk, "Here comes the lunch money." '

Had Jill witnessed this gambling disaster she might well have thought thrice about becoming seriously involved with him, but a week or two later he took her to spend another Dirty Weekend with friends in Suffolk and they found a cottage to rent in the Brett Valley village of Chelsworth, near Ipswich, one mile from Bildeston and five miles from Hadleigh. They were to live in the cottage – 84 The Street, now Meadow Cottage – for six years, until 1972. The rent, which they paid to an eccentric old lady called Mrs Petch, was at first just three shillings a week, 15p in decimal coinage. 'When it went up to 3/6d I had a row with the landlady!' Bernard told me. 'I'd always fancied the idea of living in the country. I've always had this silly notion that geographical changes will make life better and of course they don't because wherever you go the first person you meet when you get there is yourself.' Another reason for moving to Suffolk was that his agent, Irene Josephy, who was also the agent of Frank Norman and Dan Farson – a truly intrepid woman – had told him that he would never write that novel he kept promising unless he distanced himself from the pubs, clubs, betting shops and girls of Soho and that it was time he pulled his socks up and stopped being so emotionally immature.

It was a rustic idyll that at first seemed to match his every dream. Chelsworth was said to be one of the prettiest villages in England, with its thatched roofs and orchards, and opposite the Peacock Inn there was a bridge over the gurgling River Brett and swans glid between the water lilies. Bernard began to fancy himself as a country gent and soon hired a gardener to work for two hours a week. The five-room cottage in Chelsworth was thatched and there was sweet-smelling honeysuckle around the front door and a wishing well in the garden and a real live summerhouse where he began at last to write his Great Novel. Before long he was not only playing for the village cricket team but captaining it and bringing a team from Soho to play against the village. In the winter he would go to Ipswich to watch the local Ipswich Town soccer team's home games 'because there was nothing else to do except, as Oscar Wilde once said of the country, to be good.' In typical Bernardine fashion he came to admire the Ipswich Town team 'because they were a team of non-stars'.

To make his rural retreat perfect, he had a good gun and would go out poaching with his pale Labrador bitch Smedley – 'the most human of all the females that lived in my village' – shooting rabbits, pigeons and pheasant in the misty evenings, and now and then he would delight in the sight of a barn owl swooping above the darkening river. When he returned home in the twilight Jill would have cooked a fish pie with cheese sauce which they would eat lovingly as Smedley snored in front of the log fire.

His proposal of marriage was equally romantic. *Town* sent him to Gloucestershire to interview an expert on race-horse breeding who was married to Robert Newton's sister, Joy. Bernard took Jill with him for the weekend and while they were there Valentine Thynne, the son of the Marquis of Bath, telephoned to invite Joy and her husband to dinner and told them to bring their guests as well. 'I had no clothes whatsoever,' Jill remembered, 'but we went round to Valentine Thynne's and there were about six people plus the four of us and they were all dressed very exotically with chiffons and I looked as though I'd just cleaned out the pigs, so I felt a degree of disadvantage the whole time.' During dinner Thynne's unconventional hippy brother Viscount Weymouth, who sported a ponytail and a harem of beautiful 'wifelets', telephoned to invite them all to the family's country mansion, Longleat, for a drink or three. 'As I say, I looked like the pig cleaner,' said Jill, 'but we went into Longleat, this fantastic house. It was twilight, and I couldn't believe the whole scene. The room was huge, in darkness, just candles, and there were all these half-caste Indian ladies lying out on divans and candles everywhere, and this beautiful fireplace. We could hardly see, but Weymouth was offering us drinks and saying, "Oh, this is Queensberry, and this is thingy, and this is so-and-so" and they're all lying around on sofas playing backgammon and there were all these beautiful women, and I thought, "I can't *handle* this, it's ridiculous". I sat on the floor in front of this beautiful Adam fireplace and Jeff said, "Will you marry me?" No, we weren't pissed. It was quite romantic. I was stupid. I was a fool. But I had told Mrs Petch we were already married and it was quite *naughty* then to live in sin. I was certainly the little toy-girl.'

They were married at Sudbury register office on 23 August 1966, just three months after they had met. But almost as soon as they returned to Chelsworth they discovered that the reality of life there was to be very different from the idyll that they had imagined. For a start, the village was divided into two, the snobs and the yobs, and Bernard, no mean snob himself, quickly found that he was at the wrong end among the vests, bicycle clips and rusting junk and was being excluded from the smart Sunday cocktail parties. Chelsworth 'was so posh that at one jumble sale I saw six pith helmets and an Admiral's full dress uniform on one stall,' he wrote in the *Daily Express* ten years later. The cottage's thatch was very patchy ('imagine a roof with alopecia'). They had no drains. They had to wash in a bowl and empty the water in a ditch at the end of the garden. The lavatory was outside. The water in the well was undrinkable. No wonder the rent was only three shillings a week. And then the Great Novel stubbornly refused to allow itself to be written.

Bernard's main employment at the end of 1966 was with
Town – which was owned by Michael Heseltine and edited
by Julian Critchley – and the £15 a week that it paid him
was enough for him to rent a flat in Pimlico as well as the
cottage in Chelsworth. In September the magazine carried
a report of how he had spent a night out riding with
three Chelsea policemen in a squad car. The style is as
distinctively Bernardine as ever: 'Chelsea Police station is
very quiet and the desk sergeant says good evening very
nicely, in case I haven't come to give myself up.' Later,
in the police car, 'the radio comes to life but it's not for us,
it's for a car in the East End. "GOT A FUNNY ONE FOR
YOU HERE. WOMAN IN THE STREET IN BARKING
IN HER UNDERCLOTHES!" We all go in to a little dream
wondering what that must look like.'

For the November issue *Town* sent him to Hamburg to
investigate prostitution on the Reeperbahn, where the hotel
he stayed in 'was the sort of place where travelling salesmen
leave their pubic hair embedded in the pink Camay'. When
he tried to take some photographs of the whores he was chased
down the street by two giant pimps. Michael Heseltine would
have been proud of him. After Hamburg he was sent to Spain
to report on a school for matadors, got dysentery and was
robbed by a girl in Seville who claimed to be a flamenco
singer from Cadiz. In January 1967 he was writing an
open letter to the boxer Mark Rowe, in February a piece
bemoaning the boredom of life in the country – an article
he was to write in various forms over and over again for the
next twenty-five years. 'I just *can't* destroy myself here in the
country,' he wrote, seriously underestimating his impressive
talent for self-destruction. At every opportunity he high-tailed
it back to London and his beloved Soho.

He was also sent by *Town* to interview the sex-symbol
actress Raquel Welch over tea at the Dorchester. Unfortunately she sat on a low couch on the other side of a low
table and Bernard could see right to the top of her legs and
trembled so much at the sight of the Welch knickers that he

poured the tea over her sandwiches. When she realised what had happened she was not pleased and the following week had him ordered off the set of the film she was making. Another star who crossed his path was the Rolling Stones singer Mick Jagger, who was drinking in the Kismet Club in Little Newport Street one lunchtime when Bernard also popped in for just the one. A couple of hours later they were still there. It was the year of the huge Stones hit *Jumpin' Jack Flash* and the album *Beggar's Banquet* and Jagger was already immensely rich. But he was inconsolable, reported Bernard: 'He ended up bloody crying. He said "I've got all this money and all these birds are after me and I don't know what to do." I said, "Give half the fucking stuff to me, you cunt." Pressure, it's called, I think. I suppose the tears were just drink.'

Town gave him plenty of scope for his mischievous sense of humour. In one four-page feature he wrote a series of spoof pieces as an agony aunt (Marje Bernard), a cleric (Archbishop Bernard), a fey women's magazine writer (Godfrey Bernard), a medic (Dr Stafford Bernard) and a writer of doggerel verse (Patience Bernard) – all illustrated with appropriate photographs of Bernard dressed up to suit each persona.

In another article he wrote with startling honesty about the joys, anxieties and remorse of his heavy drinking ('If I had all the money I've spent on drink – I'd spend it all on drink') and described how he had suffered blackouts, physical collapse, depression, tears, self-pity, 'a tendency to punch walls and smash hands' and an 'inability to conduct affairs ending with falling asleep during sexual intercourse'. With sharp self-knowledge he admitted that his boozing was due to emotional immaturity and he wrote: 'The more necessary it becomes to stop, the more impossible it becomes to stop.' It was a remarkable public confession.

He had found his main subjects for a long career in journalism: booze, racing, sex and moaning about his lack of money. He was not to change them for the rest of his life. And for the rest of his life he seemed truly to believe, as he did at the end of that *Town* article, that 'starting tomorrow it's all going to be different'.

He was also working occasionally now on the *Sunday Times*'s Atticus diary column with Allan Hall, Tim Heald, Nick Tomalin and eventually Hunter Davies, who became the column's editor. 'Jeffrey was a walking disaster even then,' Heald remembered, 'but a lovely writer.' He was also brilliant at making the most of his expenses. When the Editor of the *Sunday Times*, Harold Evans, gave him the money to write an article about spending a night with an expensive prostitute, he 'settled for a short time and spent the remaining cash on an excellent dinner and wine', he confessed years later. Meanwhile he was fully living up to being The Godfather when he gave his godson Sean Dunbar, Peter and Marsh's son, an illegal dice game for his ninth birthday in June, a Crown and Anchor board. 'It's illegal because if you own the board you can't lose,' said Marsh. 'Jeff taught him the rules of the game, Sean took it to school and for ages I never understood why Sean always had money, sixpences and shillings. He used to win money off the other boys in the lavatory. The teacher finally took it away.'

Bernard's third marriage was of course even more boozy than the previous two. He could afford it now, and drank so much that the landlady of the Peacock Inn in Chelsworth, Gwen, a 'querulous, vaguely upper-class widow who had had a tragic war', barred him once for a couple of months, even though he must have been her best customer. When he wanted a drink he had to walk to the next village, Bildeston, where he would drop in to see his old Soho friends Bobby Hunt or Elinor Bellingham Smith, John Moynihan's mother, both of whom had moved to the country.

'I thought it was a *normal* marriage, not having had any experience,' said Jill. 'We weren't pissed all the time, no, but it was like a three-month cycle and we'd start with him in hospital with a drip, with the pancreatitis, then he would be terribly contrite and ashamed – deeply, bitterly ashamed – and he would be sober for about a month. It drove me mad because he was dreadful when he was sober: he was sullen, depressed, a miserable sod; I'd want to go down to the bar for a drink, I'd take the dogs for a walk at night and nip into the bar just to see someone. He'd go into sulks for days and he wouldn't talk for days. He was only all right when he was between being on the wagon and the pancreatic attacks, which were quite regular. I can't *remember* any fun times. There *were* good bits, but I can't remember them.'

Jill certainly enjoyed a few drinks herself and it would be unfair to blame the drunkenness of the marriage on Bernard alone. Even Jill's daughter Isabel, who was to be born in 1970, later spotted the alcoholic collusion between her mother and Bernard. 'My mother always really enjoyed being married to him,' Isabel told me, 'simply because she loved drinking and he was always a lot more badly behaved than her so she could do outrageous, disgusting things because she could always get away with murder!'

Jill was also unhappy sexually. 'You couldn't cuddle Jeff because he'd want to fuck you. I think he probably suffers from satyriasis. I don't really want to be screwed three times a day every bloody day and I don't want to be able not to cuddle someone without him getting a bloody hard-on.' Foolishly, considering the volatility of their relationship, they had a typically permissive Sixties open marriage where they each felt free to have affairs. Bernard, true to form, had an affair with his great friend Allan Hall's wife, Connie. Eventually the Halls divorced. Bernard's infidelities were so blatant that Jill once played a practical joke on him by borrowing a black, curly wig from her antique dealer friend Beverley, changing her usual style of make-up by using plenty of black eyebrow pencil, and walking into the saloon bar of the Peacock, where Bernard was drinking. 'I did a bit of eye fluttering at Jeffrey, who was staring at me,' she recalled, 'and he started to chat me up and I just fell about laughing. I couldn't keep a straight face. He was quite pissed off with me.'

She too had numerous affairs and was unimpressed when I told her that Bernard had claimed to have had two hundred and fifty lovers, a figure he later revised to five hundred. 'Two hundred and fifty's not many,' she shrugged and seemed to think that most people who were young in the Swinging Sixties would have had similar totals. 'Fool that I was,' Bernard said later, 'I didn't realise that the entire village was lusting after her. And a pretty ugly and repressed bunch they were.'

In 1992 Jill was quite open about her infidelities: 'I was unfaithful to Jeffrey quite a few times during the marriage. It upset him dramatically. I got pregnant in 1968 and had an abortion. The story was going to be that I had fibroids and I had to have them removed, but Jeffrey found out. I can't remember how. I really wanted that child, actually, and I think he knew I really wanted it.' To make matters worse, Bernard was convinced that he was sterile and could never become a father. 'I'm sure of it,' he said. 'I've never used a contraceptive in my life. Jill owned up to me and it was the beginning of the end for us. She had been to work for a magazine in Spain and she came back and owned up that she'd had an affair and I was very upset and I think I made a mistake, I *made* her go to a doctor and get an abortion. I don't think I should have done that. If I'd really loved her, I suppose I ought to have been willing to take it on.'

Already the idyll was over. Nor did they keep the pregnancy secret and soon it was common knowledge. 'Oska' Wood remembered that one night in the Peacock at Chelsworth the Bernards invited him back to their cottage: 'They were a bit subdued. "You know that I can't have children?" said Jeff. "Well, Jill's pregnant."'

In November 1968 a rich American friend of Bernard's, Jane Morrison, asked him one day in the pub if he had ever been to New York and when he said no she promptly paid for his return airfare. Unhappy with Jill, he flew off alone to the States for a month and took his revenge by having a brief affair with a friendly woman called Ricki Rheingold. He stayed in a cockroach-infested room above a jazz club and the weather was freezing. 'It was so cold it was physically painful,' he told me, 'and I didn't have enough money to buy an overcoat. I was desperate. I think I would have died if I hadn't bumped into Francis Bacon, who bought me an overcoat and gave me several champagne breakfasts at the Algonquin Hotel. We would always have a bottle of Dom Perignon for breakfast and then he would give me a $100 bill. He saved my life.' Bernard also suffered an attack of pancreatitis in New York and was rushed to the Roosevelt hospital for a week, at the end of which he was presented with a bill for $1,000. Two young doctors, realising that he simply could not pay, smuggled him out of the hospital through the basement kitchens.

Meanwhile, Jill was to go to Spain again in 1969, to Barcelona, and Bernard was so jealous and suspicious that he went with her to keep an eye on her. She was there to play the lead as a model for several photo-novels opposite some dashing Spaniards and he was taking no chances, especially since she was again with her randy friend called Pam who later hanged herself but was then sexually rampant. 'When Pam was in Spain,' said Jill, 'she'd fuck the entire Sixth Fleet when it was in Barcelona.' This cannot have helped to lessen Bernard's unease about his wife. 'I loved making the photo-novels,' Jill told me. 'They were all love affairs and I was the heroine in them. They wanted a blonde English girl. I thought it was wonderful, a dead easy way of making loadsamoney. I was earning £60 a week at least, a lot of money then. In spite of the fact that I couldn't speak Spanish I seemed to know exactly what the next thing was in the script although I didn't understand what they were telling me ... I loved it.'

While Bernard was in Barcelona keeping a beady marital eye on Jill that summer of 1969 he was also writing an article for the *Daily Mirror*'s new colour magazine about the pain in Spain of an advertising crew that was making a thirty-second TV commercial for a tin of fruit. He did not allow the Mediterranean sun or his personal problems to interfere with his regular bet on the Derby. He was in

Barcelona on Derby day and was convinced that Blakeney was going to win the race but could not think how to place a bet on the horse. In a moment of inspiration he went to the British Consulate and asked if he could use their telephone to call his 'dying grandmother' in England, who had in fact been dead for decades. Using the consulate telephone, he rang the only bookmaker in London to whom he owed nothing and bet £10 on Blakeney. In the afternoon the consulate contacted him with an urgent message: they had had a call from London to say that his grandmother had won.

After two weeks Bernard had to return to England. Jill stayed in Spain for another month and became pregnant again. This time she was to have the child, who was born on 4 March 1970 and named Isabel after Bernard's friend Isabel Rawsthorne. Jeffrey attended the birth, drunk. 'OK, he was there,' Jill said. 'But it had nothing to do with him.' Isabel was traumatic for Bernard. Carol Bennett, who was Deputy Art Editor of the *Mirror Magazine*, remembered that he was distraught at the time. 'Jeffrey used to come into the office very early every morning,' she told me in 1992. 'He had terrible DTs – his hands shook very badly – and one morning he told me he was thinking of committing suicide by jumping off the roof because he knew he was not the father of his wife's child.'

'I'm sure I'm not her father,' Bernard told me. 'The times indicate to me that Jill had a short job in Barcelona and the dates made me pretty sure she's not mine. Also I was vaguely suspicious when she wanted to go into hospital to the Middlesex before proper pains had started. She got them to break the waters to bring it on a few days. I know Isabel is not mine, though Jill wouldn't admit it to me. I asked her a couple of times round about the time Isabel was born, and when she was a baby I got drunk on a couple of occasions and said to Jill, Come on, tell me the truth . . .' For more than twenty years he wrote about 'my daughter Isabel' regularly in his articles, even though he told most of his friends that he was not her father, and as late as 1992 he was still keeping up the pretence, mainly to protect her feelings because he did not believe that she knew or ever would know. But in fact Isabel was told the truth by Derek Brook and Jill when she was seventeen.

'Jill and I and Izzy were all together one night when it happened,' Brook told me. 'We were in the kitchen/dining room of Jill's flat in Chiswick. It sort of *happened*. Izzy didn't break down and cry or get upset. She was sort of relieved. I think she was glad that she knew for sure at last. I got the impression that she knew or suspected already.' Isabel herself told me that she felt more like a Spanish gipsy than a middle-class English girl.

Bernard was often criticised later for his cavalier attitude towards her and for not contributing to her upkeep and upbringing after Jill left him in 1972, taking the child with her. Since the child was not his, and since Jill soon married again, it is at least understandable that Bernard should not have felt any particular responsibility for the child, who was just two when Jill left him. He may be castigated for many weaknesses and vices but not for his treatment of another man's daughter.

Bernard worked on the *Mirror Magazine* for almost a year, alongside Mike Molloy (its Editor), Bill Hagerty (Assistant Editor), Keith Waterhouse (who wrote a regular column), Eve Pollard (who was Fashion Editor), Delia Smith (who was starting to write about cooking) and the astrologer Patric Walker.

When the *Mirror Magazine* was closed in July 1970 it had lost nearly £2 million in a year, an enormous amount then, not all of it, to be fair, because of Bernard's lavish expenses. He had actually started to write a regular sports column for the magazine but the staff had to work ten weeks ahead of publication and his first column never appeared. He was working in Paris and Chantilly on a racing article when he opened an English newspaper and read the awful news. He burst into tears and returned to London, broke again.

11

The Sport of Kings

Towards the end of 1970 Bernard landed the job of his dreams. On 24 July 1970 there had already been a good omen for Bernard's future as a racing correspondent when his one and only ever win-Yankee combination bet came in with four winners at Ascot at 4–1, 10–1, 2–1 and 8–1. The last two horses seemed particularly appropriate: Mummy's Pet and Country Retreat. He was even able to pay some bills with the winnings. Two months later he was asked to write a racing column for the *Sporting Life*.

The *Sporting Life* column was a watershed in Bernard's life. It was his first fulltime job as a journalist and was finally to stamp him as a professional national newspaper writer. It was to inspire many of his funniest anecdotes, which he was to tell and retell for the next twenty years. It was also to inspire his most disgraceful behaviour. And the ferocious drinking that seemed to come with the job finally destroyed his health and nearly killed him.

For exactly a year he wrote two half-page horse-racing columns a week for £50 a week. He started on 1 October 1970 and was sacked on 1 October 1971. He heard about the job when a bookmaker who reckoned that he was a mug punter and knew nothing at all about horses remarked jokingly in the pub that the *Sporting Life* was advertising for a columnist and perhaps he ought to apply for it. Bernard was even to admit in print six months later that he was *frightened* of horses, so he and the bookie were both amazed when he was actually hired to do the job. Carolyn Cluskey, who was then a young secretary on the *Sporting Life* but went on to become Administration Manager, was 'totally in awe of this rather glamorous columnist who used to get drunk a lot'. When she gave him his first metal racecourse badge, which permitted entry to any course in Britain, he clutched it to his chest and said 'in the manner of a small boy who might have been allowed to drive a steam train: "Oh! I've always wanted one of these. I can't believe it. I've just fulfilled a lifetime's ambition."' She remembered that he 'used to exist from expense claim to expense claim, and often used to offer the bribe of lunch with him if his exes sheets could be processed as soon as possible.'

The column caught on immediately and quickly became immensely popular. 'I think I was the first person to write about things like losing in an official racing organ,' said Bernard. 'The punters identified with it and really loved it because I took the piss out of racing people. They're very self-important. They don't like you to tease them.' Geoffrey Wheatcroft agreed: 'The *Life* column was just terribly funny. Trainers were used to being taken with deadly seriousness but he took the piss out of them.' Jonathan Powell, who was then the racing correspondent of the *News of the World*, agreed: 'He didn't know much about racing but he immediately sussed out the characters and got them right. He had that wonderful instinct of picking up where they were in the game – the pompous people, the fun people, he got them all right. He was brilliant. I was very fond of him, even though he pinched one of my best lines when I said to him once "It's all the same with John Meacock's horses, it's slowly away and then they fade." He used it the next week.'

Bernard's first column for the *Sporting Life* appeared on Saturday 3 October in the prime features position on page three and right from the start it was unlike any other racing column that anyone could remember. He led the page by reviewing William Douglas-Home's play *The Jockey Club Stakes* at the Vaudeville Theatre, starring Alistair Sim and Julia Lockwood, and he introduced himself to his new readers thus: 'I was born four days before that rather moderate animal April the Fifth won the Derby and like most other people born under the sign of Gemini, I wake up every morning convinced that I shall break the bookmakers by five o'clock. So far, I've given the enemy very few anxious moments, but I live in hope.'

The next day, the Sunday, he was in France to see the Prix de l'Arc de Triomphe and on the Wednesday his column was headed 'My Paris Diary' and he was reporting that on the cross-Channel boat he saw a man reading his first column and then being sick. At midnight on the Saturday he was ogling the girls in the Paris streets and on the Sunday at the races he succumbed to the alcoholic charms of four jolly, champagne-swilling Irishmen and stayed with them at the course until 9.30 p.m. drinking £15 magnums of Dom Perignon and singing *Sur le Pont d'Avignon*. It was the start of an astonishingly euphoric, boozy, roller-coaster year. He was writing columns on Saturdays and Wednesdays, and he was going to the races four or five times a week – Newmarket, Newbury, Ascot, Sandown and almost every other track in the land – but he later confessed that the entire year had been spent 'in a drunken haze'.

Among those he met for the first time in these first few weeks – some of whom were to remain friends for years – were the trainers Vincent O'Brien, Paul Cole, Peter Walwyn, Gavin Hunter, Eddie Reavey and Doug Marks, the jockeys Lester Piggott and Kipper Lynch, the rich racehorse owner and insurance broker Charles St George, and the commentators Peter O'Sullevan and Clive Graham. And of course, true to form, he quickly fell in love with a couple of trainers' wives, notably Caroline Balding and 'Bonk' Walwyn.

Within two weeks of joining the *Life* the paper had given Bernard a whole page to fill, and a week after that a huge picture-byline showed him sporting a rather nasty moustache. By early November he had already made a notable impact on the racing world. 'Thank you for introducing Jeffrey Bernard to your diary page,' one clerk of the course wrote to the Editor. 'He is like a breath of fresh air.'

Bernard's own theory to explain his immediate success,

that he wrote about *losing*, was to develop in such depth over the next twenty years that eventually he had almost cornered the market in writing about failure, whether it were about losing on the horses or losing wives or your looks or even your marbles. He was eventually to become the Prophet of Loss.

The other great attraction of his column was its impish unpredictability. In November he described the runners in the Miss World beauty contest: the 12–1 second favourite, Miss Australia, Valli Kemp, 'has an intelligent head, extremely long cannon bones and very fine pasterns. She certainly isn't what Mr John Hislop would call "a bit straight in front" . . . her skirt moved up and revealed two powerful gaskins.' He once printed on his page a picture of a topless model and the photocopy of a bet (5–2 against) that he had had with a Brighton bookmaker that the Miss World winner would have a 36-inch chest: she did. The following week he was recalling the famous Battersea Cat Race yet again. Bernard even reported that he had asked the bookmakers to lay him odds against his living for another year, since the insurance companies were not too keen to cover him because although he was only thirty-eight his smoking and drinking habits made him a bad risk. Victor Chandler suggested 25–1 but John Banks would offer only a cruel 10–11.

Bernard's tipsy irreverence was of course bound to make him enemies among some of the rich and powerful in racing. At a dance at the Subscription Rooms in Newmarket on 2 December Lady Aitken reprimanded him for his lack of respect for some people in racing. Bernard declared: 'I can only say that training a lot of horses to go faster than some others or having half a million in your current account doesn't warrant respect willy nilly.' When a reader wrote and accused him of having a chip on his shoulder he admitted in print that he would have liked to be a wealthy racehorse owner, trainer or breeder but insisted that he only attacked in his column people who took themselves and racing far too seriously. He was sometimes, however, as usual, his own worst enemy. He offended some racing people by refusing to wear a hat at the races and at Cheltenham in December, while queuing to place a bet on the Tote, he indicated one old battleaxe and remarked to the man standing beside him that he had never seen such a collection of repulsive old boots in his life. 'Actually,' said the man, 'that's my wife.' It did not help a great deal that strangers were increasingly recognising him at the races because of the photograph above his column, and that it was in fact now illustrated by a new picture that showed him smirking like an East End spiv.

But already, before the end of the year, there was a warning that Bernard's endless drinking at the races was putting his health in hock. In November he went to see Reavey's horses at East Hendred and felt so ill that he stayed for three days and nights, being nursed by Jocelyn Reavey.

He was suddenly being hailed as a brilliant columnist and being recognised, feted and bought bottles of champagne wherever he went. It must have been almost impossible to resist such lionisation. He quickly became so celebrated that he was asked to go on the TV panel game *Call My Bluff*, appearing for Patrick Campbell's team against Frank Muir's team.

Despite his obvious talent and charisma, Bernard's selfishness and lack of imagination were awesome. He spent New Year's Eve at the Sportsman's Aid Society dinner getting legless at the Grosvenor House Hotel in London while Jill sat at home alone.

Even his readers had begun to notice and had started writing to the *Life* to say that he wrote too much about drinking and not enough about racing. He ignored all the warning signs. He was having far too much fun. He was also travelling all over the British racing world and to Ireland, which he always loved. He once checked in to a Dublin hotel, unpacked his suitcase, went to the bathroom to shave, and heard a knock at the door. A very young messenger's voice piped up: 'Mr Bernard, I've got a message for you.'

'Shove it under the door,' boomed Bernard.

'I can't, sir,' squeaked the leprechaun, 'it's on a salver.'

He was in Dublin again in 1971 and telephoned London to place the biggest bet he had ever had, a monstrous £100, on the boxer Muhammad Ali to beat Joe Frazier in the overnight world heavyweight title fight. He asked the night porter to wake him very early, at 5 a.m., because he had a plane to catch back to London. While he slept Ali was beaten and at 5 a.m. there was a bang on the door and a voice shouted excitedly: 'Mr Bernard, sor, it's five o'clock and you've done your ton.'

Back in England the racing game kept delighting him. One of the many racehorse trainers Bernard met was Ryan Price, who once employed a stable girl who was so well endowed that when she seemed to be having trouble mounting a horse he cried: 'Just throw your tits over and the rest will follow.'

Another wonderfully lively trainer was Richard Hannon, whose taste for the bizarre gamble inspired one of Bernard's favourite anecdotes, which found its way into Keith Waterhouse's play and caused Peter O'Toole to juggle on-stage with three dolls. Bernard described Hannon thus in his book *Talking Horses* (Fourth Estate, 1987): 'His wife had triplets, two boys and a girl. One night after his wife and children had gone to bed, Richard was downstairs enjoying a drink with a merry band of lunatic, punting-mad Irishmen when he had a brilliant idea. He crept upstairs, got hold of the triplets, brought them down to the sitting room and arranged them on the sofa. "Now," he announced, "we're going to play Find The Lady." When Hannon's companions had finished betting on which triplet was the odd girl out, he removed their nappies with the panache of a bullfighter about to administer the *coup de grace*. But that wasn't the end of the game. "All out of the room," Hannon bellowed, "while I shuffle them." '

Bernard's own sense of humour could be mischievously wicked. Once at a Derby racing lunch at the Dorchester he saw at another table the beautiful Sally Croker Poole, the wife of the Aga Khan, and asked an Irish waiter to carry a note to her which read: 'Although I am only a humble Irish waiter, I think I am in love with you.' She looked stunned when she unfolded it but Bernard gave the game away by grinning when she looked up and she sent the waiter back with a reply that said 'I love you too.'

The drawback of all this fun was that because of the nature of the job Bernard was not only drinking too much but drinking stupidly. 'Whenever I went racing people kept buying me drinks and I never refused them,' he told me. 'I was very childish and greedy.' He was drinking so much that he set fire accidentally to the London flat that he had kept on in Westminster. The flat cost him £15 a week but it did mean that he could get to Soho easily and he was better placed than in Suffolk to go racing as often as possible, even down to the West Country if necessary. 'He set fire to the mattress,' Jill remembered, 'and he woke up because the smoke was suffocating him and he dragged the mattress into the bathroom and he attempted to put the mattress out but it exploded.' And it was the *Sporting Life*, not *The Spectator*, that was first privileged to inform its readers that Jeffrey Bernard was too 'ill' to produce his column.

'That column went to my head physically and metaphorically,' Bernard admitted, 'because I used to go on the racecourse, people would recognise me because I had a photograph on the top of the column, and people used to send me drinks all afternoon, and like an idiot I drank them all. I never learned how to say no, so I used to get absolutely paralytic: not at a good time, because Isabel had just been born and I was supposed to be a responsible parent and husband. But I used to go racing three or four times a week and always would get drunk with trainers and owners who became great friends and showed me the ropes, like Charles St George, Dave Hanley, Doug Marks, Bill Marshall and Eddie Reavey. I drank a hell of a lot. I'd get pancreatitis again and again: the mortality rate from that is very high, I don't know why I'm still alive. I used to get really horribly drunk and sick. I'd be drinking whisky and then some well-wisher would send over a bottle of champagne, a disastrous mix, *fatal*.'

Mike Molloy remembered that he and his wife Sandy and Irma Kurtz were once invited to the Pimlico flat for a Sunday lunch that Bernard, a good cook, was going to prepare. 'When we arrived he was clearly very pissed,' said Molloy, 'and Irma and Sandy and myself sat at the table with Jill and we were all talking very brightly because it was clear that Jeff was comatose by this time. The meal had been cooked, and Jill was unhappy that this social occasion had just disintegrated before we'd arrived and the meal was served and we ate it but there was no Jeff sitting at the table. We sat talking and laughing rather nervously and pretending that he's probably outside knocking up a pudding. And then we heard the distant sounds of snoring. We all crept away and there was Jeff as we passed the bedroom lying on the bed snoring, absolutely out.'

The marriage was by now in a terminal condition. The Bernards had finally, once and for all, been struck off the Chelsworth cocktail party circuit after he had relieved himself in the rector's flower bed. Bernard had begun increasingly to console himself with other women, including the wives of friends. 'I don't think he ever made a pass at Sandy,' said Mike Molloy, 'but I think he had that bohemian idea, rather like Eskimos do, that there was a general pool of women for the consumption of everyone. Jeff would have had an Eskimo's idea about relationships with people's wives. He had started young. He started with mature women and every now and again you'd meet a tottering old lady in Gerry's Club and Jeff would be talking to her quite sweetly and she'd totter off into the night and he'd say "what a fuck she was in 1949."' It did not help that Jill too was quite happy to flirt with other men and make him jealous.

That year a man drew Bernard aside at a Christmas party and pointed at Jill on the other side of the room. 'Bit of a knockout, isn't she?' he leered.

'Yes,' said Bernard. 'I think she's very attractive.'

'Well, I'll tell you something,' said the stranger. 'She's available. Very available.'

1971 was not to be a very good year.

- 2 -

After his misbehaviour on New Year's Eve Jill must have had a strict word with him because before the end of January he was even taking the baby Isabel for a walk in Chelsea Royal Hospital gardens at 9.30 in the morning, before the pubs opened. 'I'm talking to the baby all the time although she can't understand a word,' he wrote in the *Sporting Life*. 'Dr Spock says it's good for babies to hear long conversations.'

His gambling was not always entirely his own fault. In February he claimed that Jill had told him to go out and gamble that evening because she wanted a colour television set. He had played craps, won £120 (more than a fortnight's wages) and duly bought her the TV. But his drinking had by now become so excessive that he admitted even in his column that it could eventually cost him his job, which he had been doing for less than a year. Looking back on his first twenty weeks he wrote: 'If I was completely honest, there's a strong chance that I'd get the sack, but unlike most, I've never been exactly terrified of being out of work. After all, it does provide sufficient leisure for getting on with the important things in life.' He even added: 'As anyone will tell you, I'm drunk at the time of writing this.' He was not only about to hang himself, he was also buying the rope and knotting it.

He had some sort of breakdown at the end of February and saw a psychiatrist in a Surrey hospital but it only lasted a couple of weeks and by 6 March he was writing jauntily in the *Sporting Life*: 'Would the married lady who wasn't with her husband, but with the other chap, please contact me? I enjoyed drinking with her at Lingfield, have forgotten her name and wish to repeat the performance.' It is difficult to escape the conclusion that he was trying now to enrage not only his employers but also his wife. How did he expect Jill to take such open infidelity in print? Three weeks later he reported trying to pick up a 'very flashy' woman in a Newmarket pub and in May he wrote: 'Two days in Newmarket hasn't filled me with a great amount of optimism on the picking-up birds front. It's always very depressing to discover that the best racing crumpet is usually accompanied by racehorse trainers and/or millionaires.' He was either by now utterly indifferent to Jill's feelings or inflamed beyond reason by booze. He was also beginning to regret his decision to live in the country. He felt that the village was far too insular and respectable for him.

In March he had four very drunken days in Ireland and then took a week's holiday, but even then this was spent in Newmarket 'to get material for a satirical novel about racing'. He saw a psychoanalyst, and at last he met his hero Lester Piggott properly. Piggott gave him a lift to Newmarket but because of Bernard's 'dreadful inferiority complex', he told his readers 'we said hello, goodbye, lovely weather, see you again, thanks for the lift and it was a pleasure'.

It was not to be long, however, before he and Piggott were sharing entire sentences of dialogue. Once, when they were together on Newmarket Heath, Bernard spotted a loose horse on the road and suggested that they should catch it. 'Never catch a loose horse,' muttered Piggott. 'You can end up holding on to it all fucking day.' Bernard then cadged a lift to Newbury racecourse in Piggott's aeroplane and was incensed to be sent a week later a bill for £35 which of course he never paid.

Bernard used to send out an entire cantering string of Lester Piggott anecdotes all dressed up in his own bright colours. One told of the stable lad who asked the notoriously tight-fisted Piggott for a £1 tip for looking after one of his winning horses. 'What?' said Piggott. 'I can't hear. That's my bad ear.' The lad tried the other side. 'What about a £2 tip?'

he bellowed. Piggott shook his head. 'Try the £1 ear again', he said.

Bernard's sense of humour remained unimpaired by the deluge of alcohol. On 1 April he tried to stage an April Fools' Day hoax at Stafford races by standing beside a Rolls Royce and pretending to be a beggar. Most of the passers-by recognised him from the photograph at the top of his column, but one old lady pressed 25p into his hand and said: 'You poor man. It must be terribly hard to run a car like that.'

A week later, on the train to Worcester, he met the boozy but breezy Labour politician George Brown, who had recently been made a peer. Brown told him that he had been approached the previous year by a spiv who had told him that if he gave him some money he could make him £200 by betting on a certain winner. 'Don't tell me the name of the horse,' said Brown, 'just give me the £200 now.' Other noblemen who impressed Bernard less were Lord Wigg, the chairman of the Tote Race Betting Levy Board, and the Duke of Norfolk, about both of whom he was constantly rude in his column.

He was too ill to write a column on 22 May but a week later he was ferociously drunk in Lambourn, in training for playing the following day in an All-Stars cricket team in a match against Gay Kindersley's XI at the nearby village of East Garston. After a lunch of salmon and strawberries, Bernard went in at number three, was bowled for three, and 'went behind the tea tent for a good cry'. During the tea interval he was embarrassed that several children approached him for his autograph but ignored Fred Winter, who was standing beside him. Bernard was now such a star in the racing world that in June he was one of the judges who chose Miss Royal Ascot at a lavish charity ball at the Hilton Hotel.

On Wednesday 16 June the column did not appear again, quite probably because he had become so drunk at Ascot races that he had either vomited all over the Queen Mother or at least all over the flowers in front of the Royal Box.

Bunny May was with him and remembered that they had been freeloading champagne off rich contacts all afternoon and were very drunk indeed when Bernard at the end of the day made the mistake of suddenly downing a large whisky on top of all the champagne. 'As we get to the door of the bar by the lift we're stopped by the security men,' said May. 'The lift comes down, the doors open, the Queen Mother, all in the blue, with the hat, absolutely charming, nodding away, and out she comes, and at that precise moment Jeff's neck went back and up came the champagne, the scotch and the dried tomato skins all over the Queen Mother's feet. He did. Not a pretty sight. Things like this did not go down well at the *Sporting Life*. I just got hold of him and took him away. I thought he might get nicked. He didn't say anything, he was pissed. Her legs were actually spattered with all the little tomato skins. There were lots of people standing around. And there it is. He's done it. He's just barfed.'

Readers of the *Sporting Life* were now beginning increasingly to write to the paper about Bernard's mischievous column. When one sneering letter was published it was answered by five others, one of which said that Bernard was 'the first journalist to understand the average punter – self-destructive, paranoiac, a loser, yet richly human. Mr Bernard has captured the comedy of racing: that a punter is someone who expects Lester Piggott to win every race, believes all jockeys and trainers are crooked, and never forgets his losers.' But his column also attracted piles of angry letters from readers and at least twice he was challenged by readers to a fight, once by the trainer Taffy Salaman (for insulting apprentice jockeys) and once by a taxi driver for insulting cabbies. One reader even sent him a turd through the post because he had been rude about the Government.

His drunkenness had now become legendary in racing, which had always known many heavy drinkers and alcoholics but none quite as amusing and bizarre as Bernard.

'Odd things used to happen to me on the *Life*,' he wrote sixteen years later in his book about racing, *Talking Horses* (Fourth Estate, 1987). 'One night I woke up in a field outside Pontefract and I still have no idea how I got there. Another time I remember opening my eyes to find myself in bed with Barry Brogan – a great jockey, it is true, but not my idea of a desirable bed companion. And I once spent the night with a girl in the ditch of the celebrated Pond Fence at Sandown. I don't know how we met or what was so enticing about the Pond Fence – perhaps I was pointing out to her that obstacle's peculiar hazards.' When he had woken up in bed with Barry Brogan that morning in Huntingdon he had found himself also sharing the bed with a local charwoman, had no idea how they had all arrived there together, and was asked by the hotel and an official from the local council never to return to Huntingdon again.

He once filed the same column five times from Newmarket to the *Sporting Life* in one afternoon, on Two Thousand Guineas day, and it was also at Newmarket – at Tattersalls yearling sales – that he made a rash drunken bid of more than £100 (two weeks' wages) for a horse. 'I used to think I was Lord Rothschild when I was drunk,' he explained. By the next morning, when he returned to the Sales, he had of course completely forgotten his purchase of the previous day until the trainer Henry Cecil walked up to him and said 'I hope you've watered and fed your horse this morning.'

'What the fuck are you talking about?' enquired Bernard. 'I haven't got a horse.'

'You have,' said Cecil. 'We all watched you buy it yesterday, with some amazement.'

Bernard was appalled to learn that while he had bid £100 for the horse, the underbidder, Peter Poston, a butcher from Bury St Edmunds who was also a small-time horse trainer, had bid only £50. Doug Marks apologised to Tattersalls on Bernard's behalf, pointed out that he had been drunk and did in fact have no more than eleven shillings in his bank account, and suggested that they ought to take the horse back. Eventually Bernard agreed to pay the £50 difference between his and Poston's bids. Even then he did not actually part with the £50 himself: that was eventually paid for him by Anne Pacey, the film critic of the *Daily Mirror*.

But he loved racing, of course, and despite the suicidal drinking he could write with love about it, touching it with magic. At the end of August he described lyrically the early morning scene at Newmarket as the racehorses were exercised soon after dawn, 'ghost-like columns coming out of the mist, stirrups and bits jangling, horses snorting. As they peeled in twos and galloped off, the slamming of hooves into damp turf produced that intoxicating rhythm which somehow always makes the hair stand up on the back of your neck and the pulse beat a little faster.'

His job on the *Sporting Life* was still the job of his dreams but sadly he was not to enjoy it for much longer. He had only another month to go before the Editor, Ossie Fletcher, could stand no more and sacked him.

On 29 September there appeared a rambling and much shorter column than usual. It had obviously been written when he was very drunk and in it he was unwisely angry about letters that readers had written to the Editor complaining about him. 'If people had various things to occupy their minds,' he wrote childishly, 'they wouldn't have the time or the energy to write complaining letters to newspapers. If you fancy the job, write to the Editor.' He was tempting fate and it was an unworthy end to his *Sporting Life* career.

In fact it was the national point-to-point dinner at the Kensington Close Hotel in London that finally destroyed Bernard's career at the *Sporting Life*. Michael Williams, the newspaper's point-to-point correspondent and member of the organising committee for the dinner, had the bright idea of inviting Bernard to present the *Sporting Life* cup to the leading lady point-to-point rider of the season, Sue Aston, and to say a few words. Bernard was very nervous, had never spoken in public, and went to the *Sporting Life* office at 6 a.m. to write a speech. He could not think what to say and decided that just the one in a Smithfield pub would help to oil the inspiration. He took with him the *Sporting Life*'s heavy-drinking greyhound correspondent, Albert Bright. From Smithfield they went to the 'Stab In The Back', the *Daily Mirror* pub, and then on to the Colony Room club. Williams, who was still the paper's point-to-point correspondent in 1992, recalled: 'I had received an assurance from Norman Bardsley, who was the managing editor of the paper at that time, that he would get him to the dinner sober. Unfortunately, it didn't work. Jeffrey, arriving on his own after Bardsley, fell into the hotel out of his taxi. I offered him a glass of sherry, which he rejected with the remark, "What is that filthy stuff?" So I was about to hand him a gin and tonic when Bardsley remarked, "I think Jeffrey has had enough, Michael." Naturally, this didn't put him in a good mood. A little later I introduced him to Sue Aston, and he clearly frightened the life out of her before going to sleep on the sofa in the hallway. So Bardsley had to step in and present the trophy himself. He was obviously quite well prepared for this eventuality, because he made a nice little speech.' Meanwhile Bernard had been carried upstairs to bed by two waiters.

Jonathan Powell, the racing correspondent for the *News of the World*, was at the dinner. 'Jeff was legless,' he said twenty years later. 'He stood up to speak and collapsed over the table.' When Bernard recovered he went off to Paris for the weekend to see the Arc de Triomphe and was stunned when he met Henry Cecil at Longchamps the next day and the trainer remarked: 'I'm sorry to hear you've got the sack.' Bernard himself could not even remember passing out at the hotel the night before. Three days later he received this letter, dated 4 October 1971, from Ossie Fletcher, sacking him:

Dear Mr Bernard,

It will come as no surprise to you that following your unpardonable exhibition at the point-to-point dinner which you attended as a representative of the paper on Friday evening, it is no longer possible for you to continue in our employ.

This was not, you will agree, the first time your behaviour has compromised us and to protect myself and all connected with *The Sporting Life* from further embarrassment, I have no alternative but to terminate your engagement forthwith.

Although in the circumstances I do not consider there is any onus on us to pay you three months' salary in lieu of notice, I am giving you the benefit of any doubt that may exist and you will be hearing from our cashiers in due course.

I am sorry this has become necessary, but you will agree you were given every chance.

Should you wish to return to the office to collect any personal belongings, I would be glad if you would arrange with Mr Sandys to do so and I would also be obliged if you would return to me your metal Press badge at your earliest convenience.

Yours faithfully,

O. W. Fletcher

Editor

Bernard took it well. 'You should never be frightened of the sack,' he told a *Sporting Life* reporter in 1989, when he had gone on to become famous without them. 'You've got to have bottle.'

12

Jeff In Bin

Bernard's sacking by the *Sporting Life* was the final act in a drunken drama that confirmed him for life as a legend in the racing world. His misbehaviour at the point-to-point dinner made him so famous among the boozy, horsey fraternity that it was to buzz for years afterwards with almost as many apocryphal stories about him as politicians tell about Winston Churchill. 'Jeff's supposed to have gone into the Editor's office the day after the dinner,' said Jonathan Powell, 'taken his cock out, slapped it on the desk and said, "Beat that!" to which the editor Ossie Fletcher replied, "You're fired".'

The incident was so successful in polishing the Bernard legend that he was invited to speak at numerous racing dinners in the months to come. He had three months' salary from the *Life* to live on and he was still writing occasionally for the *Daily Mirror* and the *Sunday Times*, and at the beginning of May 1972 he started yet again to write his autobiography but quickly gave up. He was never to be able to write much more than a thousand words: he was simply not a long-distance writer. More important, he was now drinking so much that any serious writing was quite beyond him. He was drinking two bottles of whisky a day and heading for a major breakdown and at the end of the year he would spend three months in what he called 'a loony bin'. Because he found it so difficult to work, Jill was forced to do any dressmaking jobs she could find. Jeff seemed naively surprised that by now their love life had completely deteriorated and later complained in print about how Jill had used sex during their marriage: he was treated every now and then to an emission for good behaviour. 'My wife used sex as a reward and punishment system, an unforgivable habit with some women,' he claimed in *Men Only* in 1977.

His drinking still at times had its funny side. On his way to Paris for the Arc de Triomphe, after consuming a lunch of vindaloo curry and a bottle of whisky, he stayed overnight with the TV newsreader Sandy Gall and his wife Eleanor and blenched when he realised that dinner with the Galls was another hot curry and another bottle of whisky. Gamely he consumed them both but with terrible consequences. He spent the night in their son Alexander's vacant room and was mortified when he woke in the night to find that the curry had done its worst and he had badly fouled the bed. For hours he sat up and smoked and paced the room, wondering what to do. He could hardly creep into the bathroom to wash the sheets in the middle of the night, nor switch the machine on at dawn, nor rummage in the airing cupboard in the early hours to find clean sheets, nor just steal the dirty ones. Eventually, tortured by embarrassment and cowardice, he did nothing at all except make the bed, covering up the mess.

Off he went with the Galls for a day at the races, but he felt so bad about what he had done – and about what Eleanor Gall faced when eventually she had to make up the bed in her son's room – that he kept starting to tell her the truth and then stopping out of sheer shame.

'Eleanor . . .'

'Yes, Jeffrey?'

'Uh . . . no . . . never mind.'

This happened three or four times until eventually Bernard said: 'Eleanor, there's something I just *have* to tell you.'

Mrs Gall laid a consoling hand on his arm. 'Don't worry, Jeffrey,' she said with an understanding smile. 'I understand. I know what you're trying to tell me.'

'Good God! You do?'

'Of course I do,' she smiled. 'You're in love with me, aren't you?'

'Christ, no!' stammered Bernard. 'I've shat your son's bed.'

His drinking had started to cost him work. One glossy magazine editor, the Rev. Marcus Morris, who had previously been editor of the boys' comic the *Eagle*, decided to dispense with his services after Bernard had turned up drunk at his office, accused him of being late with a payment, and called him a cunt. '*What* did you call me?' spluttered the priest.

'I said you're a cunt,' Bernard repeated.

Morris rushed upstairs to the accounts department, returned with £60 in cash, handed the notes to Bernard and told him that he was fired.

Bernard was unrepentant. 'I should have called you a cunt before,' he said. 'It's obviously the only way to get paid.'

But there was also now a desperate compulsion about his drinking that was no longer amusing. Among Bernard's very few unpublished jottings, in a brown John Menzies exercise book, there is a vivid description of the terrible powerful grip of his alcoholism when he was on the *Sporting Life*:

'We always went to the pub at opening time. I had to get there then. Albert [Bright] used to knock his first one back and I'd stare at mine for ten minutes, sometimes more. He'd always have the shakes more badly than me, but I felt the angst he didn't seem to know about. He never seemed anxious to get to the pub on the dot of opening time and yet he had the knack of arriving as the door bolts slid back. Once I was at the bar, I felt safe. I don't exactly know what from, but I always felt secure listening to the horror and boredom of a publican's or barmaid's chit chat.'

At times Bernard seemed determined to kill himself before the booze could do so and he began to threaten yet again to commit suicide. 'I was in Suffolk,' said Jill, 'and it must have been about 11 o'clock at night and Jeff rang me: "Errr, errr, I'm gonna *kill* myself, errr, I'm *really* gonna" . . . apparently he'd phoned half of Berkshire as well. "I'm gonna *do* it, I'm gonna *kill* myself." And I thought, well, there's fuck-all I can do at 11 o'clock at night, no trains, forget it, so I rang around

Soho and eventually I got Bruce and he got somebody and they broke the door in and there was Jeff with bottles and the phone off the hook.' He was taken to Westminster Hospital.

Once he was out of hospital and back home in Suffolk the violence increased. He was barred from the Peacock and during one of his drunken rows with Jill she was about to drive away in the car when he shouted through the window: 'She's not my fucking daughter, is she?'

'*No!*' yelled Jill.

On another night, in July, she was having a drink in a pub with a male friend when Bernard walked in drunk, hit her on the neck and knocked her off the stool. 'You've fucking ruined my fucking car,' he yelled, disappearing and taking the car's distributor head with him. When she returned home and looked through the kitchen window she was faced by a shambles. 'I've never *seen* such a mess in my life,' she said. 'He'd pulled the tap out, the sink was hanging off, he'd pulled all the shelves off, there was fat everywhere, every bottle was broken, there was glass, I can't *tell* you, this mess. I got the window open and I climbed in and I walked through this mess and there were notes everywhere, "*You* have done this", "*You* have killed me", "It's all *your* fault". Once more Bernard had taken an overdose.

Jill had had enough. She told him at last to get out and leave her in peace with Isabel. He went, but kept pestering her with drunken telephone calls. By now Jill loathed him, he wrote in the *Daily Mirror* three years later, in a series about alcoholism: 'I never saw it at the time, but the hard fact of it was she dreaded my company. Filled with the usual remorse, it occurred to me too late that I loved her. By now I was drinking almost two bottles of whisky a day and my family was going without to provide it.'

In September Jill was summoned to Lambourn to collect him from the Red Lion, where he had fallen desperately ill with pancreatitis. Back in Chelsworth, Jill saw him back to full recovery and then asked him to leave again. He did, returning to live in London, but he was now on the brink

of an abyss and was undoubtedly having a nervous breakdown. On the morning of 24 October 1972 he walked into a
tobacconist's shop in Kensington High Street and when the
assistant asked, 'Can I help you, sir?' he burst into tears.
'I couldn't stop,' he told me. 'He got a very nice doctor
from over the road – coincidentally a mad Irishman who
owned racehorses, Dr Morrissey – and he packed me off
to the Alcohol and Addiction Unit of a mental hospital at
Hanwell, near Ealing.' Here, at the appropriately named St
Bernard's Hospital, to which he always referred later as 'the
loony bin' or 'the nuthouse', Bernard underwent three months
of voluntary incarceration and psychoanalysis at the hands
of Dr Max Glatt, of whom he greatly approved because he
'had the good sense to tell students: "if you want to know
about alcoholism, ask an alcoholic."' The Alcohol and Drug
Addiction Unit, which was attached to the mental hospital,
consisted of two small wards in an out-building. 'We used
to see a lot of mad people,' said Bernard, 'and I'd go to the
canteen because I thought it might be interesting to be surrounded by them but I discovered very quickly that lunatics
are terribly boring people.'

Bernard's best friend in 'the bin' was a Scots tramp,
inevitably called Jock, who had been sleeping rough on
Ealing Common but claimed to have done even that in
style, arranging for a pint of milk and the *Sporting Life* to
be delivered at his bench each morning. It was Jock who
advised Bernard that if he was ever so hard-up that he had
to resort to drinking cheap surgical spirit 'for God's sake drink
Boots' and not Timothy Whites'. It's got a better looking label
and doesn't look so sordid on the sideboard.' Another patient
was a female nurse who had eventually realised that she was
an alcoholic when she sprayed a patient's face with vaginal
deodorant. There was also a woman who had resorted to
prostitution to pay for her drinking and had once accom-
modated fifteen men in an hour as she lay on a tomb in a
Liverpool cemetery.

Among the numerous tests that Bernard underwent in

hospital was a Shipley Hartford Intelligence Test which suggested that his vocabulary was well above average (20.2 against an average of 16) but that his grasp of abstractions was lower than average (17.3 rather than 20). He also had an Eysenck Personality Inventory which found both his neuroticism and his extraversion to be 'Very High'. Other fragments that survive in his own notes of those months are tantalising. 'Ego Weakness = Feelings of inferiority', says one. 'Id tension = Subconscious Hang Ups', says another. Why should he have felt inferior? And what were these 'Subconscious Hang Ups'? What had the shrinks discovered? His lust for his mother?

After a few weeks in the unit Bernard found himself disapproving not only of drink and drugs but also of gambling and even infidelity. He was however upset by his psychology test, which had found that he was suffering from a deep inferiority complex, paranoid insecurity and guilt and was all in all an emotional mess. At the end of the treatment each patient had to write a summary of his or her life that was then discussed and taken to pieces by the group. Bernard's own memory of those numerous life stories was that 'children should shoot their parents as soon as they're old enough to pull the trigger'.

Two years later he gave a vivid glimpse of his life at St Bernard's – and his marriage – in a television play about alcoholism that he wrote when he was forty-two, *Starting Tomorrow It's All Going To Be The Same*, a play so depressing that although it was bought by the BBC it never reached the screen. Except for the booze, it has little in common with *Jeffrey Bernard is Unwell*. There are not a lot of laughs, even though the play is startlingly autobiographical. 'It's all true,' Bernard told me in 1992. 'I was never able to write fiction.'

The play opens with a forty-two-year-old alcoholic racing journalist, Jack Foster, who has been educated at Pangbourne, going into a Fleet Street pub one morning for 'just the one'. It ends months later when he comes out of an alcohol and drug addiction unit and walks immediately into the same Fleet Street pub for 'just the one'. Like Bernard himself, Jack Foster cannot beat the demon in the bottle, no matter how he tries. He is without hope. He will drink himself to death.

In his TV play Bernard wrote about his unhappy childhood: 'A day doesn't go by without my thinking of it.' Could that really be true? Surely not? Not even one day? Bernard was a schoolboy who must have been more popular at Pangbourne than most because by comparison with most schoolboys he had everything going for him: he made the other boys laugh and was very good at cricket and boxing and won a prize for reading. Could he really have been so unhappy? Yet the story of his 'childhood unhappiness' was eventually to become a banner that he was to brandish all his life to excuse his failures, bad manners and self-indulgent melancholy. He was to turn his Poor-Little-Sad-Boy act into a polished professional routine.

Most illuminating of all are the numerous flashbacks in the play that describe Foster's fictional relationship with his wife, 'Jane', who is described in the script as 'very attractive, slightly tough-looking, hard. She is twenty-eight-years-old' but obviously relates to Bernard's marriage to Jill. Foster reveals in the play that when he met his wife he had begun to become a heavy drinker and 'was getting drunk without fail': 'We met in a pub, of course, and it was what you could call love at first sight. It was either that or lust at first sight. She didn't realise how much I drank at the time and although I was, as I say, drunk for most of the time, I think she just thought I was a rather boozy "Jack the Lad". Within twenty-four hours we were living with each other and six months after that, we got married. At first we got on marvellously . . .'

If the play has any message or moral it comes in a few lines of dialogue from a homosexual nurse, Blossom: 'It's not really our *right* to be happy. You mustn't expect to be . . . life's very ordinary. You drinkers expect dreams to come true. They don't, Jack. The good times and the nice people are the exception and not the rule ... Just regard everything as being terribly unimportant.' At the end Foster is asked if he could ever be happy without a drink. 'I think it's unlikely,' he admits. 'I think life must be better without drink, but I don't *expect* happiness. I think unhappiness is a sort of disease that you catch when you're very, very young and I think you probably have it for ever. I think it's a chronic illness.'

At the end of the play, when Foster leaves the hospital, he goes straight back to the Fleet Street pub, the Stab in the Back. 'I'll have *one*, Bert. I'll take it easy and I'll be alright,' he says. 'I never ate properly, that was the trouble. I'm going to start eating two good meals a day. You remember that chap Doctor Camps? He was the Home Office pathologist. He said it's not what you drink that kills you, it's what you don't eat.'

And the very last line of the play is when Foster says: 'Oh, thanks. I'll have a scotch please. I'm taking it easy, though.'

Bernard himself went straight back into a pub as soon as he left St Bernard's, and although he subsequently gave up the booze for two-and-a-half years, from 1974 to 1976, he was ultimately as much its prisoner as was his fictional character Foster. He got drunk as soon as he had left St Bernard's 'to celebrate the fact that I'd stopped drinking. I stayed drunk for a month.'

Jill remembered those last months of their marriage as 'a complete nightmare. I was working in London. It was the year of my thirtieth birthday and I remember spending New Year's Eve 1972 in tears sobbing quietly to myself. He wasn't there and I thought "I can't stand this man any longer, no *way*, I'm going to get out of here." So I got myself a job to be a bit financially independent and I started working for Slix, which meant getting up, driving seventeen miles to Colchester, sitting on the train for fifty-five minutes, getting out at Liverpool Street, rushing to the Tube, rushing to Oxford Circus, getting out and running all the way so I got there at nine – and I did that for about three months. He was supposed to look after Isabel.

'He was nasty and violent often when he was drunk, and I came home from work one night about eight o'clock and the door was open and he was scarlet-eyed. "I've got dinner on," he said – he was pissed out of his *brain*. "I've made paella." There was a pyramid of frozen food stuck in this pan. I said, "Where's Isabel?" and he said, "Oh, she's all right, she's in bed, asleep." Then he fell on the sofa with his fag and fell asleep. I went upstairs. Isabel was fully dressed, filthy, lying on top of her bed, asleep, with her little thumb in her mouth. I thought, "This is it. I'm out of here." I put Isabel in the car, packed a few things, took my sewing machine and left. I drove to Luton where my sister had a pub.'

It was 26 April 1973. Jill had stayed with him for one month short of seven years, longer than any of his other wives had managed. She and Isabel went to stay with Jill's parents in Ealing and eventually Slix asked her to work in their new design room in Derby, where she lived in half a farmhouse in Aston-on-Trent. She spent one day returning to Chelsworth in the Cortina estate to collect her personal belongings, two cats and all Isabel's bedroom furniture, which she loaded onto the roof.

Bernard's version of the final incident that broke the marriage was completely different. 'I passed out one afternoon and Isabel got out,' he said. 'She was sitting in the middle of the road and an articulated truck had stopped about five yards away from her – so I was told by the neighbour who found her. Jill heard about this when she came home and Isabel was next door with the neighbour – I was still asleep on the sofa. When I woke up in one morning the cottage was half empty and they'd both left. I had an estate car that she used to drive: she'd filled it up with everything that she could lay her hands on. I was asleep through all this – whisky – and you could have taken an oxy-acetylene welder to me and I wouldn't have woken up. It was an amazing shock to wake up in an empty room and realise what had happened. The only thing in the room was the fucking sofa I was lying on. She'd removed everything and she never came back.'

Jill divorced him for unreasonable behaviour nine months later in the Derby County Court. She cited his drinking, violence, morose moods, incendiary tendency, suicidal episodes and neglect of Isabel. She was eventually to return to London and to marry the man she had left just before meeting Bernard in 1966, David Wilsworth.

If the marriage had done nothing else for her, it had certainly hardened her. Even so, her epitaph on the marriage itself was a sad one. 'I don't think he loved me at all,' she told me. 'I don't think Jeff loves anyone apart from himself. He loves Jeff.'

13

The Prophet of Loss

The loss of Jill hit Bernard badly and he in turn hit the bottle harder than ever. He tried to forget her by taking a girlfriend to Norfolk for a fortnight's holiday but he had a row with her on the first day, sulked for the next three days, and watched it rain for the next eleven. He tried to write his Great Novel but progressed little beyond the title, *Reach for the Ground*. He consoled himself by having an affair with Liz, the vicar's daughter. And still he could not leave Jill alone. He would telephone her in Derby about his domestic problems, how to clean a tartare sauce stain from his suit, or about his love life, and even after she married David Wilsworth he would telephone him and refer to her as '*my* wife'.

Liz was a sweet girl who did not only his ironing but also his washing and a spot of gardening. He first noticed her potential when she was squatting planting radishes and he saw that she was not wearing any knickers herself. Marsh Dunbar, whose marriage had finally broken up, remembered the vicar's daughter well. 'We called her The Angel,' said Marsh. 'She was a very *good* girl. The Rector was out and they had a bath and we all got absolutely pissed on homemade elderberry wine.'

After The Angel there was a Suffolk barmaid, Rose, who seemed astonished by his lovemaking and kept remarking with a Suffolk twang: '*No* one has ever done *that* to me before.' And then there was the twenty-seven-year-old actress Wendy Richard, who was later to become a star of the TV soap *EastEnders* and was then playing the dim but sexy young Cockney department store assistant Miss Brahms in the popular television comedy series *Are You Being Served?*

'I lived with Wendy for about six months,' Bernard claimed, although she denied this in 1992 and told me that it was more like one month. 'I met her in the French pub where she used to drink quarter-bottles of champagne.' Mike Molloy remembered that the impecunious Bernard was particularly delighted about having an affair with Wendy Richard because her parents had left her a small hotel in King's Cross, the Yorkshire Palace Hotel ('Hot and Cold Running Water'). This was 'a cheap bed-and-breakfast place,' said Bernard, 'six or so bedrooms, an old Dickensian mid-Victorian house near King's Cross station. She had a woman there all the time to run it. She had a bedroom and sitting room on the ground floor and I stayed with her for a bit. She was very attractive. When you get her on her own she can drop that silly Cockney accent of hers: she puts it on a little bit. Her father had a posh pub in Shepherd Market called the Shepherds, very fashionable it used to be, a touristy place. I don't think the gossip columnists knew about me though I remember being conscious of the fact that I was with someone who was well-known.

'I was quite shocked to discover that Wendy was a housewife manqué. She would drink champagne in pubs, which was slightly flash then, and what with her two great boobs and sexy figure I didn't realise that she half-expected me to be home for supper every night. That came as a shock to me. She wanted to mother me a bit. Wendy wants to mother people, oddly enough, and she's not that tough Cockney she pretends to be.'

Even so, he said, they had fun together inventing amusing love games: 'When she moved to Baker Street – she had a bloody enormous flat there at Chiltern Court – we'd play these silly games. I came round one morning when I lived in Marylebone, I walked round the corner to her flat and pretended that I'd come to read her meter. I climbed down to have a look at it and went through all this charade and then of course immediately . . . It was a game. I pretended to be a Cockney meter reader and she went along with the joke.'

In 1992 Wendy Richard could remember little about the affair. 'He stayed with me for a while,' she told me, 'but we weren't together for a long time. My mother had died and I had had a disastrous marriage and threw my husband out in October 1972. I met Jeff in 1973 but we weren't together for six months. It might have been a month. The only funny thing I can remember was when we went into the Stab and the barman said, "Is he with you?" and I said, "Yes" and he said, "Never mind, dear, we've all got our cross to bear."'

The affair ended with a whimper. 'There was no specific row,' said Bernard. 'I got a bit bored with her. *They* haven't always left *me*.' By then he was renting a flat in Nottingham Place, between Marylebone High Street and Baker Street, just around the corner from Madame Tussaud's. He was to live there alone for the next four years.

Work that year was hard to come by. He used to hang around Allan Hall's office at the *Sunday Times*, helping him with the Atticus diary, and bummed around, scrounging the occasional job. But already, in February, in the depths of his drunken despair, as his marriage splintered, he had written his first article for the socialist weekly journal the *New Statesman*, an article that was eventually to lead him towards the *Spectator*, his Low Life column, and fame. In February the *New Statesman* published a piece about alcohol addiction and St Bernard's and paid him £30 for it. It was the first of a string of pieces he was to write for the magazine over the next three years, all of them autobiographical, about racing, living in the country, money, women, acting, schooldays. They were usually more than a thousand words long, much longer than his later more famous articles in the *Spectator*. They were among the best work he was ever to do, and it was in the *New Statesman* that he first told many of the anecdotes that were later to appear in the *Spectator*. Anthony Howard, who was then the Editor of the *New Statesman*, claimed in later years that he had published some of Bernard's very best writing. Bernard certainly came up with some memorable lines for the *New Statesman*. In a piece about cookery after Jill had left him he wrote: 'If you haven't any salt, tears make a splendid substitute.'

Despite the high quality of Bernard's articles Richard West, who met Bernard when they were both working for the *New Statesman*, believed that Bernard was not completely happy or properly appreciated there. 'They used to employ good writers even if they weren't socialists,' West told me. 'I used to meet him in these grim socialist corridors with the terrible dirty mackintosh of H. G. Wells hanging on the back of the door: it was supposed to be the great H. G. Wells mackintosh and anyone who put it on could get the first woman that they met. I used to see Jeffrey in the corridor and raise an arm and we'd go off to a pub and he was extremely miserable because they just didn't have any real sense of humour. The *New Statesman* jokes were jokes about grouse moors and the Royal Family and Tory hangers and floggers and things like that. These were the only things you were allowed to be funny about and the things that Jeff thought were funny were drink and women and Leftwingers. He's always slightly bogus in his politics. He calls himself a socialist but he isn't really. He's a complete Tory and he's also rather a snob in a funny way. I remember him once saying that the people he wouldn't ever allow into any pub he kept were commercial travellers and people with tattoos. He's really old-fashioned Tory; he likes the working classes, especially the gamekeeper sort. So his sense of humour was completely wasted on the *New Statesman* because he was contemptuous of the very things that they valued most, like feminism, which was just coming in to fashion. Bron Waugh was also working there at the same time and the *New Statesman* readers really didn't like either Jeffrey or Bron. Bron was making fun of the working classes and Jeffrey was making fun of women. We used to go out and escape from this rather austere atmosphere of this socialist organ. The socialists really don't have much sense of humour and they can't understand that *everything* should be a subject of laughter. They couldn't appreciate that the trades unions were funny, that black Africa was funny. He just didn't *fit*. He didn't have the right audience until he went to the *Spectator*.'

Some of Bernard's later detractors suggested that the reason for the high quality of his *New Statesman* articles between 1973 and 1975 was that they coincided almost exactly with the two and a half years when he gave up alcohol. But in fact after Jill left him, and now that he was more often in Soho, he drank even more than before, and behaved even more disgracefully, and it was not to be until a year after his first *New Statesman* article that he turned teetotal, in February 1974. Until then he roistered on. Albert Finney, no mean roisterer himself in his time, took him to see the film *Blazing Saddles* along with Finney's gorgeous wife Anouk Aimee and a 'blind date' for Bernard, Lauren Bacall, and when they went for a drink afterwards Bernard overheard Mrs Finney whispering loudly to her husband: 'Be vairy carefool of zat Cheffrey Bernard. I seenk he ees a drinkair.'

'Fuck me!' said Bernard later. 'Finney was a bit of a fucking drinker too!'

'As for Lauren Bacall,' said Bernard, 'my God, she frightened me. She was very snooty.' Blind date or not, he did not suggest a legover.

There were always plenty of heavy-drinking companions to be found in Soho and once a week Bernard's playmate was Frank Norman, who had married in 1971 and now refused to get drunk except on Fridays, when he would make up for the rest of the week. 'He had a very rigid pattern to the week,' said his wife, Geraldine. 'He used to go out about eleven and carry on until two or three in the morning and then spent Saturday recovering, Sunday getting better, then working from Monday to Thursday.'

Whether or not Bernard was completely appreciated at the *New Statesman* he was certainly well enough established by December for Howard to let him loose to write the Christmas Diary on 21 December, a self-indulgent perk for the privileged contributor. Bernard used the opportunity to announce that after a row with the Chelsworth postman he was going to put up a sign on his gate reading BEWARE OF THE UNDERDOG. But despite the barmaid he spent that Christmas alone for the first time in years. 'I've got the giant box of tissues ready for when the self-pity sets in at around closing time on Christmas Day,' he told his *New Statesman* readers. It was not a joke, either. He had.

Six weeks later he did something so dreadful that it stunned him into attempting to give up alcohol for two and a half years. On 3 February 1974, in the Coach and Horses, he punched a woman in the mouth so hard that he cut his fist on her front teeth and the wound went septic. He was so appalled at punching a *woman* – a pub regular called Big Eddie – that he feared he might be going mad, and he was so frightened by his own behaviour that he went 'on the wagon' for two and a half years. 'I was telephoning someone and she cut me off,' he explained. 'She put her hand on the telephone rest and cut me off in the middle of rather an important conversation. So I punched her in the mouth and then was disgusted with myself.' It seems appropriate that Big Eddie's son was to become the lead singer with the pop group Madness.

– 2 –

Going On The Dry was to make Bernard utterly miserable but his success at not touching a drop for the next thirty months, after a quarter of a century of serious drunkenness, was awesome. On how many terrible mornings must he have forced himself past the doorways of every pub that he passed? On how many afternoons must he have lingered outside the windows of friendly off-licence shops, noticing how the sun twinkled so warmly on the bottles of whisky? On how many nights must he have sat alone and lonely in his flat in Marylebone High Street, listening to Mozart and staring at a cup of tea? He was to remain teetotal for nearly a thousand days and nights. His willpower must have been as ferocious then as his talent for survival was to be twenty years later. He had now lost not only Jill, Isabel, the rustic idyll and the job he had loved best: he had also lost the greatest love of his life, booze. On the *Sporting Life* he had specialised in writing about losing. Now he was to write about it all the time, in the *New Statesman* and the *Sunday Times* and wherever he could find an outlet. Now he was living losing: he had indeed become the prophet of loss.

By the end of May 1974 he was being paid £40 per article by the *New Statesman*, the same amount that they were paying Auberon Waugh, and Bernard was fluttering his journalistic wings nicely.

He was in fact so confident of his new determination not to drink that in May he started a six-week spell as a barman at Gerry's Club and was appalled by the drunkenness of the customers, their self-pity and the banality of their conversations. He wrote in the *New Statesman* that he was shocked to realise that this was what he had once been like and swore that he would never drink again. He went to Ireland for the Galway Oyster Festival and drank nothing but Coca-Cola. He was best man at Bunny May's wedding in December and attended his bachelor night with the actor John Alderton, and sipped soft drinks. It was a truly heroic effort.

The lack of booze did not seem to impair his wit. 'If you think that astrology is nothing more than a load of old nonsense,' he wrote in the *New Statesman* in August, 'how do you account for the fact that Edward Heath and Barbara Cartland share the same birthday?' He went on in the same article to mention that in 1876 the jockey Fred Archer had blown his brains out at Newmarket and added: 'Knowing the place pretty well I suspect he was trying to attract the attention of the staff in the Rutland Hotel.'

His spell as a non-drinking barman at Gerry's Club, a basement dive in Shaftesbury Avenue which was owned by

Bunny May, was the most extraordinary test of his willpower. 'He was a bit censorious about people getting pissed,' said May. 'It was not the ideal place for somebody to be on the wagon. It was a hole in the ground, sometimes known as Losers' Lounge, and had a lot of actors and writers getting extremely pissed. They were rat-arsed when *we* got them. God knows where they'd been before. Keith Waterhouse was a regular. He and his writing partner Willis Hall had an office across the road and they'd go in there with every intention of working, then they'd start doing the rounds, so by half past five when we opened, Keith and Willis would come in, flying, but they'd do another three or four hours in our place.'

It was in Gerry's Club one December night that Keith Waterhouse dropped in, at the end of what had obviously been a marathon pubcrawl, on his way home with a Christmas tree that was seriously inebriated. Waterhouse had been getting the tree as drunk as any giggly little Christmas secretary in club after club, first by pouring pints of Guinness over its roots and then by treating it to champagne. In one club Waterhouse decided that the tree should be made a member, so it was given a membership card. In another club the tree was refused admission because it was not wearing a tie, so Waterhouse purchased a tie and draped it about the upper branches. By now the drink was going to the tree's head, its branches were wilting, and in all those dingy little clubs it was probably also beginning to suffer from Santa Claustrophobia. By the time the tree arrived at Gerry's Club it was very much the worse for wear, decked out as it was with ties, membership cards and awash with Guinness and champagne. 'And then,' said Bunny May, 'Keith was ordering brandy, *mixing the tree's drinks*, and of course it was getting more and more battered and soon it was a wreck.'

The new, improved, sober Bernard, faced regularly with similar lunatic, drunken behaviour, began to become as quiet and thin-lipped behind the bar as any of his own disapproving

wives. He could be as bitchy as any woman, too. When one
pretty young actress who was often out of work landed a small
part in a television play and was making quite a theatrical exit
as she left the club, calling to everyone 'bye-bye, bye-bye' as
she went up the stairs, Bernard looked up from the bar and
cried: 'Oh, off home, are you, darling? Off home to learn
your line?' He even disapproved when he discovered that
Bunny May was having an affair with a friend's wife. 'He
said it was bad form,' said May. 'One night in the club he
was so miserable that I cheered him up by giving him my
girlfriend for the night. She was very pretty. I just told her
to go home with Jeffrey and be nice to him. She did. She
always did what she was told.'

Mike Molloy remembered that in Gerry's Club the sober
Bernard was wonderfully patronising towards anyone who
had had a few drinks: 'He would be slightly bored by us
laughing uproariously with the same conversations going
round and round in a circle. He could be very morose.' Bill
Hagerty was less charitable than Molloy: 'Jeffrey became
insufferable. He was so sanctimonious. Keith Waterhouse
does a wonderful impression of Jeffrey saying, "Haven't you
got no homes to go to? Get out of here, it's closing time." He
hated it when people around him were drinking. He was much
better when he was drinking in there on the other side of the
bar, when John le Mesurier was in there and John Junkin
and Molloy and I and we didn't go home nearly as much
as we should have done and he was always good company.'
Even Frank Norman's understanding wife Geraldine found
Bernard 'extremely tiresome' when he was on the wagon:
'There was this dark, angry, sober face behind the bar, deeply
disapproving. He's very puritan about anything that he isn't
doing himself at the time.'

In desperation he tried to fill his days. He wrote as
much as he could for the *Sunday Times* – where Bruce was
now picture editor on the colour magazine – as well as a
regular Saturday feature for Mike Molloy, who was now the
Editor of the *Daily Mirror* and explained why neither he nor

any other editor ever gave Bernard a full-time staff job: 'He clearly cannot take any form of imposed discipline or authority. He cannot join a company where there are parameters of behaviour, and everyone thought there'd come a time when it all had to end with Jeff and in those days it was very difficult to fire anyone, there was a very powerful NUJ, and it was like tenure for life. Nobody ever took Jeff on the staff because they feared he'd be a liability. Dear old Eric Wainwright didn't do a feature for ten years: he was something of a hero of Jeff's.' When Wainwright finally left the *Mirror*, he remarked to his colleagues at his farewell party how nice it was to meet them all.

Jeff still gambled and went racing, which was as important to him as the conquest of women and curiously connected. In his brown John Menzies Exercise Book all the Grand National winners (and sometimes Derby winners too) are listed from 1958 to 1974 – and beside them, like fillies frolicking in the starting stalls, are the names of whichever wives or mistresses were around at the time. One entry, for instance, says: '1959 . . . Oxo . . . Pebmarsh . . . Marsh'. 1964 says: 'Team Spirit . . . Northern Heights . . . Jacki.' 1973 notes poignantly: 'Red Rum . . . Chelsworth . . . Jill left.'

He played cricket too, sometimes for the *New Statesman*, and once bowled Michael Foot out during a match in Hampstead. He took up housework. And he started to cling to Isabel, who was now five, spending long, wet, desperate, Sunday afternoons in the park or at the zoo, the usual lonely weekend purgatory of the divorced father. 'I was sad to lose Isabel,' he told me. 'It was the first time I'd ever had a home unit. I was never enemies with Jill: I had access to Isabel and every time I took her out for a day it used to make me feel terribly sad when I had to return her in the late afternoon. It was awful. It nearly broke my fucking heart.' Later he admitted that he and Isabel had been very awkward together when he started exercising access rights when she was about six. 'We were embarrassed by each other,' he said. 'It was obviously difficult for her, with a strange man coming out of the blue

once a month to take her to the fucking zoo, and I didn't know
what to say to her.' When Isabel came to spend the day with
him in June 1976, he considered it suitable entertainment for
a six-year-old girl to spend the afternoon watching ten horse
races on television.

To fill his teetotal days he embarked yet again on the
hopeless task of trying to write his autobiography and sent
this letter to the *New Statesman*: 'I have been commissioned
by Michael Joseph to write my autobiography, and I would
be grateful to any of your readers who could tell me what
I was doing between 1960 and 1974.' This inspired a reply
from Mike Molloy that read:

> Dear Mr Bernard,
>   I read with interest your letter asking for informa-
> tion as to your behaviour and whereabouts between the
> years 1960 and 1974. On a certain evening in September
> 1969, you rang my mother to inform her that you were
> going to murder her only son. If you would like further
> information, I can put you in touch with many people
> who have enjoyed similar bizarre experiences in your
> company.
>   Yours sincerely,
>   Michael Molloy
>   Editor
>   Daily Mirror

There were also several letters from people claiming that
Bernard owed them money, and another from a woman in
Toronto announcing that she had given birth to twins after
enjoying moments of ecstasy with him at the last Chelsea
Arts Ball. Reporting this, the Atticus column of the *Sunday
Times* called him 'one of the funniest writers we have in this
country today' and said that he was 'elusively touched by
genius'. One does not have to be of a particularly suspicious
cast of mind to wonder whether this eulogy might have been
written by Allan Hall or even possibly by Bernard himself.
He was also quoted in the Atticus column as saying: 'I've

always criticised autobiographers for not telling the truth. I now wonder how honest I can be myself.'

Despite all this activity, despite all these busy attempts to find something to do now that he had given up drinking, he was miserable. He needed alcohol to fill and fuel his life and give it some sort of tipsy-turvey meaning. He kept a diary in 1975 and wrote in it on 4 April: 'I find it almost impossible to believe that anyone can be as unhappy as I am. Can misery cause insanity? Saved by a 32–1 double at Sandown Park.' In June he was so certain that he had beaten the booze for ever that he published a self-lacerating series in the *Daily Mirror* about his fight against alcoholism. It was illustrated by a large picture of him, captioned 'Bernard the Sober', looking into the camera. He was sober, maybe, but the picture was haunted, perhaps by memories of drunken camaraderie, and the eyes looked dead.

It was about now that Francis Bacon took him out to lunch and enquired: 'Now that you've lost your looks, Jeffrey, what are you going to do?' But Bacon could not have been less perceptive, for the forty-three-year-old Bernard was about to embark on one of the genuine love affairs of his life, with Juliet Simpkins, the twenty-eight-year-old Madame Tussaud's PR girl whom he wanted eventually to make his fourth wife. For him that summer of 1975 was a burst of lustful middle-aged glory. 'She made me laugh more than any woman I've met in my life,' he told me. 'We were always laughing. We met the day Nocturnal Spree won the Two Thousand Guineas.'

They met in the French Pub. 'He has a devastating way of making you aware of him if you're a woman,' she remembered in 1992. 'For me, it was him standing, saying absolutely nothing, just simply staring, really laser-beam staring and I found it absolutely nerve-wracking. He can be quite frightening, somewhat daunting. He was irresistible, unbelievably good-looking. Those blue eyes. He used to look absolutely tremendous. After he stood and stared the *Observer* ran a piece on him and there was a terrific picture of him and I thought how on earth am I going to get to know him better?

So I wrote to him. At that time Madame Tussaud's owned an attraction called Wookey Hole, a cave in Somerset, and I asked him if he'd be interested in writing something about Wookey Hole. He was working for Atticus and he wasn't interested in Wookey Hole but he remembered me and took me out to lunch.'

She was to spend the rest of 1975 with him (and much of 1976) revelling in 'that wonderful hot summer in 1975 which actually made it rather more romantic. He wasn't drinking and had been told that if you can crack three years then you're over the hump. He was incredibly strong-minded about it. I lived with him for three or four nights a week. I was absolutely nuts about him. Even though he was miserable he was so interesting. Women are always attracted to men who make them laugh. Not drinking brought out the best and the worst in him, the best being that he was clear-headed, extremely witty, and had a deal more energy.' She too found that he objected strongly to people drinking when he was not: 'He would stand in the pub with a Perrier staring at people and saying, "Sex should be banned amongst ugly people. I mean, look at that couple over there. Can you imagine them *doing* it?" He was miserable but still very amusing. We were both good mimics. He drank gallons of tea at the time, he had a pot constantly on the go, and coffee, and Perrier. It was awful for him. We didn't go out much but that was quite convenient because he was television critic for the *Spectator*. That job at that time fitted in perfectly because he had to watch a lot of television.'

He was undoubtedly serious about Juliet. 'At that time he was more conscious than ever of setting up a home,' she said. 'He said to my mother I should really at my age have 2.4 children, be living in a leafy suburb and mowing the lawn on Saturdays. He was watching me mowing at the time, you see!'

Some things of course never changed, even though he was now teetotal. 'Even when he wasn't drinking he was gambling heavily,' said Juliet, 'and he went into hospital several times

while he was with me. On one occasion he was in the Royal
Free and Fenella Fielding was sitting there gazing at him.'

It was now that he discovered that he had diabetes, when
the *Sunday Times Magazine* sent him to write an article about
the BUPA health screening tests. He took all the tests and
was told that he had sugar in his urine and was a diabetic.
'That was the first I knew of it,' said Bernard. 'I'd had the
symptoms before without realising it: fatigue, crashing out in
the afternoon and tremendous thirst. I don't like beer but I
used to drink pints of it – your body wants that to flush the
sugar out of the system.' His diabetes was a distant result of
that mad whisky-drinking binge with Robert Colquhoun and
Robert McBryde in Ireland ten years previously, in 1965,
when he had collapsed with chronic pancreatitis and had been
rushed to St Stephen's hospital in Chelsea. His destruction of
his pancreas had stopped the pancreas making insulin.

After that it seemed particularly unfair that he should
have been sacked from the *Sunday Times Magazine* by its
new Editor, Hunter Davies, who had succeeded Magnus
Linklater and discovered that several writers, Bernard and
the travel writer Bruce Chatwin among them, had freelance
contracts. Bernard was paid £2,000 a year not to write for
any other Sunday paper, plus a fee for each article. 'What's
that worth today?' Hunter Davies asked me in 1992. '£12,000?
I admired his stuff but he hadn't written anything for ages.
He said, "I'm ill." I said, "Do a piece on being ill." He said,
"I'm too ill to write it." But he wasn't too ill to go drinking
and eating in Soho. I didn't renew his contract.'

Help, however, was at hand. At the end of 1975 Alexander
Chancellor became the Editor of the *Spectator* and was determined to hire good writers to increase the 12,000 sales to
nearer the 40,000 that the *New Statesman* sold each week. He
was persuaded by his Assistant Editor, Geoffrey Wheatcroft,
to poach Bernard from the *New Statesman* and hire him as
television critic for £30 a week. Just as Hunter Davies was
deciding that Bernard was not worth hiring at all, Chancellor was about to take him on to the magazine that was to

allow him at last to blossom and make his name and become famous. He had no difficulty in tempting Bernard from the *New Statesman* because he was offering regular weekly employment instead of erratic occasional work. The *Spectator* also paid promptly. 'I used to have a policy on the *Spectator*,' Chancellor explained. 'We paid so badly that we paid immediately, which proved very successful with someone like Jeffrey. We'd mail the magazine and the cheque on the Thursday to the authors. It was very good psychologically and made up for paying them badly.' An added attraction was that the Editor of the *New Statesman*, Anthony Howard, would regularly make Bernard rewrite his articles before he would publish them, whereas Alexander Chancellor's approach to editorship was much more relaxed – or 'slightly bizarre', as Dick West, who was lured to the *Spectator* at the same time, put it: 'The *Spectator* was edited in a shambolic way, completely instinctively, over many drinks in the pub. It was very fluid.' Dick West used to joke that Alexander Chancellor's typical day as Editor of the *Spectator* began thus:

10.55 Arrive at Office
11.00 Lose article by Solzhenitsyn
11.05 To pub for gin and tonic

Bernard's first television review for the *Spectator* appeared on 24 January 1976 and he began in typically mischievous mood: '*Poldark* always brought me down and back to earth after the soul searching I do during *Songs of Praise*, when I wonder each week whether I might not have made a colossal mistake in being an agnostic. Closeups of the twin-setted girls who sing in church choirs lead me to believe that there might be more in church than meets the mind.' The following week he was goading the book programme presenter Melvyn Bragg, who 'is fast becoming the André Previn of paperbacks, and since André Previn is already the Michael Parkinson of music we don't want that to happen, do we? No.' Bragg was to become one of his regular butts, along with Andrea Newman, the author of steamy television love dramas. Bernard attacked

Bragg week after week with such relentless scorn that a year later the *Spectator* had to publish an apology for an 'offensive and defamatory' article by Bernard in the previous issue 'which, if taken literally, would imply that Mr Bragg had improperly exploited his position as a broadcaster'.

This sort of knockabout stuff went down very well at the *Daily Express*, where Bernard was hired in April (after he had spent ten days in hospital) to write a television column each Saturday. A month later he was also writing a general feature for the *Express* (about drinking, of course) and book reviews for the *Spectator* (about racing). On top of that he was writing a regular racing column for *Pacemaker and Horseman* magazine, all of which should have been quite enough to keep him busy and out of trouble.

But just as his journalistic career was beginning to blossom his affair with Juliet Simpkins was about to end. Juliet was one of the few women who were really important in his life, so much so that in April of that year, 1976, he asked her to marry him. 'I can remember the very words,' she told me. 'It was typical Jeff. He turned the telly off and we were having yet another cup of tea and we were both sitting on the sofa and he said, "I suppose you'd never consider marrying me, would you?" For Jeff that was a proposal. At Easter that year I thought about it very carefully, but I found it difficult to imagine being married and making the commitment because I could see how men were naturally polygamous and I didn't want to be part of that sort of relationship. But I also thought I can't possibly continue with Jeffrey if I don't actually take that step. I thought I had to end it. There was no way we could go on with that hanging in the air unanswered. We separated a few days after that.'

He was distraught. Later he would claim that the affair had ended because he didn't have enough money to give her the sort of life she wanted. 'She's not grasping,' he told me, 'but it must be very boring for a woman like that to be with a chap who's never got a fucking penny. I was very skint then, getting only £30 an article.' He was to write later of his 'miserable spell of celibacy during the long, hot summer of 1976 which was the result of a certain temporary loss of self-confidence and shortage of moving around money'.

He was so miserable that he could no longer stand going without alcohol. The loss was too much to bear. He abandoned the valiant struggle on 14 June. 'The day I cracked,' he told me, 'I called round to my best friend, Eva Johansen, and we cracked a bottle of scotch.' Then they went to the Dover Castle pub, met Frank Norman and drank more whisky. After two-and-a-half teetotal years he drank a bottle of scotch in a few hours. It is astonishing that it did not kill him. He certainly thought he was about to die when he came around the next morning. Frank Norman took him to breakfast at the Connaught.

A dozen years later Bernard explained to Dan Farson why he had finally succumbed, for good this time, to the fatal embrace of alcohol. 'I've never met such boring people as my friends when I was sober,' he said, 'never been so miserable or so lonely.' Allan Hall remembered seeing him a month previously in the French pub, where Bernard still went to sip soft drinks and torment himself by watching others drink: 'I bought him a soda-water and said, "I do admire you, it must be two years now that you've been on the wagon" and Jeffrey said, "Two years three months one week four days. God." ' Bernard's fellow Soho alcoholic Martin Tomkinson, who had just met him and was later to turn teetotal for good when his doctor told him he was killing himself, understood better than most the empty feeling of loss, the desperation of *grieving* for the loss of alcohol, that Bernard had suffered for those two and a half years. 'When Jeff went back to drinking,' said Tomkinson, 'he took his decision and made his bed and said it's this now till I die.' Not surprisingly Bernard was quite incapable of writing his *Spectator* column that week. Five days later, on 19 June, there appeared for the first time a small italic line at the bottom of page 29 that read: 'Jeffrey Bernard is ill.' It was not to be the last time by any means, but eventually the formula was to be altered to read, more accurately with its hint of self-inflicted pain: 'Jeffrey Bernard is unwell.'

Whatever damage his resumption of drinking was doing to his health, it had little lasting effect on his sex appeal. He was still so startlingly attractive that he caught the eye of the glamorous redheaded actress Adrienne Corri and consoled himself briefly with the Australian journalist Jill Neville, a friend of Elizabeth Smart and the sister of Richard Neville, who had founded the mischievous *Oz* magazine. Jill Neville first glimpsed Bernard through the open door of the York Minster, the French pub. 'He was unbelievably handsome and attractive, like a *film noir* hero, a bit like the John Garfield he always admired,' she told me in 1992. 'But he was posing nevertheless and I recognised that and chuckled. Our affair was such a brief butterfly thing that lasted about three weeks. He was going grey but he was probably chasing seven other women at the same time. "You're a knockout," he said to me that summer when I was feeling very low indeed. In the course of those turbulent three weeks he phoned late one night and proposed marriage to my husband under the impression he was talking to me. The ex did not take this at all well. But it ended as suddenly as it began.'

His resumed drinking seemed to affect his writing as little as it had dented his sex appeal. His general articles for the *Daily Express* were so successful that in mid-July he stopped writing television reviews and started a general weekly column with a big picture byline, 'Jeffrey Bernard on Saturday', in which he attacked awful pubs, the residents of Eastbourne, dieting, the cost of philandering, bores, scientists, and living in the country. Ah yes, and in an article about gambling he told yet again the story of the Great Battersea Cat Race. The article about Eastbourne attracted an avalanche of angry letters from admirers of the town, including an exceedingly rash one from a sixty-eight-year-old woman who declared: 'I am classed as a geriatric . . . but I will drink you under the table any day.'

Alexander Chancellor eventually replaced Bernard as his television critic for the understandable reason that 'he never watched television because he was always too pissed. It became more and more of a strain for him. But he was very popular and we liked him and it was very important to keep him, it was just a question of what he should do.'

So once again Bernard was writing about racing. Once again he was traipsing around the racecourses – Ascot, Newbury, Kempton – and the new job can hardly have helped his drinking even though he was now trying to stick to white wine because it was less harmful than spirits. In September he was heavily back on the booze at Peter Walwyn's Lambourn Lurcher Show lunch and at the Irish St Leger, in October at the Newmarket Sales. He was reckless, too, in writing openly about the illegal tax-free bets he was taking in the pub and mentioned them twice before the end of the year. Ten years later the law was finally to catch up with him and he seemed genuinely baffled as to how the authorities could possibly have found out about it.

Racing still gave him that buzz of adrenalin that held him in thrall for so long and he was thrilled when his trainer friend Doug Marks put his name down as the owner of a syndicated chestnut yearling filly and allowed him to choose the horse's name. Bernard did so with relish and a great delight in the cleverness of his choice. The filly was by Shiny Tenth out of Elm Leaf, so Bernard called her Deciduous. In December he was writing in the *Spectator*: 'I went down to Lambourn to see my trainer last week. God, how I've wanted to be able to say that.'

Meanwhile, despite flings with other women, he was still tormented by jealousy over Juliet Simpkins. 'After we'd split up,' she said, 'I went into the French with Bruce for a drink, perfectly innocently, and Jeffrey took one look at Bruce and one look at me – Bruce had just had a hernia operation which made the whole thing even worse – and Jeffrey came up and just rammed his fist into Bruce's stomach. I got out.' Jeffrey was still utterly miserable and on 28 October he wrote in his very occasional diary: 'When a woman says she wants or likes having you as a friend it means she just doesn't fancy you. How awful to be thought sexually safe.' The next day he noted: 'Loneliness a little better today. Cold gone. Launderette.'

Ironically it was his drinking again that persuaded Juliet to return to him at the end of the year. 'He used to ring my mother at about half-past eight at night,' she explained, 'and he'd obviously been drinking again and he'd say, "I love her." I was less anxious with him when he started drinking again. When he wasn't his moods were so exaggerated: when he was down the degree of unhappiness and withdrawal and lack of communication and irascibility was nerve-wracking.'

He was awfully pleased to have Juliet back, of course, but he was not going to let it cramp his style. On Christmas Day he celebrated her return by ravishing the daughter of the landlord of the Swiss Tavern on the floor of the saloon bar after lunch while the landlord went upstairs for a nap.

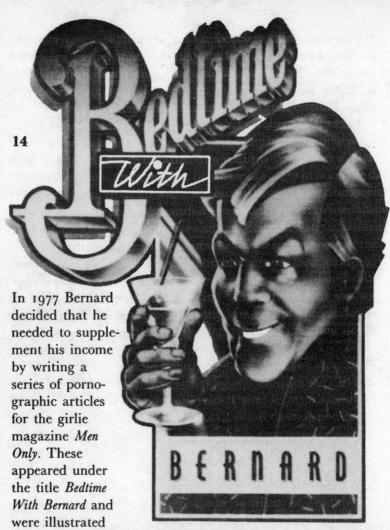

Bedtime With Bernard

14

In 1977 Bernard decided that he needed to supplement his income by writing a series of pornographic articles for the girlie magazine *Men Only*. These appeared under the title *Bedtime With Bernard* and were illustrated by a drawing of him wearing long Sixties sideboards, looking like a lounge lizard and gazing with a lecherous sneer into a cocktail glass containing – of course – a cherry. The illustration made him look unfortunately like a second-hand car salesman and although the magazine referred to him as 'our stud' and 'Soho's most rampageous man about town' and the articles were very explicit, particularly about his taste for cunnilingus, they were curiously unerotic. His heart (if you will pardon the word) was not in it. Fifteen years later he was embarrassed to have these old articles unearthed and pleaded as his excuse that he had needed the money desperately at the time. 'God, you're not going to mention *those*, are you?' he said. 'I only wrote them because they paid immediately, cash on the table, bang.'

When it came to lengths the articles were among the longest he had ever written and some of their lines deserve to become classics of the genre: 'Ann was her name and, although she was just simply attractive, she made it really jump about in my trousers.' He wrote about every sexual quirk from fellatio to masturbation and was such a connoisseur of cunnilingus that he issued a warning about the pungency of redheads, whom he claimed should be consumed only with plentiful supplies of brown bread and butter. 'I got an amazing response,' he told me. 'I got stacks of letters from husbands agreeing with me.' He was also quite shameless in openly using his experiences even with his wives and those of his mistresses whom he later claimed to have loved. He hardly bothered to camouflage any of them but simply stripped them naked for the sweaty readers of *Men Only*. Anyone who knew any of his women at all would have been able to identify them. His first night with his third wife Jill, for instance, was described in explicit lewd detail, though he did change her name to Betty.

Some of the experiences he claimed seem extremely unlikely. One of his conquests, apparently, was a 'very grand' black bus conductress who woke him at the bus depot in Battersea after he had become drunk and had fallen asleep on her bus, took him back to her bedsitter and violated him. This must have taken place no more than a few hundred yards from the venue of the Great Battersea Cat Race. In the same month it seems that he also enjoyed the intimate attentions of 'an Australian intellectual' (not you, doctor) as well as 'an American nut case', a 'nice English girl', 'an East End girl with a father fixation' and an 'upper class' girl who distressed Bernard by screaming that she was on her way. One paramour, Ann, was apparently always ready on her back on

the floor of her flat in case Bernard should call. This appears
from internal evidence to have been the same Ann who once
developed a bruised jaw due to her serious interest in fellatio.
He even claimed that in Suffolk he had debauched the vicar's
daughter in church while she was playing a thunderous Bach
climax on her father's organ.

So how much of all this tawdry sleaze by the Soho
Simenon was just fantasy? One of his *Men Only* articles which
was surely quite untrue claimed that he had been seduced at
the age of twelve by a beautiful blonde German woman in her
mid-thirties who invited him in when he stood on her doorstep
singing carols just before Christmas in 1944 in Holland Park.
She was of course wearing a silk dressing gown, black knickers
and sexy stockings. Hello, Marlene. Bernard never explained
what a German woman was doing in Holland Park during the
Second World War and never referred to this incident in any
of his other writings. He went on in that *Men Only* article to
claim that on the day after his encounter with the luscious
blonde, on Christmas Eve, he went to Harrods, where Santa
Claus invited him into the fairy grotto and placed a special
Christmas present in Jeffrey's hand: Santa's massive erection.
'Talk about a baby's arm with an orange in its fist,' wrote
Bernard. 'No wonder he couldn't get down chimneys and had
to work in a shop!' Bernard apparently fled and returned to
the Nazi blonde for second helpings. This time it seems she
was wearing a dressing gown and leather boots. Hitler would
have been proud of her.

Bernard was often amusing about sex – 'It is, after all, an
extraordinary way to say Hallo to another human being,' he
once wrote in the *Spectator* – and his own theory of successful
seduction was simple. 'Women don't care very much what
you look like,' he told me. 'If you can make them laugh you
can lower their knickers. A friend of mine said rather naively,
but I think he was right: "You can get any woman to bed
as long as you ask nicely." It's not very difficult if you work
at it. You can almost wear them down, but I'm too lazy for
that. If a woman doesn't go to bed with me immediately I

think she's a bad judge and mad. That's the vanity I've got. If I'm not good enough they must be certifiable.'

Another useful ploy was to let his intended know that he was sterile, which made her feel safe and meant that he never had to fiddle about with contraceptives, which were never the most appealing aids to romance. The story of his sterility was in fact true, perhaps because of the two operations on his penis that Dora had forced him to undergo when he was twelve. He could also rely on rumours of his impotence to excite any woman who was game for a challenge, and impotence did indeed plague him all his life, not surprisingly considering the amount he drank.

He tended in fact to prefer women who liked a challenge. 'I can't bear The Girl Next Door type,' he told me, 'and I can think of two Girls Next Door whom I couldn't fuck to save my life, straight out of *Playboy* magazine: Marilyn Monroe and Brigitte Bardot. They had no brains and they offered no threat. I like danger. I like to get the adrenalin going. I like a woman who's a challenge and tough but witty. I bet Marilyn Monroe couldn't tell a joke to save her fucking life. I had a couple of very ugly ones when I was very young and there was nothing else and I was very lonely and desperate – but no, I've been very lucky and had a lot of attractive women. Nonentities but attractive ones.'

According to Irma Kurtz there was always about Bernard a bewildered Little Boy Lost air, a Peter Pan appeal, that excited the mothering instincts of all sorts of women, who often thought they could sort him out or even reform him. They never did and they never learned from the failures of all those women who had come before. Bernard denied that he had always played on this Little Boy Lost look of his. 'I'm very grateful if that comes over,' he told me, 'but I promise you it's not intentional. It never has been. In fact I always wanted to be the opposite: John Wayne or Clint Eastwood instead of the little boy lost. I can't imagine Clint Eastwood lost, can you?'

There was certainly never any doubt about Bernard's charm. Even the craggy and not noticeably romantic landlord of the Coach and Horses, Norman Balon, spotted it. 'He's got a personality which can charm women from one end of the bar to the other,' Balon told me with a touch of envy. 'He has an amazing facility with women. I can always remember one occasion when he was standing at one end of the bar and some nurse looked in and she just glanced at him and in two minutes time she was round the other side of the bar and having a drink with him and the next thing I knew they were living together.'

The question every man will want to ask, after learning that Bernard managed to seduce five hundred women, is this: *was he actually any good in bed?* 'I don't think any of his women will remember him for his qualities as a great lover,' Irma Kurtz reported from the bottlefront. 'It's other things you'd remember Jeff for. I don't think the women who have had Jeffrey as a lover would remember him for his actual qualities in bed, his prowess. I think they'd remember him for making them laugh and for being terribly flirtatious in a way that didn't stop.'

In fact it seems that the thrill of the chase was always more important for Bernard than the consummation of an affair. 'Once I've fucked someone,' he said, 'I'm like a hero in the Bomb Disposal unit: I've de-fused an enemy and we can now be friends. Because *before* you fuck someone – God, the feminists would kill me for saying this – there is *tension* because every woman is a potential fuck. But being older and wiser I've suddenly realised it might have been the other way round, that *they* were de-fusing *me*.'

He would certainly treat women often as though they were the enemy. One of the few occasions on which I wrote something that made him laugh – he was not a great laugher, preferring the wry smile – was when I wrote in the *Sunday Express* that he had 'had a lot of wives, four of them his own'. It was of course true. Bernard had never had any compunction about seducing even the wives of his best friends. The wife of one of his oldest friends once treated him many years ago to what she described as 'a sympathy fuck' and regretted it ever after. 'He's a little shit,' she told another mutual friend afterwards. 'He always bit the hand that fed him.' Another old friend who had better remain anonymous once buttonholed Bernard during a drunken pub session and said: 'All right, Jeffrey, I know: you've fucked my wife, haven't you?'

'Yes,' said Bernard, 'and your mother and daughter as well.'

He could also be unattractively ungallant towards his lovers. He always kissed and told, which would never have gone down well in the Mess at Pangbourne, and he would sometimes jeer in a most unpleasant fashion even at the women he pretended to love. When he was with Juliet Simpkins he would refer sneeringly to Jean Marsh as 'Hatchet Face', but behind Juliet's back he would dismiss her to another mistress as 'The Wax Woman' because she worked at Madame Tussaud's.

It was Finola Morgan, the last of the Great Bernardine Handmaidens, who came up with one of the most intriguing theories about Bernard's sexuality, especially considering his reputation as a macho man, a male chauvinist pig. 'He's passive,' she told me. 'He waits for somebody else to do it. It's a very feminine trait, and he'd *like* to be a woman. He imagines that if you're a woman that all these jobs are done for you, that men will run around and do them for you. His favourite film is *An Officer and a Gentleman* and I'll tell you why. He identifies with Debra Winger because if he and I watch the film together we both think, "One day my prince will come and take me away from all this." Jeffrey dreams that someone else will sort it out for him and take him away from all this and it'll all be all right. When he had his last birthday party at Geraldine Norman's and there was an overspill from his room into Geraldine's sitting room, corridor and kitchen and the place was throbbing with a great Soho hubbub, above this hubbub Jeffrey's voice rose: "I wish *I* had a cunt." He was very wistful and loud. What he means is that he thinks the world would be his oyster. He's got an old-fashioned Hollywood view of what it would be like as a woman.'

His other great love of the mid-1980s, Deirdre Redgrave, seemed to agree with this revealing assessment of Bernard's femininity when she told me: 'I wouldn't call him a passive tart, exactly, but he said something to me which makes a lot of sense. This was some time ago, after we were together, he said, "I don't go to parties any more because the only point in going to a party is to meet somebody unbelievably interesting and seductive and then have an affair with them", which I tend to agree with. He was always on the lookout for ego reassurance.' It is also, without any doubt, the approach of a woman.

Marsh Dunbar went even further. Remembering the affair she had had with Bernard in 1959 she said: 'He'd revert into a baby, clinging on to you, not being a lover but pleading *look after me*. It was complete self-pity and sentimentality.' This did not sound much like *Men Only*'s ideal 'stud' and 'most rampageous man about town'.

'I think I have a clue as to why he's so self-destructive,' Deirdre Redgrave told me. 'He always told me, "My trouble is that I'm in love with my mother."' Indeed, Bernard admitted himself in a startlingly honest spoof obituary in the *Spectator* in 1978 that it was quite possible that his life 'was a never ending cliché of a search for his mother'. In 1989 he confessed to Martyn Harris of the *Sunday Telegraph*: 'I found her very difficult to cope with. Mothers are supposed to be rather small and dumpy with grey hair, but she looked like Sophia Loren, and I found that very disturbing. I actually fancied her when I was sixteen, so I had an enormous amount of guilt about that . . . She was irreplaceable. It's why I've had so many girlfriends and wives I suppose. I've never found her again since she died.'

Bernard denied that he had married women who looked like Dora. 'None of my wives looked like my mother,' he said. 'Hollywood films in the war, plus my mother, somehow contrived to involve me in a sartorial time-warp so that I've always liked glamorous, well-dressed filmstars. Deirdre

Redgrave, for example: in my brief affair with her I used to have the odd argument with her because I insisted that she looked like a fucking animated jumble sale. She looked awful, and I always liked Rita Hayworths, Ava Gardners, like poor old Mum, who was a bit like that. So I've never been attracted to badly presented women.'

Irma Kurtz, the magazine agony aunt, should perhaps have one of the last words on the question of Bernard's sexuality. 'On the one hand he lacks self-confidence,' she told me, 'on the other hand he thinks he's pretty damned great. I think it's got to do with being the baby son of a doting mother, or something. I think his mother possibly wanted a girl and really babied the last one, because there is in Jeff something that's both the favourite son and the neglected child and I don't understand it except that she died when he was young.'

Jill Neville, who had had a fling with Bernard in 1976, came up with the most intriguing theory of all about Bernard's sexuality. 'He had a thing about salmon-pink underwear,' she told me in 1992. 'He remembers sitting in his mother's dressing room in Covent Garden a lot and she had this very 1930s salmon-pink underwear. After years of observing and talking to Jeff and Bruce I developed a theory that these boys were so in love with their mother that even after she died they had to walk round and round and round the square mile around Covent Garden, and they still do. It was the Enchanted Wood. It was an eroticism that went on between mother and sons, not particularly physical but very Oedipal.'

Perhaps that was it. Perhaps that was why all his life he could never really escape the neighbourhood of Soho and Covent Garden because that was Mummy's Enchanted Wood, and there you could still find Cinderella's Coach and Horses, and most girls turned out in the end to be wicked witches.

And that's enough bedtime stories. No, they didn't all live happily ever after.

15

Ashley and Colonel Mad

Bernard seemed to be suddenly struck by the Old Testament gifts of tongues and prophecy when he wrote his first article of 1977 for his 'Jeffrey Bernard on Saturday' column in the *Daily Express*. 'It's . . . on the cards that I'll fall in love in the spring,' he wrote on 8 January, 'and that's a form of temporary insanity that could keep me away from the office for anything up to six months.' Was that remarkable prescience, or was he simply determined to find some unfortunate woman to marry? However it happened, he found her three months later, in the spring as he had prophesied. The unlucky lady was Sue Ashley – he was always to call her Ashley rather than Sue – and he was to pursue her relentlessly with his dogged devotion until she succumbed. She struggled and wriggled, and tried to escape her fate, and broke off the affair, but a year later, mesmerised into submission, she became the fourth and last Mrs Jeffrey Bernard.

Their love story began thanks to a most unlikely Cupid, Richard Ingrams, the Editor of the scurrilous fortnightly scandal rag *Private Eye*, who wanted to start a racing column in the *Eye* and asked a mutual acquaintance, the cartoonist Michael Heath, to introduce him to Bernard. Ingrams was so keen to meet Bernard that he was even persuaded to go to the French, into which he had never deigned to venture before. Bernard agreed to produce a fortnightly column but first wrote for *Private Eye* a 'letter from Soho' that was published on 29 April under the pseudonym Spoofer. In it he wrote: 'More frequently seen in Soho these days is cartoonist Michael Heath. He was last seen holding a conversation in the gutter in Old Compton Street with the Pernod-addicted hack Jeffrey Bernard. He in turn is reported to be love-sick over one Sue Ashley, an advertising worker and Wine Bar habituée. Will these two pathetic men ever pull themselves together?' Sue was intrigued. Who was this pathetic Pernod-addicted hack who apparently fancied her rotten? She was already hooked. Within a few days Bernard was reeling her in.

In a Soho restaurant, the Paparazzi in Dean Street, he had spotted no more than her legs, adorned with nylon stockings and a pair of high-heeled, ankle-strap shoes, sticking out from a table around a corner but he had vowed immediately that he would get to know this girl and go to bed with her. *Men Only* would have been proud of him. He discovered her name, wrote the article, and a mutual acquaintance, Jim Baker, introduced them one night in a wine bar. The 'Letter from Soho' was a novel but completely calculating and won-derfully successful seduction technique. 'Then I bought her the contents of a flower shop one day, when I was pissed,' he told me. 'Mind you, it was 3 in the afternoon and most of it was being sold cheaply, but it was still a lot of flowers! I had them sent round to her office. I was potty about her.'

Sue was twenty-nine, a producer of television commercials for a Soho production company, Jennie & Co, and had been living for five years in Chelsea with a fifty-seven-year-old American. But Bernard was relentless in his pursuit. He was forty-four, fifteen years older, but still determined to have her. By comparison with the American, he was a boy. A week earlier, even before meeting her, he had already begun to refer to Sue in his *Daily Express* column. The first occasion was on 22 April, when he was suggesting that men should keep women rather than dogs as pets: 'Women, let me tell you, have several and various advantages over dogs ... there are fields of domestic, sporting endeavour where women far outshine the ordinary dog.' A week later he was musing: 'The continuing search for Miss Right is an expen-sive affair – if affair is the right word.' On 17 June, by which time his *Daily Express* column was appearing every Friday, he reported that he had on the previous morning been playing the part of a live chess piece in a human game between the chess correspondents of the *Spectator* and the *New Statesman* in Lincoln's Inn Fields: 'Muggins here played a white knight on behalf of the *Spectator*, dressed in an extremely hot robe with a rather heavy papier mâché horse head on his head, and stood about being moved from here and there in unusual heat. I actually took a rather poker-faced bishop, then a succulent teenage pawn before I was nicked, but standing there in the gardens, being moved from square to square by my master, it did occur to me that we're all going quite bonkers. My life is crumbling around me – I'm in love and up to my eyeballs in debt – and I'm sure I'm not alone, and yet there I was involved in a farce worthy of the likes of Ivor Novello.'

'He was gorgeous,' sighed Sue in 1992, remembering those early days together. 'He looked lovely. He was a very handsome guy. But I must have been bloody mad. I did know him by sight already, I used to nod to him in the street for years around Soho when he had the moustache and he was quite chubby then, spivvy, with those white shoes and everything. Of course I couldn't resist meeting him, so we conducted this little affair while the man I was living with – Win Levine – was abroad. One night after Win had come back from one of his trips the bloody doorbell goes at 10.30 and it was Jeffrey there, drunk, saying "Howreyoudo. Mynamesheffrey Bernard and I'M IN LOVE with Sue" and I heard this and thought *shit!* and I came to the top of the stairs and saw Jeffrey standing there and Win turned and said, "D'you know this man, honey?" I said, "Well, we have met" and Win said to him "I think you'd better leave, it's half-past ten at night and you'd better go." Anyway, blow me, ten minutes later there's a knock on the door again and it's Jeffrey back saying, "I don't suppose I could have a drink, could I?" Can you beat it? So the next day I had to do a lot of explaining and I couldn't even go to the office and I had several phone calls from his various friends, like Eva, and Jeffrey then took an overdose and ended up in hospital.

'He was a nutcase, he *is* a nutcase. I mean, that's an unstable person. I knew it was dangerous and so many people said to me, "Go off and live with him, but *marrying* him, you must be nuts." I even had phone calls the night before we got married.'

She knew that he was trouble right from the start. He took her to dinner at Wheeler's in Old Compton Street. 'He slept through the whole meal, all the way through his plaice and chips until they went to take it away. I thought it was half funny but I was getting more and more angry, then he suddenly put up his head and said, "I'd like some sauce tartare, IF YOU DON'T MIND. I *am* sitting here waiting." And then he went down again. I walked out and left him there and got on the bus and went home.'

To add to Bernard's fun that spring his racing gossip column in *Private Eye* – mischievously entitled *Sporting Life* – was an immediate hit. It was written over the byline Colonel Mad, a pseudonym devised by Ingrams, with the help of the *Daily Express*'s tipster, 'The Scout', Charles Benson, and the remarkably well informed Lambourn bloodstock dealer Julian Lewis, who was better known as "Screamer" Lewis because his manic laugh resembled the screech of a rutting peacock. The first mischievous Colonel Mad column appeared on 27 May as it meant to go on, describing the trainer Peter Cundell as a 'ruddy-faced buffoon' and the racing adviser Michael Wale as 'a diminutive creep' who was 'never known to have bought a round'.

That Saturday Bernard took Isabel to Sandown Park races, where he introduced her to two publicans, one of them an ex-tic-tac man, who were floating their thirsts in their eighth bottle of Bollinger. The seven-year-old Isabel regarded them with an ancient expression. 'Actually,' she announced, 'I'm not supposed to have anything to do with people like you.' A fortnight later Bernard was emulating them by going to Ireland to write a column, popping into a pub for just the one, and not emerging for seven hours.

The Colonel Mad column quickly became notorious for its impish, irreverent in-joke snippets about racehorse trainers and their owners, jockeys, bloodstock agents, bookies, Turf journalists and other examples of racecourse wildlife, and for its naughty flirtation with the libel laws. Colonel Mad, whose identity was at first a secret, swiftly achieved cult status in the racing world, especially in the equine towns of Newmarket and Lambourn and among their horsey tribes of sinewy, rat-faced men in brown trilbies and fat-arsed rat-arsed women in stained jodhpurs. In the issue of 5 August 1977, for instance, the flavour of the Colonel Mad column was as follows: 'England's largest open-air lunatic asylum, Lambourn, is shortly to be wired off in an attempt to stop the spread of drunkenness and wife-swapping that is becoming a national disgrace. The Department of the Environment are to be congratulated on appointing a committee headed by Julian Lewis, Noel Bennett and "work" rider Robert Edmundson, to look into this disturbing situation.' The in-jokes here were that Julian "Screamer" Lewis was not only Bernard's co-writer but was also renowned for his serious affection for alcohol; and that Noel Bennett (himself not entirely teetotal) was not only the landlord of The George pub in Lambourn but also unlikely to be an expert on wife-swapping on account of being homosexual.

In the same issue 'Colonel Mad' added this item: 'Saddest sight of the week was that of the pathetic drunken hack, Jeffrey Bernard, having to borrow the price of a packet of Polo Mints from Tony Stratton-Smith in order sycophantically to feed that owner's horse, Tower Walk. When will this pathetic man pull himself together?' An in-joke can hardly be inner than when it is made pseudonymously about yourself.

Some of the jokes were disgraceful, like that on 16 September when Colonel Mad suggested that '104-year-old Sir Charles Clore' had been gelded, much to the delight of 'husbands of young wives the world over'.

Many of the stories were regular running gags. One recurrent character was the socialite Lambourn trainer Anthony

BERNARD AND SHOWBIZ
Wendy Richard, the
actress (*above*), in 1974
[*Universal Pictorial Press*]

Above left: Bernard's
actor friends John le
Mesurier in *Dad's Army*
in 1970 [*Universal
Pictorial Press*] and Tom
Baker in *Doctor Who* [*Rex
Features*]

Left: Derek Jameson, the
Daily Express editor (and
future disc jockey) who
sacked Bernard in 1978,
just after this picture was
taken [*Universal Pictorial
Press*]

The cameraderie of *Private Eye*: Bernard (left), Martin Tomkinson and Richard Ingrams (right) returning to the office after lunch at the Coach and Horses in 1978 [*Eric Hands*]

The Regulars: Michael Heath's *Private Eye* cartoon strip based on the Coach and Horses, its landlord Norman Balon and the constantly absent Jeffrey (*Jeff Bin In?*) Bernard

The Regulars

Bernard and his fourth wife, Sue Ashley, on their wedding day in 1978. At the back on the left is Simon Courtauld, on the right Charles St George

Bernard's best friend, Eva Johansen, who was to die in a fire

Bernard with Norman Balon (left), 'the rudest landlord
in London', outside his Soho pub the Coach and Horses

A perceptive Michael Heath cartoon
that had been inspired by Bernard

BERNARD'S LITERARY ADMIRERS

Above: Jeffrey with Graham Greene at Greene's favourite restaurant in Antibes, the Félix au Port, in 1988. 'I have never once been bored by Jeffrey Bernard,' said Greene

Below left: John Osborne ('Bernard is the Tony Hancock of journalism . . . as astonishing and stimulating as anything in Pepys or Boswell') [*Andy Watts, Camera Press*]

Below right: Alice Thomas Ellis ('He has certain things in common with holy people') [*Mark Gerson, Camera Press*]

Bernard outside the Theatre Royal, Brighton, after the world première of *Jeffrey Bernard is Unwell* on 26 September 1989. He was fifty-seven [*Sunday Express*]

All the stars of *Jeffrey Bernard is Unwell:* from left (back) James Bolam, Jeffrey Bernard, Peter O'Toole, Tom Conti and (front) Keith Waterhouse, Ned Sherrin and Michael Redington

Bernard's 'mad' sister Sally Bonney in her sheltered bedsitter in south London in 1992

Who's a pretty boy? Bernard in his Soho flat in May 1994 with his artificial leg in his lap and his plastic inflatable Long John Silver parrot on his shoulder, three months after his right leg was amputated below the knee. By now he was drinking red wine rather than vodka because wine was kinder to his scarred pancreas [*Dod Miller*]

IMMORTALITY: A detail from the Alternative Arts mural
in Soho, on the corner of Carnaby Street and Broadwick Street.
Bernard (right) at a pub table with Dylan Thomas (left)
and Brendan Behan (centre). At the back are Jessie Matthews
and George Melly, in the foreground Ronnie Scott.

Johnson, who was continually described by Colonel Mad as 'Captain Anthony Johnson, VC, DSO and Croix de Gucci' and who was portrayed month after month as a sybaritic lounge lizard basking constantly in the Caribbean sun. Another favourite butt was the East Garston bloodstock agent John Corbett, an Irishman renowned for his constant thirst, vociferous views and endless references to aircraft, airports and their timetables – all of which led to him being dubbed by Colonel Mad 'Concorde Corbett, the legendary air ace'.

Most of the stories were so esoteric that nobody outside the racing world would have had any idea at all as to what they meant. On 9 December, for instance, Colonel Mad enquired, 'Which of the following is the odd man out? – Lord Porchester', and went on: 'Which titled trainer had to stop his car driving which titled trainer's son to Heathrow three times for the lad to get out and be sick? Why has Hilda Marshall of the *Stallion Review* asked the ageing Colonel Mad to pose for the centrefold picture in their next issue? Why has Charles Benson's tailor been described as the most patient man in England?'

Other jokes were at least a little more accessible. On 23 December, in a column distributing 'the Colonel Mad Racing Awards for 1977', the TV commentator Jimmy Lindley was chosen as Elocutionist of the Year 'just like wot he done last year'. And among Colonel Mad's cast for 'the Jockey Club Christmas pantomime production of Snow White and the Seven Dwarfs' Bernard suggested that Snow White should be played by Lady Beaverbrook and Grumpy by the trainer Barry Hills.

Bernard believed that the Colonel Mad column was successful for the same reason that his racing column in the *Sporting Life* had been successful seven years previously: 'Racing people were all frightened of getting the piss taken out of them. They couldn't take a joke very well, but they like it against their mates. I liked Peter Walwyn, Fred Winter, Doug Marks, but some of them are terribly pleased with themselves. They get very grand. Newmarket people are a stuck-up lot, people like Henry Cecil. Barry Hills thinks he's the bees' knees now.'

Bernard much enjoyed being part of the zany, laidback team that in those days produced *Private Eye* from seedy little offices in Greek Street a few yards from the Coach and Horses. 'We'd all be silly,' he remembered fondly. 'There were people like Patrick Marnham and Bron Waugh and we used to lark about in the office like bloody schoolboys. It was great fun. Patrick Marnham used to come in in the mornings sometimes and just say, "Shall we have a silly day today?" And Peter McKay, he was fun. And Richard Ingrams used to say things very seriously like, "Have you checked your facts?" Patrick and Peter would roar with laughter and say "Of course not." I think Richard used to get quite worried. I got on well with them all at the *Eye* but I didn't like Nigel Dempster. He's a cold fish.'

Bernard was always to remain something of an outsider at *Private Eye*. Ingrams told me: 'Jeff says about Bron, "I expect Bron thinks I'm just a little jumped-up navvy with a typewriter"; so he had a sort of inferiority complex.' His colleague Martin Tomkinson agreed: 'On the *Eye* he'd come in and type his copy but he'd always have the shakes and have to go out for a drink. He most certainly wasn't part of the *Eye* inner circle. It was quite exclusive: Booker and Wells and Fantoni, it was almost deliberately *ex*clusive. I was never part of it either. Jeff was only a columnist.'

Another boozing pal was Michael Heath, who described Bernard as 'a friend in a way' but reported that keeping up with him was hard work: 'If you're around him everyone has to be *on*, it's like being on-stage. One wrong word and you're in dead trouble. If you say something about Beethoven or Brahms or Napoleon and you get the date wrong, or Nelson, then you get shouted at. In the end one got fed up with it, standing around on tenterhooks. Because of the feminist movement at the time I was doing a rather successful line in anti-feminist and misogynist jokes, so his misogyny and my misogyny met and fell in love. This was a guy who I could bounce back off. I could actually make him smile, very difficult to do. I certainly thought he was original. He's got guts. If he says something, he does it. He bites the hand that feeds him, he'll be rude to people, tell his women to piss off.

'I don't remember any great times, it was just the freedom of saying "what the fuck, it doesn't matter". We just stood around in a bar talking. It sounds like old poufs or just boring drunks: I did a strip about that in *Private Eye*, "The Regulars", about Jeffrey; Jeffrey never appears in it but there's always someone saying "Jeff Bin In?" which became the catchphrase.

His favourite Soho pub was still the French, where he said you could find a publisher seriously offering an advance of £30 for a book and a writer seriously thinking of accepting it. In April in the *Spectator* he described a typical quiet drink in the French: 'I was in the middle of playing a game of spoof with a friend of mine who'd just been released from Wandsworth and at the same time trying to hit an Irishman who owed me a wrist-watch that he had promised to have repaired for me two weeks previously. In another corner, someone was being quietly sick. Two people were tapping the guvnor for fivers and a girl that I first met in Notting Hill Gate in 1949 was asking me for a return match.'

Less amusing, and unmentioned, was the fact that whenever his distressed sister Sally came into the pub to beg he would simply turn away on his bar-stool and ignore her. 'She was living on the streets,' one witness told me. 'She was about fifty but her hair was matted and she looked like a really old, old bag-lady. It was awful. He would sit in the French while she was wandering round Soho. When she came in the French Gaston would see her out very gently. Jeffrey wouldn't even say hello to her.'

But he was also increasingly drinking in the Coach and

Horses around the corner in Romilly Street, where the land-lord, Norman Balon, was at first not too keen to have him as a regular, according to Martin Tomkinson: 'Norman would say then, "We don't want Jeffrey Bernard in here. He's just trouble." '

It is not surprising either, given that rate of suicidal drinking, that Bernard was increasingly unwell. 'I have an abiding memory of Jeffrey,' said Tomkinson. 'There used to be a betting shop in Gerrard Street and it was the first time I've ever been disgusted by seeing somebody drunk but Jeff was slumped in a corner of this betting shop, grey, trying to light a cigarette, and I was trying to get him out of there and he wouldn't come, but he looked dreadful, horrifying. I remember him once falling asleep in the middle of a sentence. In fairness to Jeff he would tell these stories against himself: it was almost as if he was glorying in these things.'

The actor Tom Baker became as close a friend of Bernard's as any at this time. 'When I was doing *Dr Who* in the Seventies,' he told me, 'I spent an enormous amount of time with Jeff in the Colony, Coach and restaurants. He had a deliciously *delinquent* quality.' He was also awesomely self-destructive. 'He had an attack of pancreatitis and was rushed to the Royal Free Hospital in Hampstead,' said Baker. 'He was in excruciating pain and knelt up in bed and begged the nurse for a painkiller. That was on a Tuesday. On the Friday he was out and we were wildly pissed together in the French pub. One doctor at the Middlesex said to him, "Jeff, is there any chance of knocking off the booze? I can hear your Maker whispering 'Come, Jeffrey, come to Jesus.'"'

Early in March he forgot his insulin one morning, went to a Tote lunch at the Savoy and passed out in a diabetic coma. In July he was very ill again and he spent the last two weeks of August in hospital, yet as soon as he came out of hospital he went off to Lambourn to enjoy Peter and Bonk Walwyn's exceedingly convivial Lurcher Show lunch in the first week of September. His survival for so many years after attacks like these was miraculous. Perhaps there had been some point in all that fresh air at Pangbourne and all those heavy outdoors navvying jobs in the 1950s after all: they had made him astonishingly fit and given him stamina.

It is remarkable too how well he kept up the standard of his journalism. He did receive one exasperated letter from Miles Kington, then literary editor of *Punch*, which read simply: 'Are you going to do the fucking article or aren't you?' He had it framed and hung it proudly on the walls of every subsequent home. But he was taking on plenty of work and had by now accepted advances for his autobiography from three publishers even though he knew he would never get around to writing it. 'Newspapers and magazines used to phone up here for him – *Queen* or *Harper's* or *Men Only* – and we had to say no because he'd missed a deadline,' remembered Norman Balon. His articles for the *Daily Express*, particularly, were still surprisingly good and jaunty. After one piece in which he wrote tongue-in-cheek about Barbara Cartland's advocacy of virginity an *Express* reader in Devon, Mrs Lois Moon of Woolacombe, wrote a letter to the Editor which read: 'Some time when things are a bit dull in the Express office, please throw Jeffrey Bernard into Jean Rook's cage. Then he would know what it's like to meet a real flesh-and-blood female, instead of making rude noises from a safe distance at a sitting hen – if that is not being too rude to Barbara Cartland.'

Another splendid *Daily Express* column appeared on 30 September 1977, when Bernard chose his Seven Modern Wonders of the World: the British Railways cup of tea, the House of Commons, women, the English summer, Sunday, money, and the Swiss Tavern in Soho. Why Sunday? Because it is 'like a dress rehearsal for being dead'. And the Swiss? 'It is the only pub in England that has no mice behind the snack bar. The rats have killed them all. The chef has been charged with manslaughter and the barmen shake so much they can hardly pour a drink. Only this morning the grocer delivered an enormous 10lbs lump of cheese. The guvnor said: "Put it in the trap."' He concluded: 'There are, of course, other wonders of the world but they defy description. There is Cyd Charisse and my ex-wife, both of them wonders in entirely different spheres.'

He still went racing whenever possible and in February returned to Lambourn and was depressed to see that 'his' racehorse Deciduous – in fact he shared her with a syndicate of nine miners – 'looked horribly like a chestnut-coloured doormat'. But the filly 'looked really sweet' when she ran three months later in her first race, at Wolverhampton. His chosen colours, he admitted, were 'fairly revolting', not pink as the race card claimed but 'more like raspberries going off'. He bet £5 each way but the horse came only eighth out of fifteen runners. A month later, however, in June, she was beaten at Lingfield by no more than half a length and a couple of weeks later, when she ran at Wolverhampton, she opened the betting as the 7–2 favourite after Terry Wogan tipped her on his early morning radio show and also exposed the fact that her 'owner' was Colonel Mad of *Private Eye*.

One great friend in the racing world was the businessman Charles St George, who invited him often to the races or his home in Newmarket for lavish lunches with the likes of Lester Piggott and who would give Bernard money when he was particularly hard up. Bernard did not seem to mind that St George had a shady reputation and invited him to be his best man when he married Sue the following year. 'It was an interesting meeting of minds between those two,' said Simon Courtauld, who was also a guest at the wedding. 'St George was sharp, streetwise – a crook – but Jeff was attracted to him because he had money. They used each other, Jeff using St George to see the high life and St George using Jeff to introduce him to *Private Eye* people like Tomkinson, whom he tried to suborn in case he was ever in a spot of bother, which he was on more than one occasion with his crooked dealings. He plied Jeff and Tomkinson with champagne and good food, and Jeff liked the high life.'

Although Bernard was to marry Sue Ashley in 1978 the affair had first to survive a long hiccup in 1977. 'When I first met him he always wanted me to go off with him to those afternoon drinking clubs,' she said, 'and I'd always say no. I had an affair with Jeff and then gave it a miss for a while. I was very confused at the time. I was trying to leave one man and there was another man waiting and it's not a good idea.'

Bernard missed her. That summer 'stank', he wrote at the end of the year in the *Spectator*, and he never managed to have a holiday and the landlord increased his rent. Even at Christmas he was still moaning, playing Scrooge and complaining about the insincerity and expense: 'This year I don't expect to get any change from £100,' he whinged in the *Daily Express*. And as always he was still on the scrounge whenever possible, despite the fact that he now had three regular jobs, on the *Daily Express*, the *Spectator* and *Private Eye*, not to mention all the magazines for which he wrote occasional articles. The money, of course, was frittered away on booze, gambling and restaurants. Tom Baker put it succinctly when he remarked cynically that Bernard 'sang for his supper. He was witty, amusing and charming. You bought him a few drinks, you gave him fifty quid and he kept you amused.' He could certainly be amusing about his continual apparent poverty. On 23 December he celebrated Christmas Eve by writing in the *Daily Express* about 'my bailiff': 'The fellow has become something of a fixture in my chambers. There was a time when he used to knock fairly respectfully on my door and address me as "Sir" or at least "Mister Bernard", but familiarity, as we know, breeds contempt and he now parks himself in my kitchen, calls me Jeff and drinks my tea. So here I am, having managed to reach rock-bottom after precisely 45½ years of effort.'

In Sue's absence he consoled himself platonically with his Three Aunties. 'The Aunties were a woman called Susanna, Leila Kooros and Eva Johansen,' said Sue. 'They'd say now come along, Jeffrey, and he'd talk to them about his sadness,

and they'd look after him. They were very much part of his
life when I met him. He was always having lunch with one
or other of them. Leila was very sweet. She would help him
out with money and he used to go down to her vicarage for
weekends in Kingsclere, near Newbury.'

But if at Christmas Jeff thought he had touched the
bottom when The Festive Season cost him £100 and the
bailiff called, worse was to come in January. On 16 January
1978 he was sacked by the new Editor of the *Daily Express*,
Derek Jameson. 'The gossip machine has it that I fired him
in brutal fashion,' Jameson told me in 1991. 'Such is the stuff
of legends!' In fact he dropped Bernard's column, he said,
because he was unreliable 'and he really had only one topic
to write about – booze.'

The sacking was disastrous for Bernard, who needed his
Daily Express income desperately. He tried to come up with
other outlets for his work, like *Punch* magazine, but these
endeavours often ran into the usual buffers of booze and
belatedness.

– 2 –

Eventually Sue returned to him in February 1978. 'One night
I rang him at that dreadful sleazy bar in Shaftesbury Avenue,
Gerry's,' she told me, 'and he said, "Why don't you come and
have a drink, you silly girl?" and I did.' Ten months after first
hooking her and after months of playing her on the end of his
line, he had finally landed her.

They were married at the unusual hour of ten o'clock on
a Monday morning, just before the pubs opened, on 15 May
1978 at Marylebone Registry Office. Charles St George and
Simon Courtauld were witnesses. Bernard was almost forty-
six and Sue was thirty. At the end of the following week he
explained his fourth bout of marital optimism by writing in
the *Spectator*: 'If freedom means pottering about alone in a flat
at 7 a.m. while avoiding accusing glances from the typewriter

and while Miss Right is incommunicado at five miles distant, then I want to be captured.' He added: 'I don't think that I'm as brave and reckless as most of my men friends think. Time will tell. Lots of it, I hope.' But for all his brave words he seemed to be incapable of realising that a new bride needs to be treated like a *bride*. According to Sue's divorce petition just two years later: 'during the week immediately following the marriage the Respondent came home drunk every night.'

Sue knew very quickly that she had made a mistake marrying Bernard. 'We got married and we went to the *Spectator*, who gave us a drinks party,' she recalled, 'and then to the French pub for a drink and then to the Paparazzi for lunch with a few people. For the rest of that week he was drunk. That evening he went to Gerry's Club on his own, on our wedding night. His celebration of the marriage went on for several weeks afterwards without me. He used to celebrate the wedding every day. I once painted his toenails bright red when he was asleep having had a good drink. He didn't know a thing because he was out cold, and the next morning when he went to the loo he looked down and saw them.'

Alexander Chancellor was amused by the wedding reception in the *Spectator* office: 'Apparently I'd said we'd have this reception but I didn't remember it, I came in at 10 in the morning and suddenly a couple of large jolly Jewish ladies from North London appeared with silver bells and suddenly my office was filled up with all Jeffrey's Soho friends and all Sue's relations. It was a very funny event. It seemed awfully early in the day to be having a reception.'

The happy couple spent the following weekend on a sort of honeymoon with Simon and Philippa Courtauld at Chievely Manor, near Newbury, where Bernard had already stayed in February, March and April, and then they moved out of London altogether in June to live in the depths of Berkshire, on the outskirts of the village of East Garston, near Lambourn. It was an extraordinary decision to move back to the country after the boredom he had experienced in Suffolk with Jill, but Bernard always believed that he could escape himself by moving somewhere new. Their first East Garston home was a £10-a-week labourer's cottage at Westfield Farm and at first it seemed as idyllic as Chelsworth had been initially.

'Eva moved in to his flat in Marylebone High Street and we went down to Westfield Farm in a horsebox that he had borrowed from a trainer, with these two black kittens,' said Sue. 'The cow-parsley was out and it was absolutely lovely. When it was summertime it was gorgeous. Within a month I started working for Nicky Henderson when he first started training in Lambourn. I used to do his VAT and invoices three mornings a week for £11 a week, which used to buy a weekend joint. We used to live on belly of pork a lot in those days: we had scant supplies.'

While living in Berkshire Sue gave up work for a while. There was no telephone at Westfield Farm and they did not have a car, but Tony Lovell, the landlord of the Queen's Arms pub just up the road, was very helpful and understanding. 'We were totally detached from general life,' said Sue, 'and I'd get phone calls from New York to the Queens Arms, and then Tony would come up and say they're going to ring back in half an hour. He was sweet.'

The Lambourn Valley – a glorious fold of the Berkshire Downs between Newbury and Wantage – was not the kindest place to take a new wife unused to the drunken, heavy-gambling rivalry of the local racehorse trainers, bloodstock agents, jockeys and stable lads. 'When we arrived in East Garston,' said Sue, 'we got there late on a Saturday afternoon and in the early morning, it was lovely summertime, I heard the door open at four o'clock in the morning downstairs in this cottage where I'd never slept before. I thought "I'm hearing things", I nudged Jeffrey and said "I can hear things" and suddenly this person arrived in his dressing gown with a bottle of champagne and it was Screamer Lewis, who'd come to welcome us into the valley! He'd been out that night and staggered up the stairs – and that was my introduction to Lambourn. We didn't really fancy champagne but we got up and drank it. Screamer was still hungover: I think he'd fallen in a ditch the night before. He's a real Character.'

Bernard had long been bewitched by Lambourn and its apparently lazy and laid-back lifestyle, which was in fact unbelievably dissolute and adulterous. Lambourn, the biggest of several villages along the valley, was, like Chelsworth, divided firmly in two and ruled by a small number of immensely extravagant and wealthy racehorse trainers, jockeys and vets, many of whom seemed surprised that anybody might drink anything but champagne and who kept seducing each other's wives and mistresses. A few months before Bernard and Sue moved there he described it accurately in the *Spectator* as an 'alfresco nut house' that 'deserves a mad, bizarre and comic equivalent of *Akenfield* written about it'. He thought he might write the book himself but the problem would be that nobody would believe it: 'I swear that any book about Newmarket would find itself on a coffee table. A book on Lambourn might actually get read.' It was in fact the one book that he really should have written and would have enjoyed writing. It could well have become a classic because the Lambourn Valley had almost as many Characters per square mile as it had racehorses.

Screamer Lewis, for instance, a man who would fall into ditches and turn up with champagne at dawn, was also renowned for being able to swear not just in French but in colloquial Provencal French, for playing *boules* even after dark outside his thatched cottage in East Garston, and for the double-act that he and the Lambourn trainer Mark Smyly perfected in the South of France: Smyly looked remarkably like Prince Charles and Screamer Lewis had perfected a particularly obsequious double-act that convinced every French citizen from Juan-les-Pins to Monte Carlo that they were in the presence of the Prince of Wales and some fat, oleaginous courtier.

Among Bernard's other close Lambourn friends were the local poacher, Phil the Dustman; Mad Jack the horsebreaker;

and the rich but immensely kind racehorse trainer Gay Kindersley, an Irish Old Etonian Guinness heir and member of the Turf and Jockey clubs who had often with his wife Maggsie entertained Bernard and had him to stay at their lovely, spacious home at East Garston. When Bernard moved to East Garston, Kindersley had just left Maggsie for his second wife, Philippa. He had broken almost every bone in his body but was still extremely keen on indoor sports, tennis and caterwauling Irish republican songs late at night after a few jars had been taken. Once on an expensive whim he suddenly decided to fly The Dubliners over from Ireland for an impromptu Saturday night hooley. He was also renowned for his unfortunate habit of farting at just the wrong moment, on one occasion while escorting the Queen Mother at the races. And he once introduced me to the Australian cricket team at a Sportsmen's Club lunch at the Savoy by remarking: 'Hello, folks. I'm Gay and this is my friend Graham.'

Another great Lambourn friend of Bernard's was the eccentric trainer Peter Walwyn, who was said to bang his head against walls when frustrated. Bernard remarked that if ever a film were made about Lambourn Walwyn should be played by John Cleese after Walwyn had fallen for the third time off one of his recalcitrant horses and had been seen to shake a fist at the brute and shout: 'Right. That's it. I've had enough of this. I've got a present for you. First thing in the morning I'm taking you down to the vets and we're having your balls off.'

In one of Bernard's favourite Lambourn pubs, the Swan at Great Shefford, the landlord was Alan 'Jamie' Jamieson, an ebullient ex-*Daily Express* racing writer in his thirties who invariably wore a smart suit, a rose in his lapel and would tell any customer who was too old, young or ugly for his taste: 'Not in here, thank you, sir. There's a nice little pub for your sort in the next village.' Up the road and over the hill, in the village of Chaddleworth, the favourite pub was The Ibex, where the licensees Bill and Mary Mays were such confirmed eccentrics that two weeks after Bernard had moved into the valley they allowed him to run the pub while they went off on a Sunday evening. (It was in Chaddleworth that the local millionaire landowner and magistrate David Nugent was said by Bernard to have been appalled when his wife sacked the butler since he no longer knew who would put the lemon into his gin and tonic.) In this 'alfresco nuthouse' in the Lambourn Valley Bernard was better placed than ever to write the Colonel Mad column in *Private Eye*. It was eventually to become so renowned in racing that the Chaddleworth race-horse manager Henry Ponsonby named one of his syndicated horses Colonel Mad and sent it to be trained by the young James Bethell. Colonel Mad eventually had to be gelded. It might have been a great relief to all concerned had the real Colonel Mad been gelded at the same time.

16

Low Life

Unknown to Bernard, the Prime Minister, Jim Callaghan, was looking for a speech-writer in 1978 and some of his advisers were seriously considering Bernard for the job. They asked Harold Wilson's one-time Press secretary Joe Haines to 10 Downing Street to give his advice. He swiftly dissuaded them. 'The idea was absolutely ludicrous,' Haines told me. 'The idea of a meeting between the non-drinking, non-smoking, non-gambling and non-womanising Callaghan and Bernard was too appalling to contemplate.' Bernard may not have approved either. In fact, his favourite politician was possibly the Irish Prime Minister Charles Haughey. Bernard was drinking in the horseshoe bar of the Shelbourne Hotel in Dublin when he fell into conversation and several drinks with three Irishmen who had also dropped by for just the one. 'I didn't know who they were,' Bernard told me, 'but they were drinking at the bar and we started talking about racing and Michael Collins. The next day I said to the barman, "Who were those nice gentlemen?" and he said "That was the Prime Minister and two of his Cabinet Ministers." ' It is however enlightening to discover how firmly Bernard's reputation was already established even before he began to write his Low Life column in the *Spectator*.

He started writing Low Life in August 1978. He had been writing an early type of Low Life column in the *Spectator*, at the back of the magazine, ever since April under the title 'End piece'. His last End piece appeared on 29 July and he reappeared in the magazine two weeks later with the first Low Life column on 12 August, the start of the grouse-shooting season. It was indeed for him the Glorious

Twelfth: it was the Low Life column, complete with never ending grouses, that was to make him famous.

'It seems strangely apposite,' he wrote in that first Low Life column, 'that on the day the editor asked me to turn my attention to the "low life" I should be informed by post that there was a warrant out for my arrest.' The tone of the column had been well and truly set. He was being pursued for £325.89 in unpaid household rates and had only two days in which to give himself up and ask for time to pay. He ended the piece with a typically Bernardine promise: 'Starting tomorrow, it's all going to be different.'

It had been Simon Courtauld who had had the brilliant idea of matching Bernard with a column about low life, a column which was later to be described perfectly by Jonathan Meades as 'a suicide note in weekly instalments'. The owner of the *Spectator*, Henry Keswick, had asked Alexander Chancellor to find a gossip columnist for the magazine; Courtauld introduced Chancellor to the rich Greek socialite Taki Theodoracopulos, who had just submitted 'a very boring piece about the Greek colonels'; Taki was persuaded to write an article about Regine's nightclub in Paris, and then a weekly high-society gossip column under the title High Life; and Courtauld suggested that it should be matched by a Low Life column by Bernard. The High Life/Low Life double act was to be one of the great draws in the *Spectator* although Bernard's column was always to be much more popular than High Life, which must have been difficult for Taki to understand or accept. 'Taki is riddled with problems about his writing,' Courtauld told me, 'but I think he recognises that Jeffrey is a greater, better writer.'

In later years Bernard was to be cynical about the reason for his column's cult success. 'People like to read about someone who is deeper in the shit than they are,' he said. In fact the real reason for its popularity was much less cynical and cruel: people liked to read about someone who broke all the rules, who drank and smoked far too much, who was rude about feminists, homosexuals and ethnic minorities, who was

politically utterly incorrect, who behaved outrageously, and
yet who somehow survived and even managed to surround
himself with an ever-increasing harem of beautiful and ador-
ing women. And of course he had some wonderful anecdotes
to tell, and was astonishingly open about himself, and seemed
not to take himself at all seriously. He always seemed able
to laugh at himself. In October 1978, for instance, Bernard
wrote to *Private Eye* to complain with typical mischief that
the Grovel diary column had reprinted one of his Colonel
Mad stories in the next issue: 'If there are three things I
despise they are drunkenness, slipshod reporting and lazy
sub-editing.' Far from sneering at him for being 'in the
shit', his fans were amused by him and perhaps reluctantly
admiring and envious.

Bernard quickly became the most popular columnist on
the *Spectator*, Chancellor told me: 'I can't think of anybody
else in journalism who writes only, only about themselves.
It's a considerable achievement, I think, to (a) do nothing
at all except drink, and (b) be able to write about it every
single week and still be interesting.'

Chancellor remembered that Bernard had been 'really
surprisingly reliable' as a contributor despite his occasional 'unwell' absences and last-minute deadline crises as the
printers were baying for his copy. 'I don't think he was lazy,
he just fucked up. I think he valued his *Spectator* column too
highly, but he played it right up to deadline always. Sometimes it was just too late and that was incredibly irritating,
though I don't think I ever threatened to fire him. He had
some unpleasant characteristics to do with drunkenness. He'd
sometimes ring me up at midnight at home and start swearing
at me. But it only occasionally happened, a sudden surge of
hatred for his employer.'

Bernard was also writing for *Harpers & Queen* and *Pacemaker* but despite his productivity – and the fact that Sue
was soon to start earning a very good salary again – he was
always in financial trouble. 'He used to say he needed £25
a day then,' Sue recalled. '*Private Eye* paid him £50 a week

and so did the *Spectator*, and he liked a bit of a gamble on
the horses and he was quite a dandy. Tom Baker bought
him a couple of suits so he always looked good.' Most of his
earnings, of course, went straight down his throat and into
the huge profits of the vodka industry. He was still spending
the best part of every day in the Lambourn Valley pubs or
at one of the racing world's frighteningly boozy thrashes. At
the beginning of September he was able to enjoy for the
first time as a local one of his favourite annual events, the
Lambourn Lurcher Show, and the usual two-hundred-strong
Sunday lunch with Peter and Bonk Walwyn at Seven Barrows
that lasted until four in the morning. To make the weekend
quite perfect a trainer who was foolish enough to complain
about Bernard's treatment of him in his *Private Eye* column
was smacked across the face by a local publican's wife, and
there was also a bloody, drunken fight in Lambourn outside
the Red Lion on the Saturday night between the local stable
lads and the invading Welsh gipsies who had imported for the
show their cross-bred dogs, crystal ball gazers, palm-readers,
sprigs of lucky heather and encrusted palms prepared to be
crossed with silver. It may well have been on this particular
night that an enraged Lambourn farmer whose livestock had
been savaged by Welsh dogs staggered into the public bar of
the Red Lion with a dead sheep on his back, dropped it at
the feet of a group of startled gipsies, and then hurled one
of the Travelling People through a closed window.

Eventually Bernard's financial worries caught up with
him. On Saturday 28 October he took Isabel to the Tower
of London and on the following morning, back home in the
Lambourn Valley, he was arrested by the police and himself
incarcerated in the less ancient prison at Newbury police
station. He had still not paid the £325.89 in outstanding
rates and was to be detained in a cell in Newbury until his
appearance before the magistrates the next day. At the police
station they removed his belt in case he might be tempted to
commit suicide and after several hours they served him one of
the most gourmet lunches that can ever have been consumed

in any British jail: chicken casseroled in white wine with
mushrooms, tomatoes, carrots, cabbage and *pommes purée*.
Because it was a Sunday the police canteen was closed
and the constabulary had been forced to obtain Bernard's
lunch from the best hotel in Newbury, The Chequers. Later
he came up with a more amusing version of this story and
claimed that the police had knocked on his door and asked
if he were Jeffrey Bernard and he had replied: 'Don't talk to
me about that shit. I've been looking for him for weeks.'

Bernard was allowed to make just the one statutory telephone call. He tried Charles St George in Newmarket but
he was not at home, and then rang Simon Courtauld, who
lived just a few miles away at Chieveley, and begged him
to come and bail him out. Courtauld took his six-year-old
son Kim with him to Newbury police station, no doubt as
a warning to the child that this was how he might end up
if he refused to eat up his greens. Courtauld paid the bail,
Bernard was handed his belt and shoelaces so that he could
kill himself if he wished and they returned to Chieveley
Manor, where Courtauld was further mortified to find that
his cook-housekeeper, Miss Watts – a great *Spectator* reader
– was such an admirer of Bernard's that she treated him like
a hero and insisted on giving him a second lunch.

Bernard himself had begun yet again to feel so guilty
about his feckless existence that he swore once more to
give up drinking and gambling and managed to do so for
more than a month, during which his withdrawal agonies
were such that his face was covered in red blotches, bumps
and weals and his hands were swollen and itchy until he
could stand it no longer and started drinking again. But his
non-stop drinking and lowering moods had already alienated
his young wife. 'Our first fight was about two or three months
after getting married, I suppose because I was angry with
myself for taking it on,' she told me. 'We had a few fisticuffs.
I think I pulled some hair out and he bashed me in the head
a couple of times. I was stronger than him. I remember once
walking into the cottage and finding him slumped there on

the sofa, drunk. I walked straight into the kitchen, filled a saucepan with cold water, came out and poured it right over his face.'

To make matters worse, within weeks of moving to the Lambourn valley Bernard had already started bemoaning its remoteness and the fact that it was impossible for him to catch the one train to London from Newbury (thirteen miles away) which had a bar on it, because the bus from Lambourn arrived in Newbury three minutes after the train had left. Sue was disillusioned with rural life – and the marriage – just as swiftly. 'I think he did love me for a while but I don't know what he expected of me,' she said. 'I think we were both a bit stupid, actually, going off like we did. When I took off for the country I didn't know what it was going to mean, I was like a fish out of water. When I was down there I wanted to be up here, when I was up here I wanted to be down there. I never knew where I belonged, and I missed my friends. We didn't have a phone. I felt very cut off. I couldn't drive and we didn't have a car and the only contact I had in those days was Patsky Payne. She was my salvation. She'd give me a lift into Hungerford when she had her hair done: she'd take me there for a little outing.'

Sue could not tolerate her husband's aimless lifestyle, either. 'He expected me to be his partner in all this hanging around pubs and I just couldn't,' she said. 'It's boring.' By September she could bear it no longer and began to work again in London for three days a week, staying with her mother or friends. Bernard resented her absenses bitterly. 'As she resented my drinking, I resented her even more,' he said. 'I consider that for two years she left me every day. She'd commute for a week and then come back at weekends. I don't know where she lived, I think with a girlfriend, or her mother.'

Matters were not improved by that very cold winter. 'Westfield Farm had stone floors,' she said, 'and it didn't have an inside loo and it was freezing. It was the worst winter for years. The snow used to come through the letterbox. It was a

nightmare.' So was Christmas, when her mother came to stay
and the marriage all but ended after just seven months. 'The
big deal was the lovely fresh farm turkey Jeffrey had ordered
from someone he knew,' Sue remembered. 'Come Christmas
Eve the turkey was duly sitting there ready to be stuffed and
put in the oven for the next day but Jeffrey and I had a terrible
row over a piece of toast. He said that I'd either burned it
or hadn't cooked it enough and it was the last straw. There
was a huge row and my mother said, "Oh Jeffrey, Jeffrey,
oh stop it Jeffrey!" ' At one stage of the proceedings Bernard
remarked to his mother-in-law, 'You can fuck off!' to which
Sue replied 'Oh no she can't' and Bernard added: 'And you
can fuck off as well!' Sue and her mother left him alone on
Christmas Eve and returned to London by train with the two
cats in baskets. He spent Christmas Day alone.

At the end of that week she had not returned and he
tried again to woo her in print, just as he had done when
he had first hooked her. He wrote in the *Spectator* that the
past year could hardly be described as a vintage one, 'by
no stretch of the imagination' although Sue had brought
into his life 'a cheerful smile and a wisdom that passeth all
understanding'.

Through the first week of January 1979 Bernard made
several humble telephone calls to Sue, apologising for his
behaviour, and although her family urged her not to go back
she returned to him in the second week of the new year. But
the magic had gone from the marriage. 'We kept going until
the Easter,' Sue remembered, 'and Jeff said, "We'll have the
turkey, get the turkey out of the deep freeze." We dragged
the turkey out again and then we had another dreadful row
and I left again.' She was to keep leaving and returning for
another year until she finally went for good in 1980.

At the end of March Bernard rented for £20 a week
a beautiful but remote cottage, Crane's Farm, on the top
of the highest part of the Berkshire Downs above East
Garston and beside the sweeping Summerdown racehorse
gallops. Had his marriage been happy his life would have

been idyllic. He was living in one of the loveliest parts of England, with high, stunning views across five counties. In the spring he even began to garden and later took great pride in his lettuces, sunflowers, tomatoes, raspberries and the huge sunflower that towered beside the front door. He would be up very early to watch Peter Walwyn's or Barry Hills' racehorses pounding the gallops above Lambourn and would breakfast afterwards on egg and bacon with the trainers and jockeys before drifting sweetly into a few large ones in one of the many pubs. He went racing often, and up to London, and on Sundays he and Sue would lunch with the Walwyns, or Gay and Philippa Kindersley, or Tony Stratton Smith, or 'Screamer' and Caroline Lewis, or Richard and Mary Ingrams a few miles away at Aldworth, where he played cricket for Ingrams's *Private Eye* team. A letter from Neil Mackwood in the *Spectator* in June suggested that Bernard's life was now so upmarket that he should be writing not the 'Low Life' column but Taki's 'High Life', a suggestion that Bernard declined, pointing out that you met a better class of person in the gutter than you did in high society and that it was much more invigorating to live on the brink of poverty than it was to be rich. He was proud of Crane's Farm and almost gushed when he told Simon Courtauld of his plans for the place. He even invited Richard Ingrams to stay. Isabel, who was now nine, came a couple of times too.

Sue admitted that Crane's Farm was 'a wonderful house. There were some lovely times up there. It was very romantic, really. There was an orchard behind with strawberries and we'd go for lovely walks and gather wood for the fire, which used to smoke like crazy. But it was very cut off and I didn't like being up there on my own.' To solve the transport problem Bernard bought a huge Datsun Bluebird car from the East Garston bloodstock agent John 'Concorde' Corbett for £50, which was not a wise move considering the amount he was drinking. He did not bother to get a licence or take out any insurance, an oversight that rebounded on him when he crashed one day and had to pay £600 for repairs out of his own pocket. He also crashed through the iron railings at the Queen's Arms in East Garston, which were still buckled from the impact at the end of 1991. Whenever such disasters struck, Bernard seemed quite helpless. 'I have never in my life seen a man so ill-fitted to exist in the countryside,' the Lambourn racehorse vet Frank Mahon told me. 'He was totally oblivious to everything that went on around him. If a mountain leopard had passed him in the road he wouldn't have given it a passing thought. He had no communion with the countryside whatever. There was also this terrible *futility* about Jeff's life. When one of the Datsun's tyres punctured Jeff had no idea at all what to do. He simply rimmed it into Gay Kindersley's yard.

'He had a total inability to cope with life in the countryside. You might just as well put me in a small paddleboat in the middle of the Pacific. God knows why he came to live here: he was in love with racing and Lambourn and wanted to be part of it, I suppose. But his whole life was geared to Opening Time. He would start off in the pub being morose and would get steadily more morose as the day went on. He made a profession out of being miserable. He was permanently sorry for himself, and he had this little vicious streak, the only female trait that he had. And yet he was much loved. Yes, he was *loved*. His secret was that everybody felt sorry for him and thought, I'm superior to him because at least I don't have his problems.'

One thing he did enjoy doing was producing the Colonel Mad column for *Private Eye* each fortnight. In March he also came up with one of the very few Low Life articles he ever wrote that he would later admit he was reasonably pleased with. It was inspired by a glossy magazine article in *Health and Slimming Vogue* about Lady Antonia Fraser, the future wife of Harold Pinter, who had told the magazine that she anointed herself with Miss Dior Eau de Toilette as soon as she arose each morning, had her hair washed weekly by John of Thurloe Place 'because it's so peaceful reading a book under the drier', used Elizabeth Arden Visible Difference just before

her evening bath, which was always garnished with Mary
Chess Gardenia Foam' – and so it went on. 'Amazing, isn't
it?' wrote Bernard. 'As soon as I wake up I smoke three or
four Senior Service and then cough for ten minutes. I like
to cough into Kleenex For Men Tissues which I buy chez
Packwood of Lambourn. Then I get up and make the first
cup of tea with a Marks & Spencer teabag. I usually go
back to bed for twenty minutes and study the day's runners
and riders while my wife strokes my forehead and begs me
to pull myself together. When I get up I wash in water, if
the pipes haven't frozen and burst. I'm very fond of Thames
Water Board water which we have specially piped in.' He
concluded: 'Sleep is important to morning freshness and I
take two valium with a mug of Ovaltine and whisky before
burying my face in my pillow and sobbing myself to sleep.'

But such moments of pleasure were rare. His boredom
with the Lambourn Valley was by now so desperate that
he was even reduced to playing pool in the Swan or the
Queen's Arms for large sums of money, once against an
aggressive racing character for £100. Bernard won. He kept
as close to the racing world as he could, though even that
could sometimes make him feel a little 'unwell': one early
morning he saw a horse being gelded by an alcoholic vet
with a hangover and hands that shook like castanets, an
operation that gave Bernard nightmares for weeks.

One of the few consolations of life near Lambourn was
the elderly barmaid in the Red Lion, Flo North, with whom
Bernard had long shared a sentimental rapport. 'When I
was a young girl, in the 1920s,' she told him one morning
as he sank his fifth large one at 11 a.m., 'the mornings were
altogether different.' It was lovely then, she said. She would
get up early, pick mushrooms for breakfast in the cobwebby
mornings, and the farmworkers in the fields would cut cheese
for their lunches with penknives and drink cider and fall
asleep in the hazy days before the combine harvester, and
the bees would buzz. 'They don't buzz so much now, do
they?' she asked.

– 2 –

In January 1980 Bernard was deeply depressed by the state
of his marriage and the damp, silent countryside where he
was trapped in his remote cottage. He kept catching trains
up to London and then finding Soho equally depressing
because he was now just a visitor, not one of the natives. Yet
ironically it was now, out of his unhappiness, that he wrote
one of his funniest columns in the *Spectator*, a description of
those two pub bores Mr Backbone of England and his wife
Mrs Backbone – he of the anorak and cheery manner, she of
the sheepskin coat and headscarf – that was to cause so much
laughter in the theatre ten years later. Bernard, like Hancock,
was often funniest when he was at his most miserable.

He made one final effort to save his marriage early in
February by taking Sue for a two-week holiday (a freebie, of
course) to Barbados, where they stayed with Antony Johnson
(he of the 'Croix de Gucci') and his wife Maggsie, who had
previously been married to Gay Kindersley. Bernard was
briefly cheered by meeting the great jockey Sir Gordon
Richards. Later Bernard looked back on that fortnight as
the best holiday he had ever had. At the time he wrote in the
Colonel Mad column: 'Readers will, I hope, appreciate the
sacrifice I have made by coming to Barbados for two weeks
to collect material for our forthcoming holiday issue. So far,
I have been able to ascertain that out of the island's 250,000
population, 249,000 of them are trainers, jockeys and wives
from Newmarket, Middleham, Lambourn and Marlborough.
As you may well imagine, this leaves very few people to crush
limes for the rum punches and wash the glasses . . .

'Most sadly missed by all in Barbados this year is "Big
Pete" Walwyn who, with his charming wife Bonk, is in
Africa leading an extremely hazardous expedition into the
dark jungles where such intrepid men as Livingstone, Stanley,
Ken Cundell and Doug Marks lost their lives searching

for owners.' Colonel Mad went on to fantasise that several tribesmen had been seen struggling to put a very tall and noisy white man (obviously Peter Walwyn) into a cooking pot: 'Dis man he shout all de time. Bery, bery loud.'

When he returned to London he took another crack at Walwyn in *Private Eye*, pretending that he had written to the disc jockey Terry Wogan to request the record *Champion The Wonder Horse* for Walwyn and Barry Hills, *Money Money Money* for the notoriously tight-fisted Lester Piggott, *God Save the Queen* for Her Majesty's racing manager Lord Porchester – and for the rich Jewish racehorse owner Phil Solomons the appropriate tune *Three Cohens in a Fountain*.

Bernard was still drinking regularly in the Swiss pub in Old Compton Street but in his column on 22 March 1980 he made his first *Spectator* reference to the landlord of the Coach and Horses, Norman Balon, the crusty Walter Matthau-lookalike whom he was eventually to make almost as famous as himself by his constant remarks about Balon's alleged meanness and rudeness. On this first occasion Bernard reported that he had asked for a menu and Balon had apparently thrown one at him and then refused to accept a cheque without the backing of a bankers' card.

As his marriage collapsed and Sue prepared to leave him he also consoled himself at the end of May with a sudden two-week flurry of travel that took in Moscow, Leningrad, Beirut and Cairo. It was the bloodstock agent John 'Concorde' Corbett who took him and twenty-five horses to the Middle East and Bernard spent his forty-eighth birthday near the Syrian border on the road to Damascus, enjoying a lavish nine-course lunch with a Lebanese racehorse trainer. Bernard stayed sufficiently sober to notice that they had to keep driving through checkpoints manned by various warlike factions and that the Beirut seafront had been completely ruined by shellfire. In the evening he smoked a little sociable hashish.

In Moscow, where he was sent by the magazine *Business*

Traveller, he was delighted to see women hard at work on building sites though he was sorry that Jill Tweedie and Sally Vincent had not taken the opportunity to avail themselves of this particular form of sexual equality. He felt that Red Square and the Kremlin were genuinely sinister and menacing and allowed himself to be picked up in a restaurant by an attractive woman whom he thought was a prostitute but who turned out to be after his dollars rather than his body. He gave her $100 in exchange for 300 roubles, an illegal currency transaction that could have had him arrested and sent to Siberia. He also met the Olympic gymnast Olga Korbut, once the darling of the Western media, who took him to lunch in a forest restaurant twenty miles outside Moscow where they spent six hours drinking, she on champagne, he on vodka. This caused a problem that evening when he had to catch the overnight sleeper from Moscow to Leningrad, on which he discovered that he was sharing a compartment with three middle-aged Russian women who found it most amusing that he kept trying and failing to climb up onto the top bunk and who eventually assisted him, giggling helplessly, with firm Russian shotputters' thrusts beneath his buttocks.

Sue left him for the fifth and final time in July. Early in May he had admitted to her that an unnamed woman friend had spent the night with him. The marriage was by now long past saving. Returning to East Garston from London on 9 May Sue had taken a taxi from Newbury to pick him up at the Queen's Arms. 'When we got into the car, as he was driving drunkenly along the main road, I whacked him round the face and he threw me out of the car into some nettles.' She was stung severely and her ankle was badly bruised. On another occasion she returned home one night to find his car overturned in a ditch near Crane's Farm and in the house itself there was mud all over the light switch where Bernard had scrabbled in the dark. He was lying, badly bruised, in a drunken stupor on the sofa. Sue told him that he should have inscribed on his tombstone the words: YOUR DINNER'S IN THE OVEN AND ALWAYS WILL BE.

Sue admitted that she had agonized before she left 'but I knew I *had* to, I had to start again. I felt guilty, I just thought he couldn't survive. It was too upsetting. But the thing I felt when I did leave him was *peace*, really, because it had been so worrying and so up and down. He opened up in me an anger that was never aroused before. I found it too big to handle. I'd always been passive before that. He was too selfish, really. Everything falls apart with a drinker. They don't look after themselves. It's no way to live and it becomes intolerable.'

Sue's departure left him distraught. 'I thought I was going round the bend. I can remember standing on top of the Downs one day and I just looked at the sky and *screamed* with desolation. I thought it was the end of the world. I stood in a field baying and howling like a dog.' He was to weep for her for months. A week after she left him he tried to commit suicide again – or at least to give the impression that he had – perhaps to win Sue back. He told me that he got drunk and took a lot of sleeping pills at Crane's Farm but survived because of an extraordinary series of coincidences when a woman fan of his *Spectator* column turned up unexpectedly in the Queen's Arms, asked the landlord, Tony Lovell, where he lived, hiked up to the cottage, found him unconscious and rang for a doctor. He was rushed by ambulance to the John Radcliffe Hospital in Oxford and stomach-pumped. 'I never saw this woman again,' said Bernard. 'If she hadn't turned up I would probably have snuffed it, up there.' The story seems most unlikely and does not ring at all true, but even this suicide attempt was dyed with a deep black tinge of humour. Unknown to him, he had already come close to a violent death night after night at Crane's Farm as he had scrabbled drunkenly on all fours in the outside woodshed picking up logs for the open fire. A couple of years later it was discovered that the woodshed had been built on top of an old well that was 1,000 ft deep; all that had saved Bernard from a long drop and a bizarre death had been a few inches of earth and concrete.

But even the John Radcliffe Hospital could bear to put up with him for no more than a fortnight. His file there referred to him with nice understatement as 'a difficult patient' and he was visited by Charles St George, Mary Ingrams and other less responsible 'friends' who tried to smuggle in vodka for him. After two weeks he was asked to leave after allegedly eating illicit jam sandwiches, a foolishness for any diabetic and a charge he denied vociferously. Bernard must surely be one of the very few people to have been expelled from a hospital as well as three schools. 'The hospital placed him on a strict diet,' reported Patrick Marnham in his book *The Private Eye Story* (Deutsch, 1982). 'He was discharged by the matron after being caught *in flagrante delicto* with a strawberry jam sandwich.'

Sue went to share a flat with a girlfriend in Chiswick, London and in mid-August escaped to Majorca to recover from the trauma of her marriage. Martin Tomkinson remembered that soon afterwards he and Michael Heath were drinking in the Coach and Horses one Monday morning when Bernard was suddenly taken ill: 'I thought he'd died. We had to lay him down on the banquette, he went grey, and I thought that was curtains. It transpired he hadn't taken his insulin and there was some suggestion that it was a ruse to get Sue to feel sorry for him and go to hospital and hold his hand.'

But she did not relent. She pressed as quickly as possible for a divorce on the grounds of unreasonable behaviour and presented her divorce petition at the end of September. She did not bother to ask for costs of the suit but she did ask rather optimistically for maintenance even though she could earn more in her job as a television advertising producer – as much as £250 a week – than Bernard was making as a very part-time journalist.

With remarkable nerve Bernard responded by claiming alimony off *her* since she earned so much more than he did. 'He tried to get £15 a week,' Sue chuckled, 'and he put it through a solicitor in Newbury, the cheeky bugger! He should have been married to Norman, really. A publican would have been perfect. That would have been a perfect marriage, Norman and Jeffrey.' Later she was to marry Malcolm Gluck and to have two children. But Bernard had to have the last word, as always. When it was all over he wrote her a letter that said simply: 'Dear Sue, Can I have my balls back, please?'

17

The Academy for Young Ladies

At the end of 1980 not only did Sue divorce him but he crashed the car and lost his Colonel Mad column in *Private Eye*. Then his old friend Frank Norman died.

The car crash, when Bernard hit a Lambourn plumber's van in the narrow lane up to Crane's Farm, was his fourth shunt in eighteen months and he was so terrified of killing somebody one day while drunk that he finally gave up driving for good. He had already driven home drunk one night from the Swan at Great Shefford on the wrong side of the road after dark with no lights on and had crashed into the cabbage patch at the Queen's Arms at East Garston, narrowly avoiding killing a goat. He sold the Datsun and needed to find some way of getting down to the village from Crane's Farm each morning without having to pay for an expensive daily taxi. His solution was magnificently simple. Each day in the village he posted himself an envelope bearing a 17p First Class stamp. The next morning the postman would drive all the way up the lane to Crane's Farm to deliver the envelope. When he arrived Bernard would be standing at the gate to cadge a lift back into the village, where he would immediately post himself another 'letter'. For 17p a day he had ensured a daily taxi service. Once safely in the village of East Garston Bernard would repair to the Queen's Arms at about 9 a.m., where Tony Lovell would leave the back door open so that Bernard and some of his thirstier racing cronies could help themselves to a few heart-starters from behind the bar.

It was certainly a miserable time for Bernard. He was now drinking vodka because 'it's the only drink that doesn't make my pancreas scream' but it did not manage to diminish his drunkenness. Keith Waterhouse once attended a dinner with Bernard in London after which he realised that Bernard was so drunk he could never get back to Lambourn alone. They repaired to the Regent Palace Hotel at Piccadilly Circus, where Waterhouse tried to book him in for the night. The receptionist took one look at Bernard and declared that there was no room at the inn.

Bernard was leaning on a pillar. He glared at the receptionist. 'Give us a room, cunt,' he ventured.

This attempt at sweet-talk was unsuccessful and Waterhouse was left with no option but to take Bernard home.

Now that Sue had left him Bernard suddenly found time again for Isabel, who was now ten and whom he had not seen for nine months. He took her to Ascot, where she was kissed by Joe Mercer, won £25, and was treated to her first taste of champagne by Keith Waterhouse and Mike Molloy. She was sick all night. Their relationship was not an easy one, not only because Bernard was invariably drunk when they met but also because he had no idea at all as to how a child should be treated: he tended in so many other relationships to cast *himself* in the role of the child. Isabel, loyally, blamed herself rather than him. 'I was a very shy, only child,' she said, 'and that probably frustrated him. Maybe he wanted me to be a bit more outrageous. When I was younger we went to the zoo or the cinema but later he would take me out to lunch and get boozed up and when you're a kid you don't really want that. Sometimes he'd take me out to lunch and fall asleep and I'd be so embarrassed.'

By now Bernard was finding it too quiet and lonely in the country even to write The Novel and he yearned openly for London and some challenging conversation. It did not help that he had to appear yet again in court at Newbury over a debt incurred in a car crash the previous year or that after consoling himself briefly with a twenty-five-year-old she soon dumped him because he was too old for her. He had had

enough of rural bliss. He discovered one day that a dead
fox had been hung on his door at Crane's Farm, possibly by
a stable lad whose car he had scratched. It was a strangely
sinister rustic gesture that made him even keener to return
to civilisation.

On Sunday 16 November Phil the Dustman and Mad Jock
joined him on a farewell pub crawl around the Lambourn
Valley to say goodbye to Flo in the Red Lion and Ruby
in the George and then helped him to move at last back to
London. He rented a flat in Kentish Town, in Gaisford Street,
and on the next day, Monday 17 November, he was finally
divorced from Sue when the decree nisi came through. Two
weeks later he was also divorced from *Private Eye*. 'He was
just so hopelessly unreliable about delivering copy,' Richard
Ingrams claimed.

The issue of *Private Eye* on 5 December 1980 announced
that there would be no more Colonel Mad columns. The final
article was much shorter than usual, very brief and brusque,
as though Bernard had been suddenly sacked. 'A team of
psychiatric experts has declared me unfit to continue this
column,' he wrote, 'the strain of having done it for three years
having quite unhinged me. I carry though, to Banstead Hospital, fond memories of the Turf which are bound to comfort
me in my dotage.' He took the opportunity to have some final
cracks at the expense of Piggott ('here comes Lester hitching a
lift') and Henry Cecil ('on his way to buy another boutique')
and the Cundells, 'Laugh-a-minute Ken, slightly more Tory
than Genghis Khan, and his rosy-faced assistant Peter.' And
he couldn't resist mentioning 'the teetotal brigade', among
them his old chum and co-Mad writer, Screamer Lewis.

Nearly three weeks later came the final blow of 1980 when
Frank Norman died of Hodgkin's Disease on 23 December.
He was only fifty. Bernard probably felt even worse about
it because he had recently been less than kind towards his
old friend. 'He was very ambivalent about Frank,' Fran
Landesman told me. 'He practically made Frank cry. They
were such dear friends and then there was a period when

Jeffrey would go on about what a bore Frank was and put him down.' Bernard made up for it by being nice to Norman's widow, Geraldine. 'He came to Frank's funeral with me,' she told me. 'He was great, lovely. I was *so* unhappy but Jeff was jolly nice to me in those days. We used to go down to Soho together just after Frank died.'

He spent Christmas alone in London and spilt a few tears for what might have been. It had been a terrible year.

– 2 –

When eventually Bernard recovered from the loss of Sue, and dried his tears, he discovered what he called later 'the luxury of living alone', which he described as perfect freedom. 'I can do what I like tomorrow morning,' he said. 'Go to fucking Timbuctoo if I want, and I don't have to ask anyone.'

At his new flat in Kentish Town Bernard resumed a bachelor life so active that he must have become confused when Isabel turned eleven in March: he sent her a dozen red roses as a birthday present. He also took Isabel to the races and lost her, though the child reported loyally later: 'He lost my mum at the races as well.' He began to spend a great deal of his time drinking in the Coach and Horses, where the cry of 'Jeff bin in?' was heard increasingly, and his new girlfriends included several very good-looking younger women, among them the actress Jill Martin and the publishing publicist Belinda Harley. Jill was playing Eliza Doolittle in a West End revival of *My Fair Lady* and the ambitious Belinda, who was twenty years younger than Bernard and still in her twenties, was about to launch her own very successful PR company and was in 1991 to become a private secretary to Prince Charles. 'Belinda eventually walked out on me,' he told me, 'when I peed in the bathroom sink because I couldn't be bothered to go down two floors to the lavatory.'

He made up for the loss of the Colonel Mad column by writing increasingly throughout the 1980s for *Punch*, mainly book reviews, though the famous magazine, which was finally to close in 1992, was by now in serious decline, notoriously unfunny and laboured. Bernard also wrote some more pornography and promised Tony Stratton Smith that he would complete the script for a film *A Day at the Races*. Delighted, Stratton Smith sent him off in May on another freebie, this time to Athens and Serifos, to write the script. 'If you're reading this, Tony, don't worry that the job won't get done,' Bernard wrote in the *Spectator* as he basked in the Greek sun with his fist firmly clasped around a large Greek vodka. 'There's nothing else to do here but work.' Of course the script was never completed, though Bernard did discover rather too late that instead of saying 'good morning' to the locals he kept remarking 'octopus'. The trip was especially memorable because he met a couple of nudists who slept rough on a remote beach where he found himself one night in the same sleeping bag as a French-Canadian woman who stank of garlic and who enquired as he was screwing her: 'Do you by any chance happen to know a man called Bruce Bernard? He works for the *Sunday Times*.'

At the end of July Bernard's first book was published by Jay Landesman, *High Life, Low Life*, an anthology of his and Taki's *Spectator* articles. John Mortimer, reviewing the book in the *Sunday Times*, wrote: 'Mr Bernard's "Low Life" reads to me, in fact, like a high old time. He is a writer after my own heart and his past joys, and here I have to admit an interest, were mine also. I too have stood in the Swiss pub in Old Compton Street in the days when you waited for Dylan Thomas to do his well-known imitation of an intoxicated Charles Laughton reciting poetry. I too have sat in the Fitzroy when Nina Hamnett, whose torso once inspired a masterpiece by the sculptor Gaudier-Brzeska, then down on her luck, was sick in her handbag. I have also spent many a happy evening in the Coffee Ann where an Alsatian lay on the billiard table chewing the ivories.' When the book was published in America the following year it was given a rave review by Tom Wolfe in *The American Spectator*. 'Jeffrey Bernard and Taki are two of the hottest tickets in British journalism,' Wolfe wrote, adding that in the venerable pages of the English *Spectator* 'they stand out like a couple of yobbos looking for a brawl'. Bernard's world, he said, 'is that of the failed middle-class intellectual. His columns are like slices of the novel he says he is going to write and keeps cadging advances for and never sits down to. He has taken the intellectual's gamble – cut his ties with conventional life in favor of dreams of low-wattage glory – and lost.'

None of this seemed to impress Bernard. He had done nothing whatever towards choosing the articles for the anthology or editing it, had left all the work to Jay Landesman and his son Cosmo, and he was as ungrateful and ungracious as ever towards Landesman, who had taken such a risk in publishing it. When *Punch* asked Bernard in December to choose the worst book of the year he chose bitchily *High Life, Low Life* and called it 'a veritable can of worms, a printing error on every page, quite obviously not proof read at any stage, wrapped in an appalling jacket. It made me sick and barely a penny.' It does not seem to have occurred to him that authors ought to proof-read their own books. Landesman even gave him a Low Life launching party on 26 June at Kettner's in Greek Street and there was also a High Life party at the Turf Club. The book in fact sold three printings, Jay Landesman told me: 'The *Spectator* took two printings because they offered it as a freebie and the response was terrific.' It also went into paperback the following year. Bernard's ingratitude towards the publishers of his few books suggests that it was perhaps fortunate for everyone that he never wrote his novel or autobiography: had he done so the complaints would never have ceased.

By now he was drinking vodka, lime, soda and ice and his drunken rudeness had become legendary, though the depths of his alcoholic bitterness could still surprise friends who had known him for years. Even Simon and Philippa Courtauld were startled when they invited him to stay for the weekend at their lovely new home in Kintbury and he arrived so drunk and aggressive that he succeeded in reducing to tears two of the three women at the dinner table.

Yet despite the desperately dark side of his nature, Bernard could still be extremely funny. In August he wrote another of the very few *Spectator* articles that he would later admit to being pleased with: a piece about a young Moroccan who had been arrested on a Greek island for sexually assaulting a pelican. 'He's up before the beak next week,' reported Bernard. What's more, the pelican was male, and the Moroccan was later alleged to have attempted also to rape two German tourists.

In September Bernard went off on yet another freebie, this time to America, to Louisville, Lexington and Los Angeles. On his return to Britain he was beaten up in Soho by two Indian mini-cab drivers when he swore at them in Gerrard Street. He celebrated the assault by repairing to a bar where he told the North Country actor and playwright Colin Welland to stop making such a fucking noise playing his tape recorder, upon which Welland 'was across the room and trying to strangle me, his fingers around my old and scraggy neck,' Bernard reported in the *Spectator*. 'I began to reflect yet again on violence and the lack of love in the world today. Suddenly it hit me. The mini-cab drivers and the odious Welland were field workers for the Exit organisation who had picked me as a target for their practice. After Welland I confidently predict that Sir John Gielgud will try and snuff me with a plastic bag in Fortnum's next week. It's thugee time again and I suppose we'll all have to start walking about with T-shirts emblazoned with such messages as "I don't want to die".'

In December he dreaded as usual the arrival of the Festive Season. 'I've tried ignoring Christmas,' he wrote in the *Spectator* 'but the bastard won't go away', so the magazine sent him to enjoy December 25 alone at the Park Lane Hilton. It cost them £287.55 in bed, board and (mainly) booze. He spent the day surrounded by the modern equivalents of the Three Wise Men from the East, 'an assorted bunch of fairly revolting Arabs and Iranians', two of whom – an Arabian couple at the next table – sneered as they sipped their mineral water and watched him become legless with the Festive Spirit. He took his revenge, as he always did, in the *Spectator* the following week, writing of the Arabian wife: 'You can hardly blame Arabs for making their women cover their faces.'

A month later, at the end of January 1982, he left his flat in Kentish Town – where he had been depressed even by the sight of the historian A. J. P. Taylor standing forlornly at the bus stop each morning – and moved in platonically with Frank Norman's widow Geraldine to share her big flat in Great Portland Street, just fifteen minutes' walk from the Coach and Horses. She charged him a paltry £10 a week in rent – rather than the market rate of about £70 a week – and he was delighted to discover that nearby there were three pubs, an off licence and an undertakers. 'I haven't been so well placed for years,' he wrote in the *Spectator*.

Geraldine Norman had been lost since the death of her husband a year previously and was convinced that Bernard was not likely to last much longer and that by taking him in she would be making a dying man's last months happy and comfortable. 'I was very conscious after Frank died that Jeff was the closest friend that he'd had,' she explained, 'and he had almost the same sense of humour so that Jeff's sense of humour was a great pleasure to me because it took me back to hubby. I was here, pretty lonely and I thought like everybody else that Jeff was dying, and I hadn't got anything to do with my life, it was all ashes, so why didn't I devote myself to seeing that Jeff had a comfortable death? Which I think many women have thought, and the bugger goes on living. So it was really a romantic move in Frank's memory.'

It was a wary relationship even though they shared the flat for more than five years. 'I was always rather shy of

Jeff,' she admitted. 'We got on very well for the first few years but we never really played together. I wasn't at the stage of life when I wanted to go on benders so we lived rather separate lives here. I think he'd be absolute hell to live with if you were in love with him. I put up with it for so long because I really did come out of Frank dying with the feeling that there was absolutely nothing left that I wanted in life, a complete crash, so I really didn't mind if Jeff set fire to the sofa and was passed out on the kitchen floor when I came in, in the middle of oceans of washing up. His terrifying domestic habits didn't matter because I wasn't into possessions at the time. I was away on holiday with my mother when he burned the sitting-room down. The danger with Jeff is that he passes out with a lighted cigarette and it just depends where it falls. The insides of the sofa caught fire and melted over the carpet. He'd tidied it up by the time I got back.'

They never became lovers. 'I think he knew that he was liable to lose his lodgings if he jumped me,' said Geraldine. 'There were a couple of times when he got very drunk and started to make up to me for a cuddle and kiss and the interesting thing was that he clearly couldn't remember who I was, it was just a case of "this is the nearest woman".'

At this time, Bernard had no trouble in finding plenty of new girlfriends even though he was about to celebrate his fiftieth birthday. He still believed he was in love with Sue and when he spotted her in Wardour Street in mid-February she seemed as 'elegant as ever, quite stunning to me, and my stomach gave a lurch'. But there were also plenty of other women. 'Usually he had pretty boring girls whom he'd picked up and who fancied this famous writer,' said Geraldine. 'I remember a nurse who used to get up here in the morning and put on her hospital kit and that really turned him on, the nurse's uniform. He brought her back here quite often. There were others. They were young and only lasted a week or two but he brought them back pretty often. He did mostly have a girl.' In fact he had so many girls in these early years of the 1980s that he named the flat 'the Great Portland Street Academy For Young Ladies' and claimed that he gave them lessons in culture and deportment. Seduction was of course a costly business and he always seemed to be on the brink of bankruptcy. He was still facing a court case over an old debt involving 'a horrid suite of furniture' he had bought for Sue and he never stopped pleading poverty. Yet he was spending at least £100 a week on booze for himself alone in the Coach and Horses and nearly as much on lunching almost every day in expensive restaurants.

Not everyone was quite as impressed by 'this famous writer' as the girls were. At the end of February an article by Maureen Cleeve in the *Observer* quoted Sir Harold Acton as suggesting that the journalist Benny Green was rather too fond of pubs and 'horrid drinks'. Bernard was amused to discover that the distinguished and impressively sober Acton had in fact been thinking of him rather than Benny Green and that the *Observer* had to publish the following Sunday an apology which read: 'Sir Harold meant to refer to another person altogether. Benny Green, as his friends and colleagues know well, is a man noted for his genuine personal moderation and professional reliability.' Indeed.

At the beginning of March Bernard took Oliver's teenage daughters Emma and Kate to spend the weekend at Taki's country house in Oxfordshire, and then, back in London, had dinner at the Caprice with David Litchfield of *Ritz* magazine and the England cricketer Ian Botham, whom Bernard described later as being 'built like the proverbial brick shithouse' and 'quite delightful'. Afterwards Botham told Litchfield: 'A nice bloke, that Jeff. I'd like to meet him when he knows what he's talking about.'

At the end of March he wrote another of the few articles

of which he was proud: a piece about the man who had cut off his penis and thrown it on the fire so that he could devote the rest of his life to God after his wife had spent the previous twelve years trying to persuade him to do so. Then he was off to the South of France, this time to Montpelier, where he went to write and present a script for a Canadian television programme about the wine war. He hated it, was astonished to discover that it was actually quite hard work and was irritated by the twenty-year-old sound man who informed him: 'I've had more women that you've had hot dinners.'

On 27 May he astonished himself and everyone else by reaching fifty. *The Times*, thanks no doubt to Geraldine Norman's influence, announced his anniversary along with those of Henry Kissinger, who was fifty-nine, Christopher Lee (60) and Vincent Price (71). There were men and women who were themselves by now long dead who had sworn twenty years earlier that Bernard could never possibly reach fifty. Norman Balon did his best to ensure that he would not reach fifty-one by giving him a chocolate and cream birthday cake – 'the *ideal* present for a diabetic', remarked Bernard. The *Spectator* gave him a lunch in their boardroom in Doughty Street and for the rest of the day he sank slowly into the West in the Colony Room Club. He was also given a delightful but weird half-century *festschrift* by the musicologist 'and staff nurse of the Coach', Clive Unger-Hamilton. One entry read: '50 Today, Daddy, Be King for another 50 years with love from Isabel XXXXX'.

Some other entries were unexpected. Auberon Waugh, who was later to dismiss Bernard as a man of little account, gave him a £10 note sellotaped to a sheet of *Private Eye* paper which was inscribed 'For Jeff, the last true English Gentleman inscribed with affection on the occasion of his 50TH BIRTHDAY by his comrade in arms Bron.' Richard Ingrams produced a typically zany contribution by the celebrated *Private Eye* contributor E. J. Thribb (17):

'So. Jeffrey
Bernard
You are 50.
Keith's Mum
Says it is
High time
You settled down
Again.'

There were offerings from Sally Vincent, Dick West and Allan Hall, who wrote: 'Do not try to get hold of yourself; we've all tried it and it's impossible. I shall never stop regarding you with astonishment and affection.' Michael Heath contributed a cartoon headed '50 AND STILL GOING STRONG'. It showed Bernard at a bar counter drinking from the first of fifty glasses and remarking 'Just the one'. Heath had even taken the trouble to ensure that there were exactly fifty glasses in the cartoon. Eva Johansen scrawled: 'Darling Jeffrey, Congratulations on the birthday we never thought you'd see; and thank you for many things – above all, never marrying me. Luv Eva.' And Irma Kurtz remembered how she had first met Bernard 'under someone's table' so many years before: 'This man, I thought then, has the most beautiful smile I'm ever going to see. Indeed, many men have smiled for me since but none so like a naughty angel, or a little devil caught out in an act of charity; no, few men smile so fine as Jeff Bernard . . . his company is constant delight . . . with all my heart and some considerable portion of my liver, I am his. I love Jeffrey Bernard.'

18

'Jeff Bin In?'

Bernard's fiftieth birthday was also marked by a shiver from the past, a mysterious ghost from the days of his youth. His first wife Anna's long-lost illegitimate daughter, Alfreda, who had been given away for adoption but was now thirty-two and calling herself Sally Bernard, suddenly turned up in the Coach and Horses one day in May to ask 'Jeff bin in?' and to claim that he might be her father. Had he asked the simplest of questions he would have realised that this was impossible, since Alfreda had been born in 1949 and he had not seen Anna at all in 1948. But he seems to have been under the impression that she was born in 1948 and he never questioned the date or bothered to ask for her birth certificate. Perhaps he *wanted* her to be his daughter, or at least to pretend that she might be. It would not be surprising if at fifty he suddenly wished that he had not been sterile. 'The reason I wanted to see him,' Alfreda/Sally told me in 1992, 'was not because he could be my father but because he could tell me about Anna and I wanted to piece together what my mother was like and to find anybody who knew who my father was.'

The following month he was back in the Middlesex Hospital having his diabetes restabilised but his fragile health did not prevent him continuing to drink like the navvy he had once been. Soon after he came out of hospital his High Life *Spectator* colleague Taki bought him lunch at Kettners and took him back afterwards to his sumptuous Knightsbridge flat for just the one. 'He was paralytic,' Taki told me, 'and after another vodka and orange he went to sleep at about 4 p.m. I went to the park for a run and then on to do some karate. When I got back Jeff was still asleep so ten or fifteen of us went out to dinner and then to Annabel's, and then I took some dope – this was in my bad drug days – and Jeff was still asleep. Eventually at about 5 a.m. he woke up. The vodka was still in his hand. He had been asleep for thirteen hours. He looked outside. "The trouble with London," he said, "is that it gets dark so early these days."'

His financial position was also as dire as ever. Early in July he appeared in court before a registrar who ordered him to pay off a debt at the rate of £25 a month and later in the month he tried again to earn a few pounds by writing his autobiography in Leila Kooros's house in Kingsclere.

A very different sort of friend whom he met at this time was Anna Haycraft, the chain-smoking, hard-drinking London novelist who wrote under the pseudonym Alice Thomas Ellis and was married to Colin Haycraft, the Duckworth publisher. Her novel *The 27th Kingdom* had just been shortlisted for the Booker Prize for the best novel of the year and when it failed to win the prize, Bernard wrote in his column that she should have won. 'I thought that was terribly nice of him,' she told me, 'so I wrote him a postcard and said come to lunch and he came to lunch and this is terribly terribly difficult to explain because he's a very very attractive man but I see him just terribly much as a friend. Is that clear?' Soon they were close friends and Bernard became a regular lunch guest at the Haycrafts' home near Regents Park. Three years later she was to dedicate her novel *Unexplained Laughter* 'To Jeffrey Bernard with love'. She did not know, of course, that one reason for his flattery was that he had backed her novel to win the Booker at 5–1 with Ladbrokes and was annoyed at losing his money.

But despite this delightful new intellectual friendship the year was ending with nervous intimations of mortality. On 23 October he went back to Chelsworth in Suffolk for a senti-mental weekend and discovered that the scruffy old thatched cottage that he had shared with Jill had been done up, the honeysuckle had been torn down, and the lawn was now as smooth as a bowling green. He was losing weight, and the strength in his leg muscles, and had become increasingly short-sighted. 'When the door bell rang this morning I was sure it was the grim reaper but luckily it was the milkman,' he wrote in the *Spectator*. And he was becoming restless again. After Christmas he went to Dublin for a few days and was so warmly received by old friends that he wondered yet again why he didn't live there.

The years of the early 1980s, now that he was living again the life of a bachelor, followed such a similar pattern that it was difficult to tell one year from another. He lived in Great Portland Street and went every day to get drunk in the Coach and Horses, where the other regulars kept popping in to enquire 'Jeff bin in?' He wrote for the *Spectator* every Tuesday morning, for other magazines occasionally, went racing often, took Isabel out for lunch at smart restaurants time and again, accepted as many 'freebies' as he could and fornicated whenever possible, preferably with somebody new, young and female. How he managed to do so was increasingly baffling since he was also increasingly 'unwell' and his Low Life column failed to appear six times in 1983 alone.

The year started dreadfully when Eva Johansen went to bed drunk, lit a cigarette and burned herself to death. Their relationship had been stormy but he always considered her to be his best friend and she wrote to him once: 'It was good to see you the other day. I'd forgotten how much our rows meant to me.' He had always admired her style. When she stayed with him once in the country he asked what she would like for breakfast and she replied: 'A slice of cold, rare roast beef and a glass of Tio Pepe, preferably from the fridge.' 'Why can't you have a fucking egg like anyone else, you flash cow?' snapped Bernard. 'Because I'm not anyone else,' she said.

One consolation was that he was getting on better than ever with Sue, who was taking him out to dinner, buying him presents and calling him 'old bean'. She was even still laughing at his jokes.

Then, in the middle of February, he received a tax demand

for £1,760 and was threatened with prosecution if he did not pay within three days. He could not understand why the Inland Revenue refused to accept that writing the Low Life column entailed huge daily expenses, which he listed in the *Spectator*: 'Morning tea, Kleenex, cigarettes, phone call to apologise for night before £2. Copy of *The Times* and hair of the dog £1.40. Taxi to the Coach and Horses (unable to work, too down at heel) £1.60. Three large vodkas by myself to face oncoming day £3. Drinks for information, gossip, dirty jokes, tall stories and autobiographical reminiscences from Charlie, Conan, Jeremy and No Knickers Joyce £6. Two more large vodkas by myself to keep going £2. Chicken in lemon sauce, beef with spring onions and ginger, mixed vegetables in Jubilee Dragon to sooth infuriated pancreas £6.50. Iodine, sticking plaster and bandages for wounds inflicted by Chinese waiters £1.75. Drinks and fruit machine in afternoon club £6. Returned favourite 3.30 Kempton Park £5. Refresher course of vodkas in Coach at 5.30 £7. Taxi home £1.60. Money for old rope for suicide attempt £3.50. Long-distance phone calls to friends in middle of night to moan, whine and complain £4.75.'

Early in June he borrowed a villa with a private pool in Southern Spain, in Tarifa, and went there on holiday alone to recuperate and to give his lung a healthy airing, after a dangerous bout of pneumonia and pleurisy, travelling by train from Madrid so that he could see the countryside. It took thirteen hours, he complained later, and all the way he was surrounded by 'Moroccan shepherds shitting on the floor'. In Tarifa he met an English widow who took charge of him and drove him every day to the market or the beach. But one afternoon by the pool he was stricken by a fearsome pain in the chest and suddenly he was terrified of dying in Spain. He took a hundred-mile taxi ride to Malaga and then a plane to Madrid and London. His wallet cringed at the expense. Back in London he worried for a fortnight that he had lung cancer but as soon as he was cleared by a specialist he lit a cigarette.

Early in July he reported with his usual endearing optimism that he had 'just discovered Miss Right again' and in August it seemed that the *Sporting Life* had at last forgiven him for the fiasco of the 1971 National Hunt dinner: he started writing a racing column for them again in the *Sporting Life Weekender* for £70 a week, which he continued to do for several years. He was also contributing to the racing magazine *Pacemaker*.

At the beginning of September he was deeply impressed to meet Anthony Burgess in the Colony and chatted with him for half an hour. The following week there was another Trust House Forte freebie to Paris and in October, while the lawyers pursued him with garnishee orders for unpaid debts, he was back in Barbados on yet another freebie, this time provided by a public relations company and Caribbean Airways, along with eight other journalists, four men and four women. When three of the four women failed to buy him what he considered to be a sufficient number of drinks Bernard denounced them loudly in the hotel, to the embarrassment of the other residents, as 'a bunch of slags'.

On his return to England he was arrested for abusing the waiters in the Raj of India restaurant in Old Compton Street and for assaulting a rubber plant in the said restaurant and had to appear at Bow Street Magistrates Court, where he was fined £10 and ordered to pay £15 damages. The following day his foot was so painful and swollen after he had cut it on a piece of coral in Barbados that he took it to the Middlesex Hospital, where they kept him in because of the danger of diabetic gangrene. He thought they might have to amputate the foot, which irritated him almost as much as the naive young doctor who looked at his records and remarked: 'You drink and smoke a horrendous amount. Why do you drink?'

'To stop myself jogging,' replied Bernard.

In December he tried to keep his hand in at the old boxing game by getting himself knocked to the ground with one punch during a drunken dispute in the Swiss Tavern in

Old Compton Street and he noted in the *Spectator* that it had
been a particularly bad year for taking women on: 'Not since
1950 have the enemy been so thin on the ground and I like
a good fight.'

Early in the new year Jonathan Meades sent him out to
eat a hearty meal in a series of restaurants and then to tell
the waiters that he couldn't pay. 'At the first one he went
to,' said Meades, 'the owner said, "You're writing an article,
aren't you, Jeffrey?" ' But his burgeoning fame was not *always*
good for his reputation. In January he had to withdraw his
application to join the Turf Club (£280 a year subscription)
after being told that he might be blackballed, which would
have forced his proposer (the Marquess of Hartington) and
seconder (his old chum Peter Walwyn) to resign. 'They told
me I was unsuitable,' Bernard told the *Evening Standard* diary.
'What do they mean, unsuitable? I can talk proper and I don't
owe my bookmakers half as much as most of them do.' He
conceded, however, that his Colonel Mad column had 'upset
a few people'.

Even people Bernard had never met seemed to know all
about him by now. Once, a plain-clothes detective arrested
him at the Coach and Horses in January for kicking a car
that he had found parked on the pavement and obstructing
his passage. As the CID man took him away to be charged
with criminal damage at Vine Street police station, where he
was fingerprinted and photographed, they passed the Swiss
pub, where the detective remarked with eerie accuracy: 'You
screwed the landlord's daughter here in 1976, didn't you?'
When Bernard appeared yet again at Bow Street Court the
magistrate sighed: 'The last time it was rubber plants, Mr
Bernard. Now it's cars. What next?'

Soon it became quite obvious that it was absurd for Bernard
to be writing a column called 'Low Life'. At Sandown Park
he was drinking with Robert Sangster ('a delightful fellow
in spite of having £100 million in his current account'), in
London he was partying with Taki, at Newmarket he was
lunching and going to the races with Charles St George in

the Rolls-Royce. His own body was also given a full service and oil-change at the Middlesex Hospital.

At the end of September there was another Press freebie, once again to Barbados, this time along with those journalistic giantesses Irma Kurtz, Ann Leslie, Suzanne Lowry and Sally Vincent. Despite their beauteous presences he was propositioned by a prostitute who threw a glass of beer in his face when he asked her for time to think about it. It was a jaunt that Dick West would never forget — when they visited a run-down bar, a wooden shack in a slum area, the barman said to Bernard: 'The usual, Sir?' 'After lunch this Englishman got up and said in a very plummy Empire voice, "I would like to introduce myself, I'm Admiral Something, formerly of the Royal Navy, and I've been living in Barbados for many years, wonderful place, absolutely first-class people, absolutely lovely, wonderful to see people from the United Kingdom, greatest affection." He sat down and Jeffrey staggered to his feet and said "Royal *Fucking* Navy. I was educated at Pangbourne and all I can remember was that I was getting caned so much my arse was bleeding. I *hate* the Royal Navy." Then he suddenly turned his attention to me and he looked round and said "Richard, *you* were educated at Marlborough, weren't you? I bet *you* had a sore arse all the time." '

Then, on 14 October he was suddenly re-admitted to the Middlesex Hospital, this time for a biopsy of a large lump that had appeared behind his left ear. It was eventually found to be benign but before long another had developed behind the right ear — they were in fact fatty lipomas — and for the next seven years they were to grow until they had become one huge growth that swelled the back of his head so grotesquely that in 1992 he was to insist on their amputation despite the danger to his life.

19

The Last of the Handmaidens

Taki was rotting in prison on a cocaine-smuggling charge and Bernard seemed to be trying to do his best to join him at the start of 1985. In January he was barred from the Coach and Horses 'for life' by Norman Balon after he had squirted the contents of a soda siphon over a barmaid who had told him to put his own ice and soda in his vodka. A week later he was arrested 'for falling asleep in a taxi'. Another writ arrived, this time from Robson Books, who sent in the bailiffs to serve him with a bankruptcy order over a debt of £564.50 for not writing the anthology of Lester Piggott anecdotes for which they had long ago paid him a £500 advance. The extra £64.50 was for legal fees in issuing the summons. Bernard considered improving his bank balance by selling to some newspaper for £25,000 a photostat of a letter that the racehorse trainer Henry Cecil had sent to owners pointing out rather blatantly that Piggott liked to be paid in cash, but at the last minute – after floating the photostat in the direction of the *Mail on Sunday* and the *Sunday Express* – Bernard decided that even the anorexic state of his finances did not justify him in selling his hero to the taxman for 25,000 pieces of silver. He was however thoroughly fed up that Piggott found out about his crisis of conscience but said nothing: 'a thank you or a large vodka would have sufficed,' Bernard wrote in the *Spectator*. The final horror was when Bernard was told by Richard West that the tax inspector who was pursuing him with such ferocity (and had now garnered sixty per cent of his income) was a woman. 1985 did not look as though it would be a good year. But in fact it was to be a vintage one. In the nine months between May 1985 and February 1986 he was to meet the last two women who seriously mattered to him, Deirdre Redgrave and Finola Morgan, the last of the Great Bernardine Handmaidens, the last before his libido finally surrendered, exhausted.

Before those double items of good luck, however, he suffered a long bout of ill health. At the end of January he managed to fall *up* some steps, breaking several ribs and infecting this time his left lung. He took to his bed again. A month later he developed a bladder infection and had to have it treated at a VD clinic, a venue that annoyed him not because of embarrassment but because the infection had not even been any fun to catch.

So it was with joy and relief that he fell in love, for the last time in his life, early in May, when he met Deirdre Redgrave, the ex-wife of the Left-wing actor Corin Redgrave and sister-in-law of Vanessa and Lynn. It was a splendidly unlikely autumn romance since he had already attacked Deirdre in print for her Left-wing, feminist opinions without ever meeting her. She had never been as rabidly militant as her ex-husband but she had been sufficiently Far Left to demonstrate against nuclear weapons at Greenham Common.

They met on 8 May, the day after Bernard was presented with £500 as the Periodical Publishers' Association's Writer of the Year for his Low Life articles. He celebrated this accolade by getting so drunk that he lost the cheque, which was later returned by a stranger after it had been discovered, appropriately, lying in the gutter. Despite Bernard's own proximity to the gutter he was looking increasingly like a star: twelve days later the *Observer* quoted him in their Sayings of the Week feature as having written: 'When people say, "You're breaking my heart", they do in fact usually mean that you're breaking their genitals.' Whenever he was embarking on a new love affair he always wrote about sex.

He was introduced to Deirdre in the Coach and Horses by their mutual friend John Hurt. Deirdre was designing clothes in Soho for a commercial at the time but had popped into the Coach for just the one with Hurt. 'I noticed this man *staring* at me across the bar,' she told me, 'and I didn't know who he was. Jeffrey came over and said, "Would you please introduce me?", which John did, and I said, "I'm sorry, I can't speak to you", and he said, "Why?" So I said, "Because you wrote a horrible article about women protesting against the Bomb in which you included my name and you had never met me. I will not shake your hand." He retreated to his corner to rethink the situation but he came back and he said, "I have won this free champagne lunch at Kettners, would you care to come with me?" Well, of course, I *did* care to go with him, so off we go to Kettners, and we're sitting having a drink and everyone's rushing around saying, "Jeffrey, it's wonderful you've won the award", so I suddenly became rather impressed and slightly overawed by this situation. Then he looked at me and he said, "I very much want to spend the night with you." I looked at him with all the hauteur I could acquire and I said, "I'm very sorry but I'm not a one-night stand", and he took my hand and looked at me very intensely and said, "I'm not thinking of *one* night, I'm thinking of a *thousand* and one nights." That got me. I looked at him and to my *horror* heard myself say, "I want to drown in your eyes."'

He was to immortalise her in his column – and eventually to ridicule her – as She Who Would Drown In My Eyes.

After dinner they went to bed together, twelve hours after meeting. It was not greatly successful physically. 'When he first took his clothes off he was like a Biafran,' she told me. 'I'd never seen a body so raddled. And the combination of alcohol and diabetes made it difficult for us to make love often, and that's not very good for a relationship.'

It was to be an unusual courtship. A couple of nights after that first meeting Deirdre received a midnight telephone call from Bernard asking her to go over to the flat in Great Portland Street. She protested that it was midnight and she was half asleep but he persuaded her to 'throw on some jeans and come over' and promised to pay for the taxi when she arrived. When she got there, of course, he was so drunk that

he was in a deep sleep. The doorbell went unanswered, much
to her embarrassment and the suspicious irritation of the cabbie, whose meter was ticking away like a bomb. Eventually
Geraldine Norman answered the door and Deirdre found
Bernard upstairs in his room 'snoring away, sound asleep'.
Later he woke up, started staggering around and disappeared
into the lavatory for ages. Eventually Deirdre went in search
of him and found him wedged so far down the lavatory bowl
that he could not move. 'He was so drunk he was right down
in the *water*,' she said, 'virtually unconscious.' Eventually she
pulled him free and lugged him back to bed.

Three weeks after they met he threw a big birthday party in
the flat at Great Portland Street and invited dozens of friends.
Jonathan Meades, the journalist who had first described the
Low Life column as 'a suicide note in weekly instalments',
was not completely surprised to find himself in the middle
of a bacchanalian orgy despite the moderating presence of
Rebecca John, Alexander Chancellor and 'a lot of suits'. What
made this celebration particularly bizarre, however, was the
fact that by some strange quirk of party-giving etiquette the
host himself was for a change 'reasonably sober'.

'There were lots of very grown-up people like Jo Grimond
leaning against walls, absolutely legless,' said Meades. 'There
was whisky, vodka and gin but no mixers, and po-faced flunk-
eys in bow ties. The chaos was unbelievable. Elizabeth Smart
had passed out on the floor, Graham Mason fell at Jeffrey's
feet and Jeffrey kicked him very hard and said, "I don't want
any fucking drunks at this party, cunt." I don't know how I
got home. People were talking to themselves.'

For months afterwards Bernard mentioned Deirdre in
the *Spectator* almost every week and jeered affectionately
at her pink socks and baggy trousers and her belief that
Everton was a suburb of London. 'I am going to lend
her to a farmer to frighten the crows,' he once wrote. She
looked 'like a walking jumble sale' and she was causing
him 'a fiscal haemorrhage' with her taste for booze and
Greek restaurants and was 'becoming as impossible as Lady

Caroline Lamb'. He even referred to her once as a 'demented frog'.

Bernard was now such a famous London media figure that his public courtship of Deirdre through his column in the *Spectator* resulted in them being interviewed together by the *Sunday Times*. 'She is the most stupid person that I ever met,' he told the paper in July. 'She is as daft as a fucking brush but she's got good legs.'

'Come on, Jeffrey,' she replied. 'Only last weekend you threatened to blow up my block of flats if I left you . . . Do you know he suggested someone ought to make a movie of our romance? He said he would be best played by Paul Newman. Personally I think Quentin Crisp would fit the part very well.'

This was to be the last great love affair of his life even though it was constantly threatened by tears and impotence. He even forgave her for not buying him drinks. When she said to him once 'Isn't it a lovely day?' he found himself replying, 'Any day that you are in is lovely' and then heard her say: 'Jeffrey, you make my heart sing with happiness.' Embarrassed by such sentimentality, he wrote in the *Spectator* that they both needed new scriptwriters but in reality he was extremely happy. He was suddenly boyish again, as bubbly as a young man in love, and his column sang too.

One morning Deirdre saw Francis Bacon sitting on the top of a bus and went up to him to introduce herself. 'I'm Jeffrey Bernard's fiancée,' she said.

'I'm sorry,' he said, 'that's *your* problem.'

'Jeffrey asked me to marry him after about two weeks,' Deirdre said. 'I said yes but he just drank too much and I couldn't cope with it in the end. In the morning, before he's had "just the one", he's seriously bad tempered, *really* grotty and awful, and he had to be spoonfed his breakfast and I used to make him scrambled egg because he was very careful about his diabetes and I made sure he always had proper meals.'

At the end of May Bernard had his first drink in the

new Groucho Club in Dean Street, which had been founded mainly by a group of feminist publishers who had become fed up with not being able to join one of the great male London clubs. At first Bernard was cool towards the Groucho, tending to sneer at the trendy people who went there, but before long it was to become his second home and he was to become its most famous habitué.

But his openness about himself in the Low Life column was beginning to become foolhardy. In July he wrote again about the illegal bets he was taking in the Coach and Horses without realising that by now the Customs and Excise officials were taking an interest in his open lawbreaking. Even when Deirdre persuaded him to see a Harley Street psychiatrist, a friend of hers called Barrington Cooper, in the hope of curing his nightmares, Bernard reported the encounter in the *Spectator*. The shrink told him perceptively that the reason he was always broke was that he wanted to remain an adolescent for ever. 'He had *terrible* nightmares,' Deirdre recalled. 'There'd always be great black boars *eating* him and lurking. Usually the things that were attacking him were animal. They were very very frightening and he reached the point where he could hardly bear to go to sleep sometimes because he was frightened of what would be shown to him, which is why I sent him to the shrink. He's terribly expensive, £200 for three-quarters of an hour, and he sent Jeffrey some mammoth bill which he never paid.'

Deirdre was disturbed by Bernard's deep unhappiness. 'There has to be a reason why somebody destroys himself like that,' she said. 'I used to sit and talk to him for hours and try to find out what made him so bloody unhappy because he's a very unhappy man. That was one of the things that touched me about him because there's great sadness there and all women fall for it: they think they can make him happy, but I don't think anybody can. His parents did die when he was young but that can't explain the basic distrust of everything which he's got. There's a kind of wistful sorrow in Jeffrey that you can't resolve.'

Sadly, by September the affair was over. 'I was working quite hard at the time,' said Deirdre 'and we just drifted apart but he finished it off with a seriously horrible piece saying thank God it's over with She – really horrible – and nobody would speak to him in the Coach because actually people quite liked me and thought I was putting up with a lot. I was really hurt by it. It was a public courtship. When he wrote a seriously vicious, unpleasant piece it really hurt me a lot.' Bernard, as ungracious as ever, told the *Standard* diary that he had called it off because 'She hadn't bought him a drink for eight weeks.'

– 2 –

In October Bernard was unwell again and spent another ten days in bed. Then he was housebound for three more weeks and had become so thin and haggard that he began to wonder whether he might have Aids. In December he spent Christmas Day in the Middlesex Hospital. His friends began to count the weeks: it seemed inevitable that he would soon be dead. But once again he dodged the undertaker and before the end of January he had embarked on yet another love affair, less charged than the one with Deirdre and less sparky, but real all the same. It was to be his last.

Sally Vincent introduced him to a friend of hers, Finola Morgan, a divorced forty-three-year-old part-time teacher of English whom he was to enshrine in the Low Life column as 'She Who Would Iron 14 Shirts'. He took her for lunch to one of his favourite expensive Soho restaurants, L'Epicure, and they arranged to meet at his flat the following week when Bernard promised that he would cook for her himself. 'But he was dreadfully ill,' Finola told me. 'I'd never seen anybody looking that ill, and the place was chaos, of course. I sat with him that day and he was in a very bad state, so I took some shirts of his to iron and unfortunately it went on. You always think "soon he'll be able to stand

on his feet and I won't have to do this any more". Now
I've learned that chaos is his natural condition and there's
nothing you can do about it. As soon as you've tidied it up
he will introduce more chaos.' He was still good-looking
but Finola was seduced by something else. 'He's got this
gift of offering instant intimacy and it's very unusual and
very seductive,' she explained. 'The instant you meet him
he never holds anything back. His charm is that he's the
same with everybody, no matter what they are. He doesn't
have different personas for different people. You're charmed
straight away.' No wonder that he was by now also writing
a regular column in *Punch* called 'Jeffrey Bernard on Women.'
Jeff and Finola soon became lovers but it was to be a friendly
rather than a passionate affair: Finola was still ministering to
him in 1992 but by then she had long become his nurse and
nanny rather than his mistress.

By now he was a media celebrity in London. An increasing
number of newspapers and magazines were running interviews and photographs and asking him to write for them.
The *Observer* magazine commissioned him to write about the
room he lived in and on 31 January he was followed around
from the flat to the Coach and Horses to Kettners to the
Colony by a BBC television crew filming him for an *Arena*
programme about people who live an essentially nocturnal life
during the day, *Night and Day*. He took an immediate fancy to
a young American researcher, Debbie Geller, who was working on the documentary and by some miracle turned on the
charm to such an extent that they had an affair. 'I suppose
you could call it that,' she told me six years later, 'but it was
like being around a sick uncle. What I liked about him was
that he didn't seem like an English person because he was so
demonstrably emotional and self-involved to the exclusion of
other people. You don't see many English people like that.
I was in my early thirties, he was so much older than me.
That straightforwardness appealed. He is not a liar and he
doesn't disguise much of anything. He's like a kid so it was
a weird combination of clapped-out and childlike, and he

can be really sweet. It was touching how nice he was. The only time he ever got angry with me – he *screamed* at me – was for comparing cricket pitching to baseball pitching and I said I thought it was harder to pitch in baseball.'

By the end of February he had become quite taken by the Groucho Club, and went there increasingly to sleep in the afternoons. It was not however always safe. One afternoon in mid-March he was approached there by a drunken young man who punched him in the face. When Bernard asked the reason the fellow replied: 'You're Michael Foot, aren't you?' It was true that Bernard's hair was already white, like Foot's, but he was obviously ageing badly elsewhere too since Foot was nineteen years older than he.

Then he went to New York for ten days and spent most of his time in one bar fraternising with his boxing hero Rocky Graziano. He did not mention in his column that he went with the youthful Debbie Geller, perhaps because he did not want to antagonise She Who Would Iron 14 Shirts and have to start doing his own laundry again.

The affair was quickly over but Bernard was undeterred. That year of 1986 was to see a final burst of the Bernardine libido. As soon as he returned to London in mid-April he was smitten by a dark-haired Groucho Club waitress called Bettina. 'Her eyes are like a summer sky and the whites of them are as clear as the sparkle of her teeth behind lips that beg kissing,' he wrote in the *Spectator*. He realised that nowadays he was hardly irresistible but cried in despair: 'How can I tell her that the inside of the top of my skull is like the ceiling of the Sistine Chapel?'

At the end of April he began to write a regular 'Low Life' type Saturday column for the tabloid *Sunday Mirror* entitled 'My Life'; at first it was quite different from his *Spectator* column, but within a month it was already showing signs of becoming almost a duplicate, though he resorted to using shorter words because he felt he had to write down to tabloid readers. 'It was not as good as the *Spectator* stuff,' Molloy admitted, 'because he thought he'd got to write it for *Mirror* readers. When he writes for the *Spectator* he knows exactly who he's talking to, they're people he understands and knows.'

His evenings had by now become something of a magical mystery tour and he would awake the next morning to find curry in one of his shoes, or a raw shish kebab in his blazer pocket, or an unsigned note on the bedside table from someone he could not remember at all that read simply: 'Would you like to try again some time?' In June he arose from his bed one morning to find a paperclip in his pubic hair. He was baffled. He had not even been near a secretary in months. 'It was what Holmes would have called a five pipe problem,' he mused in the *Spectator*.

On 4 June he was off again to the Epsom Derby in an open-topped bus loaded with champagne, a buffet lunch and fifty assorted Soho spivs and bohemians. He took Finola. She was never to forget it. 'I'd never been to the Derby,' she told me, 'and the anxiety started early. Bookshop Billy's friends were all drinking ferociously from the time they left Soho so by the time they got to Epsom they were jumping off the bus and peeing in people's front gardens, which was quite an alarming experience for somebody like me. The day went on like that. Jeffrey decided to take bets and a couple of Billy's friends who had recently come out of Her Majesty's care advanced him the start-up money and he kept a marker on a sheet of cardboard which he duly lost as he got drunker. The day passed quite well but on the journey back the company was drunker than it had been on the way out and they stopped at some pub in South London that a friend had taken over and then it became clear that Jeffrey had lost the marker and there was a ruction brewing about what money he owed these chaps. It really got quite nasty. On the final stretch back to Soho there were menaces and they pushed one bloke off in Westminster. They were getting quite nasty and I wasn't quite sure how it would end. I've never been so *glad* to see the Coach and Horses, it felt like a safe haven. I felt quite relieved to see Norman.'

The mood aboard the bus would have turned even uglier had they known that Bernard was later to claim that he had won £3,000 during the day. He also claimed later that it was this big win that made his old friend Conan Nicholas 'severely sick' and caused the end of their friendship.

Bernard then went to Portugal with his old friend Michael Elphick, the actor, and enjoyed a holiday on Elphick's small cabin cruiser. He returned to find that he had been served with yet another bankruptcy order by the Inland Revenue, which was now demanding £2,000 in unpaid taxes. In desperation he placed with his bookie Victor Chandler a four-horse combination bet, a Yankee, that won him £2,535 on the evening races at Pontefract when all four of the horses won. Bernard asked Chandler to write out a cheque to the Inland Revenue 'to show them it didn't come from hard labour.'

At the end of September the inevitable happened: he was at last arrested for taking illegal bets in the Coach and Horses. On the afternoon of Saturday 20th he was in the pub taking bets as usual on the televised races. One customer put a £2 bet on a horse called Irish Passage, which was running in the 1.40 at Ayr, and won £12. Then a gang of police and Customs and Excise officers raided the pub, the winning punter was revealed as a Customs officer, and Bernard was arrested on a charge of acting as a bookmaker without being the holder of a bookmaker's permit, contrary to Section 2 of the *Betting, Gaming and Lotteries Act 1963*, an offence for which he could be fined £2,000. Astonishingly, he was arrested by three Customs and Excise men and *nine* policemen. Perhaps they had all come along for his autograph. He was taken to Vine Street police station to be fingerprinted and grilled by the police, one of whom enquired blithely whether he knew what had won the three o'clock at Newbury. He told them he had been accepting bets from regulars in the Coach for about five months and had taken bets totalling about £30 every Saturday – not for profit but for 'Saturday-only childish excitement'.

Bernard appeared on Monday 22nd at Bow Street Magistrates' Court and was remanded for a month on unconditional
bail to allow the Customs officers 'to make further inquiries'.

On Monday 20 October, at Bow Street Court, a group
of friends – among them Taki, Charles Moore, Geoffrey
Wheatcroft and John McCririck, the TV racing commentator – turned out to support him when he pleaded 'guilty,
m'lud'. Bernard was fined £200 – and £75 in costs – after
pleading guilty to two charges of taking a few illegal bets
in the Coach and Horses and evading paying £31.12 betting
duty. He admitted taking £389 in bets in the three summer
months that he had been under observation. The Excise
officers had been watching the pub for three months and
placed bets with Bernard on four Saturdays between June
and September. He had said at the police station that he took
bets only from friends. When asked whether he had realised
that he had been betting with Excise officers he had replied:
'If I did, I must have been pissed, which is quite likely.' He
went on to remark that if by some dreadful mischance the
undercover spooks had lost in their bets with him he very
much hoped that they would be entitled to reclaim their
stakes on expenses. He was defended in court by Geoffrey
Robinson, who criticised the officers for 'inciting' Bernard
to continue to break the law instead of warning him it was
illegal on their first visit. Robinson said: 'The last horse they
bet on with Mr Bernard was called Aid And Abet and that
is in fact what they were doing.'

The manner of Bernard's arrest came in for particular
criticism in the Press. The following day Geoffrey Wheatcroft
wrote in the *Daily Telegraph*: 'You wonder what assistance the
constabulary will need next time they come to feel the collar
of some frail and tipsy scribbler who has forgotten to pay his
gas bill. Mounted police? Sniffer dogs? Police marksmen?'

With typical style, just before the hearing, Bernard gave
the Excise men a cheque for £31.12, the betting duty they
claimed was due.

After the case Bernard told *The Sporting Life* (which splashed the story across the top of the front page the next day): 'It's vindictive and a total waste of public money. It's the inalienable right of every free Englishman to have a £1 bet with a friend over whether horse A finishes ahead of horse B.' And he told the *Evening Standard*: 'This kind of thing goes on in pubs all over the country. I will now be going to the Coach and Horses to acquire a hangover and to receive bets on England winning the Ashes this winter.'

The first hardback collection of his *Spectator* articles was published in November: *Low Life* (Duckworth, *1986*). It was dedicated somewhat sentimentally 'For Isabel Bernard with love.' It also carried a foreword by John Osborne, a man almost as demanding and irascible as Bernard himself, who claimed that Bernard 'possesses courage and style in abundance and his eye for physical detail, both in delight and distress, is as astonishing and stimulating as anything in Pepys or Boswell.' He added: 'Jeffrey Bernard is the Tony Hancock of journalism.'

But even Hancock would have drawn the line at posing nude. Bernard was invited to pose in the nude for Taki's photographer friend Katya Grenfell's book of celebrity pin-ups, *Naked London*. He was pictured with his genitals tastefully covered by a *Timeform* book about racehorses.

By now, Bernard had indeed become so celebrated that even the police who had arrested him invited him bizarrely to their CID Christmas party in December. Equally bizarrely, he accepted, and there met a delightful woman detective who showed him that while he might no longer have a pistol in his pocket she did have one of her own in her handbag, a revelation that made him fall in love with her on the spot.

But she was hardly one of the Handmaidens and the halcyon days of the Great Bernardine Handmaidens were nearly over. Apart from Finola Morgan, who continued to put up with his abuse for many more years, most of them had had enough. Geraldine Norman, one of the first of the many women who had taken pity on him in the 1980s, finally decided that she could no longer stand having him living in her flat in Great Portland Street. She asked him to find somewhere else. 'The reason that I finally asked him to leave was actually not because of his domestic habits at all but I couldn't bear living with his unhappiness,' she told me. 'He was so *intensely* unhappy, he *hated* himself. He was frightened of dying. There was a *deep* unhappiness around the place. It's difficult dealing with one's own life. He had to drink to get himself out of that depression. I used to reckon his high point was from about eleven in the morning – whenever he'd had a second double vodka – through to about three, when he was charming, wonderful company, very funny, and then he went down into the slough again.'

It was the start of two years of even greater unhappiness and insecurity for Bernard. Once again he had no home.

20

The Vultures Gather

At first he simply refused to face up to the fact that Geraldine wanted him to leave and for several weeks he made no effort at all to find another flat. Early in January he tootled off to Lambourn for the weekend as though nothing had happened and the next week he went to Berlin for three days to write a magazine article. He even told Jeremy Lewis, who was writing a profile of him for *Midweek* magazine, that he had stopped hating himself at last 'because of the small amount of success I've had with my columns, and silly things like people coming up and buying me drinks. I suppose, unconsciously, I one day started thinking, "Well, perhaps you're not quite the c--- you thought you were."'

This was not an opinion shared by the Marylebone County Court, which issued at the end of February a warrant for his arrest for contempt of court and threatened to imprison him if he did not turn up in court on 4 March in The Case of the Sueing Dentist, who wanted £100. Then another large bill arrived from the Inland Revenue demanding £7,500 in unpaid back taxes. Bernard happened to be staying with us in Lambourn that weekend and he showed me the bill and whimpered: 'What shall I do?'

Pay it, I said.

This astonished him. 'That is fantastic and so simplistic,' he wrote in the *Spectator*. 'It has never occurred to me before that you can get these people off your back by paying up.' He did not of course mention that just before showing me the tax demand he had also shown me his bank statement and that there was more than £10,000 in his current account. He was to spend the next couple of years constantly on the run from the taxman, changing his address every few months and blitzed from one home to the next by a bombardment of buff-coloured envelopes. It was not until 1990 that the taxman (or – horrors – the taxwoman) eventually caught up with him and finally managed to seize eighty per cent of all his royalties from *Jeffrey Bernard is Unwell*, about £40,000 out of the £50,000 that the play was to earn him. Even then he moaned and solicited for sympathy. He seemed incapable of understanding that many of his friends had paid twice as much as that in tax over the years even though they had earned no more than he had. For some mysterious reason he always seemed to think that the rules of ordinary life should not apply to him, that he should be let off, that he was *different*. After all, only *grown-ups* pay tax.

Then, at the beginning of May, Jeffrey suddenly left Great Portland Street after five years, even though he felt sick with worry at the prospect of being homeless. 'I went away somewhere,' Geraldine remembered, 'and he'd said he wouldn't move till I came back but I came into the flat and the sink was completely piled with washing up and there were slices of bread and marmalade on the floor and he'd gone. The vodka and fresh oranges had gone. I laughed and then had this idea that I'd write about it for the *Spectator*.'

Bernard was incensed when Geraldine submitted the article. He had always boasted that he couldn't care less what anyone wrote or said about him but he prevented the piece being published by protesting to the Editor, Charles Moore. It was the second time that Bernard had censored an article about himself – the first was when he had persuaded *Harper's & Queen* to kill an unflattering profile by Craig Brown.

The paragraph that now offended Bernard the most read: 'While he was in Tenerife last month I opened his bank statement by mistake and discovered that he had £13,500 in his current account. That made it easier to harden my heart. If he wanted he could afford a suite at the Ritz.'

Bernard's ostensible excuse for preventing the publication of the article was that it breached his financial privacy but it seems more likely that he did so because it threatened to reveal at last the unattractive truth about his real nature and to expose him not as the devil-may-care Fuck-You swashbuckler of the legend that he had created about himself but as the miserable, moaning, depressing old sod that he had in fact become.

The news that Bernard was comparatively well-off electrified Soho. 'All this time I've been *conned*,' said one friend off whom Bernard had often cadged money. 'Jeff showed her article to everyone but for the amount of money: that was Tippexed out!'

Bernard left most of his possessions behind in Great Portland Street without bothering too much as to whether this might inconvenience Geraldine and he was to remain homeless for eight traumatic months, during which he scuttled from one small borrowed room to another and lived out of a few carrier bags.

He tried to cheer himself up by going off to the Derby as usual in a bus full of champagne and Soho cronies. When the bus driver (from Yorkshire) lost his way and started heading towards Brighton, Bernard directed the bus back in the right direction towards Epsom. He was once again taking illegal bets even though he knew that if he were caught again he could go to prison.

Back in London it was such a glorious evening and his spirits were still so high that he startled Ian Board the bar of the Colony Club by suddenly appearing outside an open first-floor window at the top of a ladder and announcing volubly, as though he were Eamonn Andrews on *This Is Your Life*: 'Ian Board, you're a stupid fucking cunt.' Board nearly fell off his barstool and it is a miracle that Bernard did not fall off the ladder. By the time Board had staggered down the stairs and into the street Bernard had somehow negotiated his way back to ground level and had fled.

Not surprisingly, considering the amount he had drunk at the Derby, he was again very unwell with pancreatitis. He moved to Finola Morgan's house for a couple of days' cossetting, then into a Soho hotel, and then stayed with Isabel at Jill's flat in Chiswick while Jill was away.

By now Bernard was constantly being interviewed and photographed and strange young women whom he had never met kept nodding at him in the Groucho Club and commenting on the quality of the afternoon. He pretended to be disconcerted but in fact loved it all, though he seemed now increasingly to be Taking Himself Very Seriously Indeed: when he called out to Anthony Burgess in Old Compton Street and the Sage of Monaco appeared not to hear, Bernard was convinced that he had been snubbed.

Yet despite his fame he remained homeless and the flat-hunting was becoming a nightmarish obsession. In August he was even reduced to cat-sitting for a friend in Belsize Park. He then moved into a room at the Chelsea Arts Club for a few weeks while a Norfolk nun, a friend of Oliver, prayed daily that he might find a flat. His peace of mind was not eased by the news that Isabel had started working as a waitress in a wine bar. He was even more disconcerted by a caustic attack on him in a new novel that was published in September.

Jane Ellison's novel, *Another Little Drink* (Secker & Warburg), was a light-hearted satire in which she lampooned the boozy journalistic world of *Private Eye* and the *Spectator*, which she renamed in the book the *Commentator*. Bernard appeared in it – not even lightly disguised – as Jerry Gude, a 'has-been writer' and 'notorious philanderer and drunk'. The novel's description of 'Jerry Gude' was brutally accurate and the book's cover, a cartoon by Michael Heath, depicted Norman Balon swearing at his customers in the Coach and Horses, which appears in the novel as the Dog and Biscuit. In the book the foul-mouthed regulars of the Dog and Biscuit are astonished to hear that the has-been alcoholic 'Gude' is to be the subject of a television documentary in which all three of his ex-wives are encouraged to tell the truth.

– 2 –

In November Fourth Estate published his new book *Talking Horses*, a collection of his best racing stories, which was reviewed in *The Spectator* by John Lord Oaksey, who called Bernard 'the funniest living writer on the subject' and said: 'the *Sporting Life* is crazy not to have its author back.' The publishers launched the book by giving a champagne party at Lingfield races and by sponsoring the 2.15 Jeffrey Bernard Handicap, after which he was to present the winning owner with a signed copy of the book, a cut-glass bowl and a bottle of vodka. The day was to bring him a sudden miraculous £10,000 libel windfall when the *Evening Standard* suggested that he had been drunk and he decided to sue them. Once again it seemed that he cared more about the opinions of others than he would admit. His new maxim seemed to be 'Publish and Be Sued.' His libel action seemed particularly hypocritical in view of what he had written in the *Spectator* just four months previously, in June: 'Why are people so touchy about what is said about them? Most of us are being slandered every minute of the day.'

Those of his friends who accompanied him to Lingfield – Norman Balon, Gordon Smith – swore later that he had indeed been sober that day. Bernard did however admit in the *Spectator* the following weekend that he had no idea why he had thought it might be a good idea to pour all the vodka into the bowl, that he had behaved so badly that he would probably be warned off the racecourse, and that he had slept nearly all the way back to London and had then managed to cook some fish cakes without burning down the entire block of flats.

The *Evening Standard* obviously went too far when it claimed in its Londoner's Diary the next day that when the race ended he was 'snoring peacefully' in the weighing room, 'a skinny hand clutching the glass bowl trophy that he was meant to present to the winner'. It also reported inaccurately that 'the day ended in tears when Bernard and his entourage boarded the train to London, fighting broke out and several arrests were made at Victoria Station.' There was indeed a fight on the train back to London but it did not involve Bernard, who had returned on an earlier train. The *Standard* story added that Bernard was ten years behind with his tax returns and quoted one friend as saying: 'Jeffrey's off to Kenya on Thursday to forget about his little problem. Some of us think he might be gone a long time.'

A few days later Bernard did indeed go to Kenya for a month, taking Irma Kurtz with him, and stayed in a house lent to him by a complete stranger who was a fan who read the *Spectator*. He went to Nairobi and much enjoyed having a maid and a chauffeur to minister unto him, and then to Lake Naivasha, Mombasa and Lake Victoria and saw some hippopotami and a giraffe. He wrote in the *Spectator* that Kenya was the only country that he would like to live in. Indeed, he enjoyed Kenya so much that on two consecutive weeks he filed identical columns to the *Spectator*.

And yet it seemed that nothing would ever really please him. His summing-up of 1987 was devastating. He had been down the Nile and to Lanzarote, Dublin, Paris, Kenya. He had had a book published and a race named after him. He had even at last found somewhere permanent to live, in the attic of his old friend Pete Arthy's house in Covent Garden. But he was still determined to be unhappy. 'The trouble is that I bore myself,' he wrote in the *Spectator*. 'When even a self-obsessed man is made to yawn by his own day-dreams then there's nowhere to go.'

At times it seemed that he thoroughly deserved his unhappiness for the way he treated other people. 'Just before Christmas 1987 Jeff lent me £50 which I was due to repay by the end of January,' his old friend Conan Nicholas told me, 'but on 6 January 1988 he saw me drinking in the Swiss and sent his girlfriend over to ask for the £50 back. I had to borrow it from the chap next to me, and I paid him.' Yet Bernard was renowned for not repaying his own debts. 'There was a time when he was short of money to pay an income tax bill and five or six people contributed to pay what was due but none of it ever came back,' Norman Balon told me. 'One or two people are still aggrieved about it. Michael Elphick gave him some money to pay the income tax: it was supposed to be a loan and he asked me if he should ask for it back and I said, "Don't waste your time, all you'll get is a mouthful of abuse."'

– 3 –

He moved in January to the attic in Covent Garden, in Betterton Street just a few hundred yards' stagger from the Coach and Horses and immediately opposite the twinkling lights of a handy genito-urinary hospital specialising in Aids, syphilis, bemused bladders and other afflictions of the southern regions. The next month he was reunited with his bed, pictures and books, which had been stored at Geraldine Norman's flat ever since he had left in a huff, and their return pleased him so much that he promised himself that now, at last, he would write That Book. But his eyes were beginning to fail and by the end of April his weight had fallen to 8st 6lbs, not much more than he had been as a boxing bantamweight when he was seventeen. This did not prevent the arrival of fan letters from women who seemed to have sexual designs on him. 'I'm not very interesting,' wrote one Spanish groupie, 'sometimes with a bit of efforts I attain to be, but I have a pair of boots that it can be lace up, up.'

In March he was off to Thailand, where he was so impressed that when he returned to Britain he did something that seemed to be completely out of character: he contacted the Children's Christian Aid society and sponsored a twelve-year-old Thai girl, Sum Pettikum, whose father had died (sadly but appropriately) from a liver disease. This act of charity cost Bernard £12 a month by banker's order – 'just two drinks a week,' as he put it – and the charity spent the money on food and medicine for the child, who had two sisters and a brother. He was sent a photograph of the child and occasional reports.

He then won £1,000 on the Grand National and was rich enough to have a £500 bet on the American Presidential election with Jay Landesman's daughter-in-law Julie Burchill, the *Mail on Sunday* columnist, who wagered £1,000 that Michael Dukakis would win while Bernard and Landesman each backed George Bush for £500. Later in the year, however, the *Evening Standard* reported that Burchill had backed out of the wager and returned Bernard's cheque. 'She's got no bottle,' he told the paper. 'A gentleman would never do that.'

He was never to be poor again. Early in 1988 he was drinking in the Groucho Club when Keith Waterhouse suggested he might write a stage show based on Bernard's Low Life columns. Bernard was not impressed. 'I thought the man was mad,' he told Brigit Grant of the *Ham & High*. 'It was something I would never have considered doing myself. I've been asked to write my autobiography many times, but who wants to read about my bloody boring life?' Waterhouse went home to start writing and a legend was in the making. On 4 July the news of the new play was reported in the *Evening Standard* diary, which tipped Walter Matthau to play the part of Norman Balon and John Hurt to play Bernard, and remarked of Hurt: 'Friends say it would be his most taxing role since playing Merrick in *The Elephant Man*, and will require almost as much make-up.' It quoted Bernard as saying: 'I hope I live till then, but I'll probably make a balls-up and die on opening night.'

His health was certainly deteriorating. In May he was ill again in bed at home with pancreatitis and in June he was back in hospital, this time in Avon, where he felt as though he were on holiday. The nurses could not understand why he alone was allowed to drink (to restabilise his body, weight and strength) and one nurse made a friend of him for life when she asked earnestly: 'Mr Bernard, are you *sure* you're drinking enough?' Despite his frailty he was still determined to live dangerously. As soon as he emerged from hospital he tottered into a betting shop in Greek Street to listen to a race commentary and found himself informing 'an enormous' football fan who was listening to a noisy soccer commentary that this was a betting shop, not a fucking football ground. The large fan invited Bernard to step outside, where a right-hander on the chin felled him so efficiently that he went down like a tropical sunset. His assailant was arrested by plainclothes policemen who happened to be in the betting shop and was fined £100.

At the end of July Finola went to the South of France for a few days' holiday with her brother and sister-in-law, to Haut de Cagnes, near Nice, and Bernard decided to escape doctors, taxwomen, publicans and all the other endless aggravations by going down by train to join her. By coincidence his old Colonel Mad co-writer 'Screamer' Lewis and I were there at the same time, 'Screamer' to enjoy a long weekend at his favourite auberge up in the hills at Rocquefort-les-Pins and I to interview Graham Greene in Antibes for the *Sunday Express*.

At my suggestion, Greene booked Bernard into a hellishly seedy and noisy hotel that was apparently considered suitable even for Greene's posh Russian friends and visitors, like the traitor Kim Philby's widow. After my interview with Greene on 2 August Bernard joined us at Greene's flat above the roaring, buzzing, hooting traffic of the harbour at Antibes, where Greene was expecting a visit from the local Mafia at any time and kept a gas bomb to deal with intruders. We were to lunch at his favourite restaurant, the Félix au Port, a noisy, smelly pavement café near the port but only a five-minute stroll away. I had rented a car but suggested we should walk to the restaurant, as he usually did. The great man was shocked. 'We must drive,' he insisted. 'Jeffrey's legs will never make it.' Bernard was just fifty-six, Greene all of eighty-three. Greene told me later that within half-an-hour of meeting Bernard he felt he had known him all his life. They became surprisingly good friends. Greene took him out for lunch three more times in five days, gave him a copy of his new book and a tube of vitamin and caffeine pills that he told Bernard would give him 'the courage to go on', suggested that he might write some excellent short stories, and even introduced him to his mysterious French mistress, Yvonne Cloueta. Bernard was so flattered and encouraged by Greene's attention that he started to write a short story though he never finished it. Subsequently they met several times in London, where they lunched at the Ritz and Greene offered to write a quote for the Pan paperback *More Low Life* which was to be published the following year: 'In all the years I have never once been bored by Jeffrey Bernard.'

The friendship could not be explained solely by the fact that Greene, like Bernard, relished a deep daily morning dive into a couple of vast frosty vodkas well before noon, followed by generous helpings of wine at lunch and a nap and drinks again before dinner. There was more to it than that. Greene's motto as a writer had always been this Browning quote: 'Our interest's on the dangerous edge of things, the honest thief, the tender murderer, the superstitious atheist.' Greene was himself what he liked to call 'an agnostic Catholic' and perhaps he enjoyed the notion of seeing in Bernard somebody similarly contradictory, the puritan cavalier, the sober drunk, the split Gemini personality. Whatever the reason, their mutual warmth was undoubtedly genuine.

During one game of *boules* with 'Screamer' Lewis and me at the Auberge du Colombier up in the hills at Rocquefort-les-Pins Bernard needed to buy his usual Senior Service cigarettes and was told that he would have to walk fifty yards down the road to buy them. He was away for twenty-five minutes.

'Why did you take so long?' Lewis asked him.

'There was a pub next door,' explained Bernard. As usual his capacity for booze was limitless.

Bernard's ex-wife Jill was once told by a diabetes and pancreatitis specialist that patients like Bernard never lived beyond forty-five and when she told him that her ex-husband was in fact fifty-six he said: 'Christ, I'd love to cut him up when he's dead.' He would have to join the queue. As the vultures circled and contemplated the prospect of feasting on Bernard's corpse he punched Lord Patrick Coyningham in the face (at the Coach and Horses) because 'he was sniggering at me and said, "I'm having bets on how much longer you've got to live." I didn't like that so I whacked him. When we had those bets years before in the Swiss that was in a more friendly way, a joke.'

But however thin-skinned Bernard was about himself he was still vicious about others, even the gentle Isabel. When she went to look for work in Australia in November he wrote cruelly in the *Spectator* that she seemed to know nothing and reported that when he had asked her who had succeeded Lenin she had replied 'Stanley Baldwin.'

Yet he could be remarkably kind. At Christmas, which he usually hated, he suffered another sudden gush of generosity when Conan Nicholas's house in Hounslow was badly damaged by fire and Bernard asked him for lunch on Christmas Day and gave him £500, knowing how hard-up Nicholas was. But that magnificent Christmas present was finally to destroy their friendship. 'Three times I asked him if it was a loan or a gift,' said Nicholas, 'and he said it was a gift – no question. But soon afterwards he regretted it, and he wrote a piece saying I hadn't paid him back.' They were still not speaking to each other in 1992. It was a sad end to a long friendship that had included so long ago the Great Battersea Cat Race.

As the year ended Bernard was sunk in gloom and the outlook did indeed look pretty grim for 1989. He weighed a frail 8st 12lbs and his legs had become so weak that he kept falling backwards off the stairs in Betterton Street. To pick anything up off the floor he had to go down on all fours. In the last *Spectator* issue of the year he wrote miserably that his life in the Coach and Horses had become monotonously predictable: 'I am late this morning but I know that Gordon is already on his third large Bells and that Eric, the French barman, is staring out of the window when he should be looking to see if anyone needs serving, Mary is preparing the salad, Norman is screaming at the nurses in his posh clinic and Graham [Mason] is holding his head in his hands and moaning, "Oh no, oh no", time and again. There must be something else somewhere.'

There was, of course. Keith Waterhouse was finishing his play *Jeffrey Bernard is Unwell*. It was to transform Bernard's life.

21

Jeffrey Bernard is Unwell

That year of 1989 was to be Jeff Bernard's *annus mirabilis*, the year of Keith Waterhouse's play and astonishing fame and wealth. As the year began it seemed quite possible that he would never see the end of it. In January, as he went into his flat, he suddenly keeled over with all the symptoms of a heart attack and woke up in University College hospital. The next morning a chest X-ray showed nothing amiss so of course he lit a cigarette. The consultant admitted that he was baffled. Bernard repaired immediately to the Coach and Horses for a couple of heart-starters.

At first he simply refused to believe that Waterhouse was seriously intending to stage a play about *him* in the West End and at the end of February he took himself off to Australia to see Isabel for two weeks. He enjoyed Sydney especially, because it was full of good pubs. As usual he saw nothing much of the country or its people but he returned to announce that he could live there. Then, as the truth about the play began to seep into his consciousness, he became increasingly convinced that he would not live to see it. In April he was unwell again and had to spend four days in bed at home. By June he was so weak that he had to sit down to put his trousers on and he was now so renowned for his illnesses and frailty that the health insurance company BUPA asked him to write a quarterly column in their house magazine about being unwell. At the end of July he was exhausted after standing for four hours umpiring a cricket match between the *Spectator* and the Coach and Horses at the Oval and he was so worried about his health that for the first time in his life he consulted a private doctor, who

seemed less concerned about the drinking than about the
fifty cigarettes he was smoking each day.

It was now that he fell out finally and irrevocably with
his old love Sally Vincent when he wrote about her once too
often in the *Spectator*. He reported that he had said that he
shared a birthday with Amelia Bloomer and that Sally had
replied: 'Well, you've had your hands in a few pairs, haven't
you?' She was incensed, feeling that he had damaged her pro-
fessionally as a journalist by portraying her as being vulgar
and she sent him a letter that read: 'Dear Jeffrey, Would it
be possible, do you think, for you to continue to amuse your
winsome little clique without further derisive references to
me? I can easily understand that your malice is probably as
unconscious as your stance is arch, but surely you can grasp
that I don't get money for jam, either, and it's tough enough
out here without having to suffer the embarrassment of your
idle mockeries. That you are discouraging and unkind to old
friends is something you have to live with. Try not to live off
it as well.' First Conan Nicholas, now Sally Vincent. He was
beginning to lose all his oldest friends. The next would be Pete
Arthy, his Covent Garden landlord and the oldest friend of all.
It was lucky for Bernard that the play was soon to make him
so famous and lionised that he could pretend that he did not
need any of them any more.

The play was also to save him in the nick of time from
bankruptcy, though the *Evening Standard* money helped as
well. In June The Taxwoman finally lost patience and sued
him for £21,000 in unpaid tax and interest for the years
1975 to 1985, and she would doubtless have plenty of other
demands for the four years after that. As usual he tried to
escape reality by flying off for an exotic holiday in the sun.
The South Africans refused him a visa, possibly because he
abused them when they wanted to know his mother's maiden
name, so he went instead to his favourite island, Barbados.
Beneath the palm trees he tried to forget that he was due to
appear in the High Court in London the following week and
to cough up the £21,000 or else. But just then he found himself

£10,000 richer when the *Evening Standard* settled out of court in his libel case. He had been tempted to settle for £5,000 but his lawyer, the *Daily Mirror*'s libel expert Oscar Beuselinck, the father of the actor Paul Nicholas, had stiffened his backbone to hold out for more. 'That was a hell of a lot of money to me,' said Bernard. 'I haven't looked back since then and I haven't been short of funds since then. That's what did it.' God bless the *Evening Standard*.

Bernard's libel jackpot sickened Richard Ingrams, no stranger to libel actions himself as Editor of *Private Eye*. 'If I had a tenner for every time I have seen him the worse for drink,' wrote Ingrams in his column in the *Observer*, 'I would have considerably more than £10,000.'

Meanwhile, as the first night of *Jeffrey Bernard is Unwell* loomed closer, and he accepted at last that his name really was going to be up in lights in Shaftesbury Avenue, he could barely think of anything else. He began to drift in a daze of excitement and apprehension. He was valiant in refraining from mentioning it in his column until the very last moment but he hardly needed to mention it. Every other publication in Britain suddenly seemed incapable of writing about anything else.

It gradually struck Bernard that Keith Waterhouse was working some kind of miracle as the year progressed and that this play based on his life and writings – *his* life – might just become a huge success. 'Keith had thought for a long time that Jeffrey would be a marvellous character for a play,' the play's director, Ned Sherrin, told me, 'but he had the first idea when he went to *La Bohème* at Covent Garden and was sitting there bored when his mind went off onto the story of the late John Murphy, a casting director at Granada Television, who *did* get locked into Gerry's Club one night and fell asleep in the loo. Murphy was in fact let out very quickly, but Keith suddenly thought: *that*'s the play. That's how to do it.'

Waterhouse did not of course simply lift a few Low Life columns from the *Spectator* and stick them together

for the stage. Bernard himself admitted to me that Sherrin
was right in his estimate that only seventy per cent of the
play was derived directly from his own work and that the
remaining thirty per cent was due to Waterhouse alone —
not to mention the art and creative imagination that were
necessary to mould the material for the stage. Several of the
anecdotes in the play had nothing at all to do with Bernard.
'The story in it about Denis Shaw, for instance, is Keith's,
not Jeffrey's,' said Sherrin. The wonderful set-piece scene
involving The Great Egg Trick had nothing whatever to do
with Bernard: Waterhouse was its only begetter. Strangest
of all, perhaps, considering the phenomenal success of the
play, was Bernard's admission that although he had known
Waterhouse for thirty years 'I know nothing about him and
I'm sure he knows nothing about me: we just collide in pubs
and clubs and newspaper offices.'

Waterhouse and the play's producer, Michael Redington,
offered the lead at first to John Hurt. It seemed inspired
casting. 'John is not only a good actor but also the same kind
of person as Jeffrey,' Dick West suggested, 'rather sour and
angry and melancholy. Several times I've been in the Coach
with Jeffrey *and* John Hurt and they've merged into the same
person, they're exactly the same.' And as the bumps on the
back of Bernard's head grew larger he even took to calling
himself after one of Hurt's major roles, The Elephant Man.

Bernard took Hurt's rejection of the part as a personal
slight. He liked to claim later that he had shown the script
of the play to Hurt, who had said 'in a very snooty way':
'Not for me, darling, but it might make a radio play.' Hurt's
version of the story is significantly different. 'I was contacted
by the producer and Keith Waterhouse,' Hurt told me, 'and
when I read it my reaction was that I know Jeff so well and
being the kind of performer that I am I would not have
done anything that Peter did, which I think was absolutely
brilliant. When I heard Peter was going to do it I thought it
was absolutely inspired casting but I would have gone very
much more for Jeffrey and I didn't think in the way that I

approached it that it would have been a theatrical piece. It would have been much more a radio piece. Also I suppose it was partly the puritan in me, that I found it very difficult to commit myself entirely to the out-and-out adulation of self-destruction by alcohol, which I know we all laugh at and joke about and Jeffrey has become a kind of martyr to the cause. But there is a streak of puritanism in me that says this can't quite be right.' Hurt said to Ned Sherrin, the director, later: 'You're fucking lucky I said no. I wouldn't have been nearly as good as O'Toole in the theatre.'

Sherrin, who had previously worked with Waterhouse when he had asked him to write sketches for the satirical television programme *That Was The Week That Was* in the 1960s – and on Waterhouse's play *Mr and Mrs Nobody* – was himself not the first choice as director, either. That was Trevor Nunn, 'but he kept postponing his availability,' said Sherrin. Sherrin must have been a forgiving man. Thirteen years previously Bernard had written of him in one of his *Spectator* television reviews: 'I haven't often wondered what ever happened to Ned Sherrin, but now that I know, I'm going to try to forget. He looks very pleased, mind you.' Bernard must have been praying now that Sherrin had forgotten it. Sherrin in fact had no doubts about directing *Jeffrey Bernard is Unwell*. 'Well, I had some doubts about all that swearing,' he confessed, 'but I had no doubts at all about its success after Peter O'Toole came here to give a reading.'

O'Toole, who was exactly the same age as Bernard, fifty-seven, had no doubts about taking the part, either. 'When I sent Peter the script,' said Waterhouse, 'I got an offensive message on my machine that night: "Keith, I bloody hate you. I had all my plans for the year and now you've screwed them up. We're in business."' O'Toole had known Bernard for years (though not as well as Hurt). 'I used to see him in Gerry's Club occasionally,' said Bernard, 'but it was only this play that brought us together again. I like him: he's *difficult* – about giving interviews and having his photograph taken and things like that. He's vain and there's something in him that made it easy to understand the character he was playing, which a hell of a lot of actors wouldn't be able to. Had I woken up under a table in the pub, that's par for the course as far as Peter's concerned. *He* used to get up to some pretty dodgy things himself when he was younger, when he was drinking.'

The money to stage the play was quickly raised. Michael Heath put up £1,000 and even Norman Balon was persuaded to be an angel and to invest £500 in the play and was before long beside himself with excitement at the prospect of seeing the bar of his pub recreated on the West End stage. 'The play now apparently has nothing whatsoever to do with Keith Waterhouse, Peter O'Toole or Ned Sherrin,' Bernard reported in the *Spectator*. 'Oh no. It is Norman's play.' Rehearsals went smoothly and were completed without any problems in three weeks, possibly because Bernard stayed away. 'He said he was saving himself,' said Sherrin, who was later to report in his book *Theatrical Anecdotes* (Virgin, 1991): 'By a curious irony – since part of the play deals with Jeffrey's occasional impotence – one piece of scenery was labelled to enable the set constructors to identify it. The notice read: "Jeff Bernard. Centre leg. Extra stiffening".'

Early in September O'Toole and Bernard met for lunch at the Groucho Club and O'Toole told him: 'I want you to know, Jeff, that I have no intention of doing an impersonation of you.'

'Just as well,' retorted Bernard. 'I have been doing an impersonation of you since we met thirty-odd years ago.'

On Tuesday 26 September the play had its out-of-town premiere in Brighton. It was a triumph. 'I was not surprised by the play's success,' Sherrin told me. 'It sounded copper-bottomed as soon as I heard O'Toole reading it and the opening night in Brighton was so good that we *knew*.' The play caused so much laughter that Waterhouse and Sherrin had to cut half-an-hour from it before it reached London for fear of running too long. Bernard himself was so stunned by the hilarious reaction of the audience that night that he set fire to himself. 'He was wearing a dark suit but he went to bed with a cigarette still smouldering in the pocket,' said Sherrin. 'The next day he went to do radio interviews and there was this enormous hole burned in his trousers.'

The following day the entire cast went to Brighton races for champagne and steak and kidney pie and three days later, back in London, Bernard and O'Toole were mobbed by dozens of Press photographers at a publicity photocall outside the Coach and Horses. Both white-haired and emaciated, they looked remarkably alike. 'I hope you haven't come for the fiver you gave me in the 1950s,' said Bernard nervously.

'People say that Jeffrey leads a negative life,' O'Toole told the reporters. 'I don't agree. He allows people to see him as he is, with all his strengths and weaknesses.' Afterwards O'Toole kissed Bernard on the forehead. 'Goodbye darling,' he cried.

Bernard's elation was such that he took Finola to lunch at L'Epicure but his euphoria swiftly evaporated when he saw the present she had bought him. It was a rubber hospital ring to sit on now that he had become so bony with his loss of weight. 'I am geriatric before my time and it is humiliating,' he told his *Sunday Mirror* readers that weekend. 'Sitting in a bath, for example, is now quite painful, as is any contact with my pelvic bones other than a bar stool. I must get a shower fitting if I can stand up for five minutes.'

But nothing could now deny him his excitement. On 7 October the play moved to the Theatre Royal in Bath, which was said to be haunted by the ghost of a tortoiseshell butterfly after a previous actor-manager had dropped dead on stage during a sketch about a butterfly. The appearance of the ghost butterfly was said to bring good luck. 'We had an omen,' O'Toole told Victor Davis of the *Mail on Sunday*. 'I was on stage pouring a drink when a tortoiseshell butterfly landed on my newspaper. So I ad-libbed a chat with it. I said, "You are in bad company but you're welcome. Why don't you sit there? But don't make a noise – and don't get pissed." The audience fell about. And, when it finally left, I said ta-ta and the audience gave it a lovely exit round. What excited the ghostologists is that this phenomenon was witnessed by a thousand people.'

Interviews and profiles appeared in numerous papers and magazines, notably the *Telegraph Weekend Magazine*, which published a big colour portrait of Bernard, O'Toole, Waterhouse and Sherrin together and persuaded the four big names behind the play to write about each other: Waterhouse on Bernard, Bernard on O'Toole, O'Toole on Sherrin, Sherrin on Waterhouse.

Waterhouse recalled the 'appalling behaviour' of their young boozing days in Soho and went on: 'I guess I grew up after a fashion, but Jeff never did. The best and worst thing that happened to him was the gift of his Low Life column in *The Spectator*. From then on playing truant was more than a vocation, it was a commitment. Being his own Boswell meant that he had to be Jeffrey Bernard all round the clock, seven days a week. No wonder he doesn't look too clever.'

Bernard himself was embarrassingly flattering about O'Toole: 'The man is so damn good-looking it made me sick ... I just sat there looking into those pale blue eyes of his and thinking how unfair it is of God that he can't spread out good looks a little more.'

Bernard's cup of fame was running over. Two days before the play opened in London at the Apollo Theatre he appeared on Melvyn Bragg's radio chat programme *Start the Week* with the Queen's couturier Sir Hardy Amies and the genial Labour politician Denis Healey. Bernard proceeded from the programme to the Groucho Club, where he was interviewed by a woman from the *Sunday Times Magazine*, who seemed disconcerted to learn that generally he spent the first few hours of each day, from 4 until 8 a.m., lying in bed chain-smoking, drinking and staring at the photographs on his walls which (he wrote in the *Spectator*) 'trigger off a relentless speculation ending in remorse. (There are three ex-wives staring at me at this very moment.)' He told the interviewer, Ginny Dougary, that it would be 'a warning light' if he started wearing the same shirt two days running: 'Another warning light is to find a load of curry in your typewriter the next morning.' After the interview Bernard staggered up two floors to attend the launch party for his paperback anthology *More Low Life*. After the party Bernard lunched with Keith Waterhouse, his very own Fairy Godfather.

The play opened in London on Wednesday 18 October. That afternoon Bernard tottered down Shaftesbury Avenue to gaze up at his name in lights outside the Apollo Theatre: *JEFFREY BERNARD IS UNWELL.* He stood and looked, and stood and looked. He could hardly believe it. Once he had worked just a couple of hundred yards away as a builder's navvy, forty years ago. Once he had worked in this very theatre as a stagehand, thirty years ago. Just up the road at the Palace Theatre his parents had met nearly seventy years ago. The ghosts of Bunny and Dora must surely have flitted like tortoiseshell butterflies across the auditorium of the Apollo that night.

O'Toole's performance that first night was magnificent. He had told Bernard that he was not going to impersonate him but many in the audience were stunned by the resemblance he achieved, the trembling, the pathos, the cigarette smouldering between just the right two fingers. 'At times O'Toole was so much like Jeff it was creepy,' said Mike Molloy. 'A couple of times he caught him to the point where it almost made the hairs on your neck stand up. It was absolutely breathtaking. Chilling.' Simon Courtauld agreed. 'O'Toole was very like Jeffrey,' he said. 'Some of his gestures and movements were uncannily like Jeffrey.'

Keith Waterhouse told magazine writer Graham Hassell why O'Toole was so good in the play by saying: 'Peter knows Jeffrey of course, as well as I do. We all used to roister in the Sixties. It's just that Jeffrey never stopped. So Peter has observed and heard much of what's on stage first hand. He personally sees Jeffrey's pieces of journalism as a tremendous affirmation of life, and not as pathologically despondent. And as for playing a drunk, it's easier if you've been there yourself a few times, even if it's not very recently.'

Time Out reported a week later that the first night 'was a glittering occasion attended by an astonishing assembly of drinkers, hacks and hangers-on, not to mention the usual theatre reviewers *wearing ties*. Prominent in the audience were Norman Balon, self-styled "rudest landlord in London" and presiding deity of the evening's entertainment, and Jeff himself, who sat smoking and muttering in the stalls.' The magazine claimed that the applause at the end was led by a standing ovation from Michael and Mary Parkinson – and that one American 'was heard in the interval asking why Peter O'Toole's diction was so bad, apparently unaware that the great actor was pretending to be drunk'.

Not everyone was dazzled by the play. Francis Bacon, taken to see it by Dan Farson, failed to return after the interval, apparently because he was incensed at being portrayed by Royce Mills as a mincing homosexual. 'Pity,' Ned Sherrin told the *Sunday Correspondent*'s diarist Neil Mackwood afterwards. 'I gather it's only the second time Francis has been to the theatre. The first time was to see *Cats*.' Ian Board also caused a disturbance when he considered that one of the anecdotes was slightly inaccurate: the one about the time that Bobby Hunt was going to a fancy dress party and Muriel Belcher suggested that he ought to go as himself, 'a bald-headed cunt.' On the first night he shouted out during the play 'She never said that at all.'

Michael Redington gave a first night party afterwards at the Groucho Club and the reviews the next day were raves. 'This exultant evening of pure theatre,' Jack Tinker enthused in the *Daily Mail*, 'a glorious entertainment', Irving Wardle in *The Times* described Bernard as 'a national institution in the same way as Falstaff or Mr Micawber' and the play as 'a brilliant company comedy'. Milton Shulman wrote in the *Evening Standard*: 'Anyone who cannot be amused at the concept of a cat race when horse racing was frozen out, need not come. The rest of us will forgive him everything because he makes us laugh so much.' Michael Billington said in *The Guardian* that it was 'a first-rate play . . . a very funny show indeed'. Charles Spencer wrote in the *Daily Telegraph* 'a magnificent performance, at once touching and hilarious' and his *Sunday Telegraph* colleague John Gross recommended it as 'an exceptionally enjoyable evening'.

There were a few dissenters. Brighton journalist Mike Howard had raved about O'Toole's performance ('two-and-a-half hours of magic . . . this is splendid entertainment') but added: 'The underlying morality of portraying such a man on stage is questionable.' Nor was everyone in stitches. Hilary Bonner was not sure that we ought to be laughing at a man drinking himself to death. Miss Bonner's reaction was not simply that of a killjoy. Indeed, she was renowned for her rich sense of humour. One legendary Fleet Street story told of how she had once been approached in a bar by a very small male journalist who had announced that he would very much like to make love to her. 'If you do,' she said, 'and if I ever find out about it, I shall be very, very cross.'

O'Toole had no time for the begrudgers. He refused to accept that Bernard had wasted his life. 'Wasted? Jeff is a gutter poet,' he told Michael Owen of the *Evening Standard*.

Some critics, not surprisingly, were rude about Bernard himself. In the *Financial Times* Michael Coveney suggested that the play owed little to Bernard and remarked: 'The man in question is very probably a shit of the first order.' In *The Spectator* (of all places) Christopher Edwards praised the play but suggested that Bernard in real life might not be as engaging as O'Toole on stage and drew attention to Bernard's 'self-pity and self-censure – the latter being, as Doctor Johnson remarked, an invidious form of self-love.' An interview with Bernard in the *Sunday Times Magazine* carried a picture with the caption: 'JEFFREY BERNARD could have been a seam bowler, but ended up plain seamy.'

Milton Shulman referred in the *Evening Standard* to 'the dead cynicism behind the eyes'. Hugo Williams sneered at Bernard's 'monotonous booze worship and bad English' and drew attention to 'the suggestion of smugness which hangs over them on the page.' John Gross wrote in his *Sunday Telegraph* review: 'Possibly we are being given a sanitised version of the real Jeffrey Bernard. I occasionally find something menacing and a bit unpleasant in the columns.' Many who knew the real Bernard agreed with the *Daily Mail*'s theatre critic Jack Tinker, who greatly admired the way that Waterhouse had created on the stage 'a modern, skeletal Falstaff, a hero for our own times' but who was brutal about Bernard himself when he wrote in the *Mail* in 1990 about the less attractive aspect of heavy drinking. 'To be honest I move tables in restaurants in order not to sit next to this selfsame Bernard,' Tinker wrote. 'He cannot be guaranteed to be the amusing creature of his own stage legend; and unfortunately I have never seen him behaving as anything other than a sad old drunken bore.'

The most powerful attack came on the Sunday after the first night at the Apollo when the *Sunday Telegraph* published a jaundiced half-page profile (headlined 'The cult hero of a decadent society') which suggested that it was 'perhaps worrying' that a middle-class audience 'rocks with helpless mirth' at a play about someone like Bernard, a play moreover that was stuffed with obscenities. It referred to Bernard's 'modest talent', described him as an 'absurd amateur' and insisted that he was just a drunk: 'there is *no* more to him than that.' It also drew attention to his 'unpleasant temper' and to the 'darker side to his personality, offensive to those who can't answer back and ingratiating to those who can' and sneered at him for 'sucking up' to Graham Greene.

Bernard, as paranoid as ever, was convinced that this profile must have been written by a woman and suspected Val Hennessy. He did not think that it could have been written by the Editor of the *Sunday Telegraph*, Peregrine Worsthorne, because 'I always got on all right with him. Wheatcroft would know who wrote it.' In fact Geoffrey Wheatcroft had put a new fear of death into Bernard's soul since he knew by now that Wheatcroft has written his obituary for the *Daily*

Telegraph and Bernard was apprehensive as to what it might say. He would not, of course, ever have a chance to read it.

But the dissenters were in a tiny minority. Among the first night crowd had been Princess Margaret's daughter Lady Sarah Armstrong-Jones, who 'shook with laughter', according to the *Evening Standard*, and right from the start the play was the one that Anyone Who Was Anyone just *had* to have seen. 'The play appealed to a lot of people who had never heard of Jeff,' said Courtauld. 'Some friends of ours who are very straightforward and strait-laced went to see it in Bath and said it was a wonderful play. They were dumbfounded. They had no idea it was based on a real character. It took the man out of his own boring life. Here was someone who could escape the 9–5 rat race and still survive. He was envious.'

Even *Private Eye* granted Bernard the accolade of one of its Great Bores of Today cartoons by Michael Heath where the caption read: '. . . apparently it's amazing all he's ever done is get pissed all day in this pub in Soho go round the betting shop and write this piece for some magazine and now they're making a whole play about him with whatsisname he used to like a drop himself probably why they chose him there was a picture of him in the paper with the other one and they both looked terrible and this play is apparently just the same as his column which is all about getting pissed and going round to the betting shop and then typing it all up I mean I don't see how you could write a play about that imagine a whole evening of it but that bloke in the Mirror has done it you might as well go and see him live well live-ish ha ha ha this mate of mine saw him in the street once swearing at this bloke he nearly ran over its amazing they can make a play out of it still if that Fergie can write a book anything can happen ha ha ha ha . . .'

Cartoons appeared in many of the national newspapers, and one in the *Evening Standard* by Jak showed an ambulance parked outside the Coach and Horses and one bystander saying to another: 'It looks like Jeffrey Bernard can afford a new car now!' He certainly could. The theatre was packed out night after night and suddenly he found himself earning an extra £1,000 a week on top of the £100 a week he received from the *Spectator* and the £200 a week he was paid by the *Sunday Mirror*, not to mention occasional other payments for articles in numerous other publications. Even though the taxwoman was demanding £20,000 in unpaid back taxes he was now so affluent, at least on paper, that he had to employ an accountant for the first time in his life – and he had to register with his old persecutors, Her Majesty's Customs and Excise, to pay Value Added Tax.

During the last few months of 1989 he floated on a cloud of euphoria towards the sudden promise of the 1990s. The play was so successful that it took only seven weeks in the West End to recoup its costs. The Apollo Theatre reported record profits in the bar and even Bernard's long-suffering editor at the *Spectator*, Charles Moore, decided that it was time for the magazine to enjoy a cut of the proceeds. 'We do own the copyright on Jeff's articles,' the *Spectator*'s publisher James Knox told me at the time. 'We aren't making a profit, so we've been generous letting him have the first £20,000. None of us expected the play to be so successful.' Bernard took Jill, who was now running a bar in Spain, to see the play one night and was astonished to learn that among the audience that night were the King of Norway, Elton John, Sean Connery and Norman St John Stevas, though the latter did not appear to be enjoying himself much.

Tourists began to invade the Coach and Horses in increasing numbers to gawp at what had by now become the megastar conjunction of Balon and Bernard, the greatest double act since Morecambe and Wise, and to revel in lines of witty dialogue like this:

'Well, you can fuck off for a start.'

'Fucking cunt.'

It was a London taxi driver who brought Bernard down to earth again and rescued him from the danger of Taking Himself Too Seriously. 'Here, you're *famous*,' said the cabbie as Bernard tottered into his vehicle. 'You're that Laurie Lee, aren't you?'

By a curious coincidence he was to sit beside Laurie Lee at the *Sunday Express* Book of the Year Award lunch at the Café Royal in November, when Lee astonished him by putting four naked lamb cutlets into his pocket and announced that these would be reheated for his supper. Bernard was slightly depressed that the author of *Cider With Rosie* should have come to this.

Because of the play Bernard now made valiant efforts not to get too drunk every afternoon but to remain upright until well into the evening so that he could hang about, hoping to be noticed, in the Apollo bar, which was presided over by his old racecourse barmaid friend Mrs Mac and where a drunken American woman one night accused him of being Peter O'Toole. During the performances he would sit in the empty bar becoming steadily stocious and listening to the glorious ego massage of endless muffled laughter from the auditorium. The sound must have resembled increasingly the flutter of banknotes. 'Once the play had started Jeffrey would settle down to his large vodka and soda and quite often drop off to sleep,' recalled Ned Sherrin. 'At the interval, punters would point him out as a tourist attraction. One night the regular front of house manager was away and a temporary replacement routinely checked the bar before the interval to make sure that all was well. Confronted by a strange, frail figure apparently incapable over his glass, he reacted strongly: "Get that drunk out of here!" he shouted.

' "You can't do that," Mrs Mac countered. "That's Jeffrey Bernard."

' "Don't try to fool me," snapped the manager, "Jeffrey Bernard's up on the fucking stage!" '

Among the thousands who flocked to see the play was Bernard's admirer John Osborne, who felt that it did not do him justice. 'I dare say I was over affected by what seemed to me a very brutal audience, who revelled only in the jokes and were impervious to the pain,' Osborne told me.

'However, that may well have been a rather priggish reaction. Sometimes I can only assume that I inhabit a remote world of my own.'

The play ran and ran at the Apollo Theatre until October 1990 and became such a fashionable success that it appeared on every hotel porter's list of sights of London not to be missed and the most unlikely audiences flocked to see it. Leslie Thomas, the author, saw a party of bewildered Japanese tourists sitting transfixed one night in one of the expensive boxes while Peter O'Toole on stage was setting fire to a bed. 'They were completely mystified,' Thomas told me, 'and kept trying to laugh when everyone else did but they were always thirty seconds late. Then all the smoke drifted into their box and they were all coughing, with tears streaming down their faces. It was very funny.' Princess Margaret saw the show and enjoyed it. Joan Collins did too, and didn't: 'she didn't find it very uplifting,' reported Ned Sherrin. Jane Russell was there one night, and so was Jack Lemmon, who met Bernard at the bar during the interval and said how much he was enjoying the play. The former Prime Minister, Lord Callaghan, saw the play and remarked to Keith Waterhouse on 'the superabundance of the F word'. Perhaps it was a good thing that Callaghan had not hired Bernard as his speech writer. The play's huge success boosted the sales of the *Spectator* and Charles Moore increased his payments for the Low Life column, which was now being syndicated each week and reprinted in the *Sunday Independent* in Dublin and *Midweek* magazine in London, to £250 a week.

By now the media attention had reached saturation point. Even the American television station NBC filmed an interview and then followed him around his haunts. Strangers were asking him for his autograph in the theatre and he was besieged by admirers in the Coach and Horses, among them a female groupie who had seen the play seven times and kept giving him carrier bags full of fruit and asking him to Fortnums for tea. 'He loves the fans when they come in,' Norman Balon told me. 'He likes being lionised. Complete strangers would come up to him.' Balon himself had also become famous because of the play. 'Everybody says that,' he protested, 'but I appeared in *Private Eye* magazine long before. I was mentioned in everything and the *Jeff Bin In?* strip made me famous I suppose, just a strip about public houses and me in particular.'

For the first time Bernard was asked to write his entry for *Who's Who*. He gave his address as 29 Greek Street, Soho, the address of the Coach and Horses, and his recreations as cricket, racing, cooking and Mozart. When it came to listing his wives he seemed to have forgotten poor suicidal Anna, who was not mentioned at all: Jacki was listed as his first spouse. He was also asked to write his entry for *Debrett's Distinguished People of Today*, in which he promoted his father from the humble Oliver P. Bernard of *Who's Who* to Major Oliver Bernard, OBE, MC, FRIBA. He did not mention his mother at all and this time omitted all of his first three wives, listing only Sue. Here one of his recreations was 'drinking with friends' rather than cricket.

All this excitement was a little too much and in mid-January he was back in hospital for five days suffering from malnutrition. He found it quite impossible to put on any weight. Strangely enough it was now, at the peak of his celebrity, that the Racecourse Association rejected his annual application for a metal Press badge for the first time in twenty-years so that he could no longer go into unsaddling enclosures or weighing room areas at the races. Perhaps they objected to the levity with which the play treated the racing world. But the bookseller Christina Foyle made up for this snub on 7 February when she gave one of her famous Foyles literary lunches for Peter O'Toole at the Grosvenor House hotel in Park Lane – a rare accolade considering O'Toole had not in fact written a book – and placed Bernard in a place of honour between herself and the ballerina Dame Alicia Markova, who murmured later 'he really is a dear man', even though he fell asleep over the pudding. Aroused by Miss Foyle to make a speech, Bernard staggered to his feet, thanked her for the meal and revealed that he had stolen a book from her shop in 1948.

After the lunch Bernard looked decidedly tired and emotional and the journalist Neil Mackwood took pity on him, offered him a lift and went outside to hail a taxi. A cab stopped, Mackwood climbed in, and the dishevelled Bernard suddenly staggered into sight and lurched into the taxi as well.

' 'Ere!' said the cabbie. 'Not you! Out!'

'No, that's all right,' said Mackwood.

'Wot?' said the cabbie. ' 'E with you?'

'Yes.'

'Cor,' said the cabbie. 'I thought he were a tramp.'

'Cunt!' said Bernard.

On 5 March Tom Conti replaced O'Toole in *Jeffrey Bernard is Unwell*. O'Toole's creation of the part had been a huge financial as well as artistic triumph. He had invested £20,000 in the play and was said in the *Daily Mail* to have made £200,000 out of it in a few months. How was Conti to follow such a triumph? He was later considered by general consent not to have been quite right for the part. His performance certainly did not impress Bernard, who attended the opening night. 'You can't play me if you disapprove of me – and he does,' he told the art magazine *Antique* two years later, in April 1992. In July he complained to John Edwards of the *Daily Mail*: 'He's turned the dressing room into a church. Conti hasn't got a sip of anything in there. When I asked him for a drink the other day he looked at me as if I was mad.' Bernard was already openly looking forward to Conti's replacement later in the year by James Bolam: 'He sounds like the kind of man who'd have a drink around.'

By now so many American tourists were flocking to see the show that *Newsweek* published a full-page piece by Daniel Pedersen, who quoted Keith Waterhouse as saying that perhaps at last in America there was a backlash against the fashionable puritanism that had led Americans to invent 'the designer-water lunch'. Bernard told Pedersen that he could not possibly live for more than another three years and that Waterhouse should write a sequel entitled *Jeffrey Bernard is Dead*.

Despite the success of his professional life, Bernard's domestic life was in turmoil once again, though he was seeing more of Isabel now that she was working in the Groucho Club kitchen. In March he left Pete Arthy's attic in Covent Garden and moved to a new flat in Maida Vale, too far from Soho for comfort, only to be told by the landlady three months later that he had to leave because she was selling it. He then moved foolishly to another flat even further away, in West Hampstead, miles from Soho. Henceforth he was to spend a fortune in taxi fares to and from the Coach and Horses. 'They say that moving is third only to bereavement and divorce but, having been through three divorces, I think it is worse,' he told his *Spectator* readers. It was not as though it was a particularly desirable flat, either: the walls and floors were so thin that he could hear every morning the woman urinating in the flat above and almost every night the woman in the flat beneath enjoying a noisy orgasm. Then he was knocked down by a hit-and-run Post Office van in Brewer Street, broke six ribs, cracked his head on the pavement and was taken to the Westminster Hospital where they kept him in for a week. When he was asked to name his next of kin he replied: 'The Coach and Horses.' And finally he found himself involved in a bitter dispute with Pete Arthy over £1,000. 'I lent him £300,' claimed Bernard, 'and paid him £600 rent in advance because he was broke and I didn't take my bookshelves away, so he owed me £100 for those. It all came to £1,000. It's a pity because I've known him longer than anyone. I knew him when I was still at school and came up to Soho in the holidays. We'd been friends since 1948.' So yet another old friend had gone out of his life with bad feeling.

In August James Bolam replaced Tom Conti in the play and in September Bernard went off for another holiday in the South of France but foolishly he chose to stay in Nice and returned to London after only five days because he could find no hotel that would have him for more than a night at a time. There were two consolations: one evening in a bar in Nice he could hardly believe it and was immensely flattered when a middle-aged homosexual tried to pick him up; and in Antibes he had lunch again with Graham Greene. His friendship with Greene was undoubtedly genuine but the manner in which he wrote about it had begun to embarrass his friends. 'It is not only a pleasure to know the man but also a privilege,' he wrote in the *Spectator* on his return to England. 'He said some very amusing things about some well-known people and it is bad luck on you that I won't repeat them. I do not think it would be right . . .' Bernard's penchant for worshipping a few heroes sometimes came close to that dreadful but accurate American term 'brown-nosing'.

At the end of October the play's remarkable run of just over a year at the Apollo came to an end. He felt bereft. His name was no longer in lights and almost as distressing was the sudden evaporation of the juicy royalty cheques. But the adulation continued. A female sculptor was modelling his head in clay and on 14 November the play won the *Evening Standard* Drama Award for the best comedy of the year, a joint winner with Alan Ayckbourn's *Man of the Moment*. And five months later, in March 1991, O'Toole returned triumphantly in a revival at the Shaftesbury Theatre, where the star was so pleased with the asymmetrical set that he sent a telegram to its American designer: 'Congratulations. The set is marvellous. It's pissed.' So of course was Bernard, who became so confused that he managed to describe the new production's first night in detail in the *Sunday Mirror* four weeks before the play actually reopened. 'He described the excitement with which he had attended a preview,' Ned Sherrin remembered. 'The full house, the gales of laughter, the welcome and the vodka and soda he had received from

O'Toole after the performance.' A couple of days later, at the
Groucho Club, Bernard bumped into Keith Waterhouse, who
asked him what the hell he thought he was up to since the
play wasn't due to reopen for another month. 'Christ!' said
Bernard. 'D'you mean I dreamt it?' He had.

Jeffrey Bernard is Unwell was finally laid to rest in the
West End at the end of May, although there were plans
for a tour of Australia with Dennis Waterman in the lead
and hints that O'Toole might take it to Dublin, television
or Hollywood, or even all three. It had been a triumph,
even in its second incarnation. It had earned Bernard at
least £50,000 (although a tragic £40,000 of that had been
siphoned off by the dreaded taxwoman) and had brought
Waterhouse more than £150,000. In the ten weeks of Peter
O'Toole's comeback at the Shaftesbury Theatre it broke the
theatre record and took nearly £2 million at the box office.
In one week alone Bernard's share of the take was £1,200,
and briefly he was earning the weekly equivalent of £100,000
a year.

   As a consummate actor himself, Bernard could not allow
O'Toole to have it all his own way at the end as the play
that had made him famous died at last. Finola Morgan went
to see the penultimate performance at the Shaftesbury and
as the curtain was about to go up for the second last time
Bernard emerged from the bar and sat in one of the two
empty seats beside her in the stalls. As the lights dimmed
the people who had bought the seats arrived hurriedly to
claim them and Bernard began to shout. In a voice resonant
with indignation he boomed 'Can't a man even watch his own
play?' and stormed off as the lights went down.

   Bunny and Dora would have been immensely proud of him.

22

A Star Looking at the Gutter

In Britain, at least, Bernard had become almost as big a star as O'Toole himself and ironically much more famous than Keith Waterhouse, even though Waterhouse was to be awarded the CBE in 1991. In November 1990 Bernard bashed his skull on the pavement yet again, when he fell as he alit from a taxi, and an ambulance took him to hospital, but not before a stranger had bent over him and said 'You're Jeffrey Bernard, aren't you?' He was still unwell but no longer anonymous. It helped to ease the pain.

The media refused to leave him alone. Journalists still queued to interview him and stories appeared in the gossip columns every time he fell over. Rosanna Greenstreet of the *Telegraph Magazine* took him back to Holland Park to see his childhood home in Lansdowne Walk. He had not returned since 1949. 'I've been having nightmares about this for the past few days,' he told her. 'I see myself standing on the doorstep posing for the photographer, when the front door opens and I turn around to see the ghost of my mother standing behind me.'

His fame by now was spectacular. Ordinary people all over Britain who had never heard of the *Spectator* had heard of him. Fans sent him letters even from America enclosing money or offers of marriage. Quartet Books included a photograph of him as a child – opposite one of the pre-nubile Joan Collins – in a charity paperback collection of celebrity pictures entitled *When We Were Young*. He earned £1,000 for ten minutes' work writing an advertisement for a brewery and Olympus Cameras paid him £1,250 to feature as the star of a full-page before-and-after advertisement which showed him both well and unwell and which won an award the following year. His celebrity had even infected the landlord of the Coach and Horses, Norman Balon, whose autobiography was published in March and earned 'London's rudest landlord' a simperingly embarrassing television appearance on the *Wogan* show.

In January Bernard went into brief hibernation at Stiffkey in Norfolk to compile another book about racing, *Tales From The Turf*, but he found it so difficult now to produce more than a few hundred words at a time that he needed the help of his friend Charlie Hurt, who became a sort of nanny-ghost.

He had become such a national cult figure that the *Sunday Times* asked him later in the year to join a panel of judges to find the best water in Britain. He pronounced one sample to be 'dull and sulky. It is crying out for something stronger to be put in it.' There were those who were beginning to ask whether such determinedly alcoholic jokes were still funny in the new 'designer water' Nineties. Some said that Bernard's relentless public drunkenness was finally shredding the last few tatters of his dignity and that he had become a prisoner of his own legend. 'It's a ridiculous joke that I should become well-known,' he admitted to me, 'but I love being recognised. It cheers me up. At last I've got an identity.'

He had become a notional monument in the Groucho Club, whither he repaired each afternoon to sprawl in an armchair and sleep off the morning vodka session in the Coach and Horses. He was now a tourist attraction at whose wrecked, open-mouthed, snoring figure sleek publishing bimbos and advertising yuppies gaped with awe. When Irma Kurtz's friend Michael Bywater first met him in the club Bernard enquired: 'How old are you?'

'Thirty-five,' said Bywater.

'Good,' said Bernard. 'Would you thump that fucker over there?'

'Why?'

'It's just that I think he may be a bit of a cunt.'

On 14 February 1991 he went to Broadcasting House

to appear on the radio request programme *Desert Island Discs*, onto which he had often dreamed of being invited. He was interviewed by Sue Lawley, whom he pronounced 'delightful' when she produced a bottle of vodka and a bottle of soda as soon as he sat in front of the microphones and reminded him that it was St Valentine's Day. He might well have proposed on the spot to such an understanding woman. He was less pleased with the technician who played Mozart's Piano Concerto No 24 instead of No 23. He chose Mozart's Requiem Mass, the beginning of Mozart's 23rd Piano Concerto, Elgar's Enigma Variations, Andalusia by Granados ('from a tune my mother used to play for me'), the 2nd Movement of Beethoven's String Quartet Op 27, the beginning of a Haydn Quartet, Op 20 no 1, the beginning of Sibelius's Symphony No 1 ('because it reminds me of Sue Ashley, that was one of her heirlooms'). The book he selected to read on his desert island was a collection of the complete short stories of Sherlock Holmes 'because it's absurd, bizarre and unintentionally funny'. And he chose as the one luxury he would be allowed to take to his Robinson Crusoe island a high-powered hunting rifle, for three reasons: '(a) to shoot game for food; (b) to shoot Man Friday when he told too many boring jokes; and (c) to kill myself.'

His private life was still as much of a shambles as ever. He was incensed to discover that not only had Pete Arthy declined to return his £1,000 but his Maida Vale ex-landlady was now also refusing to return his deposit of £630. 'I am trying to remember just what it was that I did to deserve this sort of treatment,' Bernard whined in the *Spectator*. He never accepted – as Finola Morgan had pointed out – that he may well have left these flats in such a disgusting condition that the owners were perfectly entitled to withhold the deposits to pay for the damage he had done.

Now that he was so famous and increasing numbers of people were reading his columns in the *Spectator* it was sad that his articles had become repetitive, rambling and only a shadow of their former standard, but every now and then he was still able to come up with a funny piece. Among them was the one suggesting a bizarre new television show, to be called *This is Your Wife*, on which ex-husbands would have to face their angry ex-wives. He imagined himself cringing with embarrassment under the harsh television lights while Jill told an audience of millions: 'On a certain night in August 1970 he came home from Newbury races drunk and penniless and then contrived to set fire to the house having telephoned my mother to tell her that she was an ugly old bitch.'

On 4 March he gave Isabel a twenty-first birthday party in an upstairs room at the Groucho Club but tragedy was about to claim another woman in his life. At the end of February Renate Sunkler, a Viennese teacher who was doing her PhD on his life, had turned up in London to continue her research and they had lunched together. 'She looked happy and well,' said Bernard, but a week later she telephoned him in tears from Austria to say that she was in a mental hospital. A week after that her boyfriend telephoned to say that she had committed suicide. Bernard, who was no stranger to suicide, was appalled. 'I didn't realise that anyone could crack so quickly and suddenly,' he said. It is chilling to remember how many of those who had tried to come close to him committed suicide: Anna Grice, John Minton, now Renate. In fact, it transpired that Renate had died after contracting pneumonia.

In April he fell on his head yet again in the street and needed seventeen stitches. His eyesight had become so bad – from diabetic retinitis – that he gave up reading newspapers, though he was still able to make black jokes about being blind drunk and soon probably legless too when they finally amputated his limbs because of the diabetic gangrene that he feared. Later in the year he had vitamin injections that caused a great improvement in his eyesight and he could read again but nothing much could be done about the terrible shakes that afflicted him: after years of drinking and smoking his nerves were simply dying before he was. When Bernard was in the Middlesex Hospital yet again his doctor, Antony Kurtz,

brought a group of students to his bedside and announced:
'This, gentlemen, is Mr Jeffrey Bernard, who closes his veins
each day with sixty cigarettes and then opens them up again
with a bottle of vodka.' He could barely get in and out of the
bath and lying in it was increasingly painful because of his
loss of weight and protruding bones.

Bernard looked increasingly like death, talked about it
more and more and muttered nervously that he knew that
The Times and the *Daily Telegraph* had already prepared his
obituaries. When Graham Greene died in April and then
George Barker died in October Bernard began to think that
it was time he made a will. The cysts on each side of the back
of his neck were now so huge that he needed 17-inch collars
and could no longer wear a tie. The cysts were vast lumps
of fat of which his body could not rid itself. 'The fat should
be cleared by the bowels, but it's not,' he explained. He then
broke his arm and was in agony for weeks but would not go
back to the Westminster Hospital for treatment because the
last time he had been there they had kept him waiting for an
hour. Yet despite his woes he treated them all with his usual
black humour. 'In reality I'm not going to last much longer,'
he wrote in the *Evening Standard*. 'I went to the doctor recently,
I was feeling so bloody awful. He said my body was a disaster
but that the smoking would kill me before the drinking would,
so I suppose that's something.'

Yet on 27 May he turned fifty-nine. By some miracle,
despite his suicidal lifestyle, he had survived for longer than
either of his parents: his father had been fifty-eight when he
died, his mother fifty-two. What was more, the doctors told
him even now that there was nothing much wrong with his
liver. His toughness was awesome. So, amazingly, was his
sex appeal, still. In May – along with yet another demand
from the Inland Revenue, this time for £3,700 – he received
a letter from a woman who declared that she had fallen in
love with him after hearing him on *Desert Island Discs*. 'I do
not want the love of a woman,' he replied cruelly. 'What I
need is a Sancho Panza.'

Despite his physical woes his taste for practical jokes also remained intact. When a man walked into the Coach and Horses one day with a mobile telephone Bernard borrowed it and from his barstool dialled 437-5920, the number of the pub. Six feet away, behind the bar, the telephone rang, Norman Balon answered it and was bewildered to hear two identical voices – one from the earpiece and one from a nearby barstool – bellow: 'Is there any chance of being served a drink in this fucking pub?' For a moment, perhaps for the only time in his life, 'the rudest landlord in London' was speechless.

Bernard's frailty did not prevent him falling in love again, either. His new love was a twenty-five-year-old receptionist at the Groucho, Deborah Bosley, who bore a striking resemblance to his fourth wife, Sue. Deborah found him at first to be exceedingly irritating and demanding and three months later she was still telling him to 'piss off, you silver-tongued bastard'. But eventually she weakened and became extremely protective of him and was soon to fill the post of Junior Handmaiden while Finola Morgan retained the Senior Handmaiden title.

In July the lease of the Hampstead flat ran out and he had to move again, willingly this time since the flat was by now resounding to the piping of a flautist upstairs and the screams of a baby next door. He was homeless again for two weeks, staying in an hotel and then finding a temporary bolthole on the eighth floor of a depressing, soulless skyscraper block of flats in Westminster, where he was incensed to be told by the agent that it was a distinguished address because several Members of Parliament had *pieds à ciel* there. His peace was continually shattered by the drills and hammering of work on the new MI5 building that loomed right in front of him, destroying any decent view of the Thames, but at least he now had the services of two home helps who washed and dressed him and cleaned the flat every morning, one an Irish woman, the other West Indian, both provided by the local taxpayers. He was at last getting his money's-worth. This did not prevent him complaining even in print that his last three landlords had 'conned' him out of £3,000.

Despite his weakness he helped briefly to umpire the Chelsea Arts Club's centenary cricket match near the Royal Hospital in August but eventually made the mistake of sitting down at square leg with a glass of vodka, was unable to rise again, and had to be carried off the field. He then went back to Chelsworth in Suffolk for a short summer break, broke his arm, was whisked by ambulance to hospital, this time the West Suffolk in Bury St Edmunds, and then returned to the Peacock Inn at Chelsworth where the landlord and landlady found themselves in the role of nurses for the next couple of weeks.

His celebrity reached a peak in November even though it was now six months since the play had reached the end of its second run. Guy Hart, the one-time jockey who was now an antique and art dealer and friend of Lucian Freud, commissioned a brilliant young painter, Michael Corkrey, to paint Bernard's portrait, which was to be exhibited in the National Portrait Gallery in 1992, appears on the jacket of this biography, and included the black walking stick with a silver collar inscribed 'To Jeffrey Bernard from The Spectator' that had just been presented to him by the *Spectator*. If that portrait were not enough to ensure Bernard some sort of immortality, November also brought another flattering accolade when the Alternative Arts street entertainment company unveiled *The Spirit of Soho*, a huge three-storey-high mural on the corner of Broadwick Street and Carnaby Street, the heart of the Swinging Sixties London of the years of Bernard's prime. The colourful mural depicted Soho's most famous residents down the ages, from Blake, Boswell, Canaletto, Dryden, Garrick, Hazlitt, Handel, Marx, Newton, Shelley and Wagner to Bernard's great role model Casanova and his hero Mozart. In the bottom right-hand corner of the mural is a panel which shows Dylan Thomas and Brendan Behan sitting drinking at a table with a bored Bernard while Jessie Matthews and George Melly loiter in the background and Ronnie Scott cavorts in the foreground with his saxophone. There was only one cloud to darken Bernard's self-satisfaction. 'They've spelt my fucking name wrong, the *cunts!*' he told me. They had, too. On the nearby crib beneath the mural, and in the glossy Alternative Arts booklet, he is doubly misspelt as Geoffrey Barnard. 'Yes, he was a bit upset about that,' I was told by Marlene Dixon of Alternative Arts. 'He rang us up one afternoon in a rage. I think he might have been drunk.'

At Waterstone's bookshop in the Charing Cross Road in the last week of November he undertook a signing session of his two 'new' books, *Tales From the Turf* and *Jeffrey Bernard is Still Unwell*, which was in fact no more than the paperback edition of *Talking Horses* with a new title to cash in on the success of the play. Waterstone's tried to make him feel at home by laying on plenty of vodka and a bowl of ice and he signed relentlessly for an hour and a half. 'There were actually queues for forty-five minutes,' said Jane Charteris of his publishers, Fourth Estate, 'and one little old woman had come all the way from South London and wouldn't leave him alone and insisted on being photographed with him.' Perhaps she hoped to persuade him to change and settle down.

He had already caused a fuss early in October when he had gone to the Chris Beetles gallery in Ryder Street for an unveiling party for Hugh Dodd's illustrations for *Tales From the Turf* but had gone off to sulk in a pub instead with Larry Adler and others after being told not to smoke in the gallery and that there was only champagne to drink. Worse was to come. In December Bernard received a letter from Christopher Falkus, the publishing director of Weidenfeld and Nicolson, demanding the return of their £3,000 advance for *Tales From the Turf* because of its striking similarity to *Talking Horses*, which was not only an old book that had first been published by Fourth Estate in 1987 but had now become the paperback *Jeffrey Bernard is Still Unwell*.

To add to his irritation, Isabel was not only unemployed now but also had a lover of whom he deeply disapproved, a middle-aged lawyer in his late forties. It annoyed Bernard even more to be told that the reason for this was that she was probably looking for a father figure since she had never had one. He agreed but added cynically: 'I suppose he's also got a few bob. I suppose he's a port in a storm. He's not skint.' Bernard also had the gall to complain that Isabel's lover did not appear to work regular hours. 'I phoned her this morning and noticed that her lover was still there at ten past ten,' Bernard told me. 'He's a solicitor. What the fucking hell is a bloke doing at home at ten past ten? He's supposed to go to an office every day.' I pointed out that Bernard had long avoided offices himself. 'But I don't pretend to be a solicitor,' he said.

There was however good news at the end of 1991: in December he moved at last to the resting place of which he had dreamed for months, a sixth-floor flat in another soulless tower block but this time one in the heart of Soho, near Berwick Street market, within a few minutes' walk of the Coach and Horses. It was to cost him £150 a week in rent but would also save him at least £50 a week in taxi fares. He could hardly believe his luck. He had come home, back to Soho. He was happy at last – at least for a day or two.

He celebrated by inviting his old friend Gordon Smith again for Christmas Day, as he had for the previous six years. Bernard was a fully paid-up Scrooge and always shunned Christmas cards, trees, decorations, holly, mistletoe and turkey but there was always a Christmas present for Gordon Smith – one year a Waterford crystal glass, the next a bottle of whisky – and he enjoyed cooking Christmas lunch, duck or chicken or beef, though this did not always turn out exactly as expected. Smith remembered that on one Christmas Day he and Stephen Pickles, who had also been invited, were sitting at the table to get out of Bernard's way when there wafted into the room the pungent smell of something burning: 'There were the sprouts merrily in the saucepan without any water. They came up black, solid like pebbles. And we ate them, they were brilliant: smoked sprouts.'

– 2 –

By some strange chance Bernard's health up to his sixtieth birthday in May was better in 1992 than it had been in the previous two years. But his muscles were weaker than ever and he was still in agony from the broken arm, which had failed to heal, and once again he had to go to hospital in January. 'I sometimes wonder if I've got AIDS,' he told me, 'because I look as though I have and I discovered that a girl I used to fuck quite a lot ten years ago was a junkie.' But despite his frailty he was in no pain except for the broken arm and in March he was tough enough to go into the Middlesex Hospital in Mortimer Street to have the giant lipomas removed from the back of his head and neck. 'Steady with your knife, surgeon!' wrote Dominic Lawson in his *Spectator* diary that weekend. 'The eyes of over a hundred thousand *Spectator* readers are on you.'

The operation went well, and by four o'clock Bernard was sitting up drinking cup after cup of tea. But just after midnight, plagued by insomnia, he struggled to sit up in bed and pulled a vital needle out of his head, tearing a small artery. 'A fountain of blood shot out of my head,' he told me when I went to visit him on the Sunday morning. 'I lost a pint of blood but a young nurse saved my life when she pressed a gauze bandage to my head and kept pressing it for two hours until the surgeon and two anaesthetists could get here for a second operation.'

There was of course no way of disguising the fact that he had become very old physically: at fifty-nine he looked as though he were eighty. His incontinence was becoming increasingly embarrassing but his effect on women seemed hardly to have diminished at all. When he lost control of his bladder in the Groucho Club one afternoon and staggered out of his armchair, leaving a wet patch, the young journalist Jaci Stephen saw it and simply said, '*Oh, poor Jeffrey!*'

By now Bernard had given up attempting to deal with the practicalities of everyday life. 'He can't cope with the flat now or things like income tax,' Finola Morgan told me. 'He simply cannot get himself together. He will not answer a letter, he will not sort out expenses, he cannot, *will* not, do any of the practical things in life. All the flats he's lived in have been found for him by somebody else during this period of peregrination. He cannot do it. He will simply sit and bemoan and someone else, quite often Norman, will read of somewhere in the *Evening Standard* and make the necessary telephone call. Those things that everybody else does for themselves he just can't do.'

Yet even in his frailty he dreamed still of women and seduction. He even cultivated a ludicrous sexual fantasy that he might be able to tempt Keith Waterhouse's cheerful, attractive 'Factotum', Jean Leyland, into having an affair with him. 'You've done a lot of shitty things in your life, Jeffrey,' I told him when he confessed this to me over lunch at Kettners, 'but the shittiest of all would be to cuckold the guy who made you famous.' He started laughing so much that he nearly choked on his food. 'But you must admit,' he said, 'that if Jean and I ran off together it would make a wonderful ending for your book.'

He also confessed that he still harboured a bizarre fantasy that he, Jill and Isabel could all live happily together as a family. He knew that the dream was quite impossible, but nevertheless hankered for a sort of Norman Rockwell vision of cosy domestic life. 'It's funny now that it's much too late,' he said, 'but I find myself thinking about Isabel's mother a lot. It's not to do with sex, and it's too late – she wouldn't entertain me – but now I like the idea of being a family.' It was a search he had been making all his life, ever since his father had died when he was seven. Even his affair with the last of his lovers, Finola Morgan, had now become no more than 'an eccentric friendship', she told me. 'It's more a

Mummy thing. It started off as jolly good fun and (I hoped) a romance but it's developed into an eccentric friendship with a strong Mummy element. I don't do the nurturing that I did, partly because I'm now working full-time and very busy. I no longer have time to iron 14 shirts but I've seen him in some awful states these past few years and I will go round and tidy up. It's easier now that he's in Soho and plugged into a Home Help who does for him, but there've been years when nobody did and I'd go and tidy up. He can't physically do it himself any more. Yes, I think I do love him. I'm quite proud of myself because I love him for being himself: I *do* get a return, amusement and company and so on, but it's not conditional: it's just Jeffrey being himself.'

Throughout 1992 Bernard's fame seemed to increase rather than diminish. 'It hasn't changed me because I think the whole thing is absolutely ridiculous,' he told me. 'It's a joke to me, but it's a nice joke.' On 9 January the Australian tour of *Jeffrey Bernard is Unwell* opened at His Majesty's Theatre in Perth, starring Dennis Waterman. Waterhouse was there for the first night – how strange that two such watery surnames should have been connected with such an alcoholic play – and so was Ned Sherrin, while Bernard sat and glowered in Soho, pretending that he could not join them because of his broken arm. He had also taken to muttering that Waterhouse had now become jealous of his fame and had never really wanted him to go to Australia anyway. 'Keith hates me to get any publicity,' he told me absurdly. Bernard often seemed to forget that it was Waterhouse who had made him really famous and that without him he would never have been known in Wigan, Wyoming and Wooroloo. Bernard's life story was bound to appeal to the boozy Aussies and on the first night in Perth Dennis Waterman took seven curtain calls. The play later went on to Brisbane and Sydney, where Bernard finally caught up with it in April after being sent out to Australia by the *Sunday Express* to write about the last night there.

He had now become so closely identified with boozing

that in February the Health Education Authority asked him to contribute to their latest anti-alcohol abuse campaign. 'They want a slogan or two for their posters,' he reported in the *Spectator*, 'and a black and white photograph of me looking awful to hold up to the youth of England so as to warn them about what "just the one" can do to a man's face.'

Even more bizarre, on the evening of 7 April, as he was flying out to Australia for eleven days, Channel 4 television's *Obituary Show* was screening his half-hour spoof obituary in the series *Without Walls*. He was shown dressed entirely in white (white sweater, white hair) and sitting on a celestial throne surrounded by heavenly blue skies and scudding white clouds and a hellish neon glow while those who had known him on Earth (Mike Molloy, Michael Heath, John McCririck, Richard Ingrams, George Melly) said what they really thought of him now that he was apparently safely dead. Jonathan Meades described Bernard's life as 'a commando course of the soul'.

On his return from Australia he was understandably sacked from his £275-a-week job on the *Sunday Mirror* by its editor, Bridget Rowe, because he had not bothered to let the paper know that he was going away and would not be producing his My Life column for two weeks. She told him in a letter that his behaviour was unforgivable, a judgment with which it is difficult to disagree. He seemed to find it hard to understand her decision even when it was explained to him that for two consecutive nerve-wracking Saturdays executives on the *Sunday Mirror* must have been trying desperately to reach him at his flat or the Coach and Horses or the Groucho Club while he was in fact asleep and drunk on the other side of the world.

His lifelong selfishness was such that he rarely bothered to try to see anything from someone else's point of view. His whole approach, even to those closest to him, was strikingly casual. He did not even have a proper address book, just a few jumbled numbers jotted at random in the middle of his diary, and he had no idea of Isabel's or Bruce's telephone numbers. He did not even know Isabel's address. 'You can get hold of her in the Coach and Horses,' he told me vaguely. 'She sometimes goes in there.'

Commenting on his sacking from the *Sunday Mirror*, he told the *Sunday Telegraph*: 'I'm financially ruined. I don't know how I'm going to pay my rent. I'll probably have to go into an old people's home.'

This seemed unlikely. His royalties from the play were probably much greater than he would ever admit and the *Spectator* was now paying him £190 a week, double the fee they normally paid for an article, and it was being suggested that Bernard was in fact rich enough to retire if he wished. He denied it. 'I'm not skint but I couldn't retire,' he told me. 'I should have made £50,000 out of the play but the Inland Revenue took about £40,000 and left me with only £10,000. Even the Australian tour of the play earned me only £1,300.' At least the Australian tour had one positive result: in May the British tabloids reported that Dennis Waterman had made it up with his estranged wife Rula Lenska. Perhaps he had learned to appreciate her – and marriage – just a little more after playing the lead in *Jeffrey Bernard is Unwell* for four months Down Under.

Around this time, Bernard professed to be just as bored with the Coach and Horses as its landlord Norman Balon was dismissive of him in his interview with me. Bernard agreed that it showed a certain lack of imagination to spend every morning in the same small pub in the same small street of the same small area of London with the same small coterie of cronies simply getting drunk enough to stagger down the street to fall asleep in the Groucho Club. 'It's laziness,' he confessed, 'but the trouble is that I work so little I've got very little to do. I drink at home but I don't like it and I come to the Coach because I'm gregarious. I know what they're going to say every day. Yes, it's boring but since I've given up the pursuit of women I may have taken up the pursuit of bores.

Maurice Richardson years ago said you've got to learn to *savour* bores and I'm sure Graham Greene savoured them. He certainly savoured Low Life characters.'

His daily routine in 1992 had become numbingly predictable. 'I don't *do* anything,' he confessed. He would wake between five and six o'clock, listen to the news on Radio 4, drink cup after cup of tea, avoid breakfast even though he needed food for his diabetes, write his *Spectator* column if it was a Monday or Tuesday, 'lie in bed and daydream' if it was a Wednesday or Thursday, start drinking at home (sometimes as early as six o'clock), drift to the Coach and Horses down the road at eleven, drink enough until one o'clock to allow himself to be inebriated at lunch either at the Ming Chinese restaurant or the Amalfi (Italian) and to sleep either face-down in the Dish Of The Day in the restaurant or face-up in an armchair in the Groucho Club around the corner in Dean Street. When Bernard awoke in the Groucho he would have just the one and eventually return to his flat at about six, 'try to summon the energy to cook something', watch some television or play some music, and retire early to bed to enjoy eight hours of insomnia and possibly a very last drink in the middle of the night. 'I do very little work,' he told me. 'It embarrasses me when I think about it. I do about four hours a week. You see, I've got very high standards.'

Market research showed that most *Spectator* readers now turned first to the Low Life column before reading anything else. They were lucky to see any column at all: week after week Bernard was so late with his copy that the Arts Editor, Jenny Naipaul, had often still received nothing on Wednesday morning, Press day, and was on the verge of panic as the hole in her pages loomed ever whiter. Dominic Lawson wrote a stern letter to Bernard claiming that he was driving Mrs Naipaul into a nervous breakdown and for three weeks his copy arrived earlier but then it was back to the last minute again. 'Sometimes we have to use that line *Jeffrey Bernard is Unwell* and I have to switch everything round and put a very large cartoon in,' said Jenny Naipaul. 'It is very irritating but Jeff gets away with things that nobody else could get away with. He's got us over a barrel, really, because he's so popular. You've got to hope till the last minute that he's going to produce a column. We had a readership survey which showed that he is the most read column in the *Spectator*. We even have to print special paper for Jeff – we've done it for years – a foolscap-sized sheet with two lines down it. It's the exact width, so that when he types on it that will be the equivalent of a line in the *Spectator* and he knows that if he goes onto the second page, about three-quarters of the way down, he's done about 600 words which is what he's supposed to do. So then he stops, more or less in mid-stream, and it's remarkable how he actually manages sometimes to wrap it up brilliantly. But he's only done it because he sees himself getting to the bottom of the second page and that's it, enough, so he wraps it up.'

She said that he was still appallingly abusive on the telephone when drunk in the afternoons. 'I pretend I'm not there,' she said. 'He's horrible and every poor receptionist that we've ever had has come up in an absolute tizzy and said, "Jeff Bernard's been on the phone to me and been absolutely horrible, so *rude*."'

As he approached his sixtieth birthday he told the *Sunday Correspondent* that his greatest fears were death by fire, heights and slugs, and his greatest hero was Byron ('mad, *good* and dangerous to know). But in fact there were much greater fears. 'He's totally and permanently insecure,' said Mike Molloy and Bernard admitted to me that he was frightened of 'being an invalid and skint. I couldn't retire. There's no pension fund. I've got to work till I die, if they'll still have me. Being an invalid and having no money really makes me sweat. The State doesn't buy you vodka.' He worried too that his legs were so bad that he would soon be unable to go to the pub: 'I dread not being able to be gregarious.' Norman Balon believed that it was these midnight terrors that made Bernard so bitter and chippy. 'It's insecurity,' said Balon. 'He's very worried that he has to live in rented accommodation and he's very worried about what's going to happen to him if he can't work: he doesn't want to wind up in the gutter, so he's defensive. It's all part of an inferiority complex. I think that's how a man with an inferiority complex would behave.'

Yet Bernard admitted that although he had often been desperately unhappy 'in the end I *have* been lucky. I've been *very* lucky with women: they've been very good to me, really, kind. They've helped me. I've a lot of women friends, a hell of a lot, and I've had some very good times.' One of his greatest pieces of good fortune was that somehow he had always managed to live that double life that seemed to him to hold the secret of good living. 'I've got talented, capable, clever friends in the world of the arts and communications and I've always kept them separate from racing people and people I pass the time of day with in pubs,' he explained, 'because inevitably if you drink a lot you're going to end up with some pretty bloody boring people: nice people, but not people you can actually have a serious conversation with.'

If he had to write his own obituary, he said, 'I'd place myself pretty low in the Valhalla of writers but I have made a few people laugh in my time.' He confessed to a general contempt for most other columnists – Bernard Levin, Craig Brown, Alan Coren – but admitted: 'I'm very well aware that the only reason I've got any sort of name in this business is not because I'm good but because I'm different. That's why the *Sporting Life* column caught on: I was the first racing bloke ever to write about losing. Jay Landesman said that I wrote better about *loss* than anyone else. I don't mean loss of money, I mean generally: women, everything, health, you name it. I understand loss, I suppose. I wouldn't say I was *attracted* to loss, no one can be, but I identify with it because I think life is fucking awful. The good day's the exception not the rule.'

On the subject of death, Bernard hated the prospect of

a hurried, furtive funeral at Golders Green, where both his parents had been cremated. He wanted to be remembered. 'Pathetic, isn't it?' he had admitted in the *Spectator* in 1987. 'I would like my coffin to be taken down Whitehall on a gun carriage preceded by the massed pipe bands of the Highland Regiments playing a dirge and followed discreetly by members of the royal family and Norman and then to be laid to rest in Westminster Abbey during a performance of Verdi's Requiem.' This was not merely a joke, according to Dan Farson, who told me: 'There's no doubt in his mind, he's going to have a memorial service in St Paul's or Westminster Abbey, there are going to be so many people there.'

Bernard's spiritual solace had always been in music, especially that of Mozart: 'It takes Mozart to give a man a leg-up from the gutter. It's not the sadness that brings a tear to the eye; it's admiration that a human being can make something so beautiful.' Bernard once wrote that when he died he wanted his ashes to be buried by the finishing post at Epsom 'so that generations of Derby winners can gallop over me.'

As usual he decided to turn even his own death into a joke. He planned to record a message to be played at his memorial service: 'I like the idea of suddenly a voice coming out and saying, "I'm sorry I cannot be here with you today due to *foreseen* circumstances."' Bill Hagerty suspected that none of us would ever live to hear the message. 'He'll see us all off in the long run,' said Hagerty. 'Even though I hope to live to be quite an old age I wouldn't be surprised if at that time Jeffrey is sitting in some bleeding Bath chair in Nice with a lot of people coming by and he'll be telling them about how he used to know Graham Greene.'

23

Wide-eyed and Legless

As his sixtieth birthday loomed closer he was given a new lease of life by the prospect of the publication of this biography. He was determined to live long enough to see it published, just as he had been determined to survive to see the play on stage in the West End. He seemed almost to 'pull himself together' to survive for however many more months might be necessary. 'It's a terrible *indulgence* talking to you, Graham,' he said with wry relish when we got around to discussing his loneliness even in a crowd, and when I let several weeks pass at the end of 1991 without going to him for yet another interview he telephoned to ask when I was going to grill him again. He started making excuses for me to go and see him almost every Sunday in his flat, or at the Coach and Horses, to collect yet another book or photograph from him, and he seemed to resent the fact that I had to interview other people too. I felt each week so much as though this book were giving him the kiss of life that I wondered whether I dared to finish it in case its completion would leave him with nothing more to live for and would finally kill him. But I never doubted that I had to tell the full truth, however sordid or censorious it might turn out to be: anything less than the truth would have been an insult to Jeffrey, who had spent so many years crucifying himself in print and whose cold translucent gull's eye could spot a fraud or a lie from across the street. I owed him nothing at all but honesty.

In honesty it had to be admitted that I was appalled by his contempt for his mentally afflicted sister Sally even after I told him that I had tracked her down at last and spoken to her in the sheltered home where she lived on after the death of her second husband. He showed no curiosity about her condition or happiness. 'She can't have told you anything worthwhile,' he sneered. 'All she does is sit there and eat fucking bananas.' I pointed out that when I had found her she had been reading the *Mail on Sunday* and there had not been a banana skin in sight. He was dismissive. 'There's no one at home,' he said cruelly. 'She's mad. I don't see her any more. I got fed up with it. She's been bonkers since she was eighteen. I don't actually like her: that sounds awful, not to like her just because she's ill.' It did indeed. When I suggested that she was not mad but affected by the ECT treatment she had suffered, he agreed reluctantly: 'OK, she's not mad, she's shell-shocked. Shock treatment should never have been allowed.' For forty years he had not bothered even to send her a Christmas card.

Just before his birthday he was visited by another ghost from the past, his first wife Anna's illegitimate daughter Alfreda, who had four illegitimate children by two men, was living in a squat in Devon and was now calling herself Sally Bernard. It was strange how many of the characters in Jeffrey Bernard's life had changed their names or thought of themselves as being somebody else. His father Oliver called himself Bunny, his mother Edith pretended to be Fedora even when she applied for Letters of Administration when her husband died intestate, Jeffrey himself was really Jerry, his sister Sonia was known first as Sally and then called herself Sonia and Sally again, his first wife Anna was really Mary, and now here was Alfreda Grice (or Walton) calling herself Sally Bernard. Even Alfreda's putative father Andrew Dirac's real name was Gabriel.

Alfreda/Sally was still hinting that she might be his daughter but it was almost certainly untrue. She had told Bernard at first that she had been born in 1948, which would have made it possible since her mother had relieved Jeffrey of his virginity in 1947. But in fact Alfreda/Sally's birth certificate shows that she was born on 9 July 1949 and Bernard insisted that he and Anna had enjoyed just the two in 1947 and did not meet again until 1951. It is possible that he had forgotten meeting her and sleeping with her casually some time in October 1948 but he was also convinced that he had always been sterile. Had he not

been sterile he would surely have impregnated at least two or
three of his five hundred lovers since he had never used any
form of contraception.

But on 27 May 1992 there was a happier occasion and Jeff
held a joint lunch party with his Junior Handmaiden, Deborah
Bosley, at the Groucho Club to celebrate his sixtieth birthday
and her twenty-seventh. Nobody would have dreamed thirty
years previously that he would ever reach his seventh decade.
By awful coincidence his great friend Charles St George was
dying that very day less than a mile away at his home on the
other side of Regent Street, in Mayfair. 'One of the reasons
Jeffrey keeps going is because he's always looked after himself,'
suggested Juliet Simpkins. 'I think the discipline of the Pangbourne routine has actually given him a sort of loose structure.
I think it enabled him to survive as long as he has.'

There were sixteen guests, among them Oliver, Bruce, Isabel, Finola Morgan, Irma Kurtz, Mike Molloy, Gordon Smith
and his new friend Sue Townsend, the creator of Adrian Mole.
His old friend and critic Richard Ingrams was there too, sitting
immediately opposite Bernard, as one of Deborah's guests. She
and Bernard sat together in the centre and looked for a
moment just like the bride and groom at a Mafia wedding. In
the street below a jazz band struck up and it seemed perfectly
possible that men with trilby hats and violin cases would be
joining us at any minute. Later, over the Groucho's birthday
cake with one candle, Deborah told me that on the previous
Friday Bernard had persuaded her to give him some LSD. He
had always been terrified of drugs but now that he was sixty –
well, what the hell. She warned him of the possible ill effects
and then gave him a quarter of a tablet. After an hour he
complained that it had had no effect, so she gave him another
quarter tablet. 'He sat there for the rest of the afternoon with a
wonderful smile on his face,' she said. 'He's such a *sweet* man.
When I first met him I hated him. He was so rude and
demanding. But one day we had a terrible row – I told him I
wasn't putting up with his behaviour any more – and he
suddenly smiled and said no one had spoken to him like that for

years, and would I have lunch with him. We've been friends ever since.' She had even taken him recently to Brighton, the only *clean* weekend in Brighton in living memory.

I looked from Deborah to Finola, who was now sitting beside Bernard, who was about to pass out for his usual afternoon crash. Finola too had used the word *sweet* to describe him. I looked at the woman of twenty-seven and the woman of forty-nine, and they both knew what a monster Bernard could be but they both loved him and thought he was *sweet*.

The first edition of this biography was published in November 1992 and Bernard was now so famous that the British newspapers gave it an astonishing amount of publicity. There were interviews or profiles of Bernard in the *Independent Magazine*, the *Evening Standard* and the *Sunday Telegraph*, and two each in the Irish *Sunday Independent* and *The Times*. Numerous diary stories and cartoons appeared, there were feature articles in the *Daily Mail*, and the book was serialised at length for a month in the *Sunday Independent*.

Among the most memorable observations in these pieces was this one by Oliver in *The Times*: 'I wouldn't say he drinks enormously, it's just that he starts quite early.' And Stan Gebler Davies recorded in the *Sunday Independent* that a Chinese waitress in Soho had just bet Bernard £500 that he could not manage an erection in a sauna bath. Gebler Davies also reported that Jeffrey had once told the aged actress Googie Withers that as a teenager he had always thought of her while masturbating. 'I think that that's the most charming thing anyone's ever said to me,' she said.

Bernard read the book in proof in September and was appalled. 'I have been feeling not a little depressed ever since,' he wrote in the *Spectator*. 'This is not Graham's fault, who has worked very hard and done a good job, it is just that it is not a nice story, not a pretty picture. I must have been mad to have looked forward to it. I wasn't daft enough to think that everybody Graham interviewed would be lovey-dovey about me – I wasn't even that myself – but some of it still came at me like a bucket of cold water in the face when I read it in the sober light of day.'

He went on: 'The book reads like an obituary without pulled punches: I wasn't "convivial", I was as pissed as a rat. And it should be required reading for any boy stupid enough to think that a glass of whisky will make him an instant Jack the Lad.' He concluded: 'What Graham Lord's book has done has been to rekindle some guilt and remorse and that is my own fault.'

The book unsettled him so much that he fell outside Kettner's, broke his hip and had to have a titanium plate fitted (when the hospital asked the name of his next of kin he said 'the Coach and Horses') – and he threatened to sue me for libel until I pointed out that everything in the book was true and that he had himself written in the *Spectator* that the book should tell the whole grisly truth. Writing again in the *Spectator* he said that after reading it again he had had to take to his bed. 'It was a great mistake that I agreed to let Graham do the book,' he told Megan Tresidder of the *Sunday Telegraph*. 'It was very childish of me. I'm easily flattered. You see, because of the play, I suddenly enjoyed a kick out of being well-known. And when the play finished, I needed another fix.' He said that the book had particularly upset him because it 'has reminded me of how incredibly unhappy I have been. Obviously, I have had some bloody marvellous times, too, but most of my life I have been unhappy. I'll tell you, it's worse than unhappiness. The word is desolate. Desolate about myself, I suppose.' He concluded with a line worthy of 'Pseud's Corner' in *Private Eye*: 'Writing is a pain. To me, it is like having cancer.'

Despite his unhappiness he turned up three days later for the boozy lunch-time launch party at the Coach and Horses, which was televised as well as reported at length in the papers, and for lunch afterwards at the Groucho Club, though he told Jenny Rees of the *Daily Telegraph* that he was especially upset by reading in the book that some of his friends had claimed that he was slow to buy his round in the pub – an allegation that was to rankle until he died. Among the guests was a horde of his closest Soho friends and enemies as well as his ex-wife Sue Gluck, Deirdre Redgrave, Finola Morgan and 'at least twenty of my ex-lady-friends', he told the *Daily Express*, 'though I can't remember all their names.' Even though he was still on crutches he was also amazingly helpful when it came to promoting the book with me, appearing on television and giving numerous newspaper and radio interviews. He simply could not resist all that attention. He was wide-eyed at the extent of his fame. 'This is what it is all about,' he confessed to Megan Tresidder and her *Sunday Telegraph* photographer, 'you being here, this guy with his Hasselblad, all this palaver, it's stroking me. That is why the column is the best thing that has happened to me; because it made me famous.'

The publication of the book resulted in a page-lead news story even in the Sunday tabloid the *People* – 'RIDDLE OF PALACE GIRL'S FLING WITH MR BOOZY' – and several articles in *The Times* and the *Daily Mail* about why women find reprobates like Bernard so irresistibly attractive. 'Why did we all love this selfish, drunken man?' asked the *Mail* across two pages and answered: 'You want to mother him.'

Every national newspaper reviewed the book and some were highly critical of him. 'WHAT A MISERABLE LIFE' said the *Literary Review*, and John Wells accused him in the *Mail on Sunday* of being 'whining, disgusting and self-pitying'. But others were much kinder. In the *Sunday Express* his old friend Irma Kurtz wrote: 'I never appreciated the extent of his courage until I read *Just the One*. Well played, Jeff.'

A week after publication I took him to Liverpool to appear on *This Morning*, the 'Richard and Judy' TV show, and when we did a joint interview with Greater London Radio one morning he asked me to pop out and get him a vodka to lubricate the throat. In an off-licence down the road I asked the young, male, pony-tailed assistant for a couple of vodka miniatures and some soda and he said excitedly: 'Is that for Jeffrey Bernard? Is he here?' Well, who else would need a couple of vodkas at 11 a.m.?

The most nerve-wracking moment was when we went to Broadcasting House one evening for him to be interviewed live on radio on the respected *John Dunn Show* and it became obvious that Bernard had drunk far too much when he staggered into the studio, demanded a vodka (in vain) and asked the producer with menace: 'What does it sound like if you're sick into the fucking microphone?'

'This could be interesting,' said the producer nervously. 'He's not going to swear, is he?'

He did not swear. In fact he gave a consummate performance – charming, witty, penetrating – although our hearts did stop several times as he took a fraction too long to answer each question, like some ramshackle aircraft that was about to stall and fall out of the sky at any moment.

Thanks to all his help the book reached number seven in the *Bookseller*'s pre-Christmas hardback biography bestseller list.

Meanwhile his spirits had been raised when the former England cricket captain David Gower sent him a get-well-soon letter and *Jeffrey Bernard is Unwell* opened in Rome under the title *Una Bottiglia Piena di Ricordi* (Memories Seen Through a Bottle). But his broken hip took a long time to mend and he felt like a prisoner in the flat in Berwick Street. 'I get on my hands and knees to get into a taxi,' he told the *Observer* in yet another interview. 'I'm disabled now, there's no doubt about it. I've come to terms in the last few weeks that I'm fucked for life.'

In April 1993 the play opened in Cardiff, with Dennis Waterman again in the lead, before embarking on a four-month national tour. Bernard attended the opening night with his 'minder' Debbie Bosley, buying two first-class rail tickets (£206 instead of £62) because 'I have to travel first-class so that I can smoke.' There was trouble, however, when Bernard, Debbie and I were given seats at the back of the stalls and Bernard moaned so much – 'we won't hear a thing here' – that eventually three paying customers were ejected from their seats nearer the stage and we took their places right behind Ned Sherrin's vast head and Keith Waterhouse's jungle of wild, white, Worzel Gummidge hair. Bernard surveyed the packed theatre, remarked 'I'll probably get enough out of this for a round of drinks', and then, as the curtain rose, gave the back of Waterhouse's head a vigorous V-sign, hissing to Debbie and me: 'I want you both to remember that all the jokes are *mine*.' Had Bernard been Cinderella he would doubtless have pulled the Fairy Godmother's wings off.

In the interval he grumbled that Waterman was no good and insisted on Debbie taking him back to the hotel so that they missed the second act and the noisy, alcoholic dinner and booze-up after the show, which kept most of us drinking champagne until 3.30 a.m. At 7.30 the telephone rang in my room. It was Bernard. 'There's a good review in the *Western Mail* but they've cocked up your name,' he chortled. 'They've called you Keith Lloyd!' It made his day.

Although Bernard and Miss Bosley shared a room at the hotel – he even announced grandly that he had 'sent her out for a packet of condoms' – she soon moved in with the one man guaranteed to inflame Bernard with jealousy: his old *bête noire* Richard Ingrams, whose marriage had ended. When the *Daily Mail* asked Bernard how he felt about her running off with his teetotal, hitherto puritan rival, he replied darkly: 'Hitler didn't drink either, you know.' A couple of months later he attempted to console himself with the Duchess of Hamilton: Jill Hamilton and I had worked together on the *Sunday Express*, I introduced them at the Chelsea Arts Club and Bernard was smitten. He proceeded to pursue Her Grace with surprising energy for several weeks but eventually told me in despair that it was all quite hopeless because she refused to sleep with him.

By now he was disillusioned even with Soho, writing in the *Oldie* that it had become 'as boring as Lanzarote, as squalid as Times Square, as porn-ridden as Amsterdam and as gay as San Francisco' and adding that Norman Balon had 'all but emptied' the Coach and Horses with his 'egomania and what passes for his wit'. Balon replied that Bernard was a has-been and that no one in the pub missed him at all but he continued to visit Bernard and bring him treats, especially in hospital.

He was in hospital a great deal during these years. At the end of 1993 he developed an infected blister on his right foot, contracted septicaemia and diabetic gangrene and had to have the bottom half of the leg amputated just below the knee on 8 February 1994 – the very day, ironically, that *Jeffrey Bernard is Unwell* opened in Dublin and (as he pointed out himself) 'the

anniversary of Mary Queen of Scots having her head amputated'. He was literally legless at last, he announced with
terrible black humour. 'I am hopping mad,' he added grue-
somely, 'and have one foot in the grave.' He acquired an
inflatable plastic parrot which he would perch on his shoulder
while attempting an impersonation of Long John Silver. Three
months later he was fitted with an artificial leg but still insisted
on exposing his shiny stump at every opportunity, especially if it
was likely to frighten pretty young women. Soon afterwards he
inserted this advertisement in the *Spectator*: 'Alcoholic, diabetic
amputee seeks sympathy fuck.'

The pain from his pancreas whenever he sipped a vodka was
now so fierce that he started drinking red wine instead and he
told Rory Knight Bruce of the *Evening Standard* in June that if
he had enough money he would abandon Soho and go and live
in a farmhouse in Andalusia or a house on stilts in Bangkok.
His last three years were spent fighting ill health and loneliness
cooped up in a wheelchair in his flat, his sufferings eased only
by the anti-depressant drug Prozac and the daily arrival of a
series of council-employed home helps, most notably 'the
sainted Vera', about whose angelic nature he wrote constantly
in his column. He rarely ventured out to his old haunts and was
constantly being rushed into the Middlesex Hospital to deal
with some crisis or other. He became so weak that one night he
had to telephone the police to fetch his insulin from his sitting
room to his bed just ten yards away. From the beginning of
October he all but gave up alcohol because even one glass
would set off an excruciating attack of pancreatitis. By November he was writing in the *Spectator* that he was actually bored at
last with booze, pubs and their customers. He became so lonely
that he even bought an aquarium and thirty-five fish so that he
would have something to stare at other than television.

Astonishingly he was still capable of writing an occasional
hilarious column, like the one that appeared in the *Spectator* on
14 May 1994 in which he reported that not only had a tax
collector just turned up at his door to demand £9,660 but the
Irishman who had put the play on in Dublin had just gone bust

without paying him any royalties. It came as no surprise, he said, to learn that the Irishman's surname was Bernard.

There were also still moments of real pleasure and he relished the day in September that he returned to Pangbourne to open a new sixth form common room that even had a bar in it and he was presented by the headmaster with a bottle of vodka. At last his loathing of the place was exorcised. But generally his loneliness during these years was palpable and I visited him every month or so to take him books or a bottle of wine (when he was still drinking) and to chat for an hour but by the end of 1994 I realised that he never telephoned me and I decided to stay away and see how long it was before he called me. He did not do so for nearly two years.

In November the taxman demanded another £40,000 and in January Bernard had a public row with Dominic Lawson, accusing him of not paying him enough, and said he was leaving the *Spectator* to write for someone else. 'We get this with him every year,' said Lawson wearily.

Despite Bernard's myriad ailments and weakness he was still gutsy enough to fly to Venice in April 1996 with Sally James in attendance for his first ever visit to Italy at the age of sixty-three – a remarkably late age to be doing so considering that his godfather J.G. Links was a worldwide authority on Venice. In June, Duckworth published a new collection of his pieces using both of the titles he had been saving for his autobiography, *Reach for the Ground: the Downhill Struggle of Jeffrey Bernard*. In it he wrote revealingly: 'I used to think that maybe drink had destroyed my life, but that was dramatic nonsense and temporary gloom. Without alcohol I could have been a shop-assistant, a business executive, or a lone bachelor bank clerk.' To coincide with the book Channel 4 screened a documentary portrait, *Jeffrey Bernard: Reach for the Ground*, and the newspapers flocked to interview him yet again.

'I can't stand being old and raddled and not good-looking any longer,' he told Jan Moir of the *Daily Telegraph*. In an interview with Nicci Gerrard of the *Observer* he said: 'I think about death all the time. I am scared of it, the complete blank.

I don't believe in God – he's always been too slow to put his hand in his pocket to buy a round of drinks. It's about time he got in his shout.' But when he spoke to Frances Welch of the *Sunday Telegraph* God had undergone a sex change. 'I know She's a woman because She's so keen on vengeance,' he announced, adding that he found Judas much more interesting than Jesus. 'Because he was tempted by thirty pieces of silver?' asked Ms Welch.

'Obviously he should have held out for a bit more,' said Bernard.

He was still astonishingly careless of his health. In July he flew to Morocco with Sally James to write a travel article, collapsed in Tangier with renal failure, nearly died on the plane to Marrakesh, briefly stopped breathing and was rushed by ambulance thirty miles to Casablanca, where he spent five days in a coma and intensive care. 'I don't think he could have got closer to dying than he did on that plane,' said Sally James. Had he done so, she reported, Bernard's famous last words would have been: 'Fuck! I think I'm fucking dying! After all these fucking years!'

'Life is like a banana,' observed Bernard, quoting an old Arab proverb. 'One minute it is in your hand and the next minute it is up your arse.'

From now on he had to go into the Middlesex Hospital every other day to have treatment on a dialysis machine for five hours at a time. He thought long and hard before agreeing. 'It is either that or die, soonish,' he said. 'In the last twelve years death has lost its charm and appeal for me although I love obituaries; I love reading about how other men die.' Miserably he agreed to avoid tomatoes, chocolate, cheese, citrus fruits, red wine and coffee. 'I can have as much fucking tapioca and sago as I want,' he told Jan Moir. 'And spirits. What a paradox. Now that I am not a boozer any more I have just been told that after all these years I can help myself to all the vodka in the world.' Yet he faced all his trials with courage and humour and remarked: 'I will surprise God because I'm late. I'm usually very punctual. I was always punctual with the Devil.'

For nearly two years Jeff did not contact me – not even when I wrote a glowing review of *Reach for the Ground* in the *Daily Telegraph* – yet in interviews he complained bitterly that few of his friends could be bothered any longer to visit him and told Jan Moir somewhat charmlessly that he could not think of one living person whom he actually liked. In September 1996 he claimed on the Radio 4 *PM* programme that I had lied about him in my biography and had stabbed him in the back. I wrote to him to point out that he had said in person and in print that I had done a very good job on the book and that as far as I was concerned our friendship, which he obviously did not value, was over. He never replied but was apparently upset by the letter and felt guilty about it. Five months later he heard that I was in London again and he telephoned one Sunday morning. It was the first contact we had had for nearly two years.

'I'm going into hospital this week for another operation and I don't think I'll come out,' he said. 'I'd like to make it up before I die by buying you lunch.'

I told him truthfully that I was launching a new novel and that every lunch and dinner date was fully booked.

'So you haven't forgiven me, then,' he said pathetically.

'Of course I have,' I said, 'but I just don't have a free day.'

'Oh, well,' he sighed, 'I can understand it if you won't forgive me.'

Exasperated but also touched, I invited him to join me that day for a lunch that I was having at the Chelsea Arts Club with my publisher Alan Brooke, whom he knew. 'Only if you'll let me pay,' said Bernard.

'That's very kind of you,' I said.

Bernard was charming and chatty throughout the meal, drinking nothing alcoholic and even boasting that he was now much richer than anyone realised. After lunch Brooke and I had to discuss my new biography of James Herriot and we left Bernard in the bar to talk to some of his old cronies. By the time we came down again he had gone. He had left, of course, without paying the bill for lunch.

End Piece

Bernard's last Christmas, in 1996, was soured by a row he had with some of his neighbours in the block of council flats when he accused them in the *Spectator* of being 'despicable, mean, small-minded and prone to malicious gossip' and they in turn retaliated by posting up an anonymous notice and sending him a threatening Christmas card. On the day itself he woke to find himself in the Middlesex Hospital yet again but was taken home by the sainted Vera, who gave him a rollneck jersey, and he was delighted when Victor Chandler gave him a bottle of Dom Perignon and Isabel telephoned from Spain, where she had been living for nearly a year.

In 1997 the quality of Bernard's life deteriorated so much that he started wondering whether it was worth living any longer. Vera retired in January, leaving him bereft, Sally James went off to New Zealand, the relentless dialysis treatment was getting him down, he was constantly itching and in pain and so weak that he could no longer type his column but had to dictate it every Tuesday to Jessica Nettleton or Lorraine White, both *Spectator* staffers. He kept being rushed into the Middlesex Hospital where the food was 'now a national disgrace' and the medics refused to prescribe pain-killers that were strong enough, and in February he began to consider whether to refuse any further dialysis and simply let himself die. 'It is very easy indeed for people with renal failure to commit suicide,' he wrote. 'I could kill myself quite easily by messing about with the diet that forbids us food containing potassium, so I can now end it all with half a dozen bananas and a bar of chocolate.'

Identified by the hospital as a possible suicide, he was interviewed by three psychiatrists who asked him foolishly if he wanted counselling. *Counselling? Jeff Bernard?* In May he turned sixty-five and against all the odds qualified for the state old-age pension. He was delighted by the number of birthday cards he received from readers and was wheeled to the Coach and Horses for a final large vodka with Norman Balon – only his fourth alcoholic drink in a year. But by now he was so weak that he had to be helped in and out of bed, could no longer cook and weighed just 7¼ stone. He faced with horror the prospect of perhaps having to lose his other leg and go into an old folks' home, which he said would probably be run by 'the descendants of people who worked as guards at Auschwitz'.

He still had one more hilarious column in him. On 19 July, seven weeks before he died, his *Spectator* piece – about the horrors of nursing homes – made me laugh aloud. 'The conversations in the dayroom with old ladies suffering from dementia and Alzheimer's,' he wrote, 'could not possibly be more incoherent than ten minutes in the Coach and Horses.'

Early in August television researcher Andy Terrington visited Bernard to ask him to appear in a TV documentary about Lester Piggott. 'He was thinking of giving up dialysis,' Terrington told me. 'We talked about his death. He was saying he didn't know what to do: he wanted to end it but he didn't want to go through any pain. I said, "You could always get somebody to do it." He said, "Would you?", and I said no. It was more a jest than a serious request. He said he wasn't afraid of dying but he was afraid of pain.'

On 11 August Bernard warned the hospital that he would discontinue dialysis unless they could ease his pain, insomnia and terrible inexplicable itching. The Middlesex had recently decided to ban all smoking, even by old or terminal patients, and he wrote: 'If a man can't take a Woodbine with him to his death then there is, indeed, a bit of hell on earth.'

On 19 August Lorraine White went to the flat to take down what was to turn out to be Bernard's last *Spectator* column. 'He was very uncomfortable, very itchy,' she told me. 'He said, "I can't write, read, watch television, I just don't want to know any more." He said, "How do I die without committing suicide?" I said, "Drink." He said, "No, I can't breathe if I drink, I panic." '

He skipped the dialysis for one day and was surprised not to feel ill. 'I keep pondering whether or not to stop altogether until the end,' he wrote in his last *Spectator* column on 23 August. 'The only trouble with the exit is that a new bunch of people at the Middlesex who call themselves the Palliative Care Team tell me that it would take three to four weeks which is, to my way of thinking, a hell of a long time. A ridiculous picture comes to mind of a man tied to a post opposite a firing squad, the squad pull their triggers and the prisoner stands there watching the bullets coming rather slowly towards him for three weeks or more.'

By now the itching – exacerbated by the amazingly hot summer – was 'almost mind-cracking' yet the medics were refusing to prescribe pain-killers that were strong enough and would not even let him enjoy a cheese, tomato and beetroot salad. Of doctors in general he wrote 'I hear endlessly how sympathetic, understanding and compassionate they are and I don't believe a bloody word of it . . . In fact, if I really thought the amount of potassium in a Chinese take-away could give me a heart attack I would be heading to Chinatown now.' And in what was to turn out to be the last sentence he wrote he said: 'I suddenly realise that what cures any itch and most complaints is £1 million in your current account.' It seems absolutely right that the last thing Jeffrey ever wrote about was money.

On Friday 29 August the editor of the *Spectator*, Frank Johnson, went to see him. 'I tried to get him to write a last column, to say goodbye,' Johnson told me. 'He half wanted to do it but he didn't have the strength. He was extremely realistic and unsentimental about his death. As I left he grasped my hand for a longer time and more strongly than in the past.'

Bernard's plight touched the heart of Simon Jenkins, an ex-editor of *The Times*, who wrote a long article in the paper the next day in which he castigated the National Health Service for not giving terminal patients like Bernard pain-killers that were strong enough and for refusing to let them enjoy a final glass of Guinness or cigarette. 'Even condemned murderers were once allowed such consolations,' wrote Jenkins. The article reinforced Bernard's decision to refuse any more treatment. On the previous day he told his brother Bruce that he was still not sure about the fatal decision, but on the Saturday he rang Irma Kurtz to ask for the name and number of a lawyer, perhaps with a view to changing his will, and by the next day, Sunday 31st, he had made up his mind. He had had enough. He was going to let himself die.

I was living in the South of France and telephoned him at his flat that Sunday morning – the morning that the Princess of Wales was killed in a car crash in Paris – and although his voice was weak he told me how nice it was to hear me and sounded genuinely pleased. All the past animosity had evaporated.

We did not mention the tragedy of Princess Diana. Her death was terrible but until that moment she had enjoyed one of the happiest months of her life and had just had an idyllic holiday with her new lover, Dodi Fayed, in Sardinia and dinner at the Ritz, whereas Jeff's approaching demise was one of long, slow agony and apprehension. Not for him a sudden merciful extinction.

'Tomorrow will be my first day off dialysis,' he told me. 'I had a long talk with my doctor on Friday and I've got nothing to live for any more. I'm either in pain òr itching or vomiting or shitting myself. I can't move, even from the sofa to the lavatory. I'm so weak, especially in my upper arms. The doctor said that if I'm really serious about stopping dialysis it'll take about ten days to die. He said, "I'll make sure you don't feel pain or anything, you'll just feel nausea and then you'll just drift off." '

I told him how sorry I was that it had finally come to this. He was philosophical. 'It's just tough tit,' he said, 'but I've had an extraordinary life—,' he chuckled, '—as you probably know! Now that I've got it off my chest and made the decision, what I really want to do is just to go to sleep – which is what I'm going to do, isn't it?'

I suggested that he ought to go into a hospice. 'Not with all those bad-tempered old drunks in there,' he said, joking until the very end.

He asked to say goodbye to Juliet and chatted to her for five minutes, reminiscing about the weekend we had all spent together in the South of France in August 1988. 'I remember lunch at the Auberge du Colombier,' he said, 'and *boules* and Jules in the sun. I even remember what I had: a ham omelette.' At the end he said: 'Is Graham behaving himself? Good. You keep his nose to the grindstone – and whatever you want to do with his other bits, I don't want to know.'

She was crying when she handed the receiver back to me and I was tearful myself as Jeff and I said goodbye, not because of his impending death, which had been delayed for far too long, but because of his immense courage in facing it.

The end was only four days away. On the Monday he refused to have the dialysis treatment. On the Tuesday Andy Terrington telephoned to check that he was still well enough to be filmed eight days later for the Piggott TV documentary and discovered that Jeff was 'a different person' whose mood was no longer quiet but decidedly forthright. 'I'm no longer in for free co-operation,' he announced. 'So how much are you going to pay me?' Terrington said he would have to ask his producer. 'You'll have to be quick,' said Bernard. 'I'm dying.' A few minutes later Terrington called back to say that they would pay him £150. 'Okay,' said Jeff. 'Bring it with you in readies.'

He did not live to collect them. On the Wednesday he again declined dialysis and began to slip in and out of consciousness, his agonies eased by morphine, tea and cigarettes. His niece Kate Bernard was with him and a stream of women friends came to say goodbye: Anna Haycraft, Sally James, Vera, and three from the *Spectator*, Jenny Naipaul, Lorraine White and Liz Anderson. They found him in bed. Typically he announced that Frank Johnson was mad and proceeded to tell a story about a one-legged rapist racehorse trainer and to reminisce about the night he met Marlene Dietrich. 'He was determined to die,' Jenny Naipaul told me and Anna Haycraft said: 'He was drifting in and out of consciousness but he was lucid. He said he'd be going very soon and that he'd had enough.'

Kate gave him his last cigarette that evening and he slipped into the terminal coma that brought him at last the blessed relief he had been seeking for so long. His last words, spoken to Kate, were 'I feel content' – perhaps for the first time in his restless life.

The following day, Thursday 4 September, the *Spectator* appeared without the time-honoured line '*Jeffrey Bernard is unwell.*' It said instead: '*Jeffrey Bernard is not writing this week.*' He never read it. He spent his last day in a coma, surrounded by family and friends, and died at 9.30 p.m. He had succeeded in committing suicide at last. 'He didn't want to die being rushed to hospital on a hospital trolley without dignity,' Kate said afterwards. 'He avoided that elegantly by choosing to die at home.'

Six years previously Bernard had told me: 'Knowing my fucking luck I'll get no obituaries at all because I'll probably die on the same day as the Queen Mother.' He was nearly right: the *Evening Standard* ran an obituary (by me) the next afternoon but the following day, Saturday 6 September, was the day of the Princess of Wales's mammoth funeral in London when all the papers were packed with stories about her and there was little space for anything else. He was upstaged too by the deaths that weekend of Mother Teresa of Calcutta and Sir Georg Solti, whose obituaries squeezed his out of most of the papers. Ironically it was the *Guardian*, at which he had sneered time and again, that gave him the biggest coverage: two full pages. The *Independent* too gave him a large news story and a huge obituary. Of the Sunday papers, which were dominated by the Princess's funeral, only the *Sunday Telegraph* mentioned him at all, in a half-page article by Keith Waterhouse. On any other Sunday he would undoubtedly have been mentioned in Taki's weekly column in the *Sunday Times* but on this particular Sunday even Taki was writing about the Princess. I can imagine Jeff on a cloud contemplating this appalling piece of timing with a decidedly sardonic smile.

The Times, Daily Telegraph and *Daily Mail* did all eventually run long obituaries on the Monday, the *Mail*'s by Keith Water-house, the *Telegraph* also printing the spoof obituary that

Bernard had written himself many years previously. The tone of all the coverage was kind, even respectful. By the nature of his dying, and the fortitude with which he had faced it, Jeffrey had become almost respectable at last.

The Princess of Wales's funeral was precisely the one that Bernard had envisaged for himself: the gun carriage, the royal mourners, Westminster Abbey, Verdi's *Requiem*. His own funeral six days later, on a miserable grey Friday at Kensal Green crematorium in west London, was not as grand or as long – it lasted fifty minutes – but it was very much more cheerful, a jolly celebration rather than a gathering of grief. 'Jeff would have liked it,' Keith Waterhouse told me. There were no hymns, prayers, priest or any mention of God and the irreligious tone was set as the mourners waited outside for the end of the preceding funeral, that of a London bookmaker called Alf Fletcher, whose main floral tribute was an incredible arrangement depicting a racehorse and jockey approaching a winning post above the words 'The Favourite'. 'So Jeff was just pipped at the post,' chuckled Keith Waterhouse, who was there along with Peter O'Toole and Ned Sherrin as well as three of Bernard's ex-editors (Alexander Chancellor, Frank Johnson and Mike Molloy), two ex-wives (Jill and Sue), Jill's daughter Isabel, several old lovers (Juliet Simpkins, Finola Morgan, Deirdre Redgrave) and nearly three hundred other mourners, among them Norman Balon, Beryl Bainbridge, Anna Haycraft, Irma Kurtz, Michael Heath, Michael Elphick, Simon Courtauld, Jonathan Meades, Gaston Berlemont, Ferdinand Mount and Richard Ingrams's squeeze Deborah Bosley although there was no sign of Ingrams himself – nor of two other ex-editors of Bernard's, Charles Moore and Dominic Lawson, nor of any of Jeffrey's racing friends, most of whom had decided to postpone their tributes to him until his ashes were buried at Lambourn.

To the strains of Mozart's Clarinet Quintet rattling out of the tinny loudspeakers, the huge throng crammed into the chapel, squatting on the floor and jammed against the walls, and there was a great deal of laughter as speaker after speaker recalled the life of the man in the cheap black coffin. Accompanied by a volley of smokers' coughs Alexander Chancellor, George Barker's widow Elspeth, Mike Molloy and Peter O'Toole all delivered tributes and O'Toole read G.K. Chesterton's glorious poem about English drunkenness, 'The Rolling English Road', which starts '*Before the Roman came to Rye or out to Severn strode, The rolling English drunkard made the rolling English road*' and ends with the wonderfully appropriate line '*Before we go to Paradise by way of Kensal Green.*'

Some of the smokers became restless when Bruce Bernard forced the congregation to endure nine long, tinny minutes of a Beethoven largo, the Piano Sonata No. 4, opus 10. Jeffrey had never been much of a Beethoven man, but the mood lightened rapidly when Oliver Bernard gave an hilarious reading of one of Jeff's columns in which he had castigated all the anti-smoking, anti-drinking moralisers, the Association for Alcohol Abuse and women who sigh. The reading was punctuated by roars of laughter and eventually applause. 'It was terribly funny,' Anna Haycraft told me afterwards. 'Oliver sounds very like Jeff and emphasises words in the same place, so it was almost as if Jeff himself were reading it.' At the end O'Toole stooped theatrically and kissed the coffin. A heavy thunderstorm broke over the cemetery and rain was pelting down as they left the chapel to further strains of Mozart. 'Perhaps someone up there is not too pleased that Jeff's on his way up,' remarked the *Evening Standard* reporter Pete Clark in the paper's final edition that afternoon.

Afterwards about thirty mourners followed O'Toole, Sherrin and Waterhouse back to the Coach and Horses, where Bernard would have been furious to know that Norman Balon was paying for all the drinks. O'Toole and co. went on to the Groucho Club, where the family had organised a bit of a do much to the irritation of Balon, who felt that his own pub was the right place for Jeffrey's wake. Waterhouse agreed with him. 'The Groucho was ill-attended,' he said, 'and Jeff would have wanted us to go to the Coach.' So even in death Jeff Bernard was the centre of ill feeling and backbiting. As for his final resting place, the family decided that they would bury his ashes on the racehorse gallops at Lambourn. 'There's no room to bury him in Soho,' Oliver explained. He and Peter Walwyn planned to erect a memorial stone on the gallops. 'Jeffrey loved Lambourn,' Walwyn told me, 'so we'll put him somewhere overlooking the places that he loved.'

'I think I'm the sort of person who'd go straight to Heaven,' he once told Frances Welch of the *Sunday Telegraph*. 'Heaven is full of piss-artists. I think God is quite perverse like that. The trouble is Heaven will be like a place designed by Terence Conran: all white and chrome, like one of his poxy restaurants. There'll be No Smoking and you won't be able to get any service.'

In his *Daily Mail* obituary of Bernard, Keith Waterhouse predicted: 'He will be talked about as long as Soho lasts.' But was he at all significant? Did he *matter*? 'Anyone who has that sort of following or strikes such a chord is significant,' said Alexander Chancellor.

It is possible to see Bernard as one of Margaret Thatcher's stranger bedfellows and as intriguing a part of the 1980s as she was. His lazy, alcoholic, nicotine-stained, determinedly unhealthy lifestyle established him as a devil-may-care anti-Thatcher symbol that suddenly appealed to millions. At a time when a Big Nanny prime minister was urging the nation to be sober, thrifty and hardworking, Bernard was famous for being precisely the opposite. He had never taken out a mortgage, insurance policy or pension or paid a penny in alimony to any of his four ex-wives. He was in effect the ultimate example of political incorrectness, a rebel who personified the naughty, irresponsible side of our natures. If Mrs Thatcher represented the lion in the British national character, Jeff Bernard was the unicorn.

Perhaps it was no mere coincidence that their careers peaked at the same time. She was elected leader of the Conservative Party in 1975 just as he was starting to write for the *Spectator*, and she fell from power in the year that packed audiences in Shaftesbury Avenue were roaring at the decidedly un-Conservative antics of Peter O'Toole in *Jeffrey Bernard is Unwell*. Both were products of the lower-middle-class – although Bernard certainly personified everything that Margaret Thatcher abhorred.

But then he also irritated many who knew him best. They said he was startlingly vicious, callous, utterly selfish, and the meanest man they had ever met – too mean even to buy his own round in the pub. Many believed he had squandered his life.

'Jeff has got such a dazzling talent,' said Mike Molloy. 'It's as if the fairies turned up in his cot and gave him all these gifts – looks, a deeply engaging personality and great talent. I think he was given everything to become an artist but not that last bit, work.'

Bernard's own verdict was typically ruthless. 'I hate people saying I'm a shit,' he told me. 'I'm not. I'm a cunt. There's a great difference. A shit is a rotter, intentionally nasty, and I've never been that. I've never deliberately caused a lot of misery. I'm not cruel. A cunt is a cunt by mistake: it's accidental.'

Despite long feuds and disagreements with Bernard, Jay Landesman and Dan Farson came up with suitable epitaphs for him. 'He certainly brightened our lives,' said Landesman. 'He brightened them and frightened them.' Farson told me: 'He made one laugh. That's enough in life.'

But it is Bernard's father's autobiography *Cock Sparrow* that provides the most appropriate motto: 'He who has courage despises the future.' It was a quotation given to Bunny Bernard as a token of peace by a beautiful French girl as he left Paris by train at the end of the First World War. It seems particularly appropriate for his youngest son, Jeffrey, who spent his whole life taking risks and defying the odds and who faced his long last illness and his death with immense style, humour and bravery.

HE WHO HAS COURAGE DESPISES THE FUTURE.

A fitting epitaph for Jeff Bernard – and the just one.

Index